Ethical Investigations

General Editor

Lawrence C. Becker
Professor Emeritus
College of William & Mary

A ROUTLEDGE SERIES

Contents of the Collection

Rights and Duties

Volume 1

Conceptual Analyses of Rights and Duties

Edited with introductions by

Carl Wellman
University of Washington,
St. Louis

ROUTLEDGE
New York/London

Published in 2002 by
Routledge
29 West 35th Street
New York, NY 10001

Published in Great Britain by
Routledge
11 New Fetter Lane
London EC4P 4EE

Routledge is an imprint of the Taylor & Francis Group.

Printed in the United States of America on acid-free paper.

10 9 8 7 6 5 4 3 2 1

Library of Congress Cataloging-in-Publication Data

Rights and duties / edited with introductions by Carl Wellman.
p. cm. — (Ethical Investigations)
Includes bibliographical references.
Contents: v. 1. The concept of a right and a duty — v. 2. The rational foundation of rights and duties — v. 3. Natural rights and duties—v. 4. Against rights and duties—v. 5. Duties and obligations to others—v. 6. Property as a right, distribution as a duty.
ISBN 0-415-93982-8 (set : alk paper) — ISBN 0-415-93983-6 (vol. 1 : alk. paper) — ISBN 0-415-93984-4 (vol. 2 : alk. paper) — ISBN 0-415-93985-2 (vol. 3 : alk. paper)—ISBN 0-415-93986-0 (vol. 4 : alk. paper)—ISBN 0-415-93987-9 (vol. 5 : alk. paper)—ISBN 0-415-93988-7 (vol. 6 : alk. paper)
1. Natural law. .2. Obedience (Law) .3. Duty. 4. Law and ethics I. Wellman, Carl II. Series.
K460.R46 2002
340'.112—dc21 2002020621

Contents

Series Introduction

This volume is part of an ambitious series designed to collect English language journal articles and book chapters of enduring philosophical interest in the field of ethics. The articles are published here in their original formats and pagination, without editorial changes of any sort. They are thus primary bibliographic documents as well as philosophical ones.

The series is organized into multivolume collections. The first of these is the six-volume collection called *Rights and Duties*, edited by Carl Wellman, of which this volume is a part. Future collections, with their projected publication dates, include *Justice and Equality* (2002); *Ethics and Public Policy Issues* (2003); *Environmental Ethics* (2003); *Moral Responsibility* (2004); and *Feminist Ethics* (2004).

For obvious reasons the series cannot reasonably aim to be comprehensive. The English language journal literature in ethics is vast, and although the common wisdom is that much of it is ephemeral, a good deal of it is clearly better than that—and there is more of that than we can possibly republish here. Moreover, we have not chosen articles simply because they are, or are likely to be, of interest to historians of philosophy. Rather, we have confined ourselves to topics of continuing philosophical interest, and articles on those topics that are either of continuing importance in themselves or of special use in orienting readers with respect to the wider literature. In addition, we have included some material from serials published in book form, and in unusual cases, we have included chapters from monographs. The focus, however, has been on the journal and serial literature, not monographs.

In an ideal world, all important journal articles in ethics would effortlessly enter into the institutional memory of professional philosophers. Our world falls short of that ideal, of course. For one thing, Anglo-American philosophers are notoriously stingy with citations, and many, on principle, resist attempts to create anything that might be misused as a closed, canonical list of worthy philosophical texts or topics. Those traits, combined with a propensity for closely focused argument on tightly defined problems, can induce a form of professional negligence in which, say, a young philosopher working on property rights in the final third of the twentieth century, circulating drafts of his manuscripts widely, can easily fail to come across Morris Cohen's useful articles on the subject. Moreover, literature searches are of limited use if the literature is difficult to access or too large to survey effectively—especially if one is unconsciously convinced of the false proposition that "If it is important, and if I don't know about it already, one of my critics will point it out to me soon." One of the aims of this series is to address the problem of professional amnesia, by pointing some things out.

Lawrence C. Becker

Volume Introduction

This is one of six volumes of collected articles and chapters on rights and duties. The others are *Rational Foundations of Rights and Duties*, *Possible Possessors of Rights or Duties*, *Human Rights and Universal Duties*, *Welfare Rights and Duties of Charity*, and *Property Rights and Duties of Redistribution*. Each is intended to be a coherent collection that presents a set of closely related debates concerning rights and duties. Together they represent the most important themes in the twentieth century theory of rights and duties. In addition to the articles and chapters that had to be omitted from each volume in order to hold them down to publishable size, there are other important publications that are not included because they do not fit neatly into any of these volumes. As I have attempted to fulfil my duties as an editor, I hope that I have not violated any right of authors I have reluctantly excluded from my selections.

When G. E. Moore published *Principia Ethica* in 1903, he set the agenda for Anglo-American ethical theory for the first half of the twentieth century. He asserted that the most fundamental question in ethics is "What does the word 'good' mean?" This is partly because he believed that all the other ethical words could be defined in terms of intrinsic goodness. For example, a "duty" means "that action which will cause more good to exist in the universe than any possible alternative." And also because one must know what ethical words mean in order to know what reasons are necessary and sufficient to establish any ethical conclusion. His view was that the word "good" is indefinable because it refers to a simple, unanalyzable, non-natural property.

W. D. Ross agreed that goodness is unanalyzable, but rejected Moore's analysis of the concept of a moral duty. He insisted that the concept of moral rightness, duty or obligation is also simple and indefinable. He argued that Moore had oversimplified our moral obligations. In addition to the positive duty to produce good for others and the negative duty not to harm others, moral agents have duties of fidelity, of reparation, of gratitude, of justice and of self-improvement.

Is it logically possible for these various duties to conflict? Moral experience suggests that this is sometimes the case. If one is on her way to meet a friend as promised but finds a victim of a serious accident without help, it is impossible for one to fulfil both one's duty to keep one's promise and one's duty to benefit or prevent further harm to another. But how is it possible for moral duties to be incompatible in practice? Kant and most other moral philosophers maintain that a defining characteristic of moral obligation is universality. Morality requires that one act on universal moral principles, and it is immoral to make an exception of oneself when one objects to acting as one's duty demands. Ross attempts to solve this conceptual puzzle by introducing the concept of a prima facie duty. To say that an act is a prima facie duty is to say that one does have a moral obligation to perform it unless one also has some more stringent contrary prima facie duty. Thus, universal moral principles are principles of prima facie duty, such as "one ought always, other things being equal, to keep one's promises. But because in some circumstances these principles can conflict, one's actual duty is to do that act with the greatest balance of prima facie rightness.

Moore and Ross treated the concepts of duty, obligation, the right act and what one ought to do as virtually interchangeable. Most philosophers doing analytical ethics during the next few decades followed their example. They were well aware of the fact that the expressions "duty," "obligation," "the right act" and "what one ought to do" are not synonymous in ordinary English, but they believed that these idiomatic differences are not important for their theoretical purposes. And for some purposes, this is probably correct. If one is trying to explain what distinguishes all ethical language from any scientific or non-ethical language, distinctions between ethical categories may be irrelevant. But ethical theory is complex. It includes at least theory of value, theory of obligation and theory of virtue, each of which may be subdivided. Thus, H. L. A. Hart, who was especially interested in the theory of rights, insisted upon distinguishing the concept of obligation from other related concepts. He takes legal obligations as his model and develops a similar, but not identical, elucidation of the concept of moral obligation. John Ladd also seems to take legal obligations as paradigms, but R. B. Brandt and James K. Mish'Alani seem to analyze the concept of a moral obligation without reference to the law. Brandt and Mish'Alani also distinguish carefully between the concepts of obligation and duty as well as the concepts of what one ought or ought not to do.

One of the tasks confronting anyone trying to analyze the concepts of moral duty or obligation is to explain the bindingness or requiredness of moral duties or obligations. Philosophers as diverse as Kant and Mill insisted that moral duties demand obedience no matter how much one wishes to evade them. One obvious explanation is that one will or could justifiably suffer negative sanctions if one fails to fulfill one's moral obligations. Although Hart rejects John Austin's view that to have an obligation is to be likely to suffer a negative sanction, he explains that obligations presuppose a rules that authorizes the imposition of sanctions upon one who violates his obligations. John Ladd also insists that one feature of obligations is that they authorize the use of sanctions in the case of nonfulfillment. P. M. S. Hacker, however, argues forcefully against every version of a sanction theory of duty. Roderick Chisholm and Joseph Raz explain the bindingness of duties in terms of practical reason. Chisholm seems to presuppose the concept of requiredness and apply it to duties through the logic of inferences to duties. Raz goes further by introducing the concept of an exclusionary reason, a reason both to do some action and to disregard most contrary reasons.

During the first half of the twentieth century, the conceptual analysis of the language of ethics became increasingly central to ethical theory. But for the most part moral philosophers limited their attention to the most general ethical words like "good," "right" and "ought" and their contraries. Only later was it widely recognized that it might be theoretically important to analyze the more specific senses of words like "duty" and "obligation." And only then did moral philosophers undertake the analysis of the concept of a moral right.

When ethicists did turn to the conceptual analysis of rights, they found that jurists had written extensively on this subject. By far the most influential were two articles of Wesley Newcomb Hohfeld published in the *Yale Law Journal* in 1913 and 1917 respectively. Hohfeld argued that in judicial decisions and jurisprudence the expression "a right" was used indiscriminately to refer to a legal claim, a legal privilege (later called "a liberty"), a legal power or a legal immunity. He showed that this ambiguity often led to invalid legal reasoning and insisted that in the strictest sense "a legal right" refers only to a single legal claim of one party against one other party.

The reason Hohfeld gave for this conclusion was that everyone recognizes that legal rights are logically correlative with legal duties. Thus, it is a conceptual truth that X has a legal right against Y that Y do act A if and only if Y has a legal duty to X to do A, where X and Y are two persons under the law. H. L. A. Hart protested this reduction of rights to duties because it made the language of rights redundant. Were Hohfeld correct, one could say everything important about law or morals in the language of duties. But this neglected what was distinctive and practically important about rights, their special relevance to the proper distribution of freedom. Although Joel Feinberg did interpret all rights as claim-rights, he argued that to reduce rights to duties omits what is of special value in rights, that the right-holder is in a position to claim the correlative duty. Most conceptual analyses of rights during the second half of the twentieth century can be seen to be attempts to explain what is distinctive and important about rights over and above any duties they might imply.

Many of these conceptual analyses of rights are also intended to be general. Hohfeld had asserted that the expression "a legal right" is ambiguous because the conceptions of a legal claim, a legal privilege or liberty, a legal power and a legal immunity are distinct, unanalyzable and have nothing in common. Why, then, did judges, jurisprudes and practicing lawyers so often use one and the same word to refer to all of them? In his inaugural address, "Definition and Theory in Jurisprudence," Hart denied that the expression "a right" is ambiguous and set himself the task of explaining what claim-rights, liberty-rights, power-rights and immunity-rights have in common. Twenty years later he published his general theory of rights in his paper "Bentham on Legal Rights." Carl Wellman subsequently modified Hart's theory to accomplish the same end. And although D. N. MacCormick did not recognize four species of rights—claim-rights, liberty-rights, power-rights and immunity-rights—he did explain how claims, liberties, powers and immunities could all enter into a right as protections for its defining interest. On the other hand, philosophers like H. J. McCloskey, Ronald Dworkin, and Joseph Raz do not analyze rights in terms of Hohfeld's fundamental legal conceptions or their moral analogues.

There is another respect in which most of the conceptual analyses of rights were intended to be general. They were intended to apply to moral rights, legal rights and other sorts of institutional rights such as the rights conferred by the rules of a private club upon the members of that club. Still, Feinberg, Hart, and Wellman take legal rights as their model and interpret moral rights as analogous to legal rights in some essential way. Thus, Feinberg interprets both legal and moral rights in terms of the activity of claiming, Hart holds that both legal and moral rights concern the proper distribution of freedom, and Wellman argues that both determine the proper allocation of autonomy (later called dominion). However, Joseph Raz rejects the legal model of rights as misleading and takes the concept of a moral right to be logically prior to that of a legal right, and H. J. McCloskey's analysis of rights, although general, seems entirely independent of any legal model.

Philosophers and jurists often distinguish between will theories of rights and interest theories. A will theory holds that what is essential to a right is that it gives some special status to the will of the right-holder; an interest theory defines rights in terms of some interest of the right-holder. Hart holds a will theory of rights because he asserts that rights by their very nature respect some choice of their possessors. In several early publications he subjected the interest theories of Bentham and Mill to severe criticism. David Lyons rebutted many of these criticisms and forced Hart to reformulate his theory of rights. It is a mistake, however, to assume that all will theories are choice or option theories of rights. Although Wellman does not place a choice at the center of every right as Hart does, his theory is still a will theory because he defines rights in terms of autonomy or dominion and analyzes these in terms of actions of freedom and control. Feinberg maintains a different kind of will theory because he explains the nature of rights in terms of the activity of claiming. (Notice, however, that he combines a will theory of the nature of rights with an interest theory of rights possession.) MacCormick rejects all will theories of rights and argues that what is essential to any right is that it protects some interest of the right-holder. Raz explains rights in terms of interests as reasons for rights rather than rights as protections of interests. Not all conceptions of rights are either will or interest theories. McCloskey does not define an entitlement in terms of either will or interest, and Dworkin's theory takes rights to be side-constraints on the pursuit of collective social goals.

Philosophers and jurists almost universally agree that the concept of a right is an essentially distributive concept. Any real right must by its very nature have a possessor and that right-holder is necessarily an individual. (Whether groups qualify as individuals in the relevant sense is a matter of much dispute.) One of the tasks of any adequate conceptual analysis of rights is to explain this distributive feature of rights. Hart's view is that rights concern the distribution of freedom by respecting some choice of the right-holder. Wellman maintains that rights concern the allocation of autonomy or dominion in some potential confrontation between the individual right-holder and some second party. On Feinberg's theory what is distinctive and valuable in any right is that it places its possessor or her representative, but not others, in a position to claim that second-parties respect her right. The interest theories of MacCormick and Raz explain the distributive aspect of rights by placing some interest of the individual right-holder central to their analyses of rights. And Dworkin conceives of rights as limiting the justifiable pursuit of overall social utility when this would invade the right of some individual member of society.

Recent conceptual analyses of rights have seldom taken the form of definitions in any strict sense. Indeed, most analysts agree with Hart and Feinberg that any such definition would be useless because any synonymous expression would pose precisely the same philosophical problems as "a right." Most interpretations of the concept of a right attempt to explain what is distinctive and important about rights in contrast to duties, obligations or more generally values. Some, like Hart and Wellman, also provide a model of a right in which rights are analyzed into component elements corresponding to Hohfeld's fundamental legal conceptions or their moral analogues. Some analyses focus on the function of a right, for Hart determining the proper distribution of freedom and for Wellman delineating the proper allocation of autonomy. For MacCormick the function of any right is to protect some interest or good of its possessor. Other analyses explain rights in terms of their role in practical reasoning. Thus, Dworkin suggests that any right worth taking seriously trumps any appeal to collective utility in the justification of social action, and Raz explains that in practical reasoning rights are intermediate premises based on some interest of the right-holder and in turn justifying the imposition of one or more duties upon second parties. Almost all analysts attempt to explain and defend some general conception of a right from which they hope to derive practical implications about what actions are legally or morally possible or permissible for the right-holder and what actions are required or possible by the duty-bearer or other second parties. Judith Jarvis Thomson develops her theory of rights by reasoning in precisely the opposite direction. She insists that what is theoretically interesting and important in practice about any right consists in its implications. Therefore, she begins by identifying the practical implications of any right and then conceives of that right in terms of these implications.

A Short List of Related Articles

C. H. Whiteley, "On Duties," *Proceedings of the Aristotelian Society* 53 (1952–53), pp. 95–104.

Alf Ross, "Tû-Tû," *Scandinavian Studies in Law* 1 (1957), pp. 139–153.

William K. Frankena, "Obligation and Motivation in Recent Moral Philosophy," in A. I. Melden (ed.), *Essays in Moral Philosophy*, Seattle WA: University of Washington Press, 1958, pp. 40–81.

Marcus G. Singer, "On Duties to Oneself," *Ethics* 69 (1959), pp. 202–205.

Joel Feinberg, "Supererogation and Rules," Ethics 71 (1961), pp. 276–288.

Joel Feinberg, "Duties, Rights, and Claims," *American Philosophical Quarterly* 3 (1966), pp. 137–144.

Michael Stocker, "Supererogation and Duties," in *Studies in Moral Philosophy*, Nicholas Rescher (ed), Oxford: Basil Blackwell, 1968, pp. 53–63.

David Lyons, "The Correlativity of Rights and Duties," *Noûs* 4 (1970), pp. 45–55.

David Braybrooke, "The Firm But Untidy Correlativity of Rights and Obligations," *Canadian Journal of Philosophy* 3 (1972), pp. 351–363.

A. I. Melden, "The Play of Rights," *The Monist* 56 (1972), pp. 479–502.

Frank Snare, "The Definition of *Prima Facie* Duties," *Philosophical Quarterly* 24 (1974), pp. 235–244.

J. Raz, "Promises and Obligations," in P. M. S. Hacker & J. Raz (eds), *Law, Morality, and Society*, Oxford: Clarendon Press, 1977, pp. 210–228.

Rex Martin & James W. Nickel, "Recent Work on the Concept of Rights," *American Philosophical Quarterly* 17 (1980), pp. 165–180.

Jeremy Waldron, "A Right to Do Wrong," *Ethics* 92 (1981), pp. 21–39.

Richard B. Brandt, "The Concept of a Moral Right and Its Function," *Journal of Philosophy* 80 (1983), pp. 29–45.

Carl Wellman, "Relative Moral Duties," *American Philosophical Quarterly* 36 (1999), pp. 209–223.

George Rainbolt, "Perfect and Imperfect Obligations," *Philosophical Studies* 98 (2000), pp. 233–256.

Rights and Duties

Volume 1

Conceptual Analyses of Rights and Duties

SOME FUNDAMENTAL LEGAL CONCEPTIONS AS APPLIED IN JUDICIAL REASONING

From very early days down to the present time the essential nature of trusts and other equitable interests has formed a favorite subject for analysis and disputation. The classical discussions of Bacon[1] and Coke are familiar to all students of equity, and the famous definition of the great chief justice (however inadequate it may really be) is quoted even in the latest textbooks on trusts.[2] That the subject has had a peculiar fascination for modern legal thinkers is abundantly evidenced by the well known articles of Langdell[3] and Ames,[4] by the oft-repeated

[1] Bacon on Uses (Circa 1602; Rowe's ed. 1806), pp. 5-6: "The nature of an use is best discerned by considering what it is not, and then what it is. * * * First, an use is no right, title, or interest in law; and therefore master attorney, who read upon this statute, said well, that there are but two rights: *Jus in re*: *Jus ad rem*.

"The one is an estate, which is *jus in re;* the other a demand, which is *jus ad rem*s but an use is neither. * * * So as now we are come by negatives to the affirmative, what an use is. * * * *Usus est dominium fiduciarium*: Use is an ownership in trust.

"So that *usus & status, sive possessio, potius differunt secundum rationem fori, quam secundum naturam rei,* for that one of them is in court of law, the other in court of conscience. * * *"

[2] Co. Lit. (1628) 272 b: "*Nota,* an use is a trust or confidence reposed in some other, which is not issuing out of the land, but as a thing collaterall, annexed in privitie to the estate of the land, and to the person touching the land, *scilicet,* that *cesty que use* shall take the profit, and that the terre-tenant shall make an estate according to his direction. So as *cesty que use* had neither *jus in re,* nor *jus ad rem,* but only a confidence and trust for which he had no remedie by the common law, but for the breach of trust, his remedie was only by *subpoena* in chancerie. * * *"

This definition is quoted and discussed approvingly in Lewin, Trusts (12th ed., 1911), p. 11. It is also noticed in Maitland, Lectures on Equity (1909), pp. 43, 116.

[3] See Langdell, Classification of Rights and Wrongs (1900), 13 Harv. L. Rev., 659, 673: "Can equity then create such rights as it finds to be necessary for the purposes of justice? As equity wields only physical power, it sems to be impossible that it should actually create anything. * * * It seems, therefore, that equitable rights exist only in contemplation of equity, *i. e.*, that they are a *fiction* invented by equity for the promotion of justice. * * *

"Shutting our eyes, then, to the fact that equitable rights are a fiction, and assuming them to have an actual existence, what is their nature, what observations of Maitland in his Lectures on Equity,[5] by the very divergent treatment of Austin in his Lectures on Jurisprudence,[6] by the still bolder thesis of Salmond in his volume on Jurisprudence,[7] and by the discordant utterances of Mr. Hart[8] and Mr.

---

their extent, and what is the field which they occupy? * * * They must not violate the law * * * Legal and equitable rights must, therefore, exist side by side, and the latter cannot interfere with, or in any manner affect, the former."

See also (1887) 1 Harv. L. Rev., 55, 60: "Upon the whole, it may be said that equity could not create rights *in rem* if it would, and that it would not if it could." Compare *Ibid.* 58; and Summary of Eq. Plead. (2nd ed., 1883) secs. 45, 182-184.

[4] See Ames, "Purchase for Value Without Notice" (1887), 1 Harv. L. Rev., 1, 9: "The trustee is the owner of the land, and, of course, two persons with adverse interests cannot be owners of the same thing. What the *cestui que trust* really owns is the obligation of the trustee; for an obligation is as truly the subject matter of property as any physical *res*. The most striking difference between property in a thing and property in an obligation is in the mode of enjoyment. The owner of a house or a horse enjoys the fruits of ownership without the aid of any other person. The only way in which the owner of an obligation can realize his ownership is by compelling its performance by the obligor. Hence, in the one case, the owner is said to have a right *in rem*, and in the other, a right *in personam*. In other respects the common rules of property apply equally to ownership of things and ownership of obligations. For example, what may be called the passive rights of ownership are the same in both cases. The general duty resting on all mankind not to destroy the property of another, is as cogent in favor of an obligee as it is in favor of the owner of a horse. And the violation of this duty is as pure a tort in the one case as in the other."

[5] Lect. on Eq. (1909), 17, 18, 112: "The thesis that I have to maintain is this, that equitable estates and interests are not *jura in rem*. For reasons that we shall perceive by and by, they have come to look very like *jura in rem;* but just for this very reason it is the more necessary for us to observe that they are essentially *jura in personam*, not rights against the world at large, but rights against certain persons"

See also Maitland, Trust and Corporation (1904), reprinted in 3 Collected Papers, 321, 325.

[6] (5th ed.) Vol. I, p. 378: "By the provisions of that part of the English law which is called equity, a contract to sell at once vests *jus in rem* or ownership in buyer, and the seller has only *jus in re aliena*. * * * To complete the transaction the legal interest of the seller must be passed to the buyer, in legal form. To this purpose the buyer has only *jus in personam*: a right to compel the seller to pass his legal interest; but speaking generally, he has *dominium* or *jus in rem*, and the instrument is a conveyance."

[7] (2nd ed., 1907) p. 230: "If we have regard to the essence of the matter rather than to the form of it, a trustee is not an owner at all, but

Whitlock[9] in their very recent contributions to our periodical literature.

It is believed that all of the discussions and analyses referred to are inadequate. Perhaps, however, it would have to be admitted that even the great intrinsic interest of the subject itself and the noteworthy divergence of opinion existing among thoughtful lawyers of all times would fail to afford more than a comparatively slight excuse for any further discussion considered as a mere end in itself. But, quite apart from the presumably practical consideration of endeavoring to "think straight" in relation to all legal problems, it is apparent that the true analysis of trusts and other equitable interests is a matter that should appeal to even the most extreme pragmatists of the law. It may well be that one's view as to the correct analysis of such interests would control the decision of a number of specific questions. This is obviously true as regards the solution of many difficult and delicate problems in constitutional law and in the conflict of laws.[10] So, too, in certain questions in the law of perpetuities, the intrinsic nature of equitable interests is of great significance, as attested

---

a mere agent, upon whom the law has conferred the power and imposed he duty of administering the property of another person. In legal theory, however, he is not a mere agent, but an owner. He is a person to whom the property of someone else is fictitiously attributed by the law, to the intent that the rights and powers thus rested in a *nominal* owner shall be used by him on behalf of the real owner."

[8] See Walter G. Hart (author of "Digest of Law of Trusts"), The Place of Trust in Jurisprudence (1912), 28 Law Quart. Rev., 290, 296. His position is substantially that of Ames and Maitland.

At the end of this article Sir Frederick Pollock, the editor, puts the query: "Why is Trust not entitled to rank as a head *sui generis?*"

[9] See A. N. Whitlock, Classification of the Law of Trusts (1913), 1 Calif. Law Rev., 215, 218: "It is submitted," says the writer, "that the *cestui* has in fact something more than a right *in personam,* that such a right might be more properly described as a right *in personam ad rem,* or, possibly, a right *in rem per personam.*"

Surely such nebulous and cumbrous expressions as these could hardly fail to make "confusion worse confounded."

[10] See Beale, Equitable Interests in Foreign Property, 20 Harv. L. Rev. (1907), 382; and compare the important cases, *Fall v. Eastin* (1905), 75 Neb., 104; S. C. (1909), 215 U. S., 1, 14-15 (especially concurring opinion of Holmes, J.); *Selover, Bates & Co. v. Walsh* (1912), 226 U. S., 112; *Bank of Africa Limited v. Cohen* (1909), 2 Ch. 129, 143.

by the well-known *Gomm* case[11] and others more or less similar. The same thing is apt to be true of a number of special questions relating to the subject of *bona fide* purchase for value. So on indefinitely.[12]

But all this may seem like misplaced emphasis; for the suggestions last made are not peculiarly applicable to equitable interests: the same points and the same examples seem valid in relation to all possible kinds of jural interests, legal as well as equitable,—and that too, whether we are concerned with "property," "contracts," "torts," or any other title of the law. Special reference has therefore been made to the subject of trusts and other equitable interests only for the reason that the striking divergence of opinion relating thereto conspicuously exemplifies the need for dealing somewhat more intensively and systematically than is usual with the nature and analysis of all types of jural interests. Indeed, it would be virtually impossible to consider the subject of trusts at all adequately without, at the very threshold analyzing and discriminating the various fundamental conceptions that are involved in practically every legal problem. In this connection the suggestion may be ventured that the usual discussions of trusts and other jural interests seem inadequate (and at times misleading) for the very reason that they are not founded on a sufficiently comprehensive and discriminating analysis of jural relations in general. Putting the matter in another way, the tendency—and the fallacy—has been to treat the specific problem as if it were far less complex than it really is; and this commendable effort to treat as simple that which is really complex has, it is believed, furnished a serious obstacle to the clear understanding, the orderly statement, and the correct solution of legal problems. In short, it is submitted that the

[11] (1882) 20 Ch. D. 562, 580, per Sir George Jessel, M. R.: "If then the rule as to remoteness applies to a covenant of this nature, this covenant clearly is bad as extending beyond the period allowed by the rule. Whether the rule applies or not depends upon this, as it appears to me, does or does not the covenant give *an interest in the land?* * * * If it is a mere personal contract it cannot be enforced against the assignee. Therefore the company must admit that somehow it *binds the land.* But if it binds the land, it creates *an equitable interest in the land.*"

[12] Compare *Ball v. Milliken* (1910), 31 R. I., 36; 76 Atl., 789, 793, involving a point other than perpetuities, but quoting in support of the decision reached Sir George Jessel's language as to "equitable interests in land." See preceding note.

right kind of simplicity can result only from more searching and more discriminating analysis.

If, therefore, the title of this article suggests a merely philosophical inquiry as to the nature of law and legal relations,—a discussion regarded more or less as an end in itself,—the writer may be pardoned for repudiating such a connotation in advance. On the contrary, in response to the invitation of the editor of this journal, the main purpose of the writer is to emphasize certain oft-neglected matters that may aid in the understanding and in the solution of practical, every-day problems of the law. With this end in view, the present article and another soon to follow will discuss, as of chief concern, the basic conceptions of the law,—the legal elements that enter into all types of jural interests. A later article will deal specially with the analysis of certain typical and important interests of a complex character,—more particularly trusts and other equitable interests. In passing, it seems necessary to state that both of these articles are intended more for law school students than for any other class of readers. For that reason, it is hoped that the more learned reader may pardon certain parts of the discussion that might otherwise seem unnecessarily elementary and detailed. On the other hand, the limits of space inherent in a periodical article must furnish the excuse for as great a brevity of treatment as is consistent with clearness, and for a comparatively meager discussion—or even a total neglect—of certain matters the intrinsic importance of which might otherwise merit greater attention. In short, the emphasis is to be placed on those points believed to have the greatest practical value.

LEGAL CONCEPTIONS CONTRASTED WITH NON-LEGAL CONCEPTIONS.

At the very outset it seems necessary to emphasize the importance of differentiating purely legal relations from the physical and mental facts that call such relations into being. Obvious as this initial suggestion may seem to be, the arguments that one may hear in court almost any day and likewise a considerable number of judicial opinions afford ample evidence of the inveterate and unfortunate tendency to confuse and blend the legal and the non-legal quantities in a given problem. There are at least two special reasons for this.

For one thing, the association of ideas involved in the two sets of relations—the physical and the mental on the one hand, and the purely legal on the other—is in the very nature of the case, extremely close. This fact has necessarily had a marked influence upon the general doctrines and the specific rules of early systems of law. Thus, we are told by Pollock and Maitland:

"Ancient German law, like ancient Roman law, sees great difficulties in the way of an assignment of a debt or other benefit of a contract * * * men do not see how there can be a transfer of a right unless that right is embodied in some corporeal thing. The history of the incorporeal things has shown us this; they are not completely transferred until the transferee has obtained seisin, has turned his beasts onto the pasture, presented a clerk to the church or hanged a thief upon the gallows. A covenant or a warranty of title may be so bound up with land that the assignee of the land will be able to sue the covenantor or warrantor."[13]

In another connection, the same learned authors observe:

"The realm of mediæval law is rich with incorporeal things. Any permanent right which is of a transferable nature, at all events if it has what we may call a territorial ambit, is thought of as a thing that is very like a piece of land. Just because it is a thing it is transferable. This is no fiction invented by the speculative jurists. For the popular mind these things are things. The lawyer's business is not to make them things but to point out that they are incorporeal. The layman who wishes to convey the advowson of a church will say that he conveys the church; it is for Bracton to explain to him that what he means to transfer is not that structure of wood and stone which belongs to God and the saints but a thing incorporeal, as incorporeal as his own soul or the *anima mundi*."[14]

A second reason for the tendency to confuse or blend non-legal and legal conceptions consists in the ambiguity and looseness of our legal terminology. The word "property" furnishes a striking example. Both with lawyers and with laymen this term has no definite or stable connotation. Sometimes it is employed to indicate the physical object to which various legal rights, privileges, etc., relate; then again—with far greater discrimination and accuracy—the word is used to denote the legal interest (or aggregate of legal relations) appertaining to such physical object. Frequently there is a rapid and fallacious shift from the one

[13] 2 Hist. Eng. Law (2nd ed., 1905), 226.
[14] *Ibid.*, 124.

meaning to the other. At times, also, the term is used in such a "blended" sense as to convey no definite meaning whatever.

For the purpose of exemplifying the looser usage just referred to, we may quote from *Wilson v. Ward Lumber Co.*:[15]

"The term 'property', as commonly used denotes any external object *over which* the *right* of property is exercised. In this sense it is a very wide term, and includes every class of acquisitions which a man can own or have an interest in."

Perhaps the ablest statement to exemplify the opposite and more accurate usage is that of Professor Jeremiah Smith (then Mr. Justice Smith) in the leading case of *Eaton v. B. C. & M. R. R. Co.*:[16]

"In a strict legal sense, land is not 'property', but the subject of property. The term 'property', although in common parlance frequently applied to a tract of land or a chattel, in its legal signification 'means only the rights of the owner in relation to it'. 'It denotes a right over a determinate thing'. 'Property is the right of any person to possess, use, enjoy, and dispose of a thing'. Selden, J., in *Wynehamer v. People*, 13 N. Y., 378, p. 433; 1 Blackstone's com., 138; 2 Austin's *Jurisprudence*, 3rd ed., 817, 818. * * * The right of indefinite user (or of using indefinitely) is an essential quality of absolute property, without which absolute property can have no existence. * * * This right of user necessarily includes the right and power of excluding others from using the land. See 2 *Austin on Jurisprudence*, 3rd ed., 836; Wells, J., in *Walker v. O. C. W. R. R.*, 103 Mass., 10, p. 14."

Another useful passage is to be found in the opinion of Sherwood, J., in *St. Louis v. Hall*:[17]

"Sometimes the term is applied to the thing itself, as a horse, or a tract of land; these things, however, though the subjects of

---

[15] (1895) 67 Fed. Rep., 674, 677. For a somewhat similar, and even more confusing, form of statement, see *In re Fixen* (1900), 102 Fed. Rep., 295, 296.

[16] 51 N. H., 504, 511. Se also the excellent similar statements of Comstock, J., in *Wynehamer v. People* (1856), 13 N. Y., 378, 396; Selden J., S. C., 13 N. Y., 378, 433-434; Ryan, C., in *Law v. Rees Printing Co.* (1894), 41 Neb., 127, 146; Magruder, J., in *Dixon v. People* (1897), 168 Ill., 179, 190.

[17] (1893) 116 Mo., 527, 533-534. That the last sentence quoted is not altogether adequate as an analysis of property will appear, it is hoped, from the latter part of the present discussion.

See also, as regards the term, "property," the opinion of Doe, C. J., in *Smith v. Fairloh* (1894), 68 N. H., 123, 144-145. ("By considering the property *dissolved* into the *legal rights* of which it consists" etc.)

property, are, when coupled with possession, but the *indicia*, the visible manifestation of invisible rights, 'the evidence of things not seen.'

"Property, then, in a determinate object, is composed of certain constituent elements, to wit: The unrestricted right of use, enjoyment, and disposal, of that object."

In connection with the ambiguities latent in the term "property", it seems well to observe that similar looseness of thought and expression lurks in the supposed (but false) contrast between "corporeal" and "incorporeal" property. The second passage above quoted from Pollock and Maitland exhibits one phase of this matter. For further striking illustration, reference may be made to Blackstone's well-known discussion of corporeal and incorporeal hereditaments. Thus, the great commentator tells us:

"But an hereditament, says Sir Edward Coke, is by much the largest and most comprehensive expression; for it includes not only lands and tenements, but whatsoever *may be inherited*, be it corporeal or incorporeal, real, personal, or mixed."[18]

It is clear that only *legal interests* as such can be inherited; yet in the foregoing quotation there is inextricable confusion between the physical or "corporeal" objects and the corresponding legal interests, all of which latter must necessarily be "incorporeal," or "invisible," to use the expression of Mr. Justice Sherwood. This ambiguity of thought and language continues throughout Blackstone's discussion; for a little later he says:

"Hereditaments, then, to use the largest expression, are of two kinds, corporeal and incorporeal. Corporeal consist of such as affect the senses, such as may be seen and handled by the body; incorporeal are not the objects of sensation, can neither be seen nor handled; are creatures of the mind, and exist only in contemplation."

Still further on he says:

"An incorporeal hereditament is a right issuing out of a thing corporate (whether real or personal), or concerning, or annexed to, or exercisable within, the same. * * *

"Incorporeal hereditaments are principally of ten sorts: advowsons, tithes, commons, ways, offices, dignities, franchises, corodies or pensions, annuities, and rents."

---

[18] 2 Black. Com. (1765), 16-43.

Since all legal interests are "incorporeal"—consisting, as they do, of more or less limited aggregates of *abstract* legal relations—such a supposed contrast as that sought to be drawn by Blackstone can but serve to mislead the unwary. The legal interest of the fee simple owner of land and the comparatively limited interest of the owner of a "right of way" over such land are alike so far as "incorporeality" is concerned; the true contrast consists, of course, primarily in the fact that the fee simple owner's aggregate of legal relations is far more extensive than the aggregate of the easement owner.

Much of the difficulty, as regards legal terminology, arises from the fact that many of our words were originally applicable only to physical things;[19] so that their use in connection with legal relations is, strictly speaking, figurative or fictional. The term, "transfer," is a good example. If X says that he has transferred his watch to Y, he may conceivably mean, quite literally, that he has physically handed over the watch to Y; or, more likely, that he has "transferred" his *legal interest*, without any delivery of possession,—the latter, of course, being a relatively figurative use of the term. This point will be reached again, when we come to treat of the "transfer" of legal interests. As another instance of this essentially metaphorical use of a term borrowed from the physical world, the word "power" may be mentioned. In legal discourse, as in daily life, it may frequently be used in the sense of physical or mental capacity to do a thing; but, more usually and aptly, it is used to indicate a "*legal* power", the connotation of which latter term is fundamentally different. The same observations apply, *mutatis mutandis*, to the term "liberty."

Passing to the field of contracts, we soon discover a similar inveterate tendency to confuse and blur legal discussions by failing to discriminate between the mental and physical facts involved in the so-called "agreement" of the parties, and the legal "contractual obligation" to which those facts give rise. Such

---

[19] Compare Poll. & Maitl. Hist. Eng. Law (2nd ed., 1905), Vol. II, p. 31: "Few, if any, of the terms in our legal vocabulary have always been technical terms. The license that the man of science can allow himself of coining new words is one which by the nature of the case is denied to lawyers. They have to take their terms out of the popular speech; gradually the words so taken are defined; sometimes a word continues to have both a technical meaning for lawyers and a different and vaguer meaning for laymen; sometimes the word that lawyers have adopted is abandoned by the laity." Compare also *Ibid.*, p. 33.

ambiguity and confusion are peculiarly incident to the use of the term "contract." One moment the word may mean *the agreement* of the parties; and then, with a rapid and unexpected shift, the writer or speaker may use the term to indicate the *contractual obligation* created by law as a result of the agrement. Further instances of this sort of ambiguity will be noticed as the discussion proceeds.

OPERATIVE FACTS CONTRASTED WITH EVIDENTIAL FACTS.

For the purpose of subsequent convenient reference, it seems necessary at this point to lay emphasis upon another important distinction inherent in the very nature of things. The facts important in relation to a given jural transaction may be either *operative* facts or *evidential* facts. Operative, constitutive, causal, or "dispositive" facts are those which, under the general legal rules that are applicable, suffice to change legal relations, that is, either to create a new relation, or to extinguish an old one, or to perform both of these functions simultaneously.[20] For

[20] Compare Waldo, C. J., in *White v. Multonomah Co.* (1886), 13 Ore., 317, 323: "A 'right' has been define dby Mr. Justice Holmes to be the legal consequence which attaches to certain facts. (The Common Law, 214). Every fact which forms one of the group of facts of which the right is the legal consequence appertains to the substance of the right."

The present writer's choice of the term "operative" has been suggested by the following passage from Thayer, Prelim. Treat. Evid. (1893), p. 393: "Another discrimination to be observed is that between documents which constitute a contract, fact, or transaction, and those which merely certify and evidence something outside of themselves,—a something valid and *operative,* independent of the writing."

Compare also Holland, Jurisp. (10th ed, 1906), 151: "A fact giving rise to a right has long been described as a 'title'; but no such well-worn equivalent can be found for a fact through which a right is transferred, or for one by which a right is extinguished. A new nomenclature was accordingly invented by Bentham, which is convenient for scientific use, although it has not found its way into ordinary language. He describes this whole class of facts as 'Dispositive'; distinguishing as 'Investitive' those by means of which a right comes into existence, as 'Divestitive' those through which it terminates, and as 'Translative' those through which it passes from one person to another."

The word "ultimate," sometimes used in this connection, does not seem to be so pointed and useful a term as either "operative" or "constitutive."

example, in the creation of a contractual obligation between A and B, the *affirmative* operative facts are, *inter alia,* that each of the parties is a human being, that each of them has lived for not less than a certain period of time, (is not "under age"), that A has made an "offer," that B has "accepted" it, etc. It is sometimes necessary to consider, also, what may, from the particular point of view, be regarded as *negative* operative facts. Thus, *e. g.,* the fact that A did not wilfully misrepresent an important matter to B, and the fact that A had not "revoked" his offer, must really be included as parts of the totality of operative facts in the case already put.

Taking another example,—this time from the general field of torts—if X commits an assault on Y by putting the latter in fear of bodily harm, this particular group of facts immediately create in Y the privilege of self-defense,—that is, the privilege of using sufficient force to repel X's attack; or, correlatively, the otherwise existing duty of Y to refrain from the application of force to the person of X is, by virtue of the special operative facts, immediately terminated or extinguished.

In passing, it may not be amiss to notice that the term, "facts in issue," is sometimes used in the present connection. If, as is usual, the term means "facts put in issue by the *pleadings,*" the expression is an unfortuante one. The operative facts alleged by the pleadings are more or less *generic* in character; and if the pleadings be sufficient, only such *generic* operative facts are "put in issue." The operative facts of real life are, on the other hand, very specific. That being so, it is clear that the *real* and *specific* facts finally relied on are comparatively seldom put in issue by the pleadings. Thus, if, in an action of tort, the declaration of A alleges that he was, through the carelessness, etc., of B, bitten by the latter's dog, the fact alleged is generic in character, and it matters not whether it was dog Jim or dog Dick that did the biting. Even assuming, therefore, that the biting was done by Jim, (rather than by Dick), it could not be said that this specific fact was put in issue by the pleadings. Similarly, and more obviously, the pleading in an ordinary action involving so-called negligence, is usually very generic in character,[21] so

---

[21] Compare, however, *Illinois Steel Co. v. Ostrowski* (1902), 194 Ill., 376, 384, correctly sustaining a declaration alleging the operative facts *specifically* instead of *generically,* as required by the more approved forms of pleading.

that any one of various possible groups of specific operative facts would suffice, so far as the defendant's obligation *ex delicto* is concerned. It therefore could not be said that any one of such groups had been put in issue by the pleadings. A common fallacy in this connection is to regard the *specific* operative facts established in a given case as being but "evidence" of the *generic* (or "ultimate") operative facts alleged in the pleadings.[22]

An evidential fact is one which, on being ascertained, affords some logical basis—not conclusive—for inferring some other fact. The latter may be either a constitutive fact or an intermediate evidential fact. Of all the facts to be ascertained by the tribunal, the operative are, of course, of primary importance; the evidential are subsidiary in their functions.[23] As a rule there is little danger of confusing evidential facts with operative facts. But there is one type of case that not infrequently gives rise to this sort of error. Suppose that in January last a contractual obligation was created by written agreement passing between A and B. In an action now pending between these parties, the physical *instrument* is offered for inspection by the tribunal. If one were thoughtless, he would be apt to say that this is a case where part of the operative facts creating the original obligation are directly presented to the senses of the tribunal. Yet a moment's reflection will show that such is not the case. The document, in its

---

The rules of pleading determining whether allegations must be generic or specific—and if the latter, to what degree—are, like other rules of law, based on considerations of policy and convenience. Thus the facts constituting *fraud* are frequently required to be alleged in comparatively specific form; and similarly as regards *cruelty* in an action for divorce based on that ground. The reasons of policy are obvious in each case.

[22] Compare *McCaughey v. Schuette* (1897), 117 Cal., 223. While the decision in this case can be supported, the statement that the specific facts pleaded were "evidentiary" seems inaccurate and misleading.

There are, of course, genuine instances of the fatally erroneous pleading of strictly evidential facts instead of either generic or specific operative facts. See *Rogers v. Milwaukee,* 13 Wis., 610; and contrast *Illinois Steel Co. v. Ostrowski, supra,* note 21.

[23] Both operative and evidential facts must, under the law, be *ascertained* in some one or more of four possible modes: 1. By judicial admissions (what is not disputed); 2. By judicial notice, or knowledge (what is known or easily knowable); 3. By judicial perception (what is ascertained directly through the senses; cf. "real evidence"); 4. By judicial inference (what is ascertained by reasoning from facts already ascertained by one or more of the four methods here outlined).

then existing shape, had, as regards its operative effect, spent its force as soon as it was delivered in January last. If, therefore, the unaltered document is produced for inspection, the facts thus ascertained must, as regards the alleged contractual agreement, be purely evidential in character. That is to say, the present existence of the piece of paper, its specific tenor, etc., may, along with other evidential facts (relating to absence of change) tend to prove the various operative facts of last January,—to wit, that such paper existed at that time; that its tenor was then the same as it now is; that it was delivered by A to B, and so forth.

It now remains to observe that in many situations a single convenient term is employed to designate (generically) certain miscellaneous groups of operative facts which, though differing widely as to their individual "ingredients," have, as regards a given matter, the same *net* force and effect. When employed with discrimination, the term "possession" is a word of this character; so also the term "capacity," the term "domicile," etc. But the general tendency to confuse legal and non-legal quantities is manifest here as elsewhere; so that only too frequently these words are used rather nebulously to indicate legal relations as such.[24]

FUNDAMENTAL JURAL RELATIONS CONTRASTED WITH ONE ANOTHER.

One of the greatest hindrances to the clear understanding, the incisive statement, and the true solution of legal problems frequently arises from the express or tacit assumption that all legal relations may be reduced to "rights" and "duties," and that these latter categories are therefore adequate for the purpose of analyzing even the most complex legal interests, such as trusts, options, escrows, "future" interests, corporate interests, etc. Even if the difficulty related merely to inadequacy and ambiguity of

---

[24] As an example of this, compare Lord Westbury, in *Bell v. Kennedy* (1868), L. R. 1 H. L. (Sc.), 307: "Domicile, therefore, is an idea of the law. It is the *relation* which the *law creates* between an individual and a particular locality or country."

Contrast the far more accurate language of Chief Justice Shaw in *Abington v. Bridgewater* (1840), 23 Pick., 170: "The *fact* of domicile is often one of the highest importance to a person; it *determines* his civil and political rights and privileges, duties and obligations. * * *"

terminology, its seriousness would nevertheless be worthy of definite recognition and persistent effort toward improvement; for in any closely reasoned problem, whether legal or non-legal, chameleon-hued words are a peril both to clear thought and to lucid expression.[25] As a matter of fact, however, the above mentioned inadequacy and ambiguity of terms unfortunately reflect, all too often, corresponding paucity and confusion as regards actual legal conceptions. That this is so may appear in some measure from the discussion to follow.

---

[25] In this connection, the words of one of the great masters of the common law are significant. In his notable Preliminary Treatise on Evidence (1898), p. 190, Professor James Bradley Thayer said:

"As our law develops it becomes more and more important to give definiteness to its phraseology; discriminations multiply, new situations and complications of fact arise, and the old outfit of ideas, discriminations, and phrases has to be carefully revised. Law is not so unlike all other subjects of human contemplation that clearness of thought will not help us powerfully in grasping it. If terms in common legal use are used exactly, it is well to know it; if they are used inexactly, it is well to know that, and to remark just how they are used."

Perhaps the most characteristic feature of this author's great constructive contribution to the law of evidence is his constant insistence on the need for clarifying our legal terminology, and making careful "discriminations" between conceptions and terms that are constantly being treated as if they were one and the same. See, *e. g.*, *Ibid.*, pp. vii, 183, 189-190, 278, 306, 351, 355, 390-393. How great the influence of those discriminations has been is well known to all students of the law of evidence.

The comparatively recent remarks of Professor John Chipman Gray, in his Nature and Sources of the Law (1909), Pref. p. viii, are also to the point:

"The student of Jurisprudence is at times troubled by the thought that he is dealing not with things, but with words, that he is busy with the shape and size of counters in a game of logomachy, but when he fully realizes how these words have been passed and are still being passed as money, not only by fools and on fools, but by and on some of the acutest minds, he feels that there is work worthy of being done, if only it can be done worthily."

No less significant and suggestive is the recent and charactistic utterance of one of the greatest jurists of our time, Mr. Justice Holmes. In *Hyde v. United States* (1911), 225 U. S., 347, 391, the learned judge very aptly remarked: "It is one of the misfortunes of the law that ideas become encysted in phrases and thereafter for a long time cease to provoke further analysis."

See also, Field, J., in *Morgan v. Louisiana* (1876), 93 U. S., 217, 223, and Peckham, J. in *Phoenix Ins. Co. v. Tennessee* (1895), 161 U. S., 174, 177, 178.

The strictly fundamental legal relations are, after all, *sui generis;* and thus it is that attempts at formal definition are always unsatisfactory, if not altogether useless. Accordingly, the most promising line of procedure seems to consist in exhibiting all of the various relations in a scheme of "opposites" and "correlatives," and then proceeding to exemplify their individual scope and application in concrete cases. An effort will be made to pursue this method:

Jural Opposites	rights	privilege	power	immunity
	no-rights	duty	disability	liability

Jural Correlatives	right	privilege	power	immunity
	duty	no-right	liability	disability

Rights and Duties. As already intimated, the term "rights" tends to be used indiscriminately to cover what in a given case may be a privilege, a power, or an immunity, rather than a right in the strictest sense; and this looseness of usage is occasionally recognized by the authorities. As said by Mr. Justice Strong in *People v. Dikeman*:[26]

"The word 'right' is defined by lexicographers to denote, among other things, *property, interest, power, prerogative, immunity, privilege* (Walker's Dict. word 'Right'). In law it is most frequently applied to property in its restricted sense, but it is often used to designate *power, prerogative,* and *privilege,* * * *."

Recognition of this ambiguity is also found in the language of Mr. Justice Jackson, in *United States v. Patrick*:[27]

"The words 'right' or 'privilege' have, of course, a variety of meanings, according to the connection or context in which they are used. Their definition, as given by standard lexicographers, include 'that which one has a *legal claim to do,' 'legal power,' 'authority,' 'immunity* granted by authority,' 'the investiture with special or peculiar rights.'"

And, similarly, in the language of Mr. Justice Sneed, in *Lonas v. State*:[28]

"The state, then, is forbidden from making and enforcing any law which shall abridge the *privileges* and *immunities* of citizens of the United States. It is said that the words *rights, privileges* and *immunities,* are abusively used, as if they were synonymous.

---

[26] (1852) 7 How. Pr., 124, 130.

[27] (1893) 54 Fed. Rep., 338, 348.

[28] (1871) 3 Heisk. (Tenn.), 287, 306-307.

The word *rights* is generic, common, embracing whatever may be lawfully claimed."[29]

It is interesting to observe, also, that a tendency toward discrimination may be found in a number of important constitutional and statutory provisions. Just how accurate the distinctions in the mind of the draftsman may have been it is, of course, impossible to say.[30]

Recognizing, as we must, the very broad and indiscriminate use of the term, "right," what clue do we find, in ordinary legal discourse, toward limiting the word in question to a definite and appropriate meaning. That clue lies in the correlative "duty," for it is certain that even those who use the word and the conception "right" in the broadest possible way are accustomed to thinking of "duty" as the invariable correlative. As said in *Lake Shore & M. S. R. Co. v. Kurtz*:[31]

---

[29] See also, for similar judicial observations, *Atchison & Neb. R. Co. v. Baty* (1877), 6 Neb., 37, 40. (The term *right* in civil society is defined to mean that which a man is entitled *to have*, or *to do*, or *to receive* from others within the limits prescribed by law."); *San Francisco v. S. V. Water Co.* (   ), 48 Cal., 531 ("We are to ascertain the *rights, privileges, powers, duties* and *obligations* of the Spring Valley Water Co., by reference to the general law.").

Compare also Gilbert, Evid. (4th ed., 1777), 126: "The men of one county, city, hundred, town, corporation, or parish are evidence in relation to the *rights privileges, immunities* and affairs of such town, city, etc."

[30] See *Kearns v. Cordwainers' Co.* (1859), 6 C. B. N. S., 388, 409 (construing The Thames Conservancy Act, 1857, 20 and 21 Vict. c. cxlvii., s. 179: "None of the powers by this act conferred * * * shall extend to, take away, alter or abridge any right, claim, privilege, franchise, exemption, or immunity to which any owners * * * of any lands * * * are now by law entitled."); *Fearon v. Mitchell* (1872), L. R. 7 Q. B., 690, 695 ("The other question remains to be disposed of, as to whether the case comes within the proviso of s. 50 of 21 and 22 Vict. c. 98, that 'no market shall be established in pursuance of this section so as to interfere with any rights, powers, or privileges enjoyed within the district by any person without his consent.'"); Cal. Civ. Code, sec. 648a: "Building and loan associations may be formed under this title with or without guarantee or other capital stock, with all the rights, powers, and privileges, and subject to all the restrictions and liabilities set forth in this title."); Tenn. Const. of 1834, Art. 9, sec. 7: "The legislature shall have no power to pass any law granting to any individual or individuals, rights, privileges and immunities or exemptions, other than * * *").

[31] (1894) 10 Ind. App., 60; 37 N. E., 303, 304.

"A duty or a legal obligation is that which one ought or ought not to do. 'Duty' and 'right' are correlative terms. When a right is invaded, a duty is violated."[32]

In other words, if X has a right against Y that he shall stay off the former's land, the correlative (and equivalent) is that Y is under a duty toward X to stay off the place. If, as seems desirable, we should seek a synonym for the term "right" in this limited and proper meaning, perhaps the word "claim" would prove the best. The latter has the advantage of being a monosyllable. In this connection, the language of Lord Watson in *Studd v. Cook*[33] is instructive:

"Any words which in a settlement of moveables would be recognized by the law of Scotland as sufficient to create a right *or claim* in favor of an executor * * * must receive effect if used with reference to lands in Scotland."

Privileges and "No-Rights." As indicated in the above scheme of jural relations, a privilege is the opposite of a duty, and the correlative of a "no-right." In the example last put, whereas X has a *right* or *claim* that Y, the other man, should stay off the land, he himself has the ***privilege*** of entering on the land; or, in equivalent words, X does not have a duty to stay off. The privilege of entering is the negation of a duty to stay off. As indicated by this case, some caution is necessary at this point, for, always, when it is said that a given privilege is the mere negation of a *duty*, what is meant, of course, is a duty having a content or tenor precisely ***opposite*** to that of the privilege in question. Thus, if, for some special reason, X has contracted with Y to go on the former's own land, it is obvious that X has, as regards Y, both the privilege of entering and the ***duty of entering***. The privilege is perfectly consistent with this sort of duty,—

---

[32] See also *Howley Park Coal, etc., Co. v. L. & N. W. Ry.* (1913), A. C. 11, 25, 27 (per Viscount Haldane, L. C.: "There is an obligation (of lateral support) on the neighbor, and in that sense there is a correlative right on the part of the owner of the first piece of land;" per Lord Shaw: "There is a reciprocal right to lateral support for their respective lands and a reciprocal obligation upon the part of each owner. * * * No diminution of the right on the one hand or of the obligation on the other can be effected except as the result of a plain contract. * * *").

Compare, to similar effect, *Galveston, etc. Ry. Co. v. Harrigan* (1903), 76 S. W., 452, 453 (Tex. Civ. App.).

[33] (1883) 8 App. Cas., at p. 597.

for the latter is of the *same* content or tenor as the privilege;—but it still holds good that, as regards Y, X's privilege of entering is the precise negation of a duty *to stay off*. Similarly, if A has not contracted with B to perform certain work for the latter, A's privilege of *not* doing so is the very negation of a duty of *doing* so. Here again the duty contrasted is of a content or tenor exactly opposite to that of the privilege.

Passing now to the question of "correlatives," it will be remembered, of course, that a duty is the invariable correlative of that legal relation which is most properly called a right or claim. That being so, if further evidence be needed as to the fundamental and important difference between a right (or claim) and a privilege, surely it is found in the fact that the correlative of the latter relation is a "no-right," there being no single term available to express the latter conception. Thus, the correlative of X's right that Y shall not enter on the land is Y's duty not to enter; but the correlative of X's privilege of entering himself is manifestly Y's "no-right" that X shall not enter.

In view of the considerations thus far emphasized, the importance of keeping the conception of a right (or claim) and the conception of a privilege quite distinct from each other seems evident; and more than that, it is equally clear that there should be a separate term to represent the latter relation. No doubt, as already indicated, it is very common to use the term "right" indiscriminately, even when the relation designated is really that of privilege;[34] and only too often this identity of terms has involved for the particular speaker or writer a confusion or blurring of ideas. Good instances of this may be found even in unexpected places. Thus Professor Holland, in his work on Jurisprudence, referring to a different and well known sort of ambiguity inherent in the Latin *"Ius,"* the German *"Recht,"* the Italian *"Diritto,"* and the French *"Droit,"*—terms used to express "not only 'a right,' but also 'Law' in the abstract,"—very aptly observes:

"If the expression of widely different ideas by one and the same term resulted only in the necessity for * * * clumsy para-

[34] For merely a few out of numberless judicial instances of this loose usage, see *Pearce v. Scotcher* (1882), L. R. 9 Q. B., 162, 167; *Quinn v. Leathem* (1901), A. C. 495 (*passim*); *Allen v. Flood* (1898), A. C. 1 (*passim*); *Lindley v. Nat. Carbonic Acid Gas Co.* (1910), 220 U. S., 61, 75; *Smith v. Cornell Univ.* (1894), 45 N. Y. Supp., 640, 643; *Farnum v. Kern Valley Bk.* (1910), 107 Pac., 568. See also *post*, n. 38.

phrases, or obviously inaccurate paraphrases, no great harm would be done; but unfortunately the identity of terms seems irresistibly to suggest an identity between the ideas expressed by them."[85]

Curiously enough, however, in the very chapter where this appears,—the chapter on "Rights,"—the notions of right, privilege and power seem to be blended, and that, too, although the learned author states that "the correlative of * * * legal right is legal duty," and that "these pairs of terms express * * * in each case the same state of facts viewed from opposite sides." While the whole chapter must be read in order to appreciate the seriousness of this lack of discrimination a single passage must suffice by way of example:

"If * * * the power of the State will protect him in so carrying out his wishes, and will compel such acts or forbearances on the part of other people as may be necessary in order that his wishes may be so carried out, then he has a 'legal right' so to carry out his wishes."[86]

The first part of this passage suggests privileges, the middle part rights (or claims), and the last part privileges.

Similar difficulties seem to exist in Professor Gray's able and entertaining work on The Nature and Sources of Law. In his chapter on "Legal Rights and Duties" the distinguished author takes the position that a right always has a duty as its correlative;[87] and he seems to define the former relation substantially according to the more limited meaning of "claim." Legal privileges, powers, and immunities are *prima facie* ignored, and the impression conveyed that all legal relations can be comprehended under the conceptions, "right" and "duty." But, with the greatest hesitation and deference, the suggestion may be ventured that a number of his examples seem to show the inadequacy of such mode of treatment. Thus, *e.g.*, he says:

"The eating of shrimp salad is an interest of mine, and, if I can pay for it, the law will protect that interest, and it is therefore a right of mine to eat shrimp salad which I have paid for, although I know that shrimp salad always gives me the colic."[88]

This passage seems to suggest primarily two classes of relations: *first*, the party's respective privileges, as against A, B, C.

---

[85] El. Jurisp. (10th ed.), 83.

[86] *Ibid.*, 82.

[87] See Nat. and Sources of Law (1909), secs. 45, 184.

[88] *Ibid.*, sec. 48.

D and others in relation to eating the salad, or, correlatively, the respective "no-rights" of A. B. C. D and others that the party should not eat the salad; *second,* the party's respective rights (or claims) as against A, B. C. D and others that they should not interfere with the physical act of eating the salad, or, correlatively, the respective duties of A, B, C, D and others that they should not interfere.

These two groups of relations seem perfectly distinct; and the privileges could, in a given case exist even though the rights mentioned did not. A. B. C. and D, being the owners of the salad, might say to X: "Eat the salad, if you can; you have our license to do so, but we don't agree not to interfere with you." In such a case the privileges exist, so that if X succeeds in eating the salad, he has violated no rights of any of the parties. But it is equally clear that if A had succeeded in holding so fast to the dish that X couldn't eat the contents, no right of X would have been violated.[39]

Perhaps the essential character and importance of the distinction can be shown by a slight variation of the facts. Suppose that X, being already the legal owner of the salad, contracts with Y that he (X) will never eat this particular food. With A, B,

---

[39] Other instances in Professor Gray's work may be noted. In sec. 53, he says: "So again, a householder has the right to eject by force a trespasser from his 'castle.' That is, if sued by the trespasser for an assault, he can call upon the court to refuse the plaintiff its help. In other words, a man's legal rights include not only the power effectually to call for aid from an organized society against another, but also the power to call effectually upon the society to abstain from aiding others."

This, it is respectfully submitted, seems to confuse the householder's privilege of ejecting the trespasser (and the "no-right" of the latter) with a complex of *potential* rights, privileges, powers and immunities relating to the supposed action at law.

In sec. 102, the same learned author says: "If there is an ordinance that the town constable may kill all dogs without collars, the constable may have a legal right to kill such dogs, but the dogs are not under a legal duty to wear collars."

It would seem, however, that what the ordinance did was to create a privilege—the absence of the duty not to kill which otherwise would have existed in favor of the owner of the dog. Moreover, that appears to be the most natural connotation of the passage. The latter doesn't except very remotely, call up the idea of the constable's accompanying rights against all others that they shouldn't interfere with his actual killing of the dog.

See, also, secs. 145, 186.

C, D and others no such contract has been made. One of the relations now existing between X and Y is, as a consequence, fundamentally different from the relation between X and A. As regards Y, X has no privilege of eating the salad; but as regards either A or any of the others, X has such a privilege. It is to be observed incidentally that X's right that Y should not eat the food persists even though X's own privilege of doing so has been extinguished.[40]

On grounds already emphasized, it would seem that the line of reasoning pursued by Lord Lindley in the great case of *Quinn v. Leathem*[41] is deserving of comment:

"The plaintiff had the ordinary *rights* of the British subject. He was *at liberty* to earn his living in his own way, provided he did not violate some special law prohibiting him from so doing, and provided he did not infringe the rights of other people. This *liberty* involved *the liberty* to deal with other persons who were willing to deal with him. *This liberty* is *a right* recognized by law; its *correlative* is the general *duty* of every one not to prevent the free exercise of this *liberty* except so far as his own liberty of action may justify him in so doing. But a person's *liberty* or *right* to deal with others is nugatory unless they are at liberty to deal with him if they choose to do so. Any interference with their liberty to deal with him affects him."

A "liberty" considered as a legal relation (or "right" in the loose and generic sense of that term) must mean, if it have any definite content at all, precisely the same thing as *privilege*,[42] and certainly that is the fair connotation of the term as used the first three times in the passage quoted. It is equally clear, as already indicated, that such a privilege or liberty to deal with others at will might very conceivably exist without any peculiar concomitant rights against "third parties" as regards certain kinds of interference.[43] Whether there should be such concomitant rights (or claims) is ultimately a question of justice and policy; and it should be considered, as such, on its merits. The only correlative logically implied by the privileges or liberties in question are the "no-rights" of "third parties." It would therefore be a *non*

---

[40] It may be noted incidentally that a statute depriving a party of privileges as such may raise serious constitutional questions under the Fourteenth Amendment. Compare, *e. g.*, *Lindley v. Nat. Carbonic Gas Co.* (1910), 220 U. S., 61.

[41] (1901) A. C., 495, 534.

[42] See *post*, pp. 38-44.

[43] Compare *Allen v. Flood* (1898), A. C., 1.

sequitur to conclude from the mere existence of such liberties that "third parties." are under a *duty* not to interfere, etc. Yet in the middle of the above passage from Lord Lindley's opinion there is a sudden and question-begging shift in the use of terms. First, the "liberty" in question is transmuted into a "right," and then, possibly under the seductive influence of the latter word, it is assumed that the "correlative" must be "the general duty of every one not to prevent," etc.

Another interesting and instructive example may be taken from Lord Bowen's oft-quoted opinion in *Mogul Steamship Co. v. McGregor.*[44]

"We are presented in this case with an apparent conflict or an inomy between two rights that are equally regarded by the law—the right of the plaintiffs to be protected in the legitimate exercise of their trade, and the right of the defendants to carry on their business as seems best to them, provided they commit no wrong to others."

As the learned judge states, the conflict or antinomy is only apparent; but this fact seems to be obscured by the very indefinite and rapidly shifting meanings with which the term "right" is used in the above quoted language. Construing the passage as a whole, it seems plain enough that by "the right of the plaintiffs" in relation to the defendants a legal right or claim in the strict sense must be meant; whereas by "the right of the defendants" in relation to the plaintiffs a legal privilege must be intended. That being so, the "two rights" mentioned in the beginning of the passage, being respectively claim and privilege, could not be in conflict with each other. To the extent that the defendants have privileges the plaintiffs have no rights; and conversely, to the extent that the plaintiffs have rights the defendants have no privileges ("no-privilege" equals duty of opposite tenor).[45]

---

[44] (1889) 23 Q. B. D., 59.

[45] Cases almost without number might be cited to exemplify similar blending of fundamental conceptions and rapid shifting in the use of terms;—and that too, even when the problems involved have been such as to invite close and careful reasoning. For a few important cases of this character, see *Allen v. Flood* (1898), A. C, 1, (Hawkins, J., p. 16: "I know it may be asked, 'What is the legal right of the plaintiffs which is said to have been invaded?' My answer is, that right which should never be lost sight of, and which I have already stated—the right freely to pursue their lawful calling;" Lord Halsbury, p. 84: "To dig into one's own land

Thus far it has been assumed that the term "privilege" is the most appropriate and satisfactory to designate the mere negation of duty. Is there good warrant for this?

In Mackeldey's Roman Law[46] it is said:

"Positive laws either contain general principles embodied in the rules of law * * * or for especial reasons they establish something that differs from those general principles. In the first case they contain a common law (*jus commune*), in the second a special law (*jus singulare s. exorbitans*). The latter is either favorable or unfavorable * * * according as it enlarges or restricts, in opposition to the common rule, the rights of those for whom it is established. The favorable special law (*jus singulare*) as also the right created by it * * * in the Roman law is termed benefit of the law (*beneficium juris*) or privilege (*privilegium*) * * *"[47]

First a special law, and then by association of ideas, a special advantage conferred by such a law. With such antecedents, it is not surprising that the English word "privilege" is not infrequently used, even at the present time, in the sense of a special or peculiar legal advantage (whether right, privilege, power or immunity) belonging either to some individual or to some particular class of persons.[48] There are, indeed, a number of judicial opinions

---

under the circumstances stated requires no cause or excuse. He may act from mere caprice, but his right on his own land is absolute, so long as he does not interfere with the rights of others;" Lord Ashbourne, p. 112: "The plaintiff had, in my opinion, a clear right to pursue their lawful calling. * * * It would be, I think, an unsatisfactory state of the law that allowed the wilful invader of such a right without lawful leave or justification to escape from the consequences of his action."); *Quinn v. Leathem* (1901), A. C., 495, 533; *Lindsley v. Natural Carbonic Gas Co* (1910), 220 U. S., 61, 74; *Robertson v. Rochester Folding Box Co.* (1902), 171 N. Y., 538 (Parker, C. J., p. 544: "The so-called right of privacy is, as the phrase suggests, founded upon the claim that a man has the right to pass through this world, if he wills, without having his picture published."); *Wabash, St. L. & P. R. Co. v. Shacklet* (1883), 105 Ill., 364, 389.

In *Purdy v. State* (1901), 43 Fla., 538, 540, the anomalous expression "right of privilege" is employed.

[46] (Dropsie Tr.) secs. 196-197.

[47] The same matter is put somewhat less clearly in Sohm's Institutes (Ledlies Tr., 3rd ed.), 28.

See also *Rector, etc. of Christ Church v. Philadelphia* (1860), 24 How., 300, 301, 302.

[48] According to an older usage, the term "privilege" was frequently employed to indicate a "franchise" the latter being really a miscellaneous complex of special rights, privileges, powers, or immunities, etc. Thus, in an early book, *Termes de la Ley*, there is the following definition: "'Privi-

recognizing this as one of the meanings of the term in question.[49] That the word has a wider signification even in ordinary non-technical usage is sufficiently indicated, however, by the fact that the term "*special* privileges" is so often used to indicate a contrast to ordinary or general privileges. More than this, the dominant specific connotation of the term as used in popular speech seems to be more *negation of duty.* This is manifest in the terse and oft-repeated expression, "That is your privilege,"—meaning, of course, "You are under no duty to do otherwise."

Such being the case, it is not surprising to find, from a wide survey of judicial precedents, that the *dominant* technical meaning of the term is, similarly, negation of *legal duty.*[50] There are two very common examples of this, relating respectively to "privileged communications" in the law of libel and to "privileges against self-crimination" in the law of evidence. As regards the first case, it is elementary that if a certain group of operative facts are present, a privilege exists, which, without such facts, would not be recognized.[51] It is, of course, equally clear that even

---

leges' are liberties and franchises granted to an office, place, towne, or manor by the King's great charter, letters patent, or Act of Parliament, as toll, sake, socke, infangstheefe, outfangstheefe, turne, or delfe, and divers such like."

Compare *Blades v. Higgs* (1865), 11 H. L. Cas., 621, 631, per Lord Westbury: "Property *ratione privilegii* is the right which by a peculiar franchise anciently granted by the Crown, by virtue of prerogative, one may have of taking animals *ferae naturae* on the land of another; and in like manner the game when taken by virtue of the privilege becomes the absolute property of the owner of the franchise."

[49] See *Humphrey v. Pegues* (1872), 16 Wall., 244, 247, per Hunt, J.: "All the 'privileges' as well as powers and rights of the prior company. were granted to the latter. A more imporant or more comprehensive privilege than a perpetual immunity from taxation can scarcely be imagined. It contains the essential idea of a peculiar benefit or advantage, of a special exemption from a burden falling upon others."

See also *Smith v. Floyd* (1893), 140 N. Y., 337, 342; *Lonas v. State* (1871). 3 Heisk., 287, 306,307; *Territory v Stokes* (1881), 2 N. M., 161, 169, 170; *Ripley v. Knight* (1878), 123 Mass., 515, 519; *Dike v. State* (1888), 38 Minn., 366; *Re Miller* (1893), 1 Q. B., 327.

Compare *Wisener v. Burrell* (1911), 28 Okla., 546.

[50] Compare *Louisville & N. R Co. v. Gaines* (1880), 3 Fed. Rep., 266, 278, per Baxter, Asso. J.: "Paschal says (the term privilege) is a special right belonging to an individual or class; *properly,* an *exemption* from some *duty.*"

[51] For apt use of the terms, "privilege" and "privileged" in relation to libel, see Hawkins, J., in *Allen v. Flood* (1898), A. C. 1, 20-21.

though all such facts be present as last supposed, the superadded fact of malice will, in cases of so-called "conditional privilege," extinguish the privilege that otherwise would exist. It must be evident also, that whenever the privilege does exist, it is not special in the sense of arising from a special law, or of being conferred as a special favor on a particular individual. The same privilege would exist, by virtue of general rules, for any person whatever under similar circumstances. So, also, in the law of evidence, the privilege against self-crimination signifies the mere negation of a duty, to testify,—a duty which rests upon a witness in relation to all ordinary matters; and, quite obviously, such privilege arises, if at all, only by virtue of general laws.[52]

As already intimated, while both the conception and the term "privilege" find conspicuous exemplification under the law of libel and the law of evidence, they nevertheless have a much wider significance and utility as a matter of judicial usage. To make this clear, a few miscellaneous judicial precedents will now be noticed. In Dowman's Case,[53] decided in the year 1583, and reported by Coke, the court applied the term to the subject of waste:

"And as to the objection which was made, that the said privilege to be without impeachment of waste cannot be without deed, etc. To that it was answered and resolved, that if it was admitted that a deed in such case should be requisite, yet without question all the estates limited would be good, although it is admitted, that the clause concerning the said privilege would be void."

In the great case of *Allen v. Flood*[54] the opinion of Mr. Justice Hawkins furnishes a useful passage for the purpose now in view:

---

[52] As regards the general duty to testify, specific performance may usually be had under duress of potential or actual contempt proceedings; and, apart from that, failure to testify might subject the wrongdoer either to a statutory liability for a penalty in favor of the injured party litigant or, in case of actual damage, to a common law action on the case.

The subject of witnesses is usually thought of as a branch of the so-called *adjective* law, as distinguished from the so-called *substantive* law. But, as the writer has had occasion to emphasize on another occasion (The Relations betwen Equity and Law, 11 Mich. L. Rev., 537, 554, 556, 569), there seems to be no intrinsic or essential difference between those jural relations that relate to the "substantive" law and those that relate to the "adjective" law. This matter will be considered more fully in a later part of the discussion.

[53] (1583) 9 Coke, 1.

[54] (1898) A. C., 1, 19.

"Every person has a privilege * * * in the interests of public justice to put the criminal law in motion against another whom he *bona fide,* and upon reasonable and probable cause, believes to have been guilty of a crime. * * * It must not, however, be supposed that hatred and ill-will existing in the mind of a prosecutor must of necessity *destroy* the *privilege,* for it is not impossible that such hatred and ill-will may have very natural and pardonable reasons for existing. * * *"

Applying the term in relation to the subject of property, Mr. Justice Foster, of the Supreme Court of Maine, said in the case of *Pulitzer v. Lumgston*:[55]

"It is contrary to the policy of the law that there should be any outstanding titles, estates, or powers, by the existence, operation or exercise of which, at a period of time beyond lives in being and twenty-one years and a fraction thereafter, the complete and unfettered enjoyment of an estate, *with all the rights, privileges and powers incident to ownership,* should be qualified or impeded."

As a final example in the present connection, the language of Baron Alderson in *Hilton v. Eckerley*[56] may be noticed:

"*Prima facie* it is the privilege of a trader in a free country, in all matters not contrary to law, to regulate his own mode of carrying them on according to his discretion and choice."[57]

The closest synonym of legal "privilege" seems to be legal "liberty." This is sufficiently indicated by an unusually discriminating and instructive passage in Mr. Justice Cave's opinion in *Allen v. Flood*:[58]

"The personal rights with which we are most familiar are: 1. Rights of reputation; 2. Rights of bodily safety and freedom; 3. Rights of property; or, in other words, rights relating to mind, body and estate, * * *

"In my subsequent remarks the word 'right' will, as far as possible, always be used in the above sense; and it is the more

---

[55] (1896) 89 Me., 359.

[56] (1856) 6 E. & B., 47. 74.

[57] For other examples of apt use of the term in question, see *Borland v Boston* (1882), 132 Mass., 89 ("municipal rights, privileges, powers or duties"); *Hamilton v. Graham* (1871), L. R. 2 H. L. (Sc.), 167, 169, per Hatherley, L. C.; *Jones v. De Moss* (1911), 151 Ia., 112, 117; *Kripp v. Curtis* (1886), 71 Cal., 62, 63; *Lamer v. Booth* (1874), 50 Miss., 411, 413; *Weller v. Brown* (1911), Cal., ; 117 Pac., 517; *Mathews v. People* (1903), 202 Ill., 389, 401; *Abington v. North Bridgewater* (1840), 23 Pick., 170.

[58] (1898) A. C., 1, 29.

necessary to insist on this as during the argument at your Lordship's bar it was frequently used in a much wider and more indefinite sense. Thus it was said that a man has a perfect right to fire off a gun, when all that was meant, apparently, was that a man has a *freedom* or *liberty* to fire off a gun, so long as he does not violate or infringe any one's rights in doing so, which is a very different thing from a right, the violation or disturbance of which can be remedied or prevented by legal process."[59]

While there are numerous other instances of the apt use of the term "liberty," both in judicial opinions[60] and in conveyancing

---

[59] For the reference to Mr. Justice Cave's opinion, the present writer is indebted to Salmond's work on Jurisprudence. Citing this case and one other, *Starey v. Graham* (1899), 1 Q. B., 406, 411, the learned author adopts and uses exclusively the term "liberty" to indicate the opposite of "duty," and apparently overlooks the importance of *privilege* in the present connection. Curiously enough, moreover, in his separate Treatise on Torts, his discussion of the law of defamation gives no explicit intimation that *privilege* in relation to that subject represents merely *liberty*, or *"no-duty."*

Sir Frederick Pollock, in his volume on Jurisprudence (2nd ed., 1904), 62, seems in effect to deny that legal liberty represents any true legal relation as such. Thus, he says, *inter alia*: "The act may be right in the popular and rudimentary sense of not being forbidden, but freedom has not the character of legal right until we consider the risk of unauthorized interference. It is the duty of all of us not to interfere with our neighbors' lawful freedom. This brings the so-called primitive rights into the sphere of legal rule and protection. *Sometimes it is thought that lawful power or liberty is different from the right not to be interfered with; but for the reason just given this opinion, though plausible, does not seem correct."* Compare also Pollock, Essays in Jurisp. & Ethics (1882), Ch. I.

It is difficult to see, however, why, as between X and Y, the "privilege + no-right" situation is not just as real a jural relation as the precisely opposite "duty + right" relation betwen any two parties. Perhaps the habit of recognizing exclusively the latter as a jural relation springs more or less from the traditional tendency to think of the law as consisting of "commands," or imperative rules. This, however, seems fallacious. A rule of law that *permits* is just as real as a rule of law that *forbids;* and, similarly,s aying that the law *permits* a given act to X as between himself and Y predicates just as genuine a legal relation as saying that the law *forbids* a certain act to X as between himself and Y. That this is so seems, in some measure, to be confirmed by the fact that the first sort of act would ordinarily be pronounced "lawful," and the second "unlawful." Compare *Thomas v. Sorrel* (1673), Vaughan, 331, 351.

[60] Compare *Dow v. Newborough* (1728), Comyns, 242 ("For the use is only a liberty to take the profits, but two cannot severally take the profits of the same land, therefore there cannot be an use upon a use." It should be observed that in this and the next case to be cited, along with the liberty

documents,[61] it is by no means so common or definite a word as "privilege." The former term is far more likely to be used in the sense of physical or personal freedom (*i. e.,* absence of physical restraint), as distinguished from a legal relation; and very frequently there is the connotation of *general* political liberty, as distinguished from a particular relation between two definite individuals. Besides all this, the term "privilege" has the advantage of giving us, as a variable, the adjective "privileged". Thus, it is frequently convenient to speak of a privileged act, a privileged transaction, a privileged conveyance, etc.

The term "license", sometimes used as if it were synonymous with "privilege," is not strictly appropriate. This is simply another of those innumerable cases in which the mental and physical facts are so frequently confused with the legal relation which

---

or privilege there are associated powers and rights, etc.: for instance, the *power* to acquire a title to the things severed from the realty).; *Bourne v. Taylor* (1808), 10 East., 189 (Ellenborough, C. J.): "The second question is whether the replication ought to have traversed the liberty of working the mines. * * * The word *liberty,* too, implies the same thing. It imports, *ex vi termini,* that it is a *privilege* to be exercised over another man's estates"); *Wickham v. Hawkes* (1840), 7 M. & W., 63, 78-79; *Quinn v. Leathem* (1901), A. C. 495, 534 (per Lord Lindley: see quotation *aent,* p.); *Pollock v. Farmers' Loan & Trust Co.* (1895), 157 U. S., 429, 652 (per White, J., "rights and liberties"); *Mathews v. People* (1903), 202 Ill., 389, 401 (Magruder, C. J.: "It is now well settled that the privilege of contracting is both a liberty, and a property right.").

For *legislative* use of the term in question, see the Copyright Act, 8 Anne (1709) c. 19 ("Shall have the sole right and liberty of printing each book and books for the term of * * *").

Like the word "privilege" (see *ante* p. 38, n. 48), the term "liberty" is occasionally used, especially in the older books, to indicate a franchise, or complex of special rights, privileges, powers, or immunities. Thus in Noy's Maxims (1641) there is this definition: "Liberty is a royal privilege in the hands of a subject;" and, similarly, Blackstone (2 Com. 37) says: "Franchise and liberty are used as synonymous terms; and their definition is, a royal privilege, or branch of the king's prerogative, subsisting in the hands of a subject."

This definition is quoted in *S. F. Waterworks v. Schottler* (1882), 62 Cal. 69, 106, and *Central R. & Banking Co. v. State* (1875), 54 Ga., 401, 409. Compare also *Rex v. Halifax & Co.* (1891), 2 Q. B., 263.

[61] Compare *Pond v. Bates,* 34 L. J. (N. S.), 406 ("With full power and free liberty to sink for, win and work the same, with all liberties, privileges, etc., necessary and convenient," etc.); *Hamilton v. Graham* (1871), L. R. 2 H. L. (Sc.), 166, 167; *Attersoll v. Stevens* (1808), 1 Taunt., 183; *Wickham v. Hawker* (1840), 7 M. & W., 63, 78-79.

they create. Accurately used, "license" is a generic term to indicate a group of *operative* facts required to create a particular privilege,—this being especially evident when the word is used in the common phrase "leave and license." This point is brought out by a passage from Mr. Justice Adams' opinion in *Clifford v. O'Neill*:[62]

"A license is merely a *permission* to do an act which, *without such permission*, would amount to a trespass * * * nor will the continuous enjoyment of the privilege *conferred*, for any period of time cause it to ripen into a tangible interest in the land affected."[63]

Powers and Liabilities. As indicated in the preliminary scheme of jural relations, a legal power (as distinguished, of course, from a mental or physical power) is the opposite of legal disability, and the correlative of legal liability. But what is the intrinsic nature of a legal power as such? Is it possible to analyze the conception represented by this constantly employed and very important term of legal discourse? Too close an analysis might seem metaphysical rather than useful; so that what is here presented is intended only as an approximate explanation sufficient for all practical purposes.

A change in a given legal relation may result (1) from some superadded fact or group of facts not under the volitional control of a human being (or human beings); or (2) from some superadded fact or group of facts which are under the volitional control of one or more human beings. As regards the second class of cases, the person (or persons) whose volitional control is paramount may be said to have the (legal) power to effect the particular change of legal relations that is involved in the problem.

The second class of cases—powers in the technical sense—

---

[62] (1896) 12 App. Div., 17; 42 N. Y. Sup., 607, 609.

[63] See, in accord, the oft-quoted passage from *Thomas v. Sorrell* (1673), Vaughan, 331, 351 ("A dispensation or license properly passes no interest, nor alters or transfers property in anything, but only makes an action lawful, which without it had been unlawful. As a license to go beyond the seas, to hunt in a man's park, to come into his house, are only actions, which without license, had been unlawful.").

Compare also *Taylor v. Waters* (1817), 7 Taunt., 374, 384 ("Those cases abundantly prove that a license to enjoy a beneficial privilege in land may be granted, and, notwithstanding the statue of frauds, without writing." In this case the license (operative facts) is more or less confused with privileges (the legal relation created); *Heap v. Hartley* (1889), 42 Ch. D., 461, 470.

must now be further considered. The nearest synonym for any ordinary case seems to be (legal) "ability,"[64]—the latter being obviously the opposite of "inability," or "disability." The term "right," so frequently and loosely used in the present connection, is an unfortunate term for the purpose,—a not unusual result being confusion of thought as well as ambiguity of expression.[65] The term "capacity" is equally unfortunate; for, as we have already seen, when used with discrimination, this word denotes a particular group of operative facts, and not a legal relation of any kind.

Many examples of legal powers may readily be given. Thus, X, the owner of ordinary personal property "in a tangible object" has the power to extinguish his own legal interest (rights, powers, immunities, etc.) through that totality of operative facts known as abandonment; and—simultaneously and correlatively—to create in other persons privileges and powers relating to the abandoned object,—*e. g.*, the power to acquire title to the later by appropriating it.[66] *Similarly*, X has the power to transfer his interest to Y,—that is, to extinguish his own interest and concomitantly create in Y a new and corresponding interest.[67] So

---

[64] Compare *Remington v. Parkins* (1873), 10 R. I., 550, 553, per Durfee, J.: "A power is an ability to do."

[65] See *People v. Dikeman* (1852), 7 Howard Pr., 124, 130; and *Lonas v. State* (1871), 3 Heisk. (Tenn.), 287 ,306-307, quoted *ante*, p.

See also *Mabre v. Whittaker* (1906), 10 Wash., 656, 663 (Washington Laws of 1871 provided in relation to community property: "The husband shall have the management of all the common property, but shall not have the *right* to sell or encumber real estate except he shall be joined in the sale or encumbrance by the wife. * * *" Per Scott, J.: "'Right' in the sense used there means power").

Compare also *St. Joseph Fire & Marine Ins. Co. v. Hanck* (1876), 63 Mo., 112. 118.

Numberless additional instances might be given of the use of the term "right," where the legal quantity involved is really a power rather than a right in the sense of claim.

[66] It is to be noted that abandonment would leave X himself with precisely the same sort of privileges and powers as any other person.

[67] Compare *Wynehamer v. People* (1856), 13 N. Y., 378, 396 (Comstock, J.: "I can form no notion of property which does not include the essential characteristics and attributes with which it is clothed by the laws of society * * * among which are, fundamentally the right of the occupant or owner to use and enjoy (the objects) exclusively, and his *absolute power to sell and dispose of them*"); *Bartemeyer v. Iowa* (1873), 18 Wall., 129, 137 (Field, J.: "The right of property in an article involves the *power*

also X has the power to create contractual obligations of various kinds. Agency cases are likewise instructive. By the use of some *metaphorical* expression such as the Latin, *qui facit per alium, facit per se,* the true nature of agency relations is only too frequently obscured. The creation of an agency relation involves, *inter alia,* the grant of legal powers to the so-called agent, and the creation of correlative liabilities in the principal.[68] That is to say, one party P has the power to create agency powers in another party A,—for example, the power to convey X's property, the power to impose (so-called) contractual obligations on P, the power to discharge a debt, owing to P, the power to "receive" title to property so that it shall vest in P, and so forth. In passing, it may be well to observe that the term "authority," so frequently used in agency cases, is very ambiguous and slippery in its connotation. Properly employed in the present connection, the word seems to be an abstract or qualitative term corresponding to the concrete "authorization,"—the latter consisting of a particular group of operative facts taking place between the principal and the agent. All too often, however, the term in question is so used as to blend and confuse these operative facts with the

---

to sell and dispose of such articles as well as to use and enjoy it"); *Low v. Rees Printing Co.* (1894), 41 Neb., 127, 146 (Ryan, C.: "Property, in its broad sense, is not the physical thing which may be the subject of ownership, but is the right of dominion, possession, and *power of disposition* which may be acquired over it.").

Since the power of alienation is frequently one of the fundamental elements of a complex legal interest (or property aggregate), it is obvious that a statute extinguishing such power may, in a given case be unconstitutional as depriving the owner of property without due process of law. See the cases just cited.

[68] For a leading case exhibiting the nature of agency powers, especially powers "coupled with an interest," see *Hunt v. Rousmanier* (1883), 8 Wheat., 173, 201.

It is interesting to note that in the German Civil Code the provisions relating to agency are expressed in terms of powers,—*e. g.*, sec. 168: "The expiration of the power is determined by the legal relations upon which the giving of the power is founded. The power is also revocable in the event of the continuance of the legal relation, unless something different results from the latter."

Incidentally, it may be noticed also, that as a matter of English usage, the term "power of attorney" has, by association of ideas, come to be used to designate the mere operative *instrument* creating the powers of an agent.

powers and privileges thereby created in the agent.[69] A careful discrimination in these particulars would, it is submitted, go far toward clearing up certain problems in the law of agency.[70]

Essentially similar to the powers of agents are powers of appointment in relation to property interests. So, too, the powers of public officers are, intrinsically considered, comparable to those of agents,—for example, the power of a sheriff to sell property under a writ of execution. The power of a donor, in a gift *causa mortis*, to revoke the gift and divest the title of the donee is another clear example of the legal quantities now being considered;[71] also a pledgee's statutory power of sale.[72]

There are, on the other hand, cases where the true nature of the relations involved has not, perhaps, been so clearly recognized. Thus, in the case of a conditional sale of personality, assuming

---

[69] For examples of the loose and confusing employment of the term "authority" in agency cases,—and that too, in problems of the conflict of laws requiring the closest reason,—see *Pope v. Nickerson* (1844), 3 Story, 465, 473, 476, 481, 483; *Lloyd v Guibert* (1865), 6 B. & S., 100, 117; *King v. Sarria* (1877), 69 N. Y., 24, 28, 30-32; *Risdon, etc., Works v. Furness* (1905), 1 K. B. 304; (1906) 1 K. B. 49.

For a criticism of these cases in relation to the present matter, see the writer's article The Individual Liability of Stockholders and the Conflict of Laws (1909), 9 Columb. L. Rev., 492, 512, n. 46, 521, n. 71; 10 Columb. L. Rev., 542-544.

[70] The clear understanding and recognition of the agency relation as involving the creation of legal powers may be of crucial importance in many cases,—especially, as already intimated, in regard to problems in the conflict of laws. Besides the cases in the preceding note, two others may be referred to, *Milliken v. Pratt* (1878), 125 Mass., 374, presenting no analysis of the agency problem; and, on the other hand, Freeman's Appeal (1897), 68 Conn., 533, involving a careful analysis of the agency relation by Baldwin, J. Led by this analysis to reach a decision essentially opposite to that of the Massachusetts case, the learned judge said, *inter alia*:

"Such was, in effect, the act by which Mrs. Mitchell undertook to do what she had no legal capacity to do, by making her husband her agent to deliver the guaranty to the bank. He had no more power to make it operative by delivery in Chicago to one of his creditors in Illinois, than he would have had to make it operative by delivery here, had it been drawn in favor of one of his creditors in Connecticut. It is not the place of delivery that controls, but the power of delivery."

[71] See *Emery v. Clough* (1885), 63 N. H., 552 ("right or power of defeasance").

[72] See *Hudgens v. Chamberlain* (1911), 161 Cal., 710, 713, 715. For another instance of statutory powers, see *Capital, etc., Bk. v. Rhodes* (1903), 1 Ch. 631, 655 (powers under registry acts.).

the vendee's agreement has been fully performed except as to the payment of the last installment and the time for the latter has arrived, what is the interest of such vendee as regards the property? Has he, as so often assumed, merely a contractual *right* to have title passed to him by consent of the vendor, on final payment being made; or has he, irrespective of the consent of the vendor the power to divest the title of the latter and to acquire a perfect title for himself? Though the language of the cases is not always so clear as it might be, the vendee seems to have precisely that sort of power.[78] Fundamentally considered, the typical escrow transaction in which the performance of conditions is within the volitional control of the grantee, is somewhat similar to the conditional sale of personalty; and, when reduced to its lowest terms, the problem seems easily to be solved in terms of legal powers. Once the "escrow" is formed, the grantor still has the legal title; but the grantee has an irrevocable power to divest that title by performance of certain conditions (*i. e.*, the addition of various operative facts), and concomitantly to vest title in himself. While such power is outstanding, the grantor is,

---

[78] Though the nebulous term "rights" is used by the courts, it is evident that powers are the actual quantities involved.

Thus, in the instructive case of *Carpenter v. Scott* (1881), 13 R. I., 477, 479, the court said, by Matteson, J.: "Under it (the conditional sale) the vendee acquires not only the right of possession and use, but the right to become the absolute owner upon complying with the terms of the contract. These are rights of which no act of the vendor can divest him, and which, in the absence of any stipulation in the contract restraining him, he can transfer by sale or mortgage. Upon performance of the conditions of the sale, the title to the property vests in the vendee, or in the event that he has sold, or mortgaged it, in his vendee, or mortgagee, without further bill of sale. * * * These rights constitute an actual, present interest in the property, which, as we have seen above, is capable of transfer by sale or mortgage."

It is interesting to notice that in the foregoing passage, the term "right" is first used to indicate *privileges* of possession and use; next the term is employed primarily in the sense of legal power, though possibly there is a partial blending of this idea with that of legal claim, or right (in the narrowest connotation); then the term (in plural form) is used for the third time so as to lump together the vendee's privileges, powers and claims.

For another case indicating in substance the true nature of the vendee's interest, see *Christensen v. Nelson* (1901), 38 Or. 473, 477, 479, indicating, in effect, that the vendee's powers as well as privileges may be transferred to another, and that a proper tender constitutes "the equivalen of payment."

of course, subject to a correlative liability to have his title divested.[74] Similarly, in the case of a conveyance of land in fee simple subject to condition subsequent, after the condition has been performed, the original grantor is commonly said to have a "*right* of entry." If, however, the problem is analyzed, it will be seen that, as of primary importance, the grantor has two legal quantities, (1) the privilege of entering, and (2) the power, by means of such entry, to divest the estate of the grantee.[75] The latter's estate endures, subject to the correlative liability of being divested, until such power is actually exercised.[76]

Passing now to the field of contracts, suppose A mails a letter to B offering to sell the former's land, Whiteacre, to the latter for ten thousand dollars, such letter being duly received. The operative facts thus far mentioned have created a power as regards B and a correlative liability as regards A. B, by dropping a letter of acceptance in the box, has the power to impose potential or inchoate[77] obligation *ex contractu* on A and himself; and, assuming that the land is worth fifteen thousand dollars, that particular legal quantity—the "power *plus* liability" relation between A and B—seems to be worth about five thousnad dollars to B. The liability of A will continue for a reasonable time unless, in exercise of his power to do so, A previously extinguishes it by that series of operative facts known as "revocation." These last matters are usually described by saying that A's "offer" will "con-

---

[74] See *Davis v. Clark* (1897), 58 Kan. 100; 48 Pac., 563, 565; *Leiter v. Pike* (1889), 127 Ill., 287, 326; *Welstur v. Trust Co.* (1895), 145 N. Y., 275, 283; *Furley v. Palmer* (1870), 20 Oh. St., 223, 225.

The proposition that the grantee's power is irrevocable is subject to the qualification that it might possibly be extinguished (or modified *pro tanto*) as the result of a transaction between the grantor and one having the position of *bona fide purchaser*, or the equivalent.

It is hardly necessary to add that the courts, instead of analyzing the problem of the escrow in terms of powers, as here indicated, are accustomed to stating the question and deciding it in terms of "delivery," "relation back," "performance of conditions," etc.

[75] In this connection it is worthy of note that Sugden, in his work on Powers (8th ed., 1861) 4, uses, contrary to general practice, the expression, "*power* of entry for condition broken."

[76] For miscellaneous instances of powers, see the good opinions in *Bk. of S. Australia v. Abrahams*, L. R. P. C., 265; *Barlow v. Ross* (1890), 24 Q. B. D., 381, 384.

[77] As to "inchoate" obligations, see *Frost v. Knight* (1872) L. R. 7 Ex. 111, per Cockburn, C. J. This matter will receive further attention in a later part of the discussion.

tinue" or "remain open" for a reasonable time, or for the definite time actually specified, unless A previously "withdraws" or "revokes" such offer.[78] While no doubt, in the great majority of cases no harm results from the use of such expressions, yet these forms of statement seem to represent a blending of non-legal and legal quantities which, in any problem requiring careful reasoning, should preferably be kept distinct. An offer, considered as a series of physical and mental operative facts, has spent its force as soon as such series has been completed by the "offeree's receipt." The real question is therefore as to the *legal effect,* if any, at that moment of time. If the latter consist of B's power and A's correlative liability, manifestly it is those *legal relations* that "continue" or "remain open" until modified by revocation or other operative facts. What has thus far been said concerning contracts completed by mail would seem to apply, *mutatis mutandis,* to every type of contract. Even where the parties are in the presence of each other, the offer creates a liability against the offerer, together with a correlative power in favor of the offeree. The only distinction for present purposes would be in the fact that such power and such liability would expire within a very short period of time.

Perhaps the practical justification for this method of analysis is somewhat greater in relation to the subject of options. In his able work on Contacts,[79] Langdell says:

"If the offerer stipulates that his offer shall remain open for a specified time, the first question is whether such stipulation constitutes a binding contract. * * * When such a stipulation is binding, the further question arises, whether it makes the offer irrevocable. It has been a common opinion that it does, but that is clearly a mistake. * * * An offer is merely one of the elements of a contract; and it is indispensable to the making of a contract that the wills of the contracting parties do, in legal contemplation, concur at the moment of making it. An offer, therefore, which the party making it has no power to revoke, is a legal impos-

[78] Compare *Boston R. Co. v. Bartlett* (1849), 3 Cush., 225: "Though the writing signed by the defendant was but an offer, and an offer which might be revoked, yet while it remained in force and unrevoked, it was a continuing offer, during the time limited for acceptance, and during the whole of the rest of the time it was an offer every instant; but as soon as it was accepted, it ceased to be an offer merely.

Compare also the forms of statement in Ashley, Contr. (1911), 16 *et. seq.*

[79] Langdell, Sum. Contr. (2nd ed., 1880), sec. 178.

sibility. Moreover, if the stipulation should make the offer irrevocable, it would be a contract incapable of being broken; which is also a legal impossibility. The only effect, therefore, of such a stipulation is to give the offeree a claim for damages if the stipulation be broken by revoking the offer."[80]

The foregoing reasoning ignores the fact that an ordinary offer *ipso facto* creates a legal relation—a legal power and a legal liability,—and that it is this relation (rather than the physical and mental facts constituting the offer) that "remains open." If these points be conceded, there seems no difficulty in recognizing an unilateral option agreement supported by consideration or embodied in a sealed instrument as creating in the optionee an irrevocable power to create, at any time within the period specified, a bilateral obligation as between himself and the giver of the option. Correlatively to that power, there would, of course, be a liability against the option-giver which he himself would have no power to extinguish. The courts seem to have no difficulty in reaching precisely this result as a matter of substance; though their explanations are always in terms of "withdrawal of offer," and similar expressions savoring of physical and mental quantities.[81]

In connection with the powers and liabilities created respectively by an ordinary offer and by an option, it is interesting to consider the liabilities of a person engaged in a "public calling;" for, as it seems, such a party's characteristic position is, one might almost say, intermediate between that of an ordinary contractual

---

[80] Langdell's *a priori* premises and specific conclusions have been adopted by a number of other writers on the subject. See, for example, Ashley, Contr. (1911), 25 *et seq.*, R. L. McWilliams, Enforcement of Option Agreements (1913), 1 Calif. Law Rev., 122.

[81] For a recent judicial expression on the subject, see *W. G. Reese Co. v. House* (1912), 162 Cal., 740, 745 per Sloss J.: "Where there is a consideration, the option cannot be withdrawn during the time agreed upon for its duration, while, if there be no consideration the party who has given the option may revoke it at any time before acceptance, even though the time limited has not expired * * * such offer, duly accepted, constitutes a contract binding upon both parties and enforceable by either."

See, to the same effect, *Linn v. McLean* (1885), 80 Ala., 360, 364; *O'Brien v. Boland* (1896), 166 Mass., 481, 483 (sealed offer).

Most of the cases recognizing the irrevocable power of the optionee have arisen in equitable suits for specific performance; but there seems to be no reason for doubting that the same doctrine should be applied in a common law action for damages. See, in accord, *Baker v. Shaw* (1912), 68 Wash., 99 103 (*dicta* in an action for damages).

offerer and that of an option-giver. It has indeed been usual to assert that such a party is (generally speaking) under a present *duty* to all other parties; but this is believed to be erroneous. Thus, Professor Wyman, in his work on Public Service Companies,[82] says:

"The duty placed upon every one exercising a public calling is primarily a duty to serve every man who is a member of the public. * * * It is somewhat difficult to place this exceptional duty in our legal system. * * * The truth of the matter is that the obligation resting upon one who has undertaken the performance of public duty is *sui generis*."[83]

It is submitted that the learned writer's difficulties arise primarily from a failure to see that the innkeeper, the common carrier and others similarly "holding out" are under present *liabilities* rather than present *duties*. Correlativly to those liabilities are the respective powers of the various members of the public. Thus, for example, a travelling member of the public has the legal power, by making proper application and sufficient tender, to impose a duty on the innkeeper to receive him as a guest. For breach of the duty *thus* created an action would of course lie. It would therefore seem that the innkeeper is, to some extent, like one who had given an option to every travelling member of the public. He differs, as regards net legal effect, only because he can extinguish his present liabilities and the correlative powers of the travelling members of the public *by going out of business*. Yet, on the other hand, his liabilities are more onerous than that of an ordinary contractual offerer, for he cannot extinguish his liabilities by any simple performance akin to revocation of offer.

As regards all the "legal powers" thus far considered, possibly some caution is necessary. If, for example, we consider the ordinary property owner's power of alienation, it is necessary to distinguish carefully between the *legal* power, the *physical* power to do the things necessary for the "exercise" of the legal power, and, finally, the *privilege* of doing these things—that is, if such privilege does really exist. It may or may not. Thus, if X, a landowner, has contracted with Y that the former will not alienate to Z, the acts of X necessary to exercise the power of alienating to Z are privileged as between X and every party other than Y; but, obviously, as between X and Y, the former has no

[82] Secs. 330-333.

[83] Compare, to the same effect, Keener, Quasi-Contr. (1893), p. 18.

privilege of doing the necessary acts; or conversely, he is under a duty to Y not to do what is necessary to exercise the power.

In view of what has already been said, very little may suffice concerning a *liability* as such. The latter, as we have seen, is the correlative of power, and the opposite of immunity (or exemption). While no doubt the term "liability" is often loosely used as a synonym for "duty," or "obligation," it is believed, from an extensive survey of judicial precedents, that the connotation already adopted as most appropriate to the word in question is fully justified. A few cases tending to indicate this will now be noticed. In *McNeer v. McNeer*,[84] Mr. Justice Magruder balanced the conceptions of power and liability as follows:

"So long as she lived, however, his interest in her land lacked those *elements of property*, such as *power of disposition* and *liability to sale on* execution which had formerly given it the character of a vested estate."

In *Booth v. Commonwealth*,[85] the court had to construe a Virginia statute providing "that all free white male persons who are twenty-one years of age and not over sixty, shall be *liable* to serve as jurors, except as hereinafter provided." It is plain that this enactment imposed only a *liability* and not a *duty*. It is a liability to have a duty created. The latter would arise only when, in exercise of their powers, the parties litigant and the court officers, had done what was necessary to impose a specific duty to perform the functions of a juror. The language of the court, by Moncure, J., is particularly apposite as indicating that liability is the opposite, or negative, of immunity (or exemption):

"The word both expressed and implied is 'liable,' which has a very different meaning from 'qualified * * *. It's meaning is 'bound' or 'obliged' * * *. A person exempt from serving on juries is not liable to serve, and a person not liable to serve is exempt from serving. The terms seem to be convertible."

A further good example of judicial usage is to be found in *Emery v. Clough*.[86] Referring to a gift *causa mortis* and the donee's liability to have his already vested interest divested by the donor's exercise of his power of revocation, Mr. Justice Smith said:

"The title to the gift *causa mortis* passed by the delivery, defeasible only in the lifetime of the donor, and his death perfects

---

84 (1892) 142 Ill., 388, 397.

85 1861) 16 Grat., 519, 525.

86 (1885) 63 N. H., 552.

the title in the donee by terminating the donor's right or *power of defeasance*. The property passes from the donor to the donee directly * * * and after his death it is *liable* to be divested only in favor of the donor's creditors. * * * His right and power ceased with his death."

Perhaps the nearest synonym of "liability" is "subjection" or "responsibility." As regards the latter word, a passage from Mr. Justice Day's opinion in *McElfresh v. Kirkendall*[87] is interesting:

"The words 'debt' and 'liability' are not synonymous, and they are not commonly so understood. As applied to the pecuniary relations of the parties, liability is a term of broader significance than debt. * * * Liability is responsibility."

While the term in question has the broad generic comnotation already indicated, no doubt it very frequently indicates that specific form of liability (or complex of liabilities) that is correlative to a power (or complex of powers)[88] vested in a party litigant and the various court officers. Such was held to be the meaning of a certain California statute involved in the case of *Lattin v. Gillette*.[89] Said Mr. Justice Harrison:

"The word 'liability' is the condition in which an individual is placed after a breach of his contract, or a violation of any obligation resting upon him. It is defined by Bouvier to be responsibility."[90]

---

[87] (1873) 36 Ia., 224, 226.

[88] Compare *Attorney General v. Sudeley* (1896), 1 Q. B., 354, 359 (per Lord Esher: "What is called a 'right of action' is not the *power* of bringing an action. Anybody can bring an action though he has no right at all."); *Kroessin v. Keller* (1895), 60 Minn., 372 (per Collins, J.: "The power to bring such actions").

[89] (1892) 95 Cal., 317, 319.

[90] We are apt to think of liability as exclusively an onerous relation of one party to another. But, in its broad technical significance, this is not necessarily so. Thus X, the owner of a watch, has the power to abandon his property—that is, to extinguish his existing rights, powers, and immunities relating thereto (not, however, his privileges, for until someone else has acquired title to the abandoned watch, X would have the same privileges as before); and correlatively to X's power of abandonment there is a liability in every other person. But such a liability instead of being onerous or unwelcome, is quite the opposite. As regards another person M, for example, it is a *liability to have created in his favor (though against his will) a privilege and a power* relating to the watch,—that is, the privilege of taking possession and the power, by doing so, to vest a title in himself. See *Dougherty v. Creary* (1866), 30 Cal., 290, 298. Contrast with this agreeable form of liability the *liability to have a duty created*—for example the liability of one who has made or given an option in a case where the value of the property has greatly risen.

Immunities and Disabilities. As already brought out, immunity is the correlative of disability ("no-power"), and the opposite, or negation, of liability. Perhaps it will also be plain, from the preliminary outline and from the discussion down to this point, that a power bears the same general contrast to an immunity that a right does to a privilege. A right is one's affirmative claim against another, and a privilege is one's freedom from the right or claim of another. Similarly, a power is one's affirmative "control" over a given legal relation as against another; whereas an immunity is one's freedom from the legal power or "control" of another as regards some legal relation.

A few examples may serve to make this clear. X, a landowner, has, as we have seen, power to alienate to Y or to any other ordinary party. On the other hand, X has also various immunities as against Y, and all other ordinary parties. For Y is under a disability (*i. e.*, has no power) so far as shifting the legal interest either to himself or to a third party is concerned; and what is true of Y applies similarly to every one else who has not by virtue of special operative facts acquired a power to alienate X's property. If, indeed, a sheriff has been duly empowered by a writ of execution to sell X's interest, that is a very different matter: correlative to such sheriff's power would be the *liability* of X,—the very opposite of immunity (or exemption). It is elementary, too, that as against the sheriff, X might be immune or exempt in relation to certain parcels of property, and be liable as to others. Similarly, if an agent has been duly appointed by X to sell a given piece of property, then, as to the latter, X has, in relation to such agent, a liability rather than an immunity.

For over a century there has been, in this country, a great deal of important litigation involving immunities from powers of taxation. If there be any lingering misgivings as to the "practical" importance of accuracy and discrimination in legal conceptions and legal terms, perhaps some of such doubts would be dispelled by considering the numerous cases on valuable taxation exemptions coming before the United States Supreme Court. Thus, in *Phoenix Ins. Co. v. Tennessee*,[91] Mr. Justice Peckham expressed the views of the court as follows:

"In granting to the De Sota Company 'all the rights, privileges, and immunities' of the Bluff City Company, all words are used which could be regarded as necessary to carry the exemption from

[91] (1895) 161 U. S., 174, 177.

taxation possessed by the Bluff City Company; while in the next following grant, that of the charter of the plaintiff in error, the word 'immunity' is omitted. Is there any meaning to be attached to that omission, and if so, what? We think some meaning is to be attached to it. The word 'immunity' expresses more clearly and definitely an intention to include therein an exemption from taxation than does either of the other words. Exemption from taxation is more accurately described as an 'immunity' than as a privilege, although it is not to be denied that the latter word may sometimes and under some circumstances include such exemptions."

In *Morgan v. Louisiana*,[92] there is an instructive discussion from the pen of Mr. Justice Field. In holding that on a foreclosure sale of the franchise and property of a railroad corporation an immunity from taxation did not pass to the purchaser, the learned Judge said:

"As has been often said by this court, the whole community is interested in retaining the power of taxation undiminished * * *. The exemption of the property of the company from taxation, and the exemption of its officers and servants from jury and military duty, were both intended for the benefit of the company, and its benefit alone. In their personal character they are analogous to exemptions from execution of certain property of debtors, made by laws of several of the states."[93]

[92] (1876) 93 U. S., 217, 222.

[93] See, in accord, *Picard v. Tennessee, etc., R. Co.* (1888), 130 U. S., 637, 642, (Field, J.); *Rochester Railway Co. v. Rochester* (1906) 205 U. S., 236, 252 (Moody, J., reviewing the many other cases on the subject).

In *Internat. & G. N. Ry. Co. v. State* (1899), 75 Tex., 356, a different view was taken as to the *alienability* of an immunity from taxation. Speaking by Stayton, C. J., the court said:

"Looking at the provisions of the Act of March 10, 1875, we think there can be no doubt the exemption from taxation given by it, instead of being a right vesting only in appellant, is a right which inheres in the property to which it applies, and follows it into the hands of whosover becomes the owner. * * * The existence of this right enhances the value of the property to which it applies. Shareholders and creditors must be presumed to have dealt with the corporation on the faith of the contract which gave the exemption, and it cannot be taken away by legislation, by dissolution of the corporation, or in any other manner not sufficient to pass title to any other property from one person to another. The right to exemption from taxation is secured by the same guaranty which secures titles to those owning lands granted under the act, and though the corporation may be dissolved, will continue to exist in favor of persons owning the property to which the immunity applies. Lawful dissolution of a corporation will destroy all its corporate franchises or privileges vested by

So far as immunities are concerned ,the two judicial discussions last quoted concern respectively problems of interpretation and problems of alienability. In many other cases difficult constitutional questions have arisen as the result of statutes impairing or extending various kinds of immunities. Litigants have, from time to time, had occasion to appeal both to the clause against impairment of the obligation of contracts and to the provision against depriving a person of property without due process of law. This has been especially true as regards exemptions from taxation[94] and exemptions from execution.[95]

If a word may now be permitted with respect to mere terms as such, the first thing to note is that the word "right" is overworked in the field of immunities as elsewhere.[96] As indicated, however, by the judicial expressions already quoted, the best synonym is, of course, the term "exemption."[97] It is instructive

legislature not to grant the benefit claimed by the bill."

---

the act of incorporation; but if it holds rights, privileges, and franchises in the nature of property, secured by contract based on valuable consideration, these will survive the dissolution of the corporation, for the benefit of those who may have a right to or just claim upon its assets."

Compare, as regard homestead exemptions, Sloss, J., in *Smith v. Bougham* (1909), 156 Cal., 359, 365: "A declaration of homestead * * * attaches certain privileges and immunities to such title as may at the time be held."

[94] See *Choate v. Trapp* (1912), 224 U. S., 665.

[95] See *Brearly School, Limited v. Ward* (1911), 201 N. Y., 358; 94 N. E., 1001 (an interesting decision, with three judges dissenting). The other cases on the subject are collected in Ann. Cas., 1912 B, 259.

[96] See *Brearly School, Limited v. Ward,* cited in preceding note; also *Internat. & G. N. Ry. Co. v. State* (1899), 75 Tex., 356, quoted from, *ante*, n. 91.

[97] Compare also *Wilson v. Gaines* (1877), 9 Baxt. (Tenn.), 546, 550-551, Turney, J.: "The use in the statutes of two only of the words of the constitution, *i. e.*, 'rights' and 'privileges,' and the omission to employ either of the other two following in immediate succession, viz.,' immunities' and 'exemptions,' either of which would have made clear the construction claimed by complainant, evidence a purposed intention on the part of the

Only very rarely is a court found seeking to draw a subtle distinction between an immunity and an exemption. Thus, in a recent case, *Strahan v. Wayne Co.* (June, 1913), 142 N. W., 678, 680 (Neb.), Mr. Justice Barnes said: "It has been held by the great weight of authority that dower is not immune (from the inheritance tax) because it is dower, but because it * * * belonged to her unchoately during (the husband's) life. * * * Strictly speaking, the widow's share should be considered as immune. rather than exempt, from an inheritance tax. It is free, rather than freed, from such tax."

to note, also, that the word "impunity" has a very similar connotation. This is made evident by the interesting discriminations of Lord Chancellor Finch in *Skelton v. Skelton*,[98] a case decided in 1677:

"But this I would by no means allow, that equity should enlarge the restraints of the disabilities introduced by act of parliament; and as to the granting of injunctions to stay waste, I took a distinction where the tenant hath only *impunitatem*, and where he hath *jus in arboribus*. If the tenant have only a bare indemnity or *exemption* from an action (at law), if he committed waste, there it is fit he should be restrained by injunction from committing it."[99]

In the latter part of the preceding discussion, eight conceptions of the law have been analyzed and compared in some detail, the purpose having been to exhibit not only their intrinsic meaning and scope, but also their relations to one another and the methods by which they are applied, in judicial reasoning, to the solution of concrete problems of litigation. Before concluding this branch of the discussion a general suggestion may be ventured as to the great practical importance of a clear appreciation of the distinctions and discriminations set forth. If a homely metaphor be permitted, these eight conceptions,—rights and duties, privileges and no-rights, powers and liabilities, immunities and disabilities,—seem to be what may be called "the lowest common denominators of the law." Ten fractions (1-3, 2-5, etc.) may, *superficially*, seem so different from one another as to defy comparison. If, however, they are expressed in terms of their lowest common denominators (5-15, 6-15, etc.), comparison becomes easy, and fundamental similarity may be discovered. The same thing is

[98] (1677) 2 Swanst., 170.

[99] In *Skelton v. Skelton*, it will be observed, the word *"impunity"* and the word *"exemption"* are used as the opposite of *liability* to the powers of a plaintiff in an action at law.

For similar recent instances, see *Vacher & Sons, Limited v. London Society of Compositors* (1913), A. C. 107, 118, 125 (per Lord Macnaghten: "Now there is nothing absurd in the notion of an association or body enjoying immunity from actions at law;" per Lord Atkinson: "Conferring on the trustees immunity as absolute," etc.).

Compare also *Baylies v. Bishop of London* (1913), 1 Ch., 127, 139, 140, per Hamilton, L. J.

For instances of the apt use of the term "disability" as equivalent to the negation of legal power, see *Poury v. Hordern* (1900), 1 Ch., 492, 495; *Sheridan v. Elden* (1862), 24 N. Y., 281, 384.

of course true as regards the lowest generic conceptions to which any and all "legal quantities" may be reduced.

Reverting, for example, to the subject powers, it might be difficult at first glance to discover any essential and fundamental similarity between conditional sales of personalty, escrow transactions, option agreements, agency relations, powers of appointment, etc. But if all these relations are reduced to their lowest generic terms, the conceptions of legal power and legal liability are seen to be dominantly, though not exclusively, applicable throughout the series. By such a process it becomes possible not only to discover essential similarities and illuminating analogies in the midst of what appears superficially to be infinite and hopeless variety, but also to discern common principles of justice and policy underlying the various jural problems involved. An indirect, yet very practical, consequence is that it frequently becomes feasible, by virtue of such analysis, to use as persuasive authorities judicial precedents that might otherwise seem altogether irrelevant. If this point be valid with respect to powers, it would seem to be equally so as regards all of the other basic conceptions of the law. In short, the deeper the analysis, the great become one's perception of fundamental unity and harmony in the law.[100]

Wesley Newcomb Hohfeld.

Stanford University, California.

---

[100] The next article in the present series will discuss the distinctions between legal and equitable jural relations; also the contrast between rights, etc., *in rem,* and rights, etc., *in personam.* The supposed distinctions betwen substantive and adjective jural relations will also be considered,—chiefly with the purpose of showing that, so far as the intrinsic and essential nature of those relations is concerned, the distinctions commonly assumed to exist are imaginary rather than real. Finally, some attention will be given to the nature and analysis of complex legal interests, or aggregates of jural relations.

RIGHTS

In this article, I propose to consider two of three closely inter-related, questions, namely : 'What is a right ?' 'Who or what may possess rights ?' The third question, 'What are the grounds and nature of the rights beings actually possess ? ', although vitally relevant to the former two questions, raises issues too extensive in scope to be treated of in a single paper.

A. Conceptual Issues : Rights as Entitlements

A moral right is commonly explained as being some sort of *claim* or *power* which ought to be recognized. D. G. Ritchie, for instance, observes that a moral right may be defined as " *the claim* of an individual upon others recognized by society, irrespective of its recognition by the State ".[1] Ryan and Boland, explaining the Catholic (Thomist) view of rights, state : " A right in the moral sense of the term may be defined as an inviolable moral *claim* to some personal good. When this claim is created as it sometimes is, by civil authority, it is a positive or legal right ; when it is derived from man's rational nature it is a natural right ".[2] T. H. Green, on the other hand, argues : " A right is *a power* of acting for his own ends, —for what he conceives to be his good, —secured to an individual by the community on the supposition that its exercise contributes to the good of the community ".[3] Plamenatz follows Green in explaining rights in terms of powers, but in other respects his definition differs substantially from that of Green. Plamenatz states : " A right is *a power* which a creature ought to possess because its exercise by him is itself good, or else because it is a means to what is good, and in the exercise of which all rational beings ought to protect him ".[4] There are obvious grounds for rejecting such accounts of the concept of a right, whether it be a legal, moral, social, or institutional right. To consider first rights other than moral rights.

To have *a legal right* is not to have a power conferred or recognized by law, nor is it a power which ought to be recognized by law or by officials administering the law. I may have a legal right to drive a car but lack the power to do so because temporarily paralysed or because too poor to buy or rent a car. A lot of laws which confer rights are called " private power-

[1]D. G. Ritchie, *Natural Rights*, London, 1894, pp. 78-9. The emphasis on the key word in this and subsequent definitions is mine.

[2]J. A. Ryan and F. J. Boland, *Catholic Principles of Politics*, New York, 1940, p. 13.

[3]T. H. Green, *Lectures on the Principles of Political Obligation*, London, 1941, p. 207.

[4]J. P. Plamenatz, *Consent, Freedom and Political Obligation*, Oxford, 1938, p. 82. Plamenatz has since rejected this definition in favour of the definition, " A man (or an animal) has a right whenever other men ought not to prevent him doing what he wants or refuse some service he asks for or needs " (Ar. Soc. Suppl. Vol. XXIV (1950), p. 75).

conferring laws " but, as Cohen has argued against Hart, they are not really power-conferring laws at all.[5] The laws giving me the right to marry, divorce, or to make a will, are not conferring powers on me ; yet they are clearly conferring legal rights. Similarly, criminal laws deny me legal rights but they do not interfere with my powers. Nor are legal rights powers recognized by the state, for legal rights may exist where there is no power to exercise the right. Similarly, a legal right does not amount to a claim upon others recognized by the state, although a right may provide a ground for such a claim. My legal right to marry consists primarily in the recognition of my entitlement to marry and to have my act recognized. It indirectly gives rise to claims on others not to prevent me so acting, but it does not primarily consist in these claims. I am legally entitled under our legal system to do whatever is not forbidden by the law. Thus I have a legal right to grow roses in my garden. This legal right is not simply a claim I can make under the law that others not interfere with me when selecting plants for my garden. It is essentially an entitlement to act as I please. It may give rise to derivative entitlements, and claims on others and the state.

With *institutional rights*, e.g. rights as a member of a religious organization or a social club, the possession of a right does not consist in some sort of power or claim. A right to vote in the election of the elders of the Church is an entitlement to take part in the election ; and an entitlement is very different from a power, whether it be a power conferred, recognized, or which ought to be recognized. To have the right to vote is not simply or necessarily to have the power to vote, nor is it a power to act which has been conferred or recognized or which ought to be recognized. In a laxly policed election non-members may have the power but not the right to vote. Similarly, the right does not consist primarily in claims on others. Consider the right of the Church member to partake of Holy Communion. The right and the power are clearly distinct, and the right is related to claims only in that, besides entitling the member to partake of Holy Communion, it also entitles him to resist any official or member of the Church who seeks to prevent him partaking. So too with rights as a member of a social club. My right to use the club—its writing room, library, bar—is an entitlement. I may lack the power to exercise this right, and still possess it ; and I may enjoy it without making claims on others—e.g. if it were a small, self-service club with no staff. The right equally exists for the member who is unable to get to the club, i.e. who cannot make claims on others, and for the member who admits himself to the club building and who makes no claims on others.

Rights also figure in *games*, although of course they are rights of a conceptually different kind from moral rights such as the right to liberty. However, the essence of rights in games as elsewhere consists in their being entitlements. In Australian Rules football players have the right to place-kick after a mark or free kick ; and it is clearly meaningful and correct to

[5]L. J. Cohen, " H. L. A. Hart, *The Concept of Law* ", *Mind*, LXXI (1962), pp. 395-412, esp. pp. 396-7.

assert that the player who doesn't know how to place-kick, and the player who never marks the ball nor receives a free kick, enjoy the right as fully as the skilful place-kick who receives many free kicks. The right consists in an entitlement, which, if denied, would provide the player with grounds for making demands and claims on others, viz., the umpire, which may or may not succeed. It is to misconstrue rights in games to construe them as the claims to which they may or may not give rise. It is a mistake comparable with that against which Hart argues, of construing rules of games as directions to scorers.[6]

If we look at *moral rights*, in particular at what we intend to claim when we claim a right, we find here too that a right is an entitlement. It may be an entitlement to do, to demand, to enjoy, to be, to have done for us. Rights may be rights to act, to exist, to enjoy, to demand. We speak of rights as being *possessed*, *exercised*, and *enjoyed*. In these respects there is an affinity between our talk about rights and our talk about capacities, powers, and the like, and a distinct contrast with talk about claims, for we *make* claims but do not possess, exercise, or enjoy them. But, since a right may exist and be possessed in the absence of the relevant power or capacity, rights are distinct from powers. I possess the rights to life, liberty and happiness ; my possession of these rights means that I am entitled to live, to act freely without interference, and be unimpeded in my search for happiness.

It is often argued that rights are conceptually linked with *rules*. Benn and Peters, for instance, state : " To say that X has a right to £5 is to imply that there is a rule which, when applied to the case of X and some other person Y, imposes on Y a duty to pay X £5 if X so chooses. Without the possibility of the correlative duty resting somewhere, the attribution of the right to X would be meaningless ".[7] Our foregoing consideration of legal rights suggests that this is not the case. We have legal rights in the absence of legal rules, and the way in which rules are relevant to legal rights varies. Sometimes the rule explicitly denies a right, other rules confer rights, other rules sustain rights which are rule-grounded only in the very weakened sense that ' what is not forbidden in our legal system is permitted ' may be said to be itself a rule of sorts. However, it is not a rule in the same sense or senses of ' rule ' as that in which criminal and power-conferring laws are rules. With rights as members of organizations, rules figure prominently, but rights may nonetheless exist which are not grounded on rules. There may be no rule concerning private worship in the church building on weekdays, but in the absence of a rule forbidding it, and even in the absence of a general rule stating that what is not forbidden is permitted, the member may reasonably claim the right to worship privately in the church each day. He could offer good reasons, not in terms of some rule, but in terms of the purpose of the building and the character of the religious organization.

[6]H. L. A. Hart, *The Concept of Law*, Oxford, 1961. See, e.g., p. 40.

[7]S. I. Benn and R. S. Peters, *Social Principles and the Democratic State*, London, 1959, p. 88.

The same is true of moral rights. We do not always have to point to a rule of some sort to show that we have a moral right. A claim to a right such as the right to life may be supported by a large variety of kinds of reasons. Indeed, the characteristic reasons appropriate as reasons in support of moral rights seem not to be reasons in terms of rules.

We speak of our rights as being *rights to*—as in the rights to life, liberty and happiness—not as *rights against*, as has so often mistakenly been claimed. Special rights are sometimes against specific individuals or institutions—e.g. rights created by promises, contracts, etc. The wife has rights against the husband, the creditor against the debtor, but these are special, non-general rights which differ from the characteristic cases of general rights, where the right is simply a right to (i.e. an entitlement to)—e.g. of the man to marry the woman of his choice. It is strangely artificial to suggest that this is a right against someone or some thing. Against whom or what is it a right ? My right to life is not a right against anyone. It is *my* right and by virtue of it, it is normally permissible for me to sustain my life in the face of obstacles. It does give rise to rights against others *in the sense* that others have or may come to have duties to refrain from killing me, but it is essentially a right of mine, not an infinite list of claims, hypothetical and actual, against an infinite number of actual, potential, and as yet non-existent human beings. Even non-moral rights such as legal rights, rights as a member of a club, rights in games, are not typically rights against but rights to have, to do, to be, to have done for us. My legal right to drive a car, having passed a test for a licence and paid the appropriate fee, is a right to do certain things, not a right against the police, magistrates, and other officials. Similarly, the right of the tennis club member to play on the club courts is a right to play, not a right against some vague group of potential or possible obstructors. Similarly, the right of the football player to place-kick if he so chooses is a right to do just that. It is not a right against his opponent or against the umpire. And if it is a right by virtue of his having taken a mark it is especially hard to see against whom it might be said to be.

Rights are entitlements to do, have, enjoy or have done. That it is a serious error to construe general rights as rights against rather than rights to or as entitlements, is confirmed by consideration of people who live in isolation. It is meaningful to speak of the hermit on an isolated island as having rights to do or have certain things, but it would be strange to speak of him as having rights against others. His rights may give rise to rights against others, but the right—e.g. to live—is not primarily against others. The infliction of avoidable suffering on animals is obviously *prima facie* wrong, but the fact that a person possesses the right to life, whether he be a hermit or not, justifies him in killing animals—and in the process causing them to suffer—in order to sustain himself. His right to life is inaptly described in such a situation as a right against the animals he kills. Many, although not myself, would wish to argue that there is no right to suicide.

Clearly it is not *prima facie* absurd so to argue. Yet if there is no such right, the hermit would not be entitled to take his own life, although he would have rights to do other things.

The difficulties of "rights against" talk, and of any attempt to write into the concept of a right, that it must be against someone, are evident if we consider the extreme case of the last person in the universe, who alone survives the nuclear war. Imagine that the last person is a woman capable of reproducing by artificial insemination, a large sperm bank having also survived. I suggest that talk about rights would have real application in such a situation. Suppose the woman had good reason to believe that if she reproduced, her off-spring would be monsters, defectives, imbeciles, doomed to life-long suffering. In such a case she would have to conclude that she did not possess the right to reproduce. If she had every reason to believe that her off-spring would be healthy, she would conclude that she had the right to reproduce, unless of course she regarded artificial insemination as wrong. This suggests that the actual existence of other human beings is irrelevant to whether rights may or may not be possessed. Clearly *the possible existence* of other human beings is more than adequate as a basis for talk about rights to have point. And, as I argued earlier, even this seems not to be necessary.

Other difficulties of "rights against" talk could be noted—e.g. the accounts it involves of what it is to lack a right, the difficulty of *possessing* rights against, where possession by us of the right depends on the existence of others. But enough has already been said to permit us to dismiss this sort of account, which seems to be adopted, where it is adopted, to fit in with a predetermined ethical theory.

So far I have spoken of rights, whether they be legal, moral, social, institutional, or in games, as essentially entitlements of some sort; yet obviously they are different sorts of entitlements, such that we should describe them as being conceptually different from one another. The concept of a legal right is a different concept from that of a right in a game, and both are different from rights which are created by membership of a club. Similarly, although all moral rights are entitlements, there are conceptual differences between various of the rights which may be characterized as moral rights, which makes it desirable to distinguish different *concepts* of moral rights, and to speak of legal, moral, social, etc. rights as rights of different *kinds*.

It is a commonplace for political philosophers to offer *the* definition of a moral right. Some such definitions were indicated at the outset. Elsewhere, in a brief discussion of the nature and grounds of rights, I have similarly assumed that there is only one concept and only one definition of a right.[8] In fact, if we look at the sorts of rights that are claimed as moral rights, at actual theories about rights, and at ordinary discourse, we find that there are at least four distinct concepts of moral rights, all of which are to be explained as entitlements.

[8] "The State and Evil", *Ethics*, LXIX, 3 (April 1959), p. 183.

(*a*) There is *the negative concept* of a right apparent in some of Locke's arguments for rights, particularly for the rights to life and liberty.[9] To have a negative right to X is for it not to be wrong for us to do or have X and for other people to lack the right or have a duty not to interfere ; and here the duty is obviously not a duty against us. For example, to have a right to life of this kind, would be for it to be right (or not wrong) for us to sustain ourselves, and for others to be obliged not to take our lives or at least not to be entitled to deprive us of our lives. This concept of a right lends itself most easily to modification to permit talk about animal rights, but it will be argued later that such modification is not in order as animals cannot be possessors of rights. Negative rights are not simply rights by analogy, nor are negative rights, rights in a sense parasitic on some other concept of a right. It is logically possible that all rights be of this negative character. A community which conceived of all rights as being of this kind would obviously be said to have grasped the concept of a right, although it would not have grasped the richest and fullest concept of a right. (It is still possible to speak of such negative rights as being possessed, but the sense of ' possessed ' is weaker than in the other cases.)

(*b*) There is also *the positive concept* of a right such that to have a right is to have a moral authority or entitlement to act in a certain way. This concept is often elucidated in terms of legitimate claims on others, but such accounts obviously will not do, for we explain and justify our claim on others in terms of having a right, i.e. in terms of our having a positive moral entitlement, to act in a certain way. It is this that entitles us to demand freedom from interference. The rights for which Thomists argue on the basis of the natural law are of this kind, e.g. rights to seek the truth, to rear one's offspring, to preserve oneself.

(*c*) There is a more positive, fuller concept which we may characterize as *the welfare concept* of a right such that a right is not merely a moral entitlement to do or to have, but also an entitlement to the efforts of others or to make demands on others to aid and promote our seeking after or enjoyment of some good. Thus, in terms of this welfare concept of a right, it is written into the concept that the conditions for its enjoyment be promoted. Such a concept underlies many arguments for welfare legislation, for many such arguments proceed by maintaining that respect for human rights involves removing not simply *man-made* obstacles but also *natural* hindrances and impediments to the enjoyment of some power or good. For example, many demands for conditions to promote the enjoyment of the rights to health, life, etc., proceed from such a welfare concept of a right. Indeed, if such a concept is denied significance, a great deal of controversy about rights in this century becomes meaningless.

(*d*) There are also *special rights* noted above as admitting of being described as rights against, and which spring from duties to particular individuals. The right of the creditor to repayment of his loan on the due date is a right or entitlement of this kind.

[9] *Civil Government*, Bk. 2, ch. 2.

The above distinctions between different concepts of rights are obviously relevant to the vexed question of the relation between *rights and duties.* And, of course, the question of the relation between rights and duties raises many important issues, not the least that concerning who or what may be the possessor of rights. It is commonly argued that there is a close conceptual connexion between rights and duties. To consider in what respects this is so. (i) Where the right is of type (*a*), its existence depends in part on there being a duty on others not to interfere *or* on others lacking a right of type (*b*) to interfere. Where the right is of type (*b*) A's right creates actual and potential duties for others and for potential and hypothetical others. To explain : My right to liberty creates no duty for the Hottentot or the Eskimo, for they cannot interfere with me and do not know of my existence. If they could come to interfere, my right would constitute a ground for the duty not to interfere. Similarly with infants. My rights do not create duties for them unless and until they become full moral agents and have some relationship or connexion with me, when my right causes them to have duties not to interfere. Similarly with those as yet unborn. (ii) Rights of type (*c*) obviously give rise to duties and to potential duties. If the blind man whose sight can be restored has a right to sight (as part of the right to health) he has a right to our efforts on his behalf ; and we have a duty to make the relevant effort. Such rights seem also to be possessed by those who are not full moral agents, for instances, by infants, curable lunatics, idiots, etc. If a minimal I.Q. idiot could be cured by a pill as cheap as an aspirin, it would be reasonable to claim that he has a right to the necessary treatment and that we have a duty to see that it is made available to him. (iii) Where the right is of type (*d*), i.e. a special right against another, the right implies a duty in the person against whom it is held. The husband of the wife who has promised to obey him has a right to her obedience, and she the duty to obey. In this case the duty is primary. It springs from the wife's promise and the right is created by the promise and the duty to keep the promise. (iv) Duties and rights. To have a duty is to have a right. One has the right to do what is necessary for the fulfilment of one's duty. But to have a duty is not necessarily for another to have a right. Ross notes the case of duties to animals, and other duties could be cited.[10] For example, the duty to perfect one's talents is not a duty against oneself, nor is it a duty to one's self. It is simply a duty and creates no rights in others. Similarly with the duty to maximize good. The last person in the universe would have the duty to maximize good and to produce other human beings if this were a means to or part of maximizing good ; but there would be no one with a right resulting from the duty. The duty of the artist to produce good and not slovenly paintings does not give to others the right to demand of the artist that he produce the best paintings of which he is capable. Again, I may have a duty to the state, e.g. to pay my income tax ; but the sense in which the state might be said to have a right to my

[10] W. D. Ross, *The Right and The Good*, Oxford, 1930, ch. 2, appendix 1.

tax is distinct from the sense of 'right' in which we speak of moral rights as possessed by individuals. The state cannot be the possessor of the sorts of rights human beings may possess. Yet it may be the object of duties. Further, not all duties to the state or to other institutions create these rights in the institutions. It does not follow that, because the Church member has a duty to give generously to his Church, the Church has a right to his gifts.[11] In brief : When a right is attributed, we cannot always significantly ask 'Who has the corresponding duties ?' And, when a duty is postulated, we cannot always find someone who possesses a corresponding right.

B. Who or What are Logically Possible Possessors of Rights ?

The issue as to who or what may be a possessor of rights is not simply a matter of academic, conceptual interest. Obviously, important conclusions follow from any answer. If, for instance, it is determined that gravely mentally defective human beings and monsters born of human parents are not the kinds of beings who may possess rights, this bears on how we may treat them. It does not settle such questions as to whether it is right to kill them if they are a burden or if they are enduring pointless suffering, but it does bear in an important way on such questions. Even if such beings cannot be possessors of rights it might still be wrong to kill them, but the case against killing those who endure pain is obviously easier to set out if they can be shown to be capable of possessing rights and in fact possess rights. Similarly, important conclusions follow from the question as to whether animals have rights. If they do, as Salt argued, it would seem an illegitimate invasion of animal rights to kill and eat them, if, as seems to be the case, we can sustain ourselves without killing animals.[12] If animals have rights, the case for vegetarianism is *prima facie* very strong, and is comparable with the case against cannibalism.

These issues, then, are not without importance, but they present very considerable difficulties. If we follow our unreflective moral consciousness we find ourselves drawn strongly to conclusions which seem radically inconsistent with one another ; yet if we attempt to reason to a conclusion

[11]The notion of *a duty to* needs examination. We often speak of duties to when we really mean duties concerning, involving, etc., as in talk about duties to oneself. However, we do have duties which are properly described as duties to—e.g. a duty of gratitude to our benefactor, a duty to our creditor, a duty of fidelity to one's spouse, a duty of loyalty to one's country. However, it is difficult to see what the principle is that leads us to speak of such duties as "duties to". With things, and even with animals, we seem to speak of duties as involving them, rather than as being to them. If institutions such as the State and the Church may be objects of duties to, why not things and animals ? Yet the duty to preserve a great painting (even if the duty of the last person in the universe) is not a duty *to* the painting. Similarly with animals. If I don't feed my cat, I can be reproached as not having done what I ought and as having no right to treat it as I did, but we should be disinclined to speak of my duty to my cat, or to justify such remarks by talk about its right to a square meal a day. Rather, we should speak of duties not to be cruel, etc. ; by contrast, if parents neglected their offspring, allusions to their duties *to* their children would be made quickly and naturally.

[12]H. S. Salt, *Animal Rights*, London, 1892.

it is extremely difficult even to begin to set out an argument, let alone develop a carefully worked out, convincing argument in favour of one conclusion rather than another. And, whilst our analysis of the concept of a right takes us some way—it excludes some possibilities and some arguments —it seems on the face of it to leave open a very large number of possibilities.

Although an important and difficult problem, this is one to which few theorists have applied themselves with the attention and critical scrutiny which might be expected in such an important issue. Ross, Plamenatz and Green are typical of thinkers in this area. Ross notes difficulties in respect of idiots, infants and animals, but seems quietly to forget to deal with them, and offers his conclusions without the support of reasons. Plamenatz seems simply to legislate. He asserts that animals do have rights, and hence states that any definition of rights must be such as to admit that animals do have rights. However, no argument is offered to support the view. T. H. Green does address himself to the problem to the extent of claiming that we have rights only as members of a community, that rights involve mutual recognition, and that they can therefore only be possessed by moral persons, i.e. rational beings.[13] However, he offers only very general, sketchy arguments for these contentions, and seems to fail to realize that besides excluding animals as possible possessors of rights, they exclude infants, imbeciles, and other mentally defective human beings. Ritchie perhaps comes closest to offering an argument when he notes the difficulties which arise if animals are attributed rights. If animals have rights, the cat invades the right of the mouse, the tiger of the cow, etc. Should we restrict the liberty of the cat and of the tiger out of respect for the rights of the mouse and the cow? And should we, out of respect for the rights of animals, allow parasites to continue to inhabit us if they do not have seriously deleterious effects on our health? Plamenatz seeks a way out of such difficulties, whilst at the same time allowing that animals have rights, by claiming that rights are *rights against rational beings*, hence the cow has no rights against the tiger but only against human beings. This obviously will not do, for the reasons noted above, namely, that rights are not primarily rights against but rights to. They may rationally be demanded only of rational beings, for the obvious reason that only rational beings are capable of complying with the demands, but this does not mean that the tiger is not invading the rights of the cow when he kills it. The absurdity of the conclusions which follow from the admission of animal rights may, as Ritchie claims, *suggest* that animals cannot be possessors of rights, but it does not *establish* that this is so.

The general tendency has been to maintain that free agents and potential free agents have rights, with idiots, and all born of human parents being treated as potentially free agents, although many are obviously not such. Those who have claimed that animals have rights have rarely explained whether they mean all animals; equally seriously, they seem not to explain

[13] *Ibid.*, pp. 44 and 144 (Lecture A, sn. 25, Lecture H, sn. 139).

why they think some or all sentient beings have rights, and why not all animate objects and even perhaps things. The unspoken premiss seems to be either that where there is a possibility of " action " of some sort there is the possibility of rights, or that where there is a possibility of pain, there is the possibility of possession of rights. But the reasons underlying the assumption are not evident. Clearly, if lower animals, especially parasitic animals such as the flea, are allowed to be capable of possessing rights, argument is needed to show why such animals, and not all animate objects, e.g. a beautiful oak or mountain ash, can possess rights. If it were allowed that all sentient beings and all animate objects possess some rights—e.g. to life—why, it might be asked, should rights be denied of inanimate things ? Might not beautiful works of art, paintings of Raphael and Leonardo da Vinci also have a right to continued existence ? Argument is needed here, yet argument is notably lacking. Where it is to be found, it is of the very unconvincing kind offered by Thomists, that rational beings, being subject to the natural law, have rights, since rights are grounded on the natural law ; that infants, lunatics, idiots have rights and are subject to natural law since they are rational beings. Obviously, even if the theory of natural law could be established—and this I should wish to deny—infants, lunatics and idiots are not subject to it as rational agents any more than is an intelligent dog or ape. The natural law is law, and is binding on men because and in so far as it is promulgated through reason. It is not promulgated to infants, idiots and certain lunatics. And, whilst it might be argued that it is promulgated potentially to infants, and hypothetically to idiots, potential and hypothetical promulgation are not promulgation, and to be a potential or a hypothetical possessor of rights is not to be a possessor of potential or hypothetical rights, nor of actual rights.

To consider what can be done towards reaching an answer. I have argued that rights are entitlements to do, have, enjoy, or have done for us, and not claims or powers. An obvious answer to the question ' Who may possess entitlements ? ' is ' Free moral agents '. They obviously may and do possess and claim entitlements of the sorts claimed in rights to life, liberty and health. However, it is unduly and arbitrarily to narrow and limit the field of possible possessors of rights to limit it to free moral agents. Consider the lunatic who has completely lost his grip on the world, who is devoid of all free choice, and who thinks (in so far as he can be said to think) that he is a cabbage. If he could be treated and made sane by being given a drug costing 1/-, would it not be meaningful to claim that he has a right to the drug, that others ought to exert themselves to respect his rights, to secure his enjoyment of his rights ? Here the difficulty lies in distinguishing an attribution of a duty and an attribution of a right or entitlement. Clearly others would have a duty towards the lunatic, hence, on that account, he might in some sort of analogous sense be said to have a right. However, I suggest that we should be inclined to assert that he can have and has rights in a fuller, more literal sense. Compare him with the blind, rational, free agent who can equally be cured of his blindness, but not by his own efforts. Each would be said to have a right to the necessary treatment ; and when we attribute the right to the one, we seem to be using language in the same meaningful way as when attributing a right to the other. We are saying that each is entitled or has an entitlement to the efforts of others for their own good. This suggests that, although free agents may possess rights, the test of who or what can be a possessor of a right or an entitlement is not that of freedom or rationality. A lunatic can be a possessor of an entitlement, of kinds (*a*) and (*c*). Further, the lunatic does not have to be one capable of attaining free will, i.e. to be a potential or hypothetical free agent. It is not *prima facie* absurd to claim that an incurable lunatic is entitled to decent treatment. His relatives can reasonably claim that his rights be respected, and if he is regularly being beaten up by a sadistic attendant, they can properly claim that his rights are being denied. So too with infants. There seems to be no logical paradox in asserting that the infant is entitled to care and nurture from his parents. This is because an entitlement does not have to admit of being demanded by its possessor any more than does a legitimate claim. Entitlements may be demanded (and claims made) by proxies on behalf of the holder of the entitlement. Logically we do not have to be able to say that we are entitled, to be entitled. The cases of the infant and lunatic suggest this, but obviously there are limits to those who/which may logically be possessors of entitlements.

Here it is useful to consider legal rights and entitlements in respect of animals. Legal claims may be made on behalf of animals, e.g. against trustees who embezzle money left for the care of a cat. In such cases we should be disinclined to speak of the courts upholding the legal rights of the cat. Our uneasiness, and the grounds for our uneasiness, can be brought out by the following examples. Suppose that, as a result of deliberate legal enactment, the kangaroo came to be accorded something like the privileged position of the cow in India, the kangaroo having full rights of movement, on the roads, on private property, etc. I suggest that we should be reluctant to speak of the legal rights of kangaroos. This is clear from our manner of speaking of native birds and animals in sanctuaries today. We speak of our being obliged to leave them alone, not of them as having legal rights, nor of them as being legally entitled to be left alone. The law confers duties on us, not rights in the animals. This is confirmed by another possible group of cases, of legal systems in which animals which kill men are tried, and if found guilty, executed. If an animal is given an unfair trial under such a system and its legal representative demands a new trial, he could perhaps say that the animal had not received its legal rights (lawyers seem inclined to speak in this way) but it seems more accurate and less misleading simply to say that the law has not been properly observed in the original trial. Compare with a trial of a man.

Why we are reluctant to speak of the legal rights of animals, even under such legal systems, becomes clearer if we consider *things*, and why things cannot have legal rights. Things do not have legal rights in our legal system, but not because this is a peculiarity of our legal system. It is because anything which might seem to come close to a thing having legal rights is not so described. A man can leave his money to preserve a building, a park, etc., and appoint trustees, but we do not say of the trustees who embezzle the money that they have failed to respect the legal rights of the building or gardens they were appointed to care for. (Similarly with legal systems where things such as cars or locomotives are given trials before being destroyed when guilty of killing men.) The reasons for this seem to be two. First, things such as parks, buildings, paintings, etc., do not have *interests* in the strict sense of interests, such that we could literally speak of the trustees caring for their interests. The trustees care for the thing, not for the interests of the thing. Secondly, and partly for this reason, the trustees could hardly be said to be the representatives of the thing. Here we might speak of them as custodians, etc.

What holds in respect of legal rights seems also to hold of moral rights. Moral rights can be possessed by beings who can claim them, and by those who can have them claimed on their behalf by others and whose interests are violated or disregarded if the rights are not respected. The concept of interests which is so important here is an obscure and elusive one. Interests are distinct from welfare, and are more inclusive in certain respects—usually what is dictated by concern for a man's welfare is in his interests. However, interests suggest much more than that which is indicated by the person's welfare. They suggest that which is or ought to be or which would be of *concern* to the person/being. It is partly for this reason—because the concept of interests has this evaluative-prescriptive overtone—that we decline to speak of the interests of animals, and speak rather of their welfare.

That the possibility of possessing rights is limited in this way is confirmed by the very fact that we speak of rights as being *possessed and enjoyed.* A right cannot not be possessed by someone ; hence, only beings which can possess things can possess rights. My right to life is mine ; I possess it. It is as much mine as any of my possessions—indeed more so—for I possess them by virtue of my rights. It is true that I may possess rights and not know or enjoy my possession of them. Thus, whilst rights must be possessed by a possessor, they need not be enjoyed. All we can say is that they may admit of enjoyment by their possessors.

All these considerations seem to exclude the lower animals in a decisive way, and the higher animals in a less decisive but still fairly conclusive way as possible possessors of rights. (Consider ' possess ' in its literal use. Can a horse possess anything, e.g. its stable, its rug, in a literal sense of ' possess ' ?) It might, however, be argued that animals can possess special rights, e.g. rights arising out of relations such as the owner's " debt of gratitude " to the animal for special services. Consider the blind man and his guide dog who repeatedly saves his life. The difficulty that rights are possessed and that animals cannot possess things remains ; and, in any case, the animal's special services are more naturally described as creating special duties rather than as giving rise to entitlements in the animal.

It would seem to follow from all this that monsters born of human parents whose level of existence falls far short of that of the highest animals would also seem not to be possible possessors of rights. However, two qualifications may usefully be made here. Animals, or at least the higher animals, may usefully be said to have *rights by analogy.* We have duties involving them, and these duties might be said to create rights by analogy. (The latter are not the same as rights in sense (*a*), for a right by analogy is not an entitlement, whereas a negative right is such ; and the difference leads to important implications). With those born of human parents, even the most inferior beings, it may be *a useful lie* to attribute rights where they are not and cannot be possessed, since to deny the very inferior beings born of human parents rights, opens the way to a dangerous slide. But whether useful or not, it is a lie or a mistake to attribute rights or the possibility of rights to such beings. More difficult are the cases of the infant, lunatic, etc. As indicated earlier, we do attribute rights and interests to infants, lunatics, and even to incurable lunatics. Part of the reason for this is the thought that such beings, unlike the congenital idiot, etc., are possibly potential possessors of interests. Hence, until it is clear that they can never really be said to have interests, we treat them as if they do. Also relevant is the fact that even a mentally defective human being—e.g. an imbecile, or a lunatic with periods of sanity—may literally demand some rights and possess others and generally be attributed interests in a literal sense.

I have not considered theories to the effect that possessors of immortal souls, and only such, are logically possible possessors of rights. This is because those who argue that possessors of immortal souls possess rights—and that animals do not—usually make their claim a factual and not a logical one. They argue that this is in fact the case, and do not concern themselves with the issue as to whether it is logically possible for a being without an immortal soul to possess rights. In any case, there is a quick answer to any such contention, namely, that it is possible to deny that man has an immortal soul, without being logically impelled to deny that he may possess rights.

H. J. McCloskey

University of Melbourne.

American Philosophical Quarterly
Volume 6, Number 3, July 1969

I. RIGHTS, CLAIMANTS, AND BENEFICIARIES

DAVID LYONS

To have a right, Bentham held, is to be the *beneficiary* of another's duty or obligation.[1] This theory, one of the more attractive and plausible suggestions about the nature of rights, appears supported by innumerable cases. It is reflected in the notion common to laymen, lawyers, and philosophers that someone with a right is on the advantageous side of a legal or moral relation. It promises to explain why rights are such valuable and important commodities. And it seems bolstered by a variety of facts, for example that compensation or reparation is often required, and might always be required, when one's rights are violated or infringed.

But Bentham's theory has been criticized, most notably by H. L. A. Hart, and it is not now, I think, very widely or seriously entertained. This is unfortunate, since none of the received arguments appears decisive against the beneficiary theory as such. In this paper I shall attempt to show that Hart's objections are weaker than they must at first appear because their force is largely dispelled against but one form of beneficiary theory. Another, "qualified," beneficiary theory is much less vulnerable to Hart's objections and still worthy of our consideration.

In the first section I develop and explain the beneficiary theory and distinguish two versions that might be attributed to Bentham. In the second section I argue that being a beneficiary, in a certain qualified sense, is sufficient for having a right. In the third section I chiefly discuss some difficulties surrounding the claim that being a beneficiary is a necessary condition as well.

In this paper I shall assume that straightforward statements about moral rights can be analyzed in terms of moral obligations in the same way that statements about legal rights can be analyzed in terms of legal obligations. I shall take the beneficiary theory to apply to moral as well as legal rights.[2]

I

Many writers have held that the notion of a right must be analyzed in terms of duty or obligation—or, more generally, in terms of requirements or prohibitions on someone's behavior.[3] This is Bentham's view.

> It is by imposing obligations, or by abstaining from imposing them, that rights are established or granted.... How can a *right* of property in land be conferred on me? It is by imposing upon everybody else the obligation of not touching its productions, &c. &c. How can I possess the *right* of going into all the streets of a city? It is because there exists no obligation which hinders me, and because everybody is bound by an obligation not to hinder me.[4]

So the idea of obligation is central to that of a right, though these ideas may be related in different ways, according to the type of right in question. Property rights, as Bentham suggests, involve others' obligations to forbear from using the property without permission. Some rights imply others' obligations even more obviously, e.g., a right to be paid ten dollars by Jones, a right to be cared for by one's parents, a right to be given equal consideration, a right not to be killed, and in such cases the state-

[1] This is my formulation, not Bentham's. It is designed to encompass the two interpretations of Bentham's theory discussed in this paper. Bentham's relevant views about rights are expressed in various ways and are spread virtually throughout his *Works* (ed. by J. Bowring, Edinborough, 1843), which include most but not all of his published writings. I give some references below; others may be found in H. L. A. Hart, "Bentham," *British Academy Proceedings*, vol. 48 (1962), pp. 297-320. See also C. K. Ogden (ed.), *Bentham's Theory of Fictions* (London, 1932; Patterson, 1959).

Note that Bentham's theory concerns what it is *to have* a right, not what "a right" itself is; it should not be confused with theories like those of Jhering and Salmond, who hold that a right is an interest. (See *Salmond on Jurisprudence*, 11th edn., by G. Williams [London, 1957], ch. 10.)

[2] Bentham restricted his theory to legal rights, and in his attack on natural rights implied that there could not be any extra-legal rights. His reasons for holding the latter view seem largely independent of his analysis of rights in terms of beneficial obligations.

[3] The differences between duties or obligations, on the one hand, and mere prohibitions or requirements, on the other, are touched on below. I assume in this paper that the differences between duties and obligations can be ignored.

[4] *Works*, vol. III, p. 181; see also pp. 159ff., 217ff.

ment of the right may be held to be equivalent to the statement of the corresponding obligation. But a right to *do* (or to refrain from doing) something has as its core the *absence* of an obligation to do otherwise.[5] Even here, however—as Bentham's second example and his general remarks suggest, and as others have agreed—one's right also seems to involve others' obligations, i.e., obligations to refrain from interfering.

Bentham held, then, that rights can be "reduced" to duties or obligations. But he did not hold the closely associated view, that rights and duties are necessarily "correlatives." That is, he did not hold that duties always imply rights. This is important to Bentham's analysis of rights. To see why, let us consider the notion of correlativity briefly.

When Bernard owes Alvin ten dollars we have equal reason to ascribe a right to Alvin (to be paid ten dollars by Bernard) and an obligation to Bernard (to pay Alvin ten dollars), and whatever would falsify one ascription would likewise falsify the other. Neither the right nor the obligation can arise without the other, and if one is discharged, waived, canceled, voided, forfeited, or otherwise extinguished the other must be extinguished as well. For the ground of the obligation—the debt—is the title of the right. Alvin's right and Bernard's obligation *necessarily coexist*, and a full statement of one logically implies a full statement of the other.

This pattern of correlations is extremely common. It obtains not only when debts are owed but also when certain other relations exist between two (or possibly more) particular individuals—as a consequence, for example, of promises and contracts, wrongful injuries that require reparation, good turns that require reciprocation, relationships such as parent to child and teacher to student. In such cases it is natural to speak of *A*'s having certain rights *against B* and of *B*'s having (or *owing*) corresponding obligations *to A*.[6] And it is important that, when obligations are so grounded on such special relations or transactions and consequently can be said to be "owed" to particular persons, we can infer that the person to whom the obligation is owed has a corresponding right and that he holds it against the person with the obligation.

It is important to note what these words will be taken to signify. When *A*, in particular, holds a certain right *against B*, *A* is a *claimant* against *B*. A "claimant" is one empowered to press or waive a claim against someone with a corresponding duty or obligation. He can, if he wishes, release the other from his obligation and cancel it, or he can insist upon its performance. A creditor, for example, is a claimant against his debtor. A promisee is a claimant against one who makes a valid and binding promise to him. So too is a person to whom a debt of reparation is owed because of wrongful injury done. A claimant is thus one to whom the performance of a duty or obligation is *owed*—he is the one who holds the claim against the other and who is entitled to administer the claim as he chooses. There are obviously moral as well as legal claimants in this sense.

The pattern of relations between rights and obligations I have just described does not seem to be universal. When behavior is simply required or prohibited by law or morals, without presupposing such special relations or transactions between particular individuals as I have mentioned, we often say that "duties" or "obligations" are imposed. But since these duties or obligations are *not* "owed" to anyone in particular, we cannot determine who, if anyone, has corresponding rights by noting to whom they are "owed." Indeed, although rights sometimes do correlate with such duties or obligations, we cannot infer *that there are* such rights merely from the fact *that there are* such duties or obligations. This point is essential to a theory like Bentham's.

Consider the following contrast. When children who have reached their majority are required by (criminal) law to support their aged and indigent parents it seems plausible to say that their parents have a legal right to such support from their children. Even though legally the parents may not be "claimants" against their children, they cannot release them from their obligations, and thus the children legally do not "owe" support *to* their parents in the full sense given above. But if children are required by law to inform the authorities of their parents' seditious remarks and activities (for which the punishment is death) we may have some hesitancy in saying that their parents have corresponding rights to be informed upon by their children. (We would be inclined to ascribe such

[5] Or perhaps a sphere of activity in which one is free to do as one pleases. It should be observed that we are ignoring here those species of rights that lawyers call "powers" or "capacities" on the one hand and "immunities" on the other. I assume that these are rights in a different sense, or senses, of the term.

[6] See Joel Feinberg's very helpful discussion in "Duties, Rights, and Claims," *American Philosophical Quarterly*, vol. 3 (1966), pp. 137–142.

rights only in very special circumstances.) This contrast is meant to suggest that from the fact that the law requires that *A* be treated in a certain way it does not follow, without any further assumptions, that *A* may be said to have a right to be treated in that way. That is, rights do not follow from duties or obligations, or from requirements or prohibitions, alone. Other conditions must be satisfied.

Bentham held that rights are conferred only by beneficial obligations. "To assure to individuals the possession of a certain good, is to confer *a right* upon them."[7] Goods are assured by imposing duties or obligations, by requiring acts or forbearances of others. Obligations do not correspond to rights unless they protect or serve rather than harm or threaten those they directly concern. So Bentham held that rights "correlate" with duties or obligations in the following way, by virtue of the very notion of a right: rights imply duties, but only beneficial ones. And thus duties do not necessarily correspond to rights; they do so only when they "assure goods."

It will be useful to characterize Bentham's theory as follows: to have a right is, essentially, to be the *beneficiary* of another's duty or obligation (or of some requirement or prohibition upon another's behavior). But this needs certain qualifications before it can properly be evaluated.

Two qualifications can safely be made before considering alternative interpretations of Bentham's theory. We may note, first, that obligations are not necessarily performed. They can be breached or not fulfilled, and then the benefits or goods their performances would confer cannot be conferred in that way. Thus, a "beneficiary" in the relevant sense is not one who actually benefits but rather one who would benefit from the performance of the obligation. Secondly, a person with a right need not positively gain even when the obligation is met or discharged. For there may be indirect and irrelevant consequences resulting from (or following) the performance of an obligation. (Alvin might spend on drink the ten dollars he receives from Bernard in payment of the debt, wreck his car, and suffer serious injury—none of which would happen if Bernard fails to perform as required.) Most important, obligations may require "negative" rather than "positive" services, as Bentham says, e.g., *not* robbing, assaulting, or killing.[8] One may "benefit" in the sense of *not losing* rather than in the sense of gaining; what may be "assured" is not so much a good as the avoidance of an evil. The term "beneficiary" can be misleading, therefore, but we shall continue to use it with these implicit qualifications.

Beyond this point, however, Bentham's precise position is difficult to determine. Two main currents run through Bentham's discussions of rights, from which one can construct two significantly different versions of beneficiary theory.

The unqualified beneficiary theory. On the one hand Bentham seems to hold that rights are conferred whenever (and only when) rules that impose duties are justified according to the utilitarian test, that is, when the rules and the duties they impose ear useful.[9] Good laws serve the interests of individuals, and these laws confer rights. But bad laws impose duties from which no one (or hardly anyone) stands to benefit and therefore fail to confer rights. Various passages suggest that Bentham held the unqualified beneficiary theory, as attributed to him by Hart: that someone with a right is simply one "likely to benefit" or "capable of benefiting" or one who "stands to benefit" by the performance of a duty.[10]

This is the theory attacked by Hart. We shall examine his objections, but we need not share his alternative view in order to see that such a theory, straightforwardly understood, could not be correct. It is open to innumerable counter-examples. Suppose that Bernard owed Alvin ten dollars and also that Alvin has privately decided to give Charles a present if and only if the debt is repaid. Let us suppose further that Alvin is in no way indebted to Charles and that he has made no promises—not even tacit promises—to gives Charles anything. It would seem then that Alvin has the right that corresponds to Bernard's obligation (the right to be paid ten dollars by Bernard) and that Charles has no relevant right (save the right to accept a gift from Alvin, which is clearly *independent* of Bernard's obligation). But the unqualified beneficiary theory does not differentiate between the positions of Alvin and Charles with respect to Bernard's obligation, and seems to imply that each has a right, since each "stands to benefit" from the performance of Bernard's obligation. (Indeed,

[7] *Works*, vol. III, p. 159.
[8] *Ibid.*, pp. 159, 181.
[9] *Ibid.*, pp. 181, 220f.
[10] See "Bentham," *op. cit.*, pp. 313–315, and also Hart's "Are There Any Natural Rights?", *The Philosophical Review*, vol. 64 (1955), pp. 180ff., where Hart criticizes the beneficiary theory without, however, attributing it to anyone.

Charles "stands to benefit" more than Alvin.) But it is absurd to suppose that Charles has a relevant right.

The qualified beneficiary theory. If the theory is to be rendered more plausible, the notion of a "beneficiary" must be refined. Two considerations seem fairly obvious. (1) Alvin's benefiting is *relevant* to Bernard's obligation in a way that Charles's benefiting is not. For Bernard's obligation directly *concerns* Alvin, that is, it requires treating *him* or behaving toward him in a certain way. But it does not similarly concern Charles, for Bernard's behavior toward Charles is not relevant to the question whether or not Bernard has met or breached his obligation. But the fact that an obligation *concerns* Alvin does not suffice to show either that he is a beneficiary in any recognizable sense or that he has a corresponding right. Brown's duty as executioner concerns the condemned Green, who (failing special circumstances) would not be called a beneficiary of the performance of Brown's duty, and who (failing certain theories of punishment) would not be said to have a corresponding right. But (2) both Alvin's benefiting and Charles's benefiting are related *contingently* to Bernard's obligation. Alvin's benefiting, or the fact that Bernard's obligation "assures" to him a certain good, *does not follow* from the obvious and literal specification of Bernard's obligation, which is simply *to pay Alvin ten dollars.* So, if the connection between Alvin's benefiting and Bernard's obligation is not *merely* accidental, and if this connection is supposed to be essential to the very notion of Alvin's right, how might it be defined?

Some remarks by Bentham suggest the view that a person with a right is a "beneficiary" in a narrower and more appropriate sense: he is *supposed* to benefit by or from the performance of another's obligation. He is the direct, intended beneficiary of that duty or obligation.[11]

If we consider the obligations we have, and in particular those that do correspond to the rights of others, we shall find this suggestion not implausible. Viewed in an obvious and literal but, I think, somewhat superficial way, obligations do not generally require the conferring of goods *as such*; like Bernard's obligation to pay Alvin they simply require certain acts or forbearances or patterns of behavior. But we would fail to *understand* the obligations we have—we would be unable to determine what we ought to do on the basis of them—unless we could also say whether or not those they directly concern are supposed to benefit from them. And it seems plausible to suggest that, when we fully understand the obligations we have that *do* correspond to others' *rights*, we also see that those they directly concern *are* supposed to benefit from them. This is patently true in some cases; obligations of indebtedness, reparation, and reciprocation, for example, essentially involve and require the returning or restoring of goods to particular persons. Other cases are more difficult, particularly obligations imposed by the criminal law and analogous rules of morality, on the one hand, and promissory or contractual obligations on the other. I shall deal with these separately and in some detail.

According to the qualified beneficiary theory, then, a person with a right is not one who merely "stands to benefit" from the performance of another's obligation. He is one for whom a good is "assured," or an evil obstructed, by requirements or prohibitions upon others' behavior, in the sense that some other person or persons are required to act or forbear in ways designed or intended to serve, secure, promote, or protect his interests or an interest of his. He is a beneficiary in what I shall call the "qualified" sense of the term; he is "the party to be benefited."[12] This is not to say that the conferring of certain benefits or the avoidance of specific losses or injuries is strictly *guaranteed* to him. For, aside from the fact that obligations can be breached, the specific performance of the relevant obligations might actually fail, for various reasons, to serve his interests. But I am suggesting that, on the basis of our understanding of the relation or transaction or rule that grounds the obligation, we can say in some cases that someone's interests are to be served. And, according to the qualified beneficiary theory, such persons and only such persons have rights.

II

Hart maintains, against Bentham, that:

> According to the strict usage of most modern English jurists following Austin . . . the person who has a right is something more than a possible beneficiary of duty; he is the person who may, at his option, demand the execution of the duty or waive it . . . and it is neither

[11] See, e.g., *Works*, vol. III, p. 159.

[12] As Bentham defines "beneficiary" in his discussion of trusts: *Works*, vol. I, p. 106. But it should be emphasized that Bentham does not argue explicitly that such beneficiaries, and only such persons, have rights in the relevant sense.

necessary nor sufficient (though it is usually true) that he will also benefit from the performance of it.[13]

In this section I shall argue, with regard to Hart's criminal law examples, that the qualified beneficiary theory gives a sufficient condition for having a right (although the unqualified theory fails to do so). In the next section I extend the argument to promissory rights and counter Hart's claim that the theory fails to provide a necessary condition as well.

Hart agrees with Bentham that rights imply duties or obligations but that the latter do not always imply the former. But Hart's reasons for saying that not all duties imply rights are different from Bentham's. Bentham, as we have seen, holds that the law can and unfortunately often does impose "barren" duties or "ascetic" obligations, that is, duties or obligations without beneficiaries, which have no corresponding rights. But Hart holds that duties without claimants have no corresponding rights. And these positions are different because being a claimant is not a necessary condition for being a beneficiary of another's duty. This is shown by the fact that there are obligations with beneficiaries but without private claimants in the sense discussed above. Under the civil (as distinct from the criminal) law, private individuals are empowered to enforce their own rights; they alone can initiate proceedings against others who violate or threaten their rights. But there are no private claimants under the criminal law—only *complainants*. For the substantive rules of the criminal law impose duties or obligations that cannot be canceled by a private party; they can be "canceled" only by a change in the rules. A private individual, such as the victim of a criminal offense, can impede or aid a prosecution, but he lacks the analogous legal "power" his counterpart has under the civil law to sue. Public officials have both the legal power and the responsibility of enforcing the criminal law. Moreover, civil law obligations typically arise from special relations or transactions between the parties, whereby such obligations are incurred or assumed, but criminal law obligations are simply laid down or imposed and thus it is less natural to speak of them as being "owed" to particular individuals, and they are not "owed" in the full sense discussed above.

A similar distinction can be drawn within the class of moral duties and obligations. Some can be incurred or assumed, by promising for example, and these can be canceled by the one to whom the promise is made and to whom its performance is owed. But some moral principles simply forbid or require, they lay down what one may not or must do, and while these may be said to impose "duties" or "obligations" they cannot always be waived or canceled.

Accordingly, Hart claims that, strictly speaking, there are no rights under the criminal law or in the analogous part of morality, because such duties or obligations are not administered by private claimants. Hart observes that jurists generally prefer not to speak of "rights" under the criminal law, for reasons akin to his. But he *also* concedes that usage differs on this point:

> that a somewhat wider usage of the expression "a right" is common among non-lawyers and especially among writers on political theory who might not hesitate to say, for example, that when the *criminal* law forbids murder and assault it thereby secures to individuals a right to security of the person, even though he is in no position to waive a duty imposed by the criminal law.[14]

The so-called "wider" usage lacks the requirement that the person with the right (or anyone else) be a claimant. Hart goes on to suggest that such a wider use of "right" can be tolerated if it retains a central feature of the allegedly strict sense explicated by his claimant theory. We might continue to speak of rights under the criminal law provided we recognize that laws which confer rights as well as impose duties "also provide, in a distinctively distributive way, for the individual who has the right." This part of Hart's argument is somewhat difficult to interpret, but his position seems roughly the following. When the term "right" is used strictly, a person with a right has *his own* special powers as a claimant, his "limited sovereignty over the person who has the duty." This is, presumably, the "distributive" feature Hart refers to. Under a tolerable wider use, a distributive feature would be retained when talk of rights under the criminal law is confined to cases in which the law protects the security *of the individual*—as opposed to, say, the security of the community as a whole—that is, where a breach of such a duty "necessarily involves the infliction of harm upon a specific or (in Bentham's language) 'assignable' individual." But

[13] "Bentham," *op. cit.*, p. 315. For criticisms of other kinds see Hart's *Definition and Theory in Jurisprudence* (Oxford, 1953). Here I deal only with Bentham's *beneficiary* theory (the first stage of Bentham's analysis of rights) and am unconcerned with, e.g., Bentham's naturalism, manifested in his further analysis of legal duty or obligation.

[14] "Bentham," *op cit.*, p. 315.

Hart claims that Bentham's analysis contains no such distributive feature, because on Bentham's theory one can qualify as having a right if he is merely "a member of a class who as a class may be indiscriminately benefited by the performance of a duty." For Bentham's theory would allegedly accord rights not only to persons protected by rules such as those forbidding murder and assault—who might be said to have "rights" under a tolerably extended usage of the term—but also to those who *might possibly* benefit by the performance of *any* useful duties, even though they do not serve the interests of individuals directly. The breach of such legal duties as income tax and military service (Hart's examples) does not necessarily involve the infliction of harm upon a specific individual, "but at the most merely makes it likely that the community as a whole will be less secure."[15]

Now Hart seems correct when he says that certain *ascriptions* of rights (e.g., under the criminal law) are "wider" than others (e.g., under the civil law) in the sense that the former lack implications which the latter have that the person with the right is a claimant. For rights under the civil law arise from special relations or transactions between the persons concerned and they, unlike rights under the criminal law, may be ascribed as rights "against" those having the corresponding duties, which are reciprocally "owed." (Similar remarks apply to classes of moral rights and their ascriptions.) But from this it does not follow that ascribing rights where there are no claimants involves a wider *sense of the term* "right" or uses an extended concept. For the differences between the ascriptions *as a whole* might be accounted for by the fact that some are qualified as rights "against" particular persons while others are not, depending on the sorts of conditions that warrant the ascription of the right. That is, unless we assume that being a claimant is essential to having a right in the "strict" sense of the term, we have as yet no reason to suppose that the concept of a right itself is extended when it happens not to be instantiated as a right "against" another.

Straightforward talk about rights is not generally confined to contexts in which there are private claimants. Rights may be ascribed, for example, in the context of the criminal law for the purpose of noting that some act or omission is not unlawful, e.g., when one is challenged, when interference is threatened, or to draw certain contrasts. For example, a motorist has a right to make a right turn on a red light in California which he lacks in New York because of differences between the respective traffic laws. Such a right is not held against or with respect to any particular person, but this does not seem to make it any less of a right or a right in only an extended or loose sense of the term.

A right not to be killed may be analogous. Is it clear that we speak loosely or that we stretch our ordinary notion of a right when we ascribe, in the context of the criminal law or on the basis of general moral prohibitions, the right not to be killed? One way of finding out is by determining whether there is a single acceptable account of rights within both sorts of context, i.e., with and without private claimants. This is what the beneficiary theory purports to give.

Now let us consider more directly the force of Hart's objection against the beneficiary theory concerning rights without claimants under the criminal law. Hart maintains that rules such as those forbidding murder and assault may be said to confer rights, as the beneficiary theory implies, but only in a wider sense of the term; while rules requiring payment of income tax and military service, even when useful, cannot be said to confer rights, even in such a wider sense, although the beneficiary theory implies they do. Hart says that rights can be ascribed in the former cases because such a usage retains a certain "distributive" feature of the notion of a right, since the breach of such a duty "necessarily involves the infliction of harm upon a specific . . . individual."

But there is another and I think more obvious and plausible way of understanding why rights are and can be ascribed when murder and assault are prohibited. Such rules "assure goods" or obstruct evils to those they are supposed to protect. The qualified beneficiary theory can account for such rights without implying that every useful duty has a corresponding right. Hart's objection is directed against the unqualified beneficiary theory and, as I shall try to show, it has no force against the qualified theory.

Any rule that has a utilitarian justification and is in that sense "useful" ultimately serves (or can reasonably be expected to serve) the interest of individuals, but rules can do so in different ways. The rules that serve individuals most directly do so by imposing *beneficial* duties, in a qualified sense, which implies that there are beneficiaries in the sense employed by the qualified beneficiary theory.

[15] *Ibid.*

Rules such as those forbidding murder and assault are of this type; they can only be understood as requiring that we not harm or injure others in certain ways. The duties they impose patently require treating others in ways designed or intended to serve, secure, promote, or protect their interests. The rules define the classes of persons protected, and any member of such a class is a beneficiary in the qualified sense. He does not merely "stand to benefit" by the performance of such a duty, nor does he merely "stand to suffer" if the duty is breached, for his loss at the hands of the person with the duty would be directly relevant to the question whether the duty is breached. From the point of view of the rules and the duties they impose, such a person is neither a lucky bystander in one case nor an unlucky one in the other. He is one who, according to the rules, is not to be harmed in such a way. And thus, despite the fact that such a person cannot be said to have a right "against" anyone in particular—since he cannot waive or cancel the corresponding obligation and it does not rest upon any *special* relation between him and those bound by the rules—and despite the fact that the duty is not "owed" to him in particular—since he is not a claimant—nevertheless, it does seem plausible to say that he is *entitled* to be treated in a certain way, e.g., not to be assaulted or killed, and that saying this is not speaking loosely. For others are duty-bound so to treat him, and his *right* does correspond to and correlate with their duties.

But other rules that can be justified on utilitarian grounds serve individuals much less directly. If there is a good utilitarian reason for requiring payment of income tax, for example, benefits to individuals must be expected ultimately to accrue. (As Bentham held, the interest or good of the community cannot be understood except in terms of the interests or good of its members.) But the possible, intended, or desired benefits that might ultimately accrue to individuals do not flow directly from the performance of such duties, and no harm results directly, if at all, from their breach. Duties imposed by such rules I shall call (merely) "useful." Such duties have no beneficiaries in the qualified sense. Money collected from income tax payments can be used to serve the community, and therefore its members, in various ways. But these ways are not determined by the act of payment itself. Most important, the content of the duty to pay income tax concerns payment and payment only. It does not concern the uses to which the revenue might be put. And one who might possibly benefit from the use of such revenues, and according may "stand to benefit" from the performance of the duty to pay income tax, is not a beneficiary in the qualified sense. His benefit or loss is not directly relevant to the question whether or not the duty is discharged.

There is not even a traceable connection, normally, between someone's gain or loss as a result of payment or nonpayment and another person's discharge or breach of his duty to pay income tax. The payment marks the beginning of a long, complex chain that may, but does not necessarily, lead to benefits to individuals. Generally speaking, a particular person's payment or nonpayment is neither necessary nor sufficient for bringing about or preventing another person's ultimate benefits or losses. Usually, benefits cannot accrue in the long run unless observance of such duties is widespread. Even if it is widespread, the actual result depends on how the money is used. Suppose, however, that individuals ultimately do receive benefits that are partly traceable to income tax revenues. It remains extremely unlikely, if not impossible, that we should be able to ascribe anyone's benefits to particular performances of the duty to pay income tax. And if harm results or benefits do not accrue because payments are commonly withheld, it is again extremely unlikely, if not impossible, that particular losses could be ascribed to particular breaches. Moreover, no loss will be caused by nonpayment unless breaches are common. So it is neither necessarily the case nor even likely that anyone will suffer or lose as a consequence of one breach (or several breaches) of a merely useful duty.

Hart's objection is, then, that the unqualified beneficiary theory implies that merely useful as well as beneficial duties give rise to rights. This is because such a weak condition as "Someone stands to benefit by the performance of another's duty" *must* be satisfied whenever useful duties are imposed. But this objection has no force against the qualified beneficiary theory, since merely useful duties have no beneficiaries in the qualified sense. So, while it may be implausible to say that a merely useful duty gives rise to a corresponding right, it is also difficult to construe the qualified beneficiary theory as implying it. Hart's objection has therefore been met. Rights correspond to obligations under the criminal law in just the way Hart claims, according to the qualified beneficiary theory. Rights correlate with beneficial duties and not with merely useful ones.

Before closing this section it may be illuminating

to note that the qualified beneficiary theory accounts for rights that are related, indirectly, to such duties as military service and payment of income tax. Consider, for example, those persons who supposedly "stand to benefit" from income tax payments. More precisely, consider those who *qualify by law* as recipients of governmental services and expenditures, e.g., public education, unemployment compensation, garbage collection, and so on. The rules that govern such expenditures also provide criteria for qualification. And if one qualifies by law it would seem that he is legally *entitled* to the benefits or services and thus has a legal right to them. These rights can readily be accounted for by the qualified beneficiary theory. For *corresponding* duties—not duties to pay income tax, but duties to distribute the benefits and administer the services—fall upon those whose job it is to do such things. So, the qualified beneficiary theory seems also to account for rights that Hart does not consider. And it does so by using one purported sense of "right," which is applied in other contexts as well.[16]

III

Hart's more formidable objection to the beneficiary theory concerns the case of the "third-party beneficiary."[17] Promises—when they are valid and binding—engender rights to promisees and obligations to promisors. A promisee often stands to benefit from the promised performance, but when a promise is meant to benefit a "third party" (i.e., one who is not a party to the agreement) then, according to Hart, the promisee as usual acquires a right even though he is not a beneficiary, while the third party, who is supposed to benefit, acquires no right. This shows that being a beneficiary is neither necessary nor sufficient for having a right.

In Hart's example, a son extracts a promise from another (let us say a friend) to care for his aged mother in his absence. Hart argues that the son has the right. The promise is made *to* him and he, therefore, has the claim against the friend. The friend's performance is *owed* to or *due* him. He alone can press or waive the claim, can insist upon its performance or release his friend from the promise. If the promise is not kept, Hart argues, the son is *wronged* even if he is not harmed. But the mother (a third-party beneficiary) has no right. She might be harmed if the promise is not kept, but she cannot be wronged. For the promise is not made *to her*, and thus the performance is not owed to or due her. One with a right admittedly may be, and usually is, a beneficiary of a duty. But this is not what it is to have a right. The promisee alone has a moral claim upon the promisor. He is

> morally in a position to determine by his choice how [the promisor] shall act and in this way to limit [the promisor's] freedom of choice; and it is this fact, not the fact that he stands to benefit, that makes it appropriate to say that he has *a right*.[18]

I shall try to show the limits of this objection to the qualified beneficiary theory. First, I shall argue that Hart's objection rests in part upon a misconstrual of the third-party beneficiary's position with respect to another's obligation. Because Hart considers only the unqualified beneficiary theory with its inadequate notion of a beneficiary, he assimilates the mother's position in his example to that of persons who merely "stand to benefit" by the performance of a duty and have no relevant rights. The alternative suggestion, offered by the qualified beneficiary theory, is that the mother, like those in other contexts who may properly be said to have rights although they are not claimants, can be accorded a right precisely because she is a beneficiary in the qualified sense. Then I shall examine the question whether claimants, who seem clearly to have rights, are necessarily beneficiaries —in other words, whether being a beneficiary is a necessary condition for having a right.

In Hart's discussion of the third-party beneficiary case, he concedes (as we saw he does also with regard to the criminal law) that "common usage" may sanction the ascription of rights to beneficiaries —to animals and infants for example, who are said to have rights to proper treatment because we have duties not to ill-treat them. But Hart maintains that this way of speaking employs only "the philosopher's generalized sense of 'duty' " and that it makes "an idle use of the expression 'a

[16] Hart's claimant theory might be extended to accommodate rights where provision of services or benefits is conditional upon application; but it cannot accommodate cases in which there is no choice or option to exercise, e.g., where free public education is also compulsory.

[17] Although Hart mentions this case in "Bentham," *op. cit.*, p. 314, his discussion of it is found in "Are There Any Natural Rights?", *op. cit.*, pp. 180ff.

[18] "Are There Any Natural Rights?", *ibid.*, p. 180.

right'." He contends that "the moral situation can be simply and adequately described here by saying that it is wrong or that we ought not to ill-treat" babies or animals. But "right" and "duty" have a "specific force" in other contexts that cannot be captured by such uses of "wrong" and "ought."[19] When "right" and "duty" are used strictly, and not merely in a "generalized" sense, the person with the duty may be said to be "bound to" the person with the right. The right-holder is a claimant, who controls the duty. Thus the friend has a duty "to" the son, to whom he *owes* the promised performance. But the friend has a duty "to" the mother only in the sense that his duty concerns her. The friend does not "owe" the performance to the mother, and thus she has no right to the promised services, for she has no right "against" the friend.

Hart's avowed purpose here is to draw our attention to special features of our discourse about rights, features that set it off from talk about what ought to be done or what it would be wrong to do or about "duties" that are not "owed" to claimants. He suggests that the beneficiary theory obscures the differences between these sectors of moral and legal discourse. Hart's view involves a threefold distinction, between (a) contexts in which rights in the "strict" sense can be ascribed; (b) contexts in which rights can be ascribed only in a wider sense; and (c) contexts in which "duties" may be ascribed, but not rights. The qualified beneficiary theory does not, however, eliminate any of these distinctions (although it draws the lines somewhat differently). Corresponding to Hart's contexts (a) and (b) are those in which ascriptions of rights can be made in a single sense of the term, although the ascriptions are warranted by different sorts of conditions (depending on whether or not the duty or obligation is "owed" to the person with the right). Corresponding to Hart's context (c) is that in which duties or obligations are not beneficial and rights cannot be ascribed, even if the duties are useful. Since such distinctions between sectors of moral and legal discourse are not obscured by the qualified beneficiary theory (although they may be obscured by the unqualified theory), we need not dwell upon them.

We may consider instead what may be *common* to the various plausible ascriptions of rights to see whether being a beneficiary is both common and essential. Hart seems to suggest here that what is common when rights are ascribed in both the strict and the wider sense of the term is that the behavior of others that is required or prohibited *concerns* the person with the right. But this condition is surely not peculiar to requirements that might be held to correspond to rights. For as we have noted, Green's duty as executioner concerns the condemned Brown, while it is doubtful that Brown acquires a corresponding right. And it concerns Brown differently than the restrictions regarding babies and animals concern them. For our duties regarding babies and animals assure goods or obstruct evils to them.

The cases of babies and animals raise complications we need not examine here, e.g., whether legal or moral personality or agency is required for the possession of rights. But it should be observed, nonetheless, that the position of the third-party beneficiary in Hart's example is different from that of babies and animals. The friend's obligation to serve the mother is not merely an instance of a general duty to refrain from harming the helpless. The friend's obligation arises from a specific agreement, and it is one he otherwise would not have. He has agreed to care for the mother. The mother is the one the promised services are intended to benefit. She is a direct, intended beneficiary.

Joel Feinberg suggests that Hart has overstated his point. Third-party beneficiaries are *sometimes* accorded rights in both morals and law. But, he says:

> it does not *follow necessarily* from the fact that a person is an intended beneficiary of a promised service that he has a right to it; whereas it always follows necessarily from the fact that a person is a promisee that he has a right to what is promised.[20]

Third-party beneficiaries can have rights, but "only in virtue of moral or judicial policies and rules." A third-party beneficiary's right seems to follow from his position as beneficiary only when, for example, it is also plausible "to say that the promisor made a *tacit promise* to the beneficiary in addition to the express promise to his promisee." The parties to the agreement let the beneficiary know of it and he thereupon "acts in reliance on its performance."[21]

[19] *Ibid.*, p. 181. On related points see also Hart's "Legal and Moral Obligation" in A. I. Melden (ed.), *Essays in Moral Philosophy* (Seattle, 1958), esp. pp. 82–84, 100–105.

[20] "Duties, Rights, and Claims," *op. cit.*, p. 138. Assuming the premiss is valid and binding, presumably.

[21] *Ibid.*

Here again, however, there is evidence that the objection hinges on a misconstrual of the mother's position. Feinberg's unwillingness to allow that third-party beneficiaries *necessarily* have rights seems based on a weak sense he (as well as Hart) attaches to "third-party beneficiary." When this expression is so used that it can apply even to those who, as he says, merely "stand to gain, if only indirectly" or "who will profit in merely picayune and remote ways" from the promised performance,[22] a third-party beneficiary does *not* necessarily have a right. But if it is used in the qualified sense, the expression better characterizes the mother in Hart's example and it seems to *follow* that she has a right. The mother's interest is directly relevant to the friend's obligation. A complete specification of the friend's obligation includes *essential* reference to the mother, who is supposed to benefit by its performance. Her loss in case the promise is broken would not be a remote, accidental consequence of the friend's behavior; it would be the predictable and relevant consequence of a dereliction. The fact that she was not cared for would be the chief ground for saying that the friend had failed to discharge his obligation. Her receipt of the services would be the chief reason for saying that he had discharged his obligation. The friend's obligation is beneficial, and the mother is the beneficiary. The mother is *entitled* to the services required by the friend's obligation as one entitled to be treated in a certain way when another has an obligation specifically so to behave. Does she not *have a right* to be cared for by him?

Of course, in such a case the mother may not be aware of the friend's promise and thus may not know that she is entitled to his services. But knowledge of the relevant facts is surely not a necessary condition for having a right. If ignorant of the agreement, she would be in no position to complain in case the friend broke his promise. But if she became aware of the relevant facts it would seem that she could legitimately complain and "press" her right (whether or not she was *further* inconvenienced because she relied upon the friend's help). Indeed, she might also refuse the services and thus effectively "release" the friend from his obligation, especially if she could care for herself and did not need the help arranged for her by her son. But this does not mean that she has a right *because* she is a *claimant*; it means, rather, that she *may act as* a claimant (if she is in a position to do so) precisely *because she has a right* to be cared for by the friend.

These considerations suggest once more that being a beneficiary is sufficient for having a right. But they do not show that being a beneficiary is a necessary condition, and thus the more serious threat posed by Hart's objection has not been met. For the son, as promisee, would seem to have a right against the friend. But the son does not appear to be a *beneficiary* in any straightforward sense. The promise is meant to benefit the mother, not the son, and she alone will benefit directly from the friend's care. Moreover, it is the friend's treatment of the mother, not his treatment of the son, that is relevant to the obligation, that determines whether or not it is discharged. This seems to indicate that being a beneficiary of a beneficial obligation is not a necessary condition of having a right.

If this part of Hart's objection is allowed, a defender of the beneficiary theory might be content with the following observations. The argument has tended to show that being a beneficiary of a beneficial obligation is, first of all, a sufficient condition for having a right. Hart's objection shows at best that being a beneficiary is not a necessary condition for having a right. But it does not show that rights are conferred even when there are no such beneficiaries. And this may not be an insignificant point. For it would seem that outside the contexts of promises (contracts, agreements) counter-examples to the qualified beneficiary theory are not easy to find. In other contexts in both law and morals it would seem that rights are ascribed when and only when obligations or restrictions upon others' behavior assure goods or obstruct evils to individuals and thus when breaches of the corresponding obligations would involve loss or harm to those with the rights. The apparent possibility of counter-examples arises because it does not seem to be a condition of a valid and binding promise that its performance serve the interests of the *promisee*. But in such cases there is at least a *third-party* beneficiary. It is difficult to imagine promises—or, generally, obligations that correspond to rights—which are valid and binding and yet serve no one's interests. On the contrary, our understanding of the nature of binding promises is shown by the fact that, when their fulfillment threatens unexpected disadvantages to those they are meant to serve, it would be wrong to keep them.

[22] *Ibid.*, p. 137; see also p. 138, including note 3.

But if we pursue this line of argument and attempt to clarify the respects in which promises may be said to "serve someone's interests," then it would also appear that a promisee, even in a third-party beneficiary case, is a "beneficiary" in the qualified sense.

Suppose that Jones extracts a promise from Brown. The promise is not intended to benefit a third party, and there is no one who could plausibly be regarded as a "third-party beneficiary" in the appropriate sense. Brown makes the promise because he is led by Jones to believe that he, Jones, wants the promised act performed. But suppose that Jones is, in fact, unconcerned whether or not the promise is kept. He extracts the promise on the merest whim or out of malice. It seems clear that the conditions of a valid and binding promise are not satisfied (whether or not Brown knows this), and thus that Jones does not acquire *a right* to what was promised and that Brown incurs no *obligation* (although he may *think* that he is obligated). But if Jones had really wanted what was promised and Brown had freely agreed to do it, then—barring immoral purposes—a valid and binding promise would have been made.

What does this show? One of the conditions of a valid and binding promise, and thus a condition of a right accruing to the promisee, is that he really wants what is promised.[23] Now this does not imply that there must be *benefits* in any straightforward sense. But it does, I think, imply that the obligation "assures a good" to the promisee. For it is the promisee's very want, wish, or desire *to have what is promised done* that the promise is *meant* to satisfy. And it is not implausible to suggest that the satisfaction of someone's (morally permissible) want, wish, or desire amounts to the conferring on him of a certain good.

If we try to imagine cases in which this claim is not satisfied, we shall find the ascription of a right and of a corresponding promissory obligation moot. Suppose, for example, that the promisee asks another to do him an injury or to kill him. We can imagine cases where, to avoid greater evil or unbearable pain, for example, such a promise might be reasonably requested and made and consequently binding. But in such cases there is also as much reason to say that the promise "assures a certain good" to the promisee. If there is no such good reason for the promise but only, say, a desire for self-destruction or mutilation, it is not at all clear that one would be morally free to make such a promise or that once made the promise could be regarded as morally binding.

Let us return now to Hart's example. If a son extracts a promise from his friend to care for his aged mother in his absence, we might reasonably suppose that he does so because, say, he is concerned, as an affectionate son, about his mother's well-being; or, perhaps, because he thinks he is serving his own interests in providing for her care; or even because he wants to discharge what is to him a totally disagreeable filial obligation. That is, we might reasonably suppose that, for one reason or another, the son really wants his mother cared for in his absence, that he has *some* interest in her being cared for, and that he extracts the promise accordingly. But let us not assume any such thing. Let us suppose instead that the son merely wants his friend to make such a promise, but that it is not part of his intention to provide for her care and that he has no interest in doing so.

Now, on the one hand, it might transpire that the friend acquires an obligation to care for the mother and that the mother acquires a right to the promised services—that the promise is binding to this degree, despite the son's secret indifference. For the mother has an interest that needs to be served and the friend freely agrees to serve it. But on the other hand, it would not seem that the son is truly entitled to complain if the friend fails to keep his promise. And that is because he has not satisfied the conditions necessary for acquiring such a right. If there is an obligation, it is not owed to the son (whether or not the friend knows it). If there is a legitimate claim it is not the son's claim but the mother's; and if there is a right it is not his either.

If there is such a difference between the son's moral status in this case and in Hart's original example, so that it is more plausible to ascribe a right to him in the latter than in the former, that difference has to do with the son's reasons for and his sincerity in extracting the promise. What is true of Hart's example that is not true here? The son wants his mother cared for, and for that reason asks his friend to do so. The reason he gives his friend is the same in both cases; but only in Hart's example is that really his reason. So, in both cases at least part of the point of the promise is to satisfy such a desire or wish on the part of the son—to provide for his mother's care—but only in Hart's

[23] For a similar point concerning promissory obligations, see Jerome Schneewind, "A Note on Promising," *Philosophical Studies*, vol. 17 (1966), pp. 33–35.

case will the keeping of the promise actually satisfy such a wish or desire.

This is not to say that the difference between the two cases, which may account for the fact that the son acquires a right in one but not the other, is the fact that in one but not the other the son "stands to *benefit*" from the promised performance. Nevertheless, the fact that the son has an interest in his mother's care and wants her cared for, coupled with the fact that it is *this* wish or desire of the son's that the friend's promise is designed to satisfy, shows that the friend's obligation "assures a good" to the son.

I do not mean to claim that this defense of the beneficiary theory is conclusive. I hope to have shown, rather, that the theory cannot be *dismissed* without further consideration. It is less vulnerable than its critics have supposed, largely because of the differences between its qualified and unqualified versions.

I shall conclude by considering an example that may indicate serious difficulties for the beneficiary theory. The example is suggested (in another connection) by Hart, who maintains that a certain class of moral rights correlates with "political obligations"—obligations to conform to certain social rules. These rights and obligations arise, Hart says, in the following circumstances:

> when a number of persons conduct any joint enterprise according to rules and thus restrict their liberty, those who have submitted to these restrictions when required have a right to a similar submission from those who have benefited by their submission. The rules may provide that officials should have authority to enforce obedience and make further rules, and this will create a structure of legal rights and duties, but the moral obligation to obey the rules in such circumstances is due to the co-operating members of the society, and they have the correlative moral rights to obedience.[24]

As I have argued elsewhere,[25] certain qualifications should be added, at least to make the character of the present argument clear. These include (a) actual conformity to the rules is sufficiently widespread to produce some shareable good or to prevent some common evil; (b) this desirable result could not be achieved without such cooperation; (c) the benefits and burdens are fairly distributed; (d) the total benefits outweigh the burdens imposed; (e) *universal* cooperation by those who stand to benefit is *not* required to achieve the desirable end. The last condition is most important, because it explains how it is possible for a "freeloader" to take advantage of others' cooperation without himself performing as the rules require. The conditions also show that the duties imposed by the rules and the moral obligations to conform to them are not beneficial in the qualified sense employed above. For a single breach of such a rule is not sufficient for anyone's loss, and the performances required by these duties and obligations do not consist in directly serving the interests of someone with a correlative right.

The sort of social rule that might satisfy such conditions as I have outlined is the legal rule requiring payment of income tax. This rule imposes a legal duty to pay income tax and, if the conditions are satisfied, then, according to the argument given, one has a moral obligation to conform to such a rule and others have a right to one's conformity or cooperation. Consequently, the qualified beneficiary theory cannot account for such rights, since the legal duties in question are merely useful and the same holds for the moral obligation to obey such a law.

What are the connections between goods and rights in this case? On the one hand, there cannot be such an obligation unless the law, or system of law, is useful (as conditions (a), (b), and (d) require), and unless everyone stands to benefit (as conditions (c) would I think require). So goods *are* essentially involved; but they are involved indirectly, as in the case of merely useful duties. For (as condition (e) seems to guarantee), the obligation to obey the law is *not* contingent on universal obedience being needed for the usefulness of the general practice. The idea that underlies such an obligation and its correlative right is that it would be *unfair* or *unjust* for someone who benefits from others' burdensome cooperation or conformity to fail to perform when his turn came. The idea is not that his failure to conform or cooperate would detract from the usefulness of the general practice or would decrease in any way the benefits that accrue to individuals. For according to the conditions of the argument, even, say, the secret and harmless breaking of necessary rationing restrictions would be wrong and would involve the violation of such a right and the breach of such an obligation.

If this is correct, then it would seem that the only good that can be assured by such an obligation to obey the law in *each* of its instances is the *abstract*

[24] "Are There Any Natural Rights?", *op. cit.*, p. 185.

[25] *Forms and Limits of Utilitarianism* (Oxford, 1965), ch. 5, Sect. A.

or *impersonal* good of justice. It is not a personal good, not a good *to* or *for* a person with a corresponding right. And this does not satisfy the conditions of the qualified beneficiary theory.

Utilitarians would, of course, deny that there is such an obligation, or would insist that it rests on the fact that nonconformity or noncooperation can reasonably be expected to have bad results, by setting a bad example which may lead others to disobey, thus tending eventually to decrease the usefulness of the law. This suggests that the good assured to individuals is simply the confidence that their burdensome cooperation will not be in vain. Alternatively, utilitarians may seek to argue that the abstract or impersonal good of justice reduces, ultimately, to personal goods.[26]

Cornell University

Received September 11, 1968

[26] Earlier versions of this paper were read at Cornell University and the Universities of Waterloo, Massachusetts, Pittsburgh, Michigan, and Texas, where I received helpful comments and criticisms. I have also benefited greatly from discussions with Norman Malcolm and Michael Stocker and from the suggestions of Ellen Coleman, Robert Monk, William Nelson, and John Turner.

THE NATURE AND VALUE OF RIGHTS * *

JOEL FEINBERG

1

I would like to begin by conducting a thought experiment. Try to imagine Nowheresville – a world very much like our own except that no one, or hardly any one (the qualification is not important), has *rights*. If this flaw makes Nowheresville too ugly to hold very long in contemplation, we can make it as pretty as we wish in other moral respects. We can, for example, make the human beings in it as attractive and virtuous as possible without taxing our conceptions of the limits of human nature. In particular, let the virtues of moral sensibility flourish. Fill this imagined world with as much benevolence, compassion, sympathy, and pity as it will conveniently hold without strain. Now we can imagine men helping one another from compassionate motives merely, quite as much or even more than they do in our actual world from a variety of more complicated motives.

This picture, pleasant as it is in some respects, would hardly have satisfied Immanuel Kant. Benevolently motivated actions do good, Kant admitted, and therefore are better, *ceteris paribus*, than malevolently motivated actions; but no action can have supreme kind of worth – what Kant called "moral worth" – unless its whole motivating power derives from the thought that it is *required by duty*. Accordingly, let us try to make Nowheresville more appealing to Kant by introducing the idea of duty into it, and letting the sense of duty be a sufficient motive for many beneficent and honorable actions. But doesn't this bring our original thought experiment to an abortive conclusion? If duties are permitted entry into Nowheresville, are not rights necessarily smuggled in along with them?

The question is well-asked, and requires here a brief digression so that we might consider the so-called "doctrine of the logical correlativity of rights and duties." This is the doctrine that (i) all duties entail other people's rights and (ii) all rights entail other people's duties. Only the first part of the doctrine, the alleged entailment from duties to rights, need concern us here. Is this part of the doctrine correct? It should not be surprising that my answer is: "In a sense yes and in a sense no." Etymologically, the word "duty" is associated with actions that are *due* someone else, the payments

---

* *Editorial Note:* The three papers and their commentaries published in this issue were read at the Conference on Political and Moral Philosophy held at Ripon College, Wisconsin, Sept. 18 and 19, 1969.

* This article was first given as an Isenberg Memorial Lecture at Michigan State University, Winter Series, 1969. Presented to AMINATAPHIL, Nov. 1969.

of debts *to* creditors, the keeping of agreements with promisees, the payment of club dues, or legal fees, or tariff levies to appropriate authorities or their representatives. In this original sense of "duty," all duties are correlated with the rights of those *to* whom the duty is owed. On the other hand, there seem to be numerous classes of duties, both of a legal and non-legal kind, that are *not* logically correlated with the rights of other persons. This seems to be a consequence of the fact that the word "duty" has come to be used for *any* action understood to be *required*, whether by the rights of others, or by law, or by higher authority, or by conscience, or whatever. When the notion of requirement is in clear focus it is likely to seem the only element in the idea of duty that is essential, and the other component notion – that a duty is something *due* someone else – drops off. Thus, in this widespread but derivative usage, "duty" tends to be used for any action we feel we *must* (for whatever reason) do. It comes, in short, to be a term of moral modality merely; and it is no wonder that the first thesis of the logical correlativity doctrine often fails.

Let us then introduce duties into Nowheresville, but only in the sense of actions that are, or are believed to be, morally mandatory, but not in the older sense of actions that are due others and can be claimed by others as their right. Nowheresville now can have duties of the sort imposed by positive law. A legal duty is not something we are implored or advised to do merely; it is something the law, or an authority under the law, *requires* us to do whether we want to or not, under pain of penalty. When traffic lights turn red, however, there is no determinate person who can plausibly be said to claim our stopping as his due, so that the motorist owes it to *him* to stop, in the way a debtor owes it to his creditor to pay. In our own actual world, of course, we sometimes owe it to our *fellow motorists* to stop; but that kind of right-correlated duty does not exist in Nowheresville. There, motorists "owe" obedience to the Law, but they owe nothing to one another. When they collide, no matter who is at fault, no one is morally accountable to anyone else, and no one has any sound grievance or "right to complain."

When we leave legal contexts to consider moral obligations and other extra-legal duties, a greater variety of duties-without-correlative-rights present themselves. Duties of charity, for example, require us to contribute to one or another of a large number of eligible recipients, no one of whom can claim our contribution from us as his due. Charitable contributions are more like gratuitous services, favors, and gifts than like repayments of debts or reparations; and yet we do have duties to be charitable. Many persons, moreover, in our actual world believe that they are required by their own consciences to do more than that "duty" that *can* be demanded of them by their prospective beneficiaries. I have quoted elsewhere the citation from H. B. Acton of a character in a Malraux novel who "gave all his supply of poison to his fellow prisoners to enable them by suicide to escape the burning alive which was to be their fate and his." This man, Acton adds, "probably did not think that [the others] had more of a right to the poison than he had, though he thought it his duty to give it to them."[1] I am sure that there are many actual examples, less dramatically heroic than this fictitious one, of persons who believe, rightly or wrongly, that they *must do* something (hence the word "duty") for another person in excess of what that person can appropriately demand of him (hence the absence of "right").

Now the digression is over and we can return to Nowheresville and summarize what we have put in it thus far. We now find spontaneous benevolence in somewhat larger degree than in our actual world, and also the acknowledged existence of duties of obedience, duties of charity, and duties imposed by exacting private consciences, and also, let us suppose, a degree of conscientiousness in respect to those duties somewhat in excess of what is to be found in our actual world. I doubt that Kant would be fully satisfied with Nowheresville even now that duty and respect for law and authority have been added to it; but I feel certain that he would regard their addition at least as an improvement. I will now introduce two further moral practices into Nowheresville that will make that world very little more appealing to Kant, but will make it appear more familiar to us. These are the practices connected with the notions of *personal desert* and what I call a *sovereign monopoly of rights*.

When a person is said to deserve something good from us what is meant in part is that there would be a certain propriety in our giving that good thing to him in virtue of the kind of person he is, perhaps, or more likely, in virtue of some specific thing he has done. The propriety involved here is a much weaker kind than that which derives from our having promised him the good thing or from his having qualified for it by satisfying the well-advertised conditions of some public rule. In the latter case he could be said not merely to deserve the good thing but also to have a *right* to it, that is to be in a position to demand it as his due; and of course we will not have that sort of thing in Nowheresville. That weaker kind of propriety which is mere desert is simply a kind of *fittingness* between one party's character or action and another party's favorable response, much like that between humor and laughter, or good performance and applause.

The following seems to be the origin of the idea of deserving good or bad treatment from others: A master or lord was under no obligation to reward his servant for especially good service; still a master might naturally feel that there would be a special fittingness in giving a gratuitous reward as a grateful response to the good service (or conversely imposing a penalty for bad service). Such an act while surely fitting and proper was entirely supererogatory. The fitting response in turn from the rewarded servant should be gratitude. If the deserved reward had not been given him he should have had no complaint, since he only *deserved* the reward, as opposed to having a *right* to it, or a ground for claiming it as his due.

[1] H. B. Acton, "Symposium on 'Rights'," *Proceedings of the Aristotelian Society*, Supplementary Volume 24 (1950), pp. 107–8.

The idea of desert has evolved a good bit away from its beginnings by now, but nevertheless, it seems clearly to be one of those words J. L. Austin said "never entirely forget their pasts."[2] Today servants qualify for their wages by doing their agreed upon chores, no more and no less. If their wages are not forthcoming, their contractual rights have been violated and they can make legal claim to the money that is their due. If they do less than they agreed to do, however, their employers may "dock" them, by paying them proportionately less than the agreed upon fee. This is all a matter of right. But if the servant does a splendid job, above and beyond his minimal contractual duties, the employer is under no further obligation to reward him, for this was not agreed upon, even tacitly, in advance. The additional service was all the servant's idea and done entirely on his own. Nevertheless, the morally sensitive employer may feel that it would be exceptionally appropriate for him to respond, freely on *his* own, to the servant's meritorious service, with a reward. The employee cannot demand it as his due, but he will happily accept it, with gratitude, as a fitting response to his desert.

In our age of organized labor, even this picture is now archaic; for almost every kind of exchange of service is governed by hard bargained contracts so that even bonuses can sometimes be demanded as a matter of right, and nothing is given for nothing on either side of the bargaining table. And perhaps that is a good thing; for consider an anachoronistic instance of the earlier kind of practice that survives, at least as a matter of form, in the quaint old practice of "tipping." The tip was originally conceived as a reward that has to be earned by "zealous service." It is not something to be taken for granted as a standard response to *any* service. That is to say that its payment is a "*gratuity,*" not a discharge of obligation, but something given apart from, or in addition to, anything the recipient can expect as a matter of right. That is what tipping originally meant at any rate, and tips are still referred to as "gratuities" in the tax forms. But try to explain all that to a New York cab driver! If he has *earned* his gratuity, by God, he has it coming, and there had better be sufficient acknowledgement of his desert or he'll give you a piece of his mind! I'm not generally prone to defend New York cab drivers, but they do have a point here. There is the making of a paradox in the queerly unstable concept of an "earned gratuity." One can understand how "desert" in the weak sense of "propriety" or "mere fittingness" tends to generate a stronger sense in which desert is itself the ground for a claim of right.

In Nowheresville, nevertheless, we will have only the original weak kind of desert. Indeed, it will be impossible to keep this idea out if we allow such practices as teachers grading students, judges awarding prizes, and servants serving benevolent but class-conscious masters. Nowheresville is a reasonably good world in many ways, and its teachers, judges, and masters

---

[2] J. L. Austin, "A Plea for Excuses", *Proceedings of the Aristotelian Society*, Vol. 57 (1956–57).

will generally try to give students, contestants, and servants the grades, prizes, and rewards they deserve. For this the recipients will be grateful; but they will never think to complain, or even feel aggrieved, when expected responses to desert fail. The masters, judges, and teachers don't *have* to do good things, after all, for *anyone*. One should be happy that they *ever* treat us well, and not grumble over their occasional lapses. Their hoped for responses, after all, are *gratuities*, and there is no wrong in the omission of what is merely gratuitous. Such is the response of persons who have no concept of *rights*, even persons who are proud of their own deserts.[3]

Surely, one might ask, rights have to come in somewhere, if we are to have even moderately complex forms of social organization. Without rules that confer rights and impose obligations, how can we have ownership of property, bargains and deals, promises and contracts, appointments and loans, marriages and partnerships? Very well, let us introduce all of these social and economic practices into Nowheresville, but *with one big twist*. With them I should like to introduce the curious notion of a "sovereign right-monopoly." You will recall that the subjects in Hobbes's *Leviathan* had no rights whatever against their sovereign. He could do as he liked with them, even gratuitously harm them, but this gave them no valid grievance against him. The sovereign, to be sure, had a certain duty to treat his subjects well, but this duty was owed not to the subjects directly, but to God, just as we might have a duty to a person to treat his property well, but of course no duty to the property itself but only to its owner. Thus, while the sovereign was quite capable of *harming* his subjects, he could commit no wrong against them that they could complain about, since they had no prior claims against his conduct. The only party *wronged* by the sovereign's mistreatment of his subjects was God, the supreme lawmaker. Thus, in repenting cruelty to his subjects, the sovereign might say to God, as David did after killing Uriah, "to Thee only have I sinned."[4]

Even in the *Leviathan*, however, ordinary people had ordinary rights *against one another*. They played roles, occupied offices, made agreements, and signed contracts. In a genuine "sovereign right-monopoly," as I shall be using that phrase, they will do all those things too, and thus incur genuine obligations toward one another; but the obligations (here is the twist) will not be owed directly *to* promisees, creditors, parents, and the like, but rather to God alone, or to the members of some elite, or to a single sovereign under God. Hence, the rights correlative to the obligations that derive from these transactions are all owned by some "outside" authority.

As far as I know, no philosopher has ever suggested that even our role and contract obligations (in this, our actual world) are all owed directly to

[3] For a fuller discussion of the concept of personal desert see my "Justice and Personal Desert," *Nomos VI, Justice*, ed. by C. J. Friedrich and J. Chapman (New York: Atherton Press, 1963), pp. 69–97.

[4] II Sam. 11. Cited with approval by Thomas Hobbes in *The Leviathan*, Part II, Chap. 21.

a divine intermediary; but some theologians have approached such extreme moral occasionalism. I have in mind the familiar phrase in certain widely distributed religious tracts that "it takes three to marry," which suggests that marital vows are not made between bride and groom directly but between each spouse and God, so that if one breaks his vow, the other cannot rightly complain of being wronged, since only God could have claimed performance of the marital duties as his *own* due; and hence God alone had a claim-right violated by nonperformance. If John breaks his vow to God, he might then properly repent in the words of David: "To Thee only have I sinned."

In our actual world, very few spouses conceive of their mutual obligations in this way; but their small children, at a certain stage in their moral upbringing, are likely to feel precisely this way toward *their* mutual obligations. If Billy kicks Bobby and is punished by Daddy, he may come to feel contrition for his naughtiness induced by his painful estrangement from the loved parent. Hy may then be happy to make amends and sincere apology *to Daddy;* but when Daddy insists that he apologize to his wronged brother, that is another story. A direct apology to Billy would be a tacit recognition of Billy's status as a right-holder against him, some one he can wrong as well as harm, and someone to whom he is directly accountable for his wrongs. This is a status Bobby will happily accord Daddy; but it would imply a respect for Billy that he does not presently feel, so he bitterly resents according it to him. On the "three-to-marry" model, the relations between each spouse and God would be like those between Bobby and Daddy; respect for the other spouse as an independent claimant would not even be necessary; and where present, of course, never sufficient.

The advocates of the "three to marry" model who conceive it either as a description of our actual institution of marriage or a recommendation of what marriage ought to be, may wish to escape this embarrassment by granting rights to spouses in capacities other than as promisees. They may wish to say, for example, that when John promises God that he will be faithful to Mary, a right is thus conferred not only on God as promisee but also on Mary herself as third-party beneficiary, just as when John contracts with an insurance company and names Mary as his intended beneficiary, she has a right to the accumulated funds after John's death, even though the insurance company made no promise to her. But this seems to be an unnecessarily cumbersome complication contributing nothing to our understanding of the marriage bond. The life insurance transaction is necessarily a three party relation, involving occupants of three distinct offices, no two of whom alone could do the whole job. The transaction, after all, is defined as the purchase by the customer (first office) from the vendor (second office) of protection for a beneficiary (third office) against the customer's untimely death. Marriage, on the other hand, in this our actual world, appears to be a binary relation between a husband and wife, and even though third parties such as children, neighbors, psychiatrists, and priests may sometimes be helpful and even causally necessary for the survival of the relation, they are not logically necessary to our *conception* of the relation, and indeed many married couples do quite well without them. Still, I am not now purporting to describe our actual world, but rather trying to contrast it with a counterpart world of the imagination. In *that* world, it takes three to make almost *any* moral relation and all rights are owned by God or some sovereign under God.

There will, of course, be delegated authorities in the imaginary world, empowered to give commands to their underlings and to punish them for their disobedience. But the commands are all given in the name of the right-monopoly who in turn are the only persons to whom obligations are owed. Hence, even intermediate superiors do not have claim-rights against their subordinates but only legal *powers* to create obligations in the subordinates *to* the monopolistic right-holders, and also the legal *privilege* to impose penalties in the name of that monopoly.

2

So much for the imaginary "world without rights." If some of the moral concepts and practices I have allowed into that world do not sit well with one another, no matter. Imagine Nowheresville with all of these practices if you can, or with any harmonious subset of them, if you prefer. The important thing is not what I've let into it, but what I have kept out. The remainder of this paper will be devoted to an analysis of what precisely a world is missing when it does not contain rights and why that absence is morally important.

The most conspicuous difference, I think, between the Nowheresvillians and ourselves has something to do with the activity of *claiming*. Nowheresvillians, even when they are discriminated against invidiously, or left without the things they need, or otherwise badly treated, do not think to leap to their feet and make righteous demands against one another, though they may not hesitate to resort to force and trickery to get what they want. They have no notion of rights, so they do not have a notion of what is their due; hence they do not claim before they take. The conceptual linkage between personal rights and claiming has long been noticed by legal writers and is reflected in the standard usage in which "claim-rights" are distinguished from the mere liberties, immunities, and powers, also sometimes called "rights," with which they are easily confused. When a person has a legal claim-right to *X*, it must be the case (i) that he is at liberty in respect to *X*, i.e., that he has no duty to refrain from or relinquish *X*, and also (ii) that his liberty is the ground of other people's *duties* to grant him *X* or not to interfere with him in respect to *X*. Thus, in the sense of claim-rights, it is true by definition that rights logically entail other people's duties. The paradigmatic examples of such rights are the creditor's right to be paid a debt by his debtor, and the landowner's right not to be interfered with by anyone in the exclusive occupancy of his land. The creditor's right against his debtor, for example, and the debtor's duty to his creditor, are precisely the same relation seen from two different vantage points, as inextricably linked as the two sides of the same coin.

And yet, this is not quite an accurate account of the matter, for it fails to do justice to the way claim-rights are somehow prior to, or more basic than, the duties with which they are necessarily correlated. If Nip has a claim-right against Tuck, it is because of this fact that Tuck has a duty to Nip. It is only because something from Tuck is *due* Nip (directional element) that there is something Tuck *must do* (modal element). This is a relation, moreover, in which Tuck is bound and Nip is free. Nip not only *has* a right, but he can choose whether or not to exercise it, whether to claim it, whether to register complaints upon its infringement, even whether to release Tuck from his duty, and forget the whole thing. If the personal claim-right is also backed up by criminal sanctions, however, Tuck may yet have a duty of obedience to the law from which no one, not even Nip, may release him. He would even have such duties if he lived in Nowheresville; but duties subject to acts of claiming, duties derivative from and contingent upon the personal rights of others, are unknown and undreamed of in Nowheresville.

Many philosophical writers have simply identified rights with claims. The dictionaries tend to define "claims," in turn, as "assertions of right," a dizzying piece of circularity that led one philosopher to complain – "We go in search of rights and are directed to claims, and then back again to rights in bureaucratic futility."[5] What then is the relation between a claim and a right?

As we shall see, a right *is* a kind of claim, and a claim is "an assertion of right," so that a formal definition of either notion in terms of the other will not get us very far. Thus if a "formal definition" of the usual philosophical sort is what we are after, the game is over before it has begun, and we can say that the concept of a right is a "simple, undefinable, unanalysable primitive." Here as elsewhere in philosophy this will have the effect of making the commonplace seem unnecessarily mysterious. We would be better advised, I think, not to attempt a formal definition of either "right" or "claim," but rather to use the idea of a claim in informal elucidation of the idea of a right. This is made possible by the fact that *claiming* is an elaborate sort of rule-governed *activity*. A claim is that which is claimed, the object of the act of claiming. There is, after all, a verb "to claim," but no verb "to right." If we concentrate on the whole activity of claiming, which is public, familiar, and open to our observation, rather than on its upshot alone, we may learn more about the generic nature of rights than we could ever hope to learn from a formal definition, even if one were possible. Moreover, certain facts about rights more easily, if not solely, expressible in the language of claims and claiming are essential to a full understanding not only of what rights are, but also why they are so vitally important.

---

[5] H. B. Acton, *Op. cit.*

Let us begin then by distinguishing between: (i) making claim to . . . , (ii) claiming that . . . , and (iii) having a claim. One sort of thing we may be doing when we claim is to *make claim to something*. This is "to petition or seek by virtue of supposed right; to demand as due." Sometimes this is done by an acknowledged right-holder when he serves notice that he now wants turned over to him that which has already been acknowledged to be his, something borrowed, say, or improperly taken from him. This is often done by turning in a chit, a receipt, an I.O.U., a check, an insurance policy, or a deed, that is, a *title* to something currently in the possession of someone else. On other occasions, making claim is making application for titles or rights themselves, as when a mining prospector stakes a claim to mineral rights, or a householder to a tract of land in the public domain, or an inventor to his patent rights. In the one kind of case, to make claim is to exercize rights one already has by presenting title; in the other kind of case it is to apply for the title itself, by showing that one has satisfied the conditions specified by a rule for the ownership of title and therefore that one can demand it as one's due.

Generally speaking, only the person who has a title or who has qualified for it, or someone speaking in his name, can make claim to something as a matter of right. It is an important fact about rights (or claims), then, that they can be claimed only by those who have them. Anyone can claim, of course, *that* this umbrella is yours, but only you or your representative can actually claim the umbrella. If Smith owes Jones five dollars, only Jones can claim the five dollars as his own, though any bystander can *claim that* it belongs to Jones. One important difference then between *making legal claim to* and *claiming that* is that the former is a legal performance with direct legal consequences whereas the latter is often a mere piece of descriptive commentary with no legal force. Legally speaking, *making claim to* can itself make things happen. This sense of "claiming," then, might well be called "the performative sense." The legal power to claim (performatively) one's right or the things to which one has a right seems to be essential to the very notion of a right. A right to which one could not make claim (i.e. not even for recognition) would be a very "imperfect" right indeed!

Claiming that one has a right (what we can call "propositional claiming" as opposed to "performative claiming") is another sort of thing one can do with language, but it is not the sort of doing that characteristically has legal consequences. To claim that one has rights is to make an assertion that one has them, and to make it in such a manner as to demand or insist that they be recognized. In this sense of "claim" many things in addition to rights can be claimed, that is, many other kinds of proposition can be asserted in the claiming way. I can claim, for example, that you, he, or she has certain rights, or that Julius Caesar once had certain rights; or I can

[6] G. J. Warnock, "Claims to Knowledge," *Proceedings of the Aristotelian Society*, Supplementary Volume 36 (1962), p. 21.

claim that certain statements are true, or that I have certain skills, or accomplishments, or virtually anything at all. I can claim that the earth is flat. What is essential to *claiming that* is the manner of assertion. One can assert without even caring very much whether any one is listening, but part of the point of propositional claiming is to *make sure* people listen. When I claim to others that I know something, for example, I am not merely asserting it, but rather "obtruding my putative knowledge upon their attention, demanding that it be recognized, that appropriate notice be taken of it by those concerned . . ."[7] Not every truth is properly assertable, much less claimable, in every context. To claim that something is the case in circumstances that justify no more than calm assertion is to behave like a boor. (This kind of boorishness, I might add, is probably less common in Nowheresville.) But not to claim in the appropriate circumstances that one has a right is to be spiritless or foolish. A list of "appropriate circumstances" would include occasions when one is challenged, when one's possession is denied, or seems insufficiently acknowledged or appreciated; and of course even in these circumstances, the claiming should be done only with an appropriate degree of vehemence.

Even if there are conceivable circumstances in which one would admit rights diffidently, there is no doubt that their characteristic use and that for which they are distinctively well suited, is to be claimed, demanded, affirmed, insisted upon. They are especially sturdy objects to "stand upon," a most useful sort of moral furniture. Having rights, of course, makes claiming possible; but it is claiming that gives rights their special moral significance. This feature of rights is connected in a way with the customary rhetoric about what it is to be a human being. Having rights enables us to "stand up like men," to look others in the eye, and to feel in some fundamental way the equal of anyone. To think of oneself as the holder of rights is not to be unduly but properly proud, to have that minimal self-respect that is necessary to be worthy of the love and esteem of others. Indeed, respect for persons (this is an intriguing idea) may simply be respect for their rights, so that there cannot be the one without the other; and what is called "human dignity" may simply be the recognizable capacity to assert claims. To respect a person then, or to think of him as possessed of human dignity, simply *is* to think of him as a potential maker of claims. Not all of this can be packed into a definition of "rights;" but these are *facts* about the possession of rights that argue well their supreme moral importance. More

---

[7] This is the important difference between rights and mere claims. It is analogous to the difference between *evidence* of guilt (subject to degrees of cogency) and conviction of guilt (which is all or nothing). One can "have evidence" that is not conclusive just as one can "have a claim" that is not valid. "Prima-facieness" is built into the sense of "claim", but the notion of a "prima-facie right" makes little sense. On the latter point see A. I. Melden, *Rights and Right Conduct* (Oxford: Basil Blackwell, 1959), pp. 18–20, and Herbert Morris, "Persons and Punishment," *The Monist*, Vol. 52 (1968), pp. 498-9.

than anything else I am going to say, these facts explain what is wrong with Nowheresville.

We come now to the third interesting employment of the claiming vocabulary, that involving not the verb "to claim" but the substantive "a claim." What is it to *have a claim* and how is this related to rights? I would like to suggest that *having a claim consists in being in a position to claim, that is, to make claim to* or *claim that*. If this suggestion is correct it shows the primacy of the verbal over the nominative forms. It links claims to a kind of activity and obviates the temptation to think of claims as *things*, on the model of coins, pencils, and other material possessions which we can carry in our hip pockets. To be sure, we often make or establish our claims by presenting titles, and these typically have the form of receipts, tickets, certificates, and other pieces of paper or parchment. The title, however, is not the same thing as the claim; rather it is the evidence that establishes the claim as valid. On this analysis, one might have a claim without ever claiming that to which one is entitled, or without even knowing that one has the claim; for one might simply be ignorant of the fact that one is in a position to claim; or one might be unwilling to exploit that position for one reason or another, including fear that the legal machinery is broken down or corrupt and will not enforce one's claim despite its validity.

Nearly all writers maintain that there is some intimate connection between having a claim and having a right. Some identify right and claim without qualification; some define "right" as justified or justifiable claim, others as recognized claim, still others as valid claim. My own preference is for the latter definition. Some writers, however, reject the identification of rights with valid claims on the ground that all claims as such are valid, so that the expression "valid claim" is redundant. These writers, therefore, would identify rights with claims *simpliciter*. But this is a very simple confusion. All claims, to be sure, are *put forward* as justified, whether they are justified in fact or not. A claim conceded even by its maker to have no validity is not a claim at all, but a mere demand. The highwayman, for example, *demands* his victim's money; but he hardly makes claim to it as rightfully his own.

But it does not follow from this sound point that it is redundant to qualify claims as justified (or as I prefer, valid) in the definition of a right; for it remains true that not all claims put forward as valid really are valid; and only the valid ones can be acknowledged as rights.

If having a valid claim is not redundant, i.e., if it is not redundant to pronounce *another's* claim valid, there must be such a thing as having a claim that is not valid. What would this be like? One might accumulate just enough evidence to argue with relevance and cogency that one has a right (or ought to be granted a right), although one's case might not be overwhelmingly conclusive. In such a case, one might have strong enough argument to be entitled to a hearing and given fair consideration. When one is in this position, it might be said that one "has a claim" that deserves to be weighed carefully. Nevertheless, the balance of reasons may turn out to militate against recognition of the claim, so that the claim, which one admittedly had, and perhaps still does, is not a valid claim or right. "Having a claim" in this sense is an expression very much like the legal phrase "having a *prima facie* case." A plaintiff establishes a *prima facie* case for the defendant's liability when the establishes grounds that will be sufficient for liability unless outweighed by reasons of a different sort that may be offered by the defendant. Similarly, in the criminal law, a grand jury returns an indictment when it thinks that the prosecution has sufficient evidence to be taken seriously and given a fair hearing, whatever countervailing reasons may eventually be offered on the other side. That initial evidence, serious but not conclusive, is also sometimes called a *prima facie* case. In a parallel "*prima facie* sense" of "claim," having a claim to *X* is not (yet) the same as having a right to *X*, but is rather having a case of at least minimal plausibility that one has a right to *X*, a case that does establish a right, not to *X*, but to a fair hearing and consideration. Claims, so conceived, differ in degree: some are stronger than others. Rights, on the other hand, do not differ in degree: no one right is more of a right than another.[8]

Another reason for not identifying rights with claims *simply* is that there is a well-established usage in international law that makes a theoretically interesting distinction between claims and rights. Statesmen are sometimes led to speak of "claims" when they are concerned with the natural needs of deprived human beings in conditions of scarcity. Young orphans *need* good upbringings, balanced diets, education, and technical training everywhere in the world; but unfortunately there are many places where these goods are in such short supply that it is impossible to provision all who need them. If we persist, nevertheless, in speaking of these needs as constituting rights and not merely claims, we are committed to the conception of a right which is an entitlement *to* some good, but not a valid claim *against* any particular individual; for in conditions of scarcity there may be no determinate individuals who can plausibly be said to have a duty to provide the missing goods to those in need. J. E. S. Fawcett therefore prefers to keep the distinction between claims and rights firmly in mind. "Claims," he writes, "are needs and demands in movement, and there is a continuous transformation, as a society advances [toward greater abundance] of economic and social claims into civil and political rights . . . and not all countries or all claims are by any means at the same stage in the process."[8] The manifesto writers on the other side who seem to identify needs, or at least basic needs, with what they call "human rights," are more properly described, I think, as urging upon the world community the moral principle that *all* basic human needs ought to be recognized as *claims* (in the customary *prima facie* sense) worthy of sympathy and serious consideration right now, even though, in many cases, they cannot yet plausibly

[8] J. E. S. Fawcett, "The International Protection of Human Rights," in *Political Theory and the Rights of Man*, ed. by D. D. Raphael (Bloomington: Indiana University Press, 1967), pp. 125 and 128.

be treated as *valid* claims, that is, as grounds of any other people's duties. This way of talking avoids the anomaly of ascribing to all human beings now, even those in pre-industrial societies, such "economic and social rights" as "periodic holidays with pay."[9]

Still, for all of that, I have a certain sympathy with the manifesto writers, and I am even willing to speak of a special "manifesto sense" of "right," in which a right need not be correlated with another's duty. Natural needs are real claims if only upon hypothetical future beings not yet in existence. I accept the moral principle that to have an unfulfilled need is to have a kind of claim against the world, even if against no one in particular. A natural need for some good as such, like a natural desert, is always a reason in support of a claim to that good. A person in need, then, is always "in a position" to make a claim, even when there is no one in the corresponding position to do anything about it. Such claims, based on need alone, are "permanent possibilities of rights," the natural seed from which rights grow. When manifesto writers speak of them as if already actual rights, they are easily forgiven, for this is but a powerful way of expressing the conviction that they ought to be recognized by states here and now as potential rights and consequently as determinants of *present* aspirations and guides to *present* policies. That usage, I think, is a valid exercise of rhetorical licence.

I prefer to characterize rights as valid claims rather than justified ones, because I suspect that justification is rather too broad a qualification. "Validity," as I understand it, is justification of a peculiar and narrow kind, namely justification within a system of rules. A man has a legal right when the official recognition of his claim (as valid) is called for by the governing rules. This definition, of course, hardly applies to moral rights, but that is not because the genus of which moral rights are a species is something other than *claims*. A man has a moral right when he has a claim the recognition of which is called for – not (necessarily) by legal rules – but by moral principles, or the principles of an enlightened conscience.

There is one final kind of attack on the generic identification of rights with claims, and it has been launched with great spirit in a recent article by H. J. McCloskey, who holds that rights are not essentially claims at all, but rather entitlements. The springboard of his argument is his insistence that rights in their essential character are always *rights to*, not *rights against*:

> My right to life is not a right against anyone. It is my right and by virtue of it, it is normally permissible for me to sustain my life in the face of obstacles. It does give rise to rights against others *in the sense* that others have or may come to have duties to refrain from killing me, but it is essentially a right of mine, not an infinite list of claims, hypothetical and actual, against an infinite number of actual, potential, and as yet nonexistent human beings . . . Similarly, the right of the

[9] As declared in Article 24 of *The Universal Declaration of Human Rights* adopted on December 10, 1948, by the General Assembly of the United Nations.

> tennis club member to play on the club courts is a right to play, not a right against some vague group of potential or possible obstructors.[10]

The argument seems to be that since rights are essentially rights *to*, whereas claims are essentially claims *against*, rights cannot be claims, though they can be grounds for claims. The argument is doubly defective though. First of all, contrary to McCloskey, rights (at least legal claim-rights) *are* held *against* others. McCloskey admits this in the case of *in personam* rights (what he calls "special rights") but denies it in the case of *in rem* rights (which he calls "general rights"):

> Special rights are sometimes against specific individuals or institutions – e.g. rights created by promises, contracts, etc. . . . but these differ from . . . characteristic . . . general rights where the right is simply a right to . . .[11]

As far as I can tell, the only reason McCloskey gives for denying that *in rem* rights are against others is that those against whom they would have to hold make up an enormously multitudinous and "vague" group, including hypothetical people not yet even in existence. Many others have found this a paradoxical consequence of the notion of *in rem* rights, but I see nothing troublesome in it. If a general rule gives me a right of noninterference in a certain respect against everybody, then there are literally hundreds of millions of people who have a duty toward me in that respect; and if the same general rule gives the same right to everyone else, then it imposes on me literally hundreds of millions of duties – or duties towards hundreds of millions of people. I see nothing paradoxical about this, however. The duties, after all, are negative; and I can discharge all of them at a stroke simply by minding my own business. And if all human beings make up one moral community and there are hundreds of millions of human beings, we should expect there to be hundreds of millions of moral relations holding between them.

McCloskey's other premise is even more obviously defective. There is no good reason to think that all *claims* are "essentially" *against*, rather than *to*. Indeed most of the discussion of claims above has been of claims *to*, and as we have seen, the law finds it useful to recognize claims *to* (or "mere claims") that are not yet qualified to be claims *against*, or rights (except in a "manifesto sense" of "rights").

Whether we are speaking of claims or rights, however, we must notice that they seem to have two dimensions, as indicated by the prepositions "to" and "against," and it is quite natural to wonder whether either of these dimensions is somehow more fundamental or essential than the other. All rights seem to merge *entitlements to* do, have, omit, or be something with *claims against* others to act or refrain from acting in certain ways. In some statements of rights the entitlement is perfectly determinate (e.g. *to* play tennis) and the claim vague (e.g. *against* "some vague group of poten-

[10] H. J. McCloskey, "Rights," *Philosophical Quarterly*, Vol. 15 (1965), p. 118.
[11] *Loc. cit.*

tial or possible obstructors"); but in other cases the object of the claim is clear and determinate (e.g. *against* one's parents), and the entitlement general and indeterminate (e.g. to be given a proper upbringing.) If we mean by "entitlement" that *to* which one has a right and by "claim" something directed at those *against* whom the right holds (as McCloskey apparently does), then we can say that all claim-rights necessarily involve both, though in individual cases the one element or the other may be in sharper focus.

In brief conclusion: To have a right is to have a claim against someone whose recognition as valid is called for by some set of governing rules or moral principles. To have a *claim* in turn, is to have a case meriting consideration, that is, to have reasons or grounds that put one in a position to engage in performative and propositional claiming. The activity of claiming, finally, as much as any other thing, makes for self-respect and respect for others, gives a sense to the notion of personal dignity, and distinguishes this otherwise morally flawed world from the even worse world of Nowheresville.

The Rockefeller University

Commentary

The thesis of Feinberg's paper is that "to have a legal right is to have a claim against someone whose recognition as valid is called for by some set of governing rules." Much of the value of his paper lies in the careful way he explains just what it is to have such a claim. To have a claim is "to have reasons or grounds that put one in a position to engage in performative and propositional claiming." I heartily endorse his strategy of explaining the noun form "claim" in terms of the verb form "claiming."

Nevertheless, some questions remain in my mind. What is it to *have* reasons or grounds? Suppose the facts are such that, if only I knew them, which I do not, I could go to court and successfully make a claim to a certain piece of property. Do I have a right to that property? It seems outrageous to deny that I have a right to my inheritance simply because my sister has hidden from me my father's last will and testament. Yet it is not clear that, as long as I am ignorant of that document, I have any grounds for making a legal claim. If one must possess the grounds in some sense, what sort of possession is required? Is it enough to have some slight evidence of the relevant factual statements or must one have conclusive evidence? Is it enough to have evidence in the epistemological sense, or must it be that special sort of evidence admissible in courtroom procedures?

To have a claim is to be in a position to engage in performative and propositional claiming. Why both? My suspicions are aroused when I reflect on the *content* of propositional claiming. What is it that one asserts when one asserts that one has a right? To assert that one is in a position to assert a claim seems a circular and empty sort of claiming. My hunch is that what one asserts is that one is in a position to claim in the performative sense. If so, then the propositional activity is parasitic upon the performative, and it would be better to omit it in any analysis of the very meaning of having a right. When Feinberg explains why he considers propositional claiming important, he continually returns to asserting rights in such a way that they are recognized. Does recognition consist in mere intellectual assent unconnected with practice or does it require that those who recognize the right refrain from infringing it and even protect it?

VII
Bentham on Legal Rights[1]

H. L. A. HART

I. INTRODUCTORY

MOST English students of jurisprudence learn to take the first steps towards the analysis of the notion of a legal right from Hohfeld's *Fundamental Legal Conceptions.*[2] In my view Bentham is a more thought-provoking guide than Hohfeld, and indeed than any other writer on the subject, though unfortunately his doctrine has to be collected from observations scattered through his voluminous and not always very readable works. Bentham certainly anticipated much of Hohfeld's work and he has moreover much to say about important aspects of the subject on which Hohfeld did not touch. But his account of legal rights is by no means free from objections; for at some important points his utilitarianism gets in the way of his analytical vision. Bentham's doctrine has however the supreme merit of confronting problems ignored by other theories, even where as in the case of 'interest-theories' of rights, they are similar to or even derived from his own.

The notion of a legal right has proved in the history of jurisprudence to be very elusive: how elusive may be judged not only from the well-known division of theories into 'Will theories' and 'Interest theories' but also from some of the

[1] The present account of Bentham's doctrine of rights is collected from his *An Introduction to the Principles of Morals and Legislation* (referred to here as *P.M.L.*), *Of Laws in General* (referred to here as *O.L.G.*) and passages in *Bentham's Works* (Bowring ed. 1843), vol. III (referred to here as Bowring, vol. III). All references here to *P.M.L.* and *O.L.G.* are to the 1970 edition of these works in the *Collected Works of Jeremy Bentham* (University of London: Athlone Press). A brief exposition and criticism of part of Bentham's doctrine, based mainly on Bowring, vol. III, was given in my lecture on 'Bentham': *British Academy Proceedings*, 48 (1962), 313–17. This was criticized by David Lyons in 'Rights, Claimants and Beneficiaries', (1969) 6 *American Philosophical Quarterly*, 173, and the present fuller and, I hope, more precise account and criticism of Bentham owes much to the stimulus of his article.

[2] 1919 (3rd reprint 1964).

interesting though also strange things that jurists and others have said about rights. They have on the whole hammered rights with sceptical doubts much harder than obligations or duties. Duguit, for example, held that there were legal duties but no legal rights;[3] Austin,[4] Bentham,[5] and in our own day, Ross,[6] while apparently admitting that there may be non-legal obligations or duties insist that 'strictly' the only rights are legal rights. It has moreover often been observed that the concept of a right, legal or moral, is not to be found in the work of the Greek philosophers, and certainly there is no noun or noun phrase in Plato or Aristotle which is the equivalent of our expression 'a right', as distinct from the 'right action' or 'the right thing to do'. Jurists of stature[7] have even held that lawyers of some sophisticated systems of law, including Roman Law, never achieved a clear concept of a legal right. Thus Maine wrote: 'singular as the fact may appear to those unacquainted with it, the Romans had not attained, or had not fully attained, to the conception of a legal Right, which seems to us elementary'[8] and 'The clear conception of a legal right . . . belongs distinctively to the modern world.'[9] He added that 'unquestionably a clear and consistent meaning was for the first time given to the expression "a right" by the searching analysis of Bentham and Austin.'[10]

Maine's reference to Bentham not as discovering or revealing the meaning of the expression 'a right', but as *giving* a clear meaning to it is accurate; and raises a methodological issue of some importance. When we ask for the analysis of such notions as that of a legal right, what precisely is it that we are seeking and by what criteria should success or failure be judged? Bentham's views on these matters are astonishingly modern and are still worth attention. He thought that the expression 'a right' was one of a fairly short list of terms including the

[3] *Traité de droit constitutionel* (1911), 1: 64, 130–45, discussed by Allen *Legal Duties* (1931), p. 158, and Ross, *On Law and Justice* (1958), p. 186.

[4] *Lectures on Jurisprudence* (5th ed.), ch. XII, p. 344.

[5] Bowring II. 501; III. 221.

[6] Ross, op. cit., pp. 248, 365.

[7] Besides Maine (see n. 8) Buckland, *Text Book of Roman Law*, 2nd ed. (1950) 58 and Villey, *Leçons d'histoire de la philosophie de droit* (1957), chs. XI and XIV.

[8] *Early Law and Custom* (1891), p. 365; cf. p. 366.

[9] Op. cit., p. 390. [10] Op. cit., p. 366.

term 'law' which were the subject matter of 'universal expository jurisprudence',[11] and its task was to expound the ideas annexed to these terms. But he did not think that in discharging this task he was strictly bound by common usage, or that definitions, if they were to be useful in jurisprudence, should merely follow or reflect that usage, which at points he found to be confused, arbitrary, and vague and in various other ways unsatisfactory. Quite frequently and explicitly, he departed from usage in order to construct a meaning for a term which, while generally coinciding with usage and furnishing an explanation of its main trends, would not only be clear, but would pick out and collect clusters of features frequently recurrent in the life of a legal system, to which it was important to attend for some statable theoretical or practical purpose. Hence Bentham spoke of himself as expounding the meaning of terms by 'fixing' rather than 'teaching' their import;[12] and when he came in *Of Laws in General* to elaborate his definition of a law he spoke of 'rather a meaning which I wish to see annexed to the term law than one which it has any settled and exclusive possession of already'.[13] In modern terminology, Bentham's conception of analysis is that of 'rational reconstruction' or refinement of concepts in use: his general standpoint is critical and corrective, and in the sequel I shall appeal to it in criticism of part of Bentham's own doctrine concerning legal rights.

II. SURVEY OF BENTHAM'S DOCTRINE

Bentham distinguishes three principal kinds of right which correspond roughly to Hohfeld's 'claim-right', 'liberty' or 'privilege', and 'power', though he does not include an element corresponding to Hohfeld's 'immunity'. In spite of this rough correspondence there are many differences of which perhaps the most important is that unlike Bentham, Hohfeld considers that the very common use of the expression of a right to cover all the four cases which he distinguishes to be a 'loose'[14] and even 'nebulous'[15] usage: the 'proper meaning'[16] of the term according to Hohfeld is to designate the element which he

[11] *P.M.L.*, pp. 6, 295. [12] Bowring III. 217. [13] *O.L.G.*, p. 11.
[14] Hohfeld, op. cit., pp. 42, 51. [15] Op. cit., p. 51.
[16] Op. cit., pp. 38, 39.

terms a claim-right, and the broad or loose use is described as 'unfortunate'[17] because it leads to confusion of thought. Notwithstanding these strictures Hohfeld recognizes that the use of the term to cover claim-right, liberty, power, and immunity is a use of the term in a 'generic'[18] sense and hints that the characteristic common to the genus is 'any sort of legal advantage'[19] though he does not explain this idea further. Bentham does not express any similar misgivings concerning the wide extension of the term in ordinary usage, and though in the cases of other terms he is prepared to distinguish what is 'strictly and properly so called' from what is not, he does not do so in the case of rights.

Bentham starts by making what he says is a fundamental distinction between two sorts of rights distinguished by different relationships to the idea of obligation or duty.[20] The first sort of rights owe their existence to (or as he says 'result from') the absence of legal obligation:[21] the second sort result from obligations imposed by law.[22] Rights of the first sort are rights to do or abstain from some action, and rights of the second sort are rights to what Bentham calls the 'services',[23] i.e. the actions or forbearance, of others. Corresponding to these two different sorts of rights are two different sorts of law or states of the law. Rights resulting from obligation are conferred by (or as Bentham puts it, 'have as their base') coercive laws; rights resulting from the absence of obligation have as their base discoercive or permissive laws.[24] In this last phrase Bentham includes three different cases. These are (i) *active* permission[25] or countermand: where the law permits some action, previously legally prohibited or obligatory, to be done or not done; (ii) *inactive* or original permission:[26] where the law simply declares that some action not previously prohibited or obligatory may be done or not done; (iii) the case where the law is silent.[27] Such permissive laws or legal silence leave the individual who

[17] Op. cit., p. 51. [18] Op. cit., p. 42. [19] Op. cit., p. 71.

[20] Obligation and duty are treated as synonymous terms by Bentham: see *O.L.G.*, p. 294.

[21] Bowring III. 181, 217–18; *P.M.L.*, p. 212.

[22] Bowring III, loc. cit., *O.L.G.*, pp. 57–8, 294.

[23] Bowring III. 159, *O.L.G.*, pp. 57–8.

[24] Bowring III. 181, *P.M.L.*, p. 302. [25] *O.L.G.*, pp. 57–8.

[26] Ibid. [27] *O.L.G.*, pp. 98–9, Bowring III. 159.

is the right-holder free or at liberty to do or not to do some action; I shall use the expression 'liberty-right' instead of Bentham's more explicit though clumsy circumlocution for this sort of right, and I shall use instead of Bentham's expression 'right resulting from obligation' the more familiar 'right correlative to obligation' for his second sort of right, which arises when the law imposes a duty not on the right-holder, but on another and thus restricts the other's freedom to act as he chooses.

A. LIBERTY-RIGHTS

Bentham in my view was certainly justified in regarding liberty-rights as of very great importance. Some later theorists have thought that so negative an idea could be of little significance for jurisprudence and could not represent 'a legal relation'.[28] This I am sure is a great mistake. Without attention to this negative and apparently insignificant element there cannot be any clear understanding of such important ideas as that of ownership, or of the legal character of the sphere left open by the law to economic competition, or any clear formulation of many legal problems to which that has given rise.[29] Indeed in the sequel I shall claim that this element of a liberty-right is involved in all the most important kinds of legal right at least in the civil law. But the notion of a liberty-right needs some further characterization beyond that given to it by Bentham's phrase, 'right resulting from the absence of obligation'. The following points in particular deserve attention.

The bilateral character of liberty-rights

In England and in most other countries a man has a right to look over his garden fence at his neighbour; he is under no obligation not to look at him and under no obligation to look at him. In this example the liberty is therefore bilateral; both the obligation not to look and the obligation to look are in Bentham's phrase 'absent'. Most of Bentham's examples of a liberty-right and his general account of them represents them as bilateral; they are, he says, such rights as men have in the state of nature where there are no obligations. But he occasionally speaks as if a unilateral liberty, that is the absence of

[28] e.g. Pollock, *Jurisprudence* (2nd ed., 1902), p. 62, but see Hohfeld op. cit., p. 48 n. [29] See below, p. 181 n. 53

either an obligation not to do something *or* an obligation to do it were enough to constitute a right of this kind.[30] On that footing a right to do an action would merely exclude an obligation not to do it, and men always have a right to do what they have an obligation to do. Hohfeld's 'liberty' or 'privilege' is by his definition a unilateral liberty,[31] and, in some special contexts, to treat unilateral liberties as rights accords with a common and intelligible usage for which I offer an explanation below.[32] But I shall treat Bentham as committed to regarding bilateral liberties as the standard type of liberty-right.

Liberty-rights and correlative obligations not to interfere

The fact that a man has a right to look at his neighbour over the garden fence does not entail that the neighbour has a correlative obligation to let himself be looked at or not to interfere with the exercise of this specific liberty-right. So he could, for example, erect a screen on his side of the fence to block the view. But though a neighbour may do this if he wishes, and so has himself a liberty-right or bilateral liberty to erect or not to erect such a fence, there are other things that, in most countries, he cannot legally do to prevent his tormentor looking at him. For he has certain legal obligations or duties, civil or criminal, or both, which preclude some, though not all forms of interference, and these in practice more or less adequately protect the exercise of the liberty-right. Thus he cannot enter the next-door garden and beat up his tormentor, for this would be a breach of certain duties not indeed correlative to his tormentor's liberty-right to look at him, but correlative at least in the case of civil duties to certain other rights, which his tormentor has and which are not mere liberties. These are the tormentor's rights not to be assaulted and his right that others should not enter on his land without his consent. These are rights correlative to obligations and to Bentham's account of these I now turn.

B. RIGHTS CORRELATIVE TO OBLIGATIONS

The right not to be assaulted and the right of an owner or occupier of land that others should not enter on it without

[30] e.g. Bowring III. 218 but cf. III. 159.

[31] Hohfeld, op. cit., p. 39.

[32] Below, pp. 182–3, 196 n. 93.

his consent are rights to what Bentham terms a negative service,[33] that is to the abstention from 'hurtful action';[34] in other cases of rights correlative to obligations, where the obligation is to *do* something rather than abstain from action the right is to an 'affirmative' or 'positive' service,[35] or, as Bentham paraphrases it, to 'a useful action'.[36] All rights correlative to obligations are rights to services which consist in the performance of their correlative obligation and with two exceptions all legal obligations or duties have correlative rights. One exception is the case of 'self-regarding duties'[37] where the duty is imposed by law solely for the benefit of the agent on whom they are imposed. Bentham's examples of self-regarding duties include duties to abstain from suicide, from 'indecency not in public', incest, idleness, gaming, and 'other species of prodigality'.[38] The other more important exception to the principle that all legal obligations have correlative rights is where the legislator has disregarded entirely the dictates of utility and created obligations by which no one at all benefits. Such obligation Bentham terms 'ascetic', 'pure', or 'barren', or 'useful to no one'[39] and he thought they had been all too numerous in the history of human law. But apart from these two cases, whenever the law creates civil or criminal obligations, it always thereby creates what Bentham terms 'an enforced service' negative or positive, for the benefit of others; and to have a right correlative to an obligation is to be the person or persons intended to benefit from the performance of the obligation.[40] But not only individuals have rights; the public and also distinct classes included in it have, according to Bentham, rights in those cases where the persons intended to benefit are what he terms 'unassignable individuals'.[41]

Accordingly, with the two exceptions mentioned, every offence, crime or civil wrong, is a violation of some right and a case of 'wrongful withholding of services'[42] so that 'there is no law whatsoever that does not confer on some person or

[33] Bowring III. 159; *O.L.G.*, pp. 58–9.
[34] Bowring III. 159.
[35] *O.L.G.*, pp. 58–9; Bowring III. 159.
[36] Bowring III. 159.
[37] *O.L.G.*, pp. 58, 294; *P.M.L.*, p. 206.
[38] *P.M.L.*, pp. 225 n., 296 n., 232 n.
[39] Bowring III. 181, 221.
[40] *P.M.L.*, p. 206; *O.L.G.*, p. 58.
[41] See below, pp. 186–8.
[42] *P.M.L.*, p. 228 n.

other a right'.[43] I shall call this identification of a right-holder by reference to the person or persons intended to benefit by the performance of an obligation 'the benefit theory' of rights; and when I come to criticize it I shall try to make precise the sense not only of benefit but of a person intended to benefit and to clarify the distinction which Bentham makes between assignable and unassignable individuals.

C. POWERS

Legal powers are for Bentham a species of right[44] and his works contain a most elaborate taxonomy of the different kinds of legal powers together with a sophisticated analysis of the idea of a legal power and of the legal provisions by which powers are conferred on individuals.[45] The simplest kind of power is that which a man has when he is allowed by law to interfere with or physically control things or the bodies of persons or animals. Bentham subsumes such interference (which of course may take a great variety of forms such as touching, holding, moving, confining) under the general notion of handling and he calls such powers 'powers of contrectation': examples are an owner's power to make physical use of his property or a policeman's power of arrest. Such powers are in fact liberty-rights differing from other liberty-rights in two respects: first the action which, in such cases, there is liberty to do is restricted to actions physically affecting things or bodies; secondly in such cases the liberty is exclusive or exceptional[46] in the sense that it is a liberty to do something that others are generally under an obligation not to do. Such powers are conferred by permissive laws,[47] but like other liberty-rights they may be protected or 'corroborated'[48] by duties imposed on others not to obstruct, or even requiring them to assist, their exercise. If they are not so corroborated, they exist as 'bare' liberties: and then like other liberty-rights their existence does not entail the existence of any correlative obligations.

[43] *O.L.G.*, p. 220. [44] *O.L.G.*, pp. 84, 220.

[45] See *O.L.G.*, *passim*, and esp. ch. IX and my 'Bentham on Legal Powers', Yale Law Review, (forthcoming).

[46] For an examination of Bentham's notion of powers of contrectation as exclusive or exceptional liberties see my 'Bentham on Legal Powers', loc. cit.

[47] *O.L.G.*, pp. 81, 86–7, 137 n.

[48] *P.M.L.*, p. 302; *O.L.G.*, p. 260 (48); *O.L.G.*, p. 261.

More important for our present purpose is the kind of power which Bentham calls 'investitive' and 'divestitive'.[49] These are the powers which a man has when he is enabled by law to change the legal position of others, or of himself and others as he does for example when he alienates property or makes a will or contract. In entering into such legal transactions he does an act (usually the writing or saying of certain words according to more or less strictly prescribed forms) which manifest certain intentions as to future rights and duties of himself and others. Such acts, or acts in the law, are not only *permitted* by the law but are *recognized* by the law as having certain legal consequences: given certain circumstances, a duly executed conveyance of land is 'valid', i.e. legally effective in divesting the transferor of certain rights and duties and in investing the transferee with similar ones. Bentham's elaborate account of the legal provisions by which such investitive and divestitive powers are conferred is designed to reconcile their existence with his general 'imperative' theory of law according to which all laws either impose duties or grant permissions.[50] There is not according to Bentham a further special kind of laws which confer powers; but powers are conferred when laws imposing duties or granting permissions are 'imperfect mandates',[51] i.e. incomplete in some respects and so contain 'blanks'[52] left to 'power-holders' to 'fill up', and when they do this they thereby determine or vary the incidence of existing 'imperfect' laws.

III. CRITICISM OF BENTHAM'S DOCTRINE

A. LIBERTY-RIGHTS

Liberty-rights and their protective perimeter

Those who have doubted the importance of liberties or mere absence of obligation for the analysis of legal rights have felt that so negative a notion without some positive correlate is not worth a lawyer's attention. This is a mistaken way of presenting the important fact that where a man is left free by the law to do or not to do some particular action, the exercise of this liberty will always be protected by the law to some

[49] *O.L.G.*, pp. 82–4; cf. *P.M.L.*, p. 217 n., Bowring III. 186–90 on 'collative and ablative events'.

[50] *O.L.G.*, pp. 95–9 and *passim*. *P.M.L.*, p. 302.

[51] *O.L.G.*, pp. 26, 80–91.

[52] Bowring III. 222; cf. III. 197.

extent, even if there is no strictly correlative obligation upon others not to interfere with it. This is so because at least the cruder forms of interference, such as those involving physical assault or trespass, will be criminal or civil offences or both, and the duties or obligations not to engage in such modes of interference constitute a protective perimeter behind which liberties exist and may be exercised. Thus, to take a trivial example, my right to scratch my head is protected, not by a correlative obligation upon others not to interfere with my doing that specific kind of act, but by the fact that obligations to refrain from assault or trespass to my person will generally preclude effective interference to it. In most cases the protection of my liberty afforded by this perimeter of obligations will be adequate but it may not be complete: if others could stop me scratching my head without any breach of these obligations e.g. by hypnotizing me, they may do so. This makes clear the difference between a liberty-right to do some kind of act protected by a strictly correlative obligation upon others not to interfere with it, and a liberty-right protected only by a normally adequate perimeter of general obligations.

It may be that jurists who have doubted the importance of the negative notion of absence of obligation or liberty have done so because the protective perimeter has obscured their view of it; but it is in fact important not to lose sight of either the liberty or the perimeter. Both are required in the analysis of many legal phenomena including that of economic competition. Two people walking in an empty street see a purse lying on the pavement: each has a liberty so far as the law is concerned to pick it up and each may prevent the other doing so if he can race him to the spot. But though each has this liberty there are also several specific things which each has a right that the other should not do; these are rights with correlative obligations and these correlative obligations together with the duties of the criminal law protect (and also restrict) each party's liberty. Thus neither of the competitors may hit or trip up the other, or threaten him with violence in order to get the prize. The perimeter of obligations to abstain from such actions constitutes the ring within which the competitors compete in the exercise of their liberties. Of course where competition is not in question, as in the case of 'fundamental' human rights or liberties, great importance may be attached to their unimpeded exercise and in such cases the law may protect the liberty by a strictly correlative obligation not to interfere by any means with a specific form of activity. But most liberties are not so protected.[53]

Bentham appreciated the importance of this combination of a liberty with a protective perimeter of obligations, but his formulations on the point are casual and somewhat ambiguous. He distinguishes between a 'naked' right and a 'vested' or 'established' one.[54] A naked light is a liberty unprotected by any obligation and are the rights which men have in the state of nature; a man has a vested or established right when he has a right that others should abstain from interfering with a liberty which he has. This language suggests that Bentham thought of rights as vested only where there was a strictly correlative obligation not to interfere, but in other passages in discussing liberty-rights he envisages their protection by a perimeter of general obligations not strictly correlative to the liberty.

I may stand or sit down—I may go in or out—I may eat or not eat etc.: the law says nothing upon the matter. Still, the right which I exercise I derive from the law because it is the law which erects into an offence every species of violence by which one may seek to prevent me from doing what I like.[55]

Notwithstanding his appreciation of the importance of the combination of liberties with a perimeter of protective though not correlative obligation, Bentham, like Hobbes in describing the state of nature, treats liberties even when 'naked' as rights. But it is not at all clear that lawyers or anyone else would speak of a completely naked or unprotected liberty as a right, or that any useful purpose would be served if they did. The

[53] Thus the famous cases *Allen* v. *Flood* (1898) A.C. 1, *Mogul Steamship* v. *Macgregor & Others* (1892) A.C. 25, *Quinn* v. *Leathern* (1901) A.C. 495 and (in part) *Rookes* v. *Barnard* (1964) A.C. 1129, are best understood as raising the question whether an individual's liberty-rights to trade or employ labour or sell his labour are protected by a perimeter consisting only of duties corresponding to the specific torts of conspiracy, intimidation, and inducement of breach of contract, or by a perimeter consisting also of a duty corresponding to a more general tort of interfering with the trade, business, or employment of a person without lawful justification or excuse.

[54] Bowring III. 218.

[55] Bowring III. 159-60.

state of nature, if worth describing at all, can be described adequately in other terms. So far as organized society is concerned there would be something not only strange but misleading in describing naked liberties as rights: if we said, for example, that a class of helots whom free citizens were allowed to treat as they wished or interfere with at will, yet had rights to do those acts which they were not forbidden by the law to do. All the very important points in Bentham's doctrine distinguishing between liberty-rights and rights correlative to obligations can be preserved by treating bilateral liberty as an essential *element* in the analysis of liberty-rights but only constituting a liberty-right in conjunction with a perimeter of some protecting obligations or duties. It is not necessary, nor I think useful for any purpose, to treat liberties without any such protection as a distinct kind of legal right.

Unilateral liberty-rights

Bentham, as I have said, occasionally speaks as if a unilateral liberty were sufficient to constitute a liberty-right. On this footing a liberty-right to do an act would be compatible with, and indeed entailed by, an obligation to do it. The right-holder would not, as in the case of bilateral liberty, be free to choose whether to do an act or not; he would be at liberty to do an act only in the sense that he was not under an obligation not to do it. Bentham does not discuss the appropriateness or otherwise of extending the notion of rights to include unilateral liberty; but it seems clear that a general extension to include all unilateral liberties would neither accord with usage nor be useful. In the ordinary case, where the law imposes general obligations, e.g. to pay taxes, or to abstain from assault or trespass, it would be pointless or even confusing to describe those who had these obligations as having rights to pay taxes or to abstain from assault. Yet there undoubtedly are certain specific contexts where unilateral liberties are intelligibly spoken of as rights to do actions even where there is also an obligation to do the same action. Among these are cases where individuals by way of exception to a general rule are not merely permitted but also legally required to do some act generally prohibited.

Thus a policeman ordered to arrest a man might be asked

'What right have you to arrest him?' and might well produce his orders as showing that he had a right to arrest. In general the query 'What right have you to do that?' invites the person addressed to show that some act of his which is prima facie wrongful because generally prohibited is one which in the particular case he is at liberty to do. The questioner is not concerned to know whether the liberty is unilateral, i.e. accompanied by an obligation, or bilateral; so the form of his question covers both.[56]

B. THE BENEFIT THEORY OF RIGHTS CORRELATIVE TO OBLIGATION

The most striking feature of Bentham's analysis of legal rights is his benefit theory of rights correlative to obligation: the view that with the exception of 'barren' and 'self regarding' obligation *all* obligations, civil or criminal, have correlative rights held by those intended to benefit by their performance. In considering this doctrine certain features of Bentham's elaborate classification of offences[57] must be kept in mind, since, according to him, every offence, i.e. every breach of obligation with the two exceptions mentioned, violates a right. Bentham distinguishes between offences which are primarily or in the first instance detrimental to 'assignable persons' (which he terms 'offences against individuals' or 'private offences')[58] and offences detrimental only to unassignable individuals.[59] Of the latter there are two kinds, viz. public offences against a whole community or state, or semi-public offences against classes of persons within the community distinguished either by some class characteristic or by residence in a particular area. Offences of the first kind violate individual rights: examples of them are murder, assault, theft, and breach of contract:[60] offences of the second kind violate the rights of the public or a class, and examples of them are failure to pay

[56] Further examples of unilateral liberties spoken of as rights are afforded by cases where duties in Bentham's phrase, are 'superadded' to liberty-rights (*O.L.G.*, pp. 270–1, 296). Thus a trustee who has equitable duties to put the trust property to a certain use may be said to have a right to do this since the equitable duty is for historical reasons conceived as something distinct grafted on to his still persistent legal bilateral liberty-rights, though its actual effect is to render the liberty-right unilateral.

[57] *P.M.L.*, ch. XVI, pp. 187 ff. [58] *P.M.L.*, p. 188.

[59] Op. cit., p. 189. [60] Op. cit., pp. 223–4, 228 n.

taxes or desertion from the army (public offences)[61] and violation of health regulations imposed for the protection of a particular neighbourhood (semi-public offences).[62]

Intended benefits to assignable versus *unassignable individuals*

Before attempting any general criticism of Bentham's benefit theory, it is necessary to explore the ambiguities of the central ideas involved in it. These ambiguities are, I think, involved in all theories which attempt to define the notion of an individual's right in terms of benefits or interests, and they concern (a) the ideas of benefit and detriment, (b) the distinction between assignable and unassignable persons, and (c) the idea of a person intended by the law to benefit. These are difficult notions requiring fuller investigation than is attempted here, but the following may suffice for the present purposes.

(*a*) *Benefit and detriment.* Bentham, though committed to the doctrine that pleasure and pain are the only things good and bad in themselves,[63] does not in his account of rights and offences simply identify benefit with pleasure or avoidance of pain or detriment with pain or loss of pleasure. Hence, for him, as for others, theft of £1 from a millionaire indifferent to the loss constitutes a detriment to him and an offence against him; while forbearance from such theft constitutes a negative service and a benefit to which he has a legal right. So, too, security of the person or of reputation are benefits, even if in some cases the particular individual concerned would have welcomed an attack or found it pleasurable or otherwise desirable. So in general the idea of benefit or services, positive or negative, includes the provision or maintenance of conditions or treatment which are regarded by human beings generally, or in a particular society, as desirable or 'in their interest' and so to be sought from others. Correspondingly the idea of a detriment or harm includes the loss of such benefits and conditions and treatment generally regarded as undesirable and to be avoided. No doubt Bentham thought also that what makes anything a benefit or desirable is its general tendency to produce pleasure or to avoid pain,[64] and if, in a particular society, the notion

[61] Op. cit., p. 262. [62] Op. cit., pp. 194 n., 225 n.
[63] *P.M.L.*, pp. 88–9, 100. [64] *P.M.L.*, pp. 191–3. Bowring III. 214.

of benefits or detriments had no such connection with pleasure and pain, this was an aberration to be deplored.

Given this conception of benefits and detriments, it follows that in the case of those offences which Bentham calls offences against individuals and regards as violating the rights of assignable individuals, the breach of the law necessarily, and not merely contingently, constitutes a detriment to individuals, and compliance with the law in such cases necessarily, and not merely contingently, constitutes a benefit to individuals. This feature is secured simply by the definition of the offence in terms of actions which constitute in themselves detriments to individuals even if they do not always cause pain. For killing or wounding or slandering an individual or thieving from him or false imprisonment or 'wife-stealing' (abduction), given the above account of detriments, necessarily constitute detriments and do not merely contingently cause them or make them more likely. Since it is perfectly reasonable, without further investigation of 'legislative intent', to ascribe to laws prohibiting offences which thus necessarily constitute a detriment to individuals, an intention to benefit them, it is by reference to this feature that Bentham's central conception of assignable individuals intended to benefit from the law is mainly to be explained.

In such cases we may call the benefit or detriment 'direct' and it is to be observed that in the case of Bentham's public and semi-public offences benefits and detriments are not involved in the same direct way. As Bentham points out[65] compliance with laws requiring payment of taxes will make funds available to a government, but whether or not benefits as above defined will result for any individuals is a contingent matter, depending on what Bentham terms 'a various and remote concatenation of causes and effects',[66] including the nature of the government's policies for use of the funds and their skill or even luck in implementing them. The same is true of laws requiring military service or prohibiting treason. General compliance with such laws will constitute certain conditions without which it would be impossible or less likely that various benefits will be ultimately received by individuals, and in that sense these conditions may be said to make their receipt more likely than

[65] *O.L.G.*, pp. 62–3; *P.M.L.*, pp. 149–51. [66] *O.L.G.*, p. 62.

would otherwise be the case. Such contingently beneficial laws may be said to provide indirect benefits.[67]

(*b*) *Assignable and unassignable individuals.* This distinction appears in many places in Bentham's works[68] and he uses it to explain what is meant by saying that certain offences are against the public or against a class, and that the public or a class are intended to benefit by a law and so have rights resulting from the obligations which it imposes. Bentham does not conceive of the public or of a class as an entity distinct from its members, and for him to speak of the public or class of persons as having rights is still to speak only of individuals, but of individuals who cannot be 'individually assigned' included in the community or class.[69] What then is it for an individual to be 'assignable'? Bentham's most explicit statement on this subject is in a footnote which merely tells us that an individual may be assignable 'by name or at least by description in such manner as to be sufficiently distinguished from all others'.[70] This leaves the notion of a law intended to benefit assignable individuals still obscure; because the various laws, such as the laws forbidding murder or assault which he does in fact regard as intended to benefit assignable individuals (and so as conferring rights upon them), do not refer to individuals either by name or by some uniquely applicable description, nor on any

[67] Of course the distinction between direct and indirect benefits will present disputable borderline cases, since whether anything is to be counted as in itself a benefit or only making the receipt of benefits more likely will often depend on degrees of likelihood, numbers of contingencies and also on analogies with standard direct individual benefits. Thus compliance by an employer with a duty to provide each of his workmen working in dangerous conditions with protective clothing might, like a law requiring him to pay each of them a sum of money, be considered as constituting a direct benefit, and its breach as constituting a direct detriment; whereas a law requiring him to fit a fence or guard on dangerous machinery while men are at work, might be considered not as constituting a direct benefit for them but only as making the avoidance of harm more likely, and so constituting an indirect benefit. It is also to be noted that if provision of such a fence or guard is treated as constituting a direct benefit it would be a *common* benefit, in contrast with the *separate* or *individual* benefits constituted by the provision of each workman with protective clothing. It seems likely that Bentham would regard all laws providing such common benefits as intended to benefit classes not 'assignable individuals'. (See below, p. 188, with regard to statutory duties.)

[68] e.g. *P.M.L.*, pp. 143, 188–9; *O.L.G.*, p. 37. It also appears in John Stuart Mill's account of rights in *Utilitarianism*, ch. V.

[69] *P.M.L.*, p. 189.

[70] *P.M.L.*, p. 188 n.

account of legislative intent does it seem that they are intended only to benefit individuals so identified,[71] if that means identified at the time when the law comes into existence.

None the less Bentham's brief explanation of his distinction can be used indirectly to determine whether or not the individuals intended to be benefited by a law are assignable, since the corresponding question whether or not an *offence*[72] is against assignable individuals can be answered by direct reference to it. Thus the laws which Bentham regards as creating offences against assignable individuals and so as conferring rights upon them are such that to establish that the offence has been committed it must be shown that an individual who *is* 'assignable' in Bentham's sense, i.e. distinguished from others in some way and so uniquely identified, has suffered some individual detriment from the commission of the offence. It seems therefore that we may interpret the statement that a law is intended to benefit assignable individuals (and so confers rights upon them) as meaning no more than that to establish its breach an assignable individual must be shown to have suffered an individual detriment.[73] This seems to give the required contrast with those laws creating offences which Bentham classes as against unassignable individuals, such as failure to pay taxes or military desertion; for in such cases it is not necessary to show that any individual has suffered any detriment and it may often be the case that no individual has suffered or will suffer thereby. On this footing, an offence may be said to be against unassignable

[71] Of course they may be said to be intended to benefit 'each individual' in the community but this does not make the individuals 'assignable' in Bentham's sense.

[72] Bentham observes that rights may best be 'expounded' by considering the corresponding offences: *P.M.L.*, p. 206 and see *O.L.G.*, p. 58.

[73] This interpretation is not I think inconsistent with Bentham's remark (*P.M.L.*, p. 189 n.) that the divisions between private, semi-public, and public offences are liable to be 'confounded'. He points out that 'the fewer the individuals of which a class is composed . . . the more likely are the persons to whom an offence is detrimental to *become* assignable.' This seems merely to point out that though an offence (e.g. breach of health regulations imposed for the benefit of a particular area) is correctly regarded as one against a class in accordance with the interpretation offered above, it will in the case of small *closed* classes be possible to determine which individuals ultimately suffer from a given offence even though proof of their suffering is not, as in the case of offences against individuals, necessary to establish that the offence has been committed. But Bentham's point here is certainly not clear.

individuals, and so one which violates the rights not of individuals but of the public or a class, if (a) it is not an offence against assignable individuals, and (b) general compliance with the law creating an offence is intended to constitute an indirect benefit for any one or more individuals who are or may be included in the community or in a class within it but who are not otherwise identified.[74]

(*c*) *Intended by the law to benefit.* If the statement that a law intends to benefit an individual and so confers a right upon him is interpreted as meaning no more than that its breach constitutes a direct individual detriment, then we have a criterion for determining when laws confer individual rights which avoids difficult inquiries into 'actual' legislative intent. More-

[74] It should be observed that Bentham's distinction between laws which confer rights on individuals and those which confer them on the public or classes, based as it is on assignability as interpreted above, is *not* the same as the apparently similar distinction which has sometimes been invoked by English courts in their attempts to formulate tests for determining whether breach of a statutory duty, such as the duty to fence dangerous machinery or provide specified forms of fire-escape, gives rise to an action for damages on the part of individuals for injuries caused by the breach. Breach of most such statutory duties would, according to Bentham's assignability test, not be offences against individuals and so would not confer a right upon them to performance of the statutory duty; since to establish their breach it would not be necessary to show that any individual had suffered any individual detriment, but only that e.g. the machinery had not been fenced as required: such an offence, for Bentham, would either be against a class (e.g. of workmen) or against the public. It is on the other hand true that in determining whether the legislature in creating such statutory duties also by implication created a statutory tort, courts have flirted with the idea that this depended on whether the statutory duty was 'owed to' individuals or imposed in their interests and not merely imposed for the general welfare of the public (see *Solomons* v. *R. Gertzenstein* [1954] 2 Q.B. 243). This test has been rejected by some judges (see per Atkin L.J. in *Phillips* v. *Britannia Hygienic Laundry* [1923] 2 K.B. 832) and indeed the finding that a statutory duty was owed to or for the benefit of individuals seems rather to be a conclusion from a finding, made on other grounds, that the statute conferred a right of action upon individuals, than a reason for such a finding. But whatever this distinction is it does not, for the reasons stated above, turn, as Bentham's does, upon assignability. It appears rather to be a distinction (which the Courts have found very difficult to apply in practice) between the cases where, on the construction of the statute, it can be said that its main purpose was to secure to each individual of a specific class some specific benefit or protection from some specific harm and those cases where either there was no such discernible purpose, or, if there was, this was merely ancillary to a dominant purpose to create or maintain conditions (e.g. the conservation of manpower or resources) whereby all or any unspecified members of the public might benefit in various unspecified ways.

over this criterion will give a decisive and at least an intelligible answer to some questions which have confronted theorists who, within the general framework of an interest- or benefit-theory of rights, have wished to limit, in some reasonable way, the class of intended beneficiaries who should count as having rights. Thus, to take an example, famous from Ihering's[75] discussion of it, in a similar context, should a law, forbidding in general terms the importation of manufactured goods, which was in fact enacted solely in order to benefit a particular domestic manufacturer be taken to confer a right upon him? Ihering was anxious to distinguish such a case as a mere '*Reflexwirkung* (reflex operation) of a duty and not as a right, and he sought for, but never clearly formulated, some criterion which would distinguish a right violated by a demonstrable 'individual breach of the law' (*Individuelle Rechtsverletzung*) from a mere reflex operation of duty.[76] Kelsen believed that no such distinction could be drawn; but Bentham's conception of a direct detriment to an assignable individual, interpreted as above, might well have served this purpose and the test later suggested by Ross[77] in discussing Ihering's case is in substance identical with it.

For the purpose of criticism of the benefit theory I shall assume that the above interpretation of Bentham is correct.[78] I do so because this is the strongest form of the benefit theory and if it is vulnerable to criticism it is not likely that a theory depending on a more extended sense of 'intended by the law to benefit' is likely to be successful. For the same reason I shall

[75] *Geist des römischen Rechts* (1924 ed.), III. 351–3, discussed by Kelsen in *Haupt probleme des Staatrechts* (1960 ed.), pp. 578–81, and Ross in *Towards a Realistic Jurisprudence* (1946), pp. 167–8, 179 ff.

[76] Ihering's earlier account of rights (op. cit., 2nd ed., III. 339) had avoided this problem since it restricted rights to cases where the enforcement by legal proceedings of duties protecting interests was left to the individual concerned. ('Selbstschutz des Interesses.')

[77] Op. cit., pp. 179 ff. Lyons's account of the 'qualified beneficiary theory' which he favours and considers may be attributable to Bentham (op. cit., pp. 173–4, 176–80) is very close to the above interpretation of Bentham.

[78] There are certainly passages in Bentham (e.g. *O.L.G.*, pp. 55–6) where he seems to contemplate that if the legislator intended an 'assignable' individual to benefit even very indirectly from the performance of an obligation this would confer a right to its performance on him. On this view the favoured manufacturer in Ihering's case would have a right that the goods should not be imported.

not consider further Bentham's account of rights of the public or a class.[79]

Absolute and relative duties

The principal advocates of benefit or 'interest' theories of rights correlative to obligations have shown themselves sensitive to the criticism that, if to say that an individual has such a right means no more than that he is the intended beneficiary of a duty, then 'a right' in this sense may be an unnecessary, and perhaps confusing, term in the description of the law; since all that can be said in a terminology of such rights can be and indeed is best said in the indispensable terminology of duty. So the benefit theory appears to make nothing more of rights than an alternative formulation of duties: yet nothing seems to be gained in significance or clarity by translating, e.g. the statement that men are under a legal duty not to murder, assault, or steal from others into the statement that individuals have a right not to be murdered, assaulted, or stolen from, or by saying, when a man has been murdered, that his right not to be killed has been violated.[80]

Ihering as I have said was visited by just such doubts. Bentham confronted them in his codification proposals in the form of an inquiry whether the law should be expounded at length in a list of rights or a list of obligations. The test which he proposed was 'Present the entire law to that one of the parties that has most need to be instructed'[81] and he thought that the law should generally be expounded at length in terms of obligations but need 'only be mentioned' in a list of rights; his principal reason for this was that because of the penalties imposed the party on whom the law imposed the obligation had most need for instruction.[82]

[79] In fact Bentham seems to have made very little use of his idea that in the sense explained the public or a class within it have legal rights. Nearly all of his examples of rights are rights of individuals. Austin expressly confines legal rights to the rights of 'determinate persons' (op. cit., Lecture XVII, p. 401).

[80] Under the American Civil Rights Act 1964 suits were brought against white men who had murdered negroes alleging 'that they had deprived their victims of their civil rights'. This desperate expedient was necessary because murder is a state crime and prosecutions in such cases were not likely to succeed in Southern state courts. I owe this point to Mrs. Carolyn Irish.

[81] Bowring III. 195.

[82] Ibid.

(*a*) *Criminal* versus *civil law.* The most cogent criticisms of the benefit theory are those that on the one hand press home the charge of redundancy or uselessness to a lawyer of the concept of right correlative to obligation defined simply in terms of the intended beneficiary of the obligation, and on the other hand constructively presents an alternative selective account of those obligations which are for legal purposes illuminatingly regarded as having correlative rights. This latter task amounts to a re-drawing of the lines between 'absolute'[83] and relative duties which for Bentham merely separated 'barren' and self-regarding duties from duties 'useful to others'. This has been done sometimes in too sweeping a fashion as a distinction precisely coinciding with that between the criminal and civil law, and on the assumption, which seems dogmatic, if not plainly mistaken, that the purpose of the criminal law is not to secure the separate interests of individuals but 'security and order', and that all its duties are really duties not to behave in certain ways which are prejudicial to the 'general interests of society'.[84]

None the less a line may be drawn between most duties of the criminal law and those of the civil law which does not depend on this assumption, but would, on principles quite distinct from those of the benefit theory, reserve the notion of relative duties and correlative rights mainly for the obligations of the civil law, such as those which arise under contracts or under the law of tort, and other civil wrongs. For what is distinctive about these obligations is not their content which sometimes overlaps with the criminal law, since there are some actions, e.g. assault, which are both a crime and a civil wrong; nor is the only distinction of importance the familiar one that crime has as its characteristic consequence liability to punishment, and civil wrong liability to pay compensation for harm done. The crucial distinction, according to this view of relative duties, is the special manner in which the civil law as distinct from the criminal law provides for individuals: it recognizes or gives them a place or *locus standi* in relation to the law quite different from that given by the criminal law. Instead of utilitarian notions of benefit or intended benefit we need, if we are to reproduce this distinctive concern for the individual, a different

[83] So Austin (op. cit., Lecture XVII, 401–2).
[84] Allen, *Legal Duties*, pp. 184–6.

idea. The idea is that of one individual being given by the law exclusive control, more or less extensive, over another person's duty so that in the area of conduct covered by that duty the individual who has the right is a small-scale sovereign to whom the duty is owed. The fullest measure[85] of control comprises three distinguishable elements: (i) the right holder may waive or extinguish the duty or leave it in existence; (ii) after breach or threatened breach of a duty he may leave it 'unenforced' or may 'enforce' it by suing for compensation or, in certain cases, for an injunction or mandatory order to restrain the continued or further breach of duty; and (iii) he may waive or extinguish the obligation to pay compensation to which the breach gives rise. It is obvious that not all who benefit or are intended to benefit by another's legal obligation are in this unique sovereign position in relation to the duty. A person protected only by the criminal law has no power to release anyone from its duties, and though, as in England, he may in theory be entitled to prosecute along with any other member of the public he has no unique power to determine whether the duties of the criminal law should be enforced or not.

These legal powers (for such they are) over a correlative obligation are of great importance to lawyers: both laymen and lawyers will need, in Bentham's phrase, 'to be instructed' about them; and their exercise calls for the specific skills of the lawyer. They are therefore a natural focus of legal attention, and there are I think many signs of the centrality of those powers to the conception of a legal right. Thus it is hard to think of rights except as capable of *exercise* and this conception of rights correlative to obligations as containing legal powers accommodates this feature.[86] Moreover, we speak of a breach of duty in the

[85] The right holder will have less than the full measure of control if, as in the case of statutory duties, he is unable to release or extinguish the duty or if principles of public policy prevent him, even after breach of the duty, making a binding agreement not to sue for injury caused by its breach (see e.g. *Bowmaker Ltd.* v. *Tabor* (1942) 2 K.B. 1). In such cases the choice left to him is only to sue or not to sue. There are suggestions, never fully developed, that such a choice is a necessary element in a legal system in Bentham's *A Fragment on Government* Ch. V para. 6 n. 1 s. 2.

[86] Where infants or other persons not *sui juris* have rights, such powers and the correlative obligations are exercised on their behalf by appointed representatives and their exercise may be subject to approval by a court. But since (a) what such representatives can and cannot do by way of exercise of such power is determined

civil law, whether arising in contract or in tort, not only as wrong, or detrimental to the person who has the correlative right, but as *a wrong to* him and a breach of an obligation *owed to* him;[87] we also speak of the person who has the correlative right as *possessing* it or even *owning* it. The conception suggested by these phrases is that duties with correlative rights are a species of normative property belonging to the right holder, and this figure becomes intelligible by reference to the special form of control over a correlative duty which a person with such a right is given by the law. Whenever an individual has this special control, as he has in most cases in the civil law but not over the duties of the criminal law, there is a contrast of importance to be marked and many jurists have done so by distinguishing the duties of the criminal law as 'absolute duties' from the 'relative' duties of the civil law.[88]

It is an incidental, though substantial merit of this approach that it provides an intelligible explanation of the fact that animals, even though directly protected by the duties of the criminal law prohibiting cruelty to them, are not spoken or thought of as having rights. However it is to be observed that if the distinction between absolute and relative duties is drawn as above suggested, this does not entail that only duties of the civil law have correlative rights. For there are cases made prominent by the extension of the welfare functions of the

---

by what those whom they represent could have done if *sui juris* and (b) when the latter become *sui juris* they can exercise these powers without any transfer or fresh assignment; the powers are regarded as belonging throughout to them and not to their representatives, though they are only exercisable by the latter during the period of disability.

[87] Lyons (loc. cit., p. 178) assumes that 'rights under the civil law' arise only from 'special relations or transactions between the parties' (e.g. contracts) and that only in such cases are the right holders 'claimants' to whom duties are 'owed'. But individuals have rights corresponding to the primary duties in tort which do not arise from such special relations or transactions and such duties are 'owed' to them.

[88] It is sometimes argued that in the case of persons not *sui juris* e.g. infants, it is only the fact that they are direct beneficiaries of the correlative duties which explains the ascription of rights to them, rather than to their representatives who alone can exercise the powers over the correlative duties. But the explanation offered above (p. 192, n. 86) seems adequate; even if it is not, this would only show that being the direct beneficiary of a duty was a *necessary* condition of a person not *sui juris* having a right. Hence it would still be possible so far as this argument goes, to distinguish the duties of the criminal law (over which there are no such powers of control exercisable by the beneficiaries' representatives) as not having correlative rights.

state where officials of public bodies are under a legal duty to provide individuals if they satisfy certain conditions, with benefits which may take the form of money payments (e.g. public assistance, unemployment relief, farming subsidies) or supply of goods or services, e.g. medical care. In such cases it is perfectly common and natural to speak of individuals who have satisfied the prescribed conditions as being legally entitled to and having a right to such benefits. Yet it is commonly not the case that they have the kind of control over the official's duties which, according to the view suggested above, is a defining feature of legal rights correlative to obligations. For though such obligations are not always supported by criminal sanctions they cannot be extinguished or waived by beneficiaries, nor does their breach necessarily give rise to any secondary obligation to make compensation which the beneficiaries can enforce, leave unenforced or extinguish. None the less there are in most of such cases two features which link them to the paradigm cases of rights correlative to obligations as these appear in the civil law. In most cases where such public duties are thought of as having correlative rights, the duty to supply the benefits are conditional upon their being demanded and the beneficiary of the duty is free to demand it or not. Hence, though he has no power to waive or extinguish the duty he has a power by presenting a demand to substitute for a conditional duty not requiring present performance an unconditional duty which does, and so has a choice. Secondly, though breach of such duties may not give rise to any secondary duties of compensation, there are in many such cases steps which the beneficiary if he has suffered some peculiar damage may take to secure its performance, and in regard to which he has a special *locus standi* so that on his application a court may make a peremptory or mandatory order or injunction directing the official body to carry out the duty or restraining its breach.[89] These two features of the case differentiate the beneficiary of such public duties from that of the ordinary duties of the criminal law. This explains why, though it is generally enough to describe the criminal law only in terms of duties, so to

[89] Difficult questions may arise concerning the nature of the interest which a successful applicant for such relief must possess. See *R.* v. *Manchester Corp.* [1911] 1 K.B. 560.

describe the law creating these public welfare duties would obscure important features. For the necessity that such beneficiaries if they wish the duty to be performed must present demands, and the availability to them of means of enforcement, make their position under the law a focus for legal attention needing separate description from that of the duties beneficial to them.[90]

(*b*) *Contracts and third parties.* The identification of a right-holder with the person who is merely benefited by the performance of a duty not only obscures a very important general dividing line between criminal and civil law, but is ill adapted to the law relating to contract. Whereas in the last paragraph it was urged that to be an intended beneficiary of an obligation is not a satisfactory *sufficient* condition of having a right, the present criticism is that it is not satisfactory as a *necessary* condition. For where there is a contract between two people, not all those who benefit and are intended to benefit by the performance of its obligations have a legal right correlative to them. In many jurisdictions contracts expressly made for the benefit of third parties, e.g. a contract between two people to pay a third party a sum of money, is not enforceable by the third party and he cannot waive or release the obligation. In such a case although the third party is a direct beneficiary since breach of the contracts constitutes a direct detriment to him, he has no legal control over the duty and so no legal right. On the other hand the contracting party having the appropriate control has the legal right, though he is not the person intended to benefit by the performance of the contract.[91] Where, however, the law is modified as it is in some jurisdictions so as to give the third party power to enforce the contract then he is consistently with the view presented here spoken of as having legal right.[92]

[90] But so far as such public welfare duties are thought of as providing for essential human needs they may on that ground alone be regarded as constituting legal rights. See below, pp. 197–200.

[91] It is sometimes argued that the fact that in some jurisdictions a third-party beneficiary may sue shows this point against the beneficiary theory of rights to be mistaken. But of course a third party entitled to sue or not to sue would on *that* account be recognized as having a legal right and this does nothing to confirm the beneficiary theory.

[92] Lyons, loc. cit., pp. 183–4, argues that 'one of the conditions of a valid and binding promise and thus a condition of a right accruing to a promisee is that he really wants what is promised' (even if this is true of 'promises' it scarcely seems applicable to legal contracts). He then suggests that performance of a contract

The analysis of a right correlative to obligation which is suggested by the foregoing criticisms of the benefit theory is that for such a right to exist it is neither sufficient nor necessary for the person who had the right to be the beneficiary of the obligation; what is sufficient and necessary is that he should have at least some measure of the control, described above, over the correlative obligation.

IV. THE LIMITS OF A GENERAL THEORY

If the arguments of the last section are accepted and if we substitute for the utilitarian idea of benefit, as a defining feature of a right correlative to obligation, the individual's legal powers of control, full or partial, over that obligation, a generalization may be made concerning all three kinds of right distinguished by Bentham. This is attractive because it imposes a pattern of order on a wide range of apparently disparate legal phenomena. Thus in all three kinds of right the idea of a bilateral liberty is present and the difference between the kinds of right lies only in the kind of act which there is liberty to do. In the case of liberty-rights such as a man's right to look at his neighbour, his act may be called a natural act in the sense that it is not endowed by the law with a special legal significance or legal effect. On the other hand in the case of rights which are powers, such as the right to alienate property, the act which there is a bilateral liberty[93] to do is an act-in-the-law, just in the sense that it is specifically recognized by the law as having legal effects in varying the legal position of various parties. The case

for the benefit of a third party must 'assure a good' to the promisee, since this satisfies his want to have what is promised done, and that it is this, not his control over the promisors obligation, which accounts for the ascription of a right to him. But if the performance of the obligation beneficial to the third party is not sufficient to lead lawyers to recognize the third party as having a legal right, surely the secondary benefit to the promisee consisting in gratification of his wish to benefit the third party is not sufficient to account for his right.

[93] As in the case of liberty-rights, duties may be superimposed on rights which are powers and such duties will render the liberty to exercise the power unilateral (a simple example from property law is where an owner of property binds himself by contract either to sell it or not to sell it). In general where there is a duty to exercise a power the resultant unilateral liberty is not described as a right nor is there usually any point in so describing it. Exceptions to this are again cases such as that of a trustee whose legal rights are theoretically distinguishable from his equitable duties (see above, p. 183, n. 56) and are thought of as coexisting even where they in fact conflict.

of a right correlative to obligation then emerges as only a special case of legal power in which the right-holder is at liberty to waive or extinguish or to enforce or leave unenforced another's obligation. It would follow from these considerations that in each of these three types of case one who has a right has a choice respected by the law. On this view there would be only one sense of legal right—a legally respected choice—though it would be one with different exemplifications, depending on the kind of act or act-in-the-law which there is liberty to do.

The merits of this analysis are therefore threefold. First, it coincides with a very wide area of common and legal usage. Secondly it explains why liberty-rights, powers, and rights correlative to obligations are all described as rights and does so by identifying as common to three superficially diverse types of case, an element which, on any theory of law or morals, is of great importance; namely an individual choice respected by the law. Thirdly, the concept which it defines is well adapted to a lawyer's purpose; for it will lead him to talk in terms of rights only where there is something of importance to the lawyer to talk about which cannot be equally well said in terms of obligation or duty, and this is pre-eminently so in the case of the civil law.[94]

However, in spite of its attractions, this theory, centred on the notion of a legally respected individual choice, cannot be taken as exhausting the notion of a legal right: the notion of individual benefit must be brought in, though *not* as the benefit theory brings it in, to supplement the notion of individual choice. Unless this is done no adequate account can be given of the deployment of the language of rights, in two main contexts, when certain freedoms and benefits are regarded as essential for the maintenance of the life, the security, the development, and the dignity of the individual. Such freedoms and benefits are recognized as rights in the constitutional law of many countries by Bills of Rights, which afford to the individual protection even against the processes of legislation. In countries such as our own, where the doctrine of legislative sovereignty is held to preclude limiting the powers of the legislature by Bills of Rights, they are, though given only the lesser

[94] But not exclusively, see pp. 194–5 above.

measure of legal protection in the form of duties of the criminal law, thought and spoken of as legal rights by social theorists or critics of the law who are accustomed to view the law in a wider perspective than the lawyer concerned only with its day-to-day working.

IMMUNITY RIGHTS

Both the benefit theory of rights and the alternative theory of a right as a legally respected choice are designed primarily as accounts of the rights of citizen against citizen; that is of rights under the 'ordinary' law. From that point of view the benefit theory was criticized above (*inter alia*) for offering no more than a redundant translation of duties of the criminal law into a terminology of rights, e.g. not be murdered or assaulted. But this accusation of redundancy is no longer pertinent when what is to be considered are not rights under the ordinary law, but fundamental rights which may be said to be against the legislature, limiting its powers to make (or unmake) the ordinary law, where so to do would deny to individuals certain freedoms and benefits now regarded as essentials of human well-being, such as freedom of speech and of association, freedom from arbitrary arrest, security of life and person, education, and equality of treatment in certain respects.

The various elements which the benefit theory uses to analyse rights correlative to obligations and those which the rival 'choice' theory uses to analyse these and other kinds of right (that is: duty, absence of duty, benefit, act, and act-in-the-law) are not sufficient to provide an analysis of such constitutionally guaranteed individual rights. These require for their analysis the notion of an immunity. Bentham, unlike Hohfeld, did not isolate this notion in distinguishing different kinds or meanings of legal right, and indeed his attention was never seriously given to the analysis of fundamental legal rights. This was, no doubt, because, although, unlike Austin, he did not think that there were logical or conceptual objections to the notion of legal limitations of a sovereign legislature[95] he viewed with extreme suspicion any legal arrangements which would prevent

[95] See for his discussion of such limitations, *O.L.G.*, pp. 18, 64–71, 306, and *A Fragment of Government*, ch. IV, paras. 23–36, and my 'Bentham on Sovereignty' (1967) Irish Jurist 327.

the legislature enacting whatever measures appeared from time to time to be required by the dictates of general utility; and suspicion became contempt at the suggestion that such arrangements should be used to give legal form to doctrines of natural or fundamental individual rights. Hohfeld, who identified among the various 'loose' uses of the expression 'a right' its use to refer to an immunity, defined an immunity as the correlative of 'disability' or 'no power';[96] so that to say that a man, *X*, had a certain immunity meant that someone else lacked legal power to alter *X*'s legal position in some respect. But, plainly, even in the loosest usage, the expression 'a right' is not used to refer to the fact that a man is thus immune from an *advantageous* change; the facts that the City Council cannot legally, i.e. has 'no power', to award me a pension, and my neighbour has no power to exempt me from my duty to pay my income-tax, do not constitute any legal rights for me. An individual's immunity from legal change at the hands of others is spoken and thought of as a right only when the change in question is *adverse*, that is, would deprive him of legal rights of other kinds (liberty-rights, powers, rights correlative to obligations) or benefits secured to him by law.

The chief, though not the only employment[97] of this notion of an immunity from adverse legal change which we may call an 'immunity right' is to characterize distinctively the position of individuals protected from such adverse change by constitutional limitations or, as Hohfeld would say, by disabilities of the legislature. Such immunity rights are obviously of extreme importance to individuals and may usually be asserted in the form of justiciable claims that some purported enactment is invalid because it infringes them. There is here an illuminating contrast with the redundancy of rights as defined by the beneficiary theory; for whereas, as I have urged above, nothing is to be gained for the lawyer, either in clarity or the focusing of legal attention, by expounding, say, the law of murder or assault in terms of rights, the case is altered if a constitutional Bill of Rights precludes the legislature from depriving individuals

[96] Hohfeld, op. cit., p. 60.

[97] Immunities against divestment of various kinds of rights are involved in the notion of ownership. See A. M. Honoré, 'Ownership' in *Oxford Essays on Jurisprudence*, First Series (1961), p. 119.

of the protections of the criminal law. For then there is every reason why lawyers and others should have picked out for them, as rights to life or security of the person, legal immunities the assertion of which on behalf of the individual calls for their advice and skill. That is why I said above that though certain legally secured individual benefits would have to be brought in to any adequate account of legal rights, they would not be brought in as the benefit theory brings them in.

WIDER PERSPECTIVES

Law is however too important a thing to leave to lawyers—even to constitutional lawyers; and the ways of thinking about rights common among serious critics of the law and social theorists must be accommodated even though they are different from and may not serve any of the specific purposes of the lawyer. Here also a concept of legal rights limited to those cases where the law, in the ways described above, respects the choice of individuals would be too narrow. For there is a distinct form of the moral criticism of law which, like the constitutional immunity rights already described, is inspired by regard for the needs of the individual for certain fundamental freedoms and protections or benefits. Criticism of the law for its failure to provide for such individual needs is distinct from, and sometimes at war with, the criticism with which Bentham was perhaps too exclusively concerned, that the law often fails to maximize aggregate utility. A critic of the former, individualistic, kind will of course not address himself only to those legal systems in which there are immunity rights guaranteed by Bills of Rights; but in scrutinizing systems like our own, where the maximum form of provision for such individual needs must fall short of constitutional immunity rights, he will count the measure of protection afforded by the ordinary criminal law as a provision for those needs, together with the duties to provide for them which fall on public bodies or officials. Viewed in this light the law against murder and assault will be considered and described quite properly as securing rights to life and security of the person; though if it were a question simply of expounding the criminal law this would be redundant and even confusing.

Hence in cases where the criminal law provides for such

essential human needs the individualistic critic of the law would agree with the benefit-theorist in speaking of rights corresponding to certain duties of the criminal law. They would however differ in two ways: first the critic need entertain no *general* theory that every direct beneficiary of a legal obligation had a corresponding legal right and he could therefore consistently subscribe to all the criticisms of the beneficiary theory made above; secondly the individualistic critic implicitly draws a distinction quite foreign to the letter and the spirit of the beneficiary theory between the legal provision of benefits simply as a contribution to general utility and as a contribution to the satisfaction of individual needs. It is the latter which leads him to talk of rights secured by the duties of the criminal law.

The upshot of these considerations is that instead of a general analytical and explanatory theory covering the whole field of legal rights I have provided a general theory in terms of the notion of a legally respected individual choice which is satisfactory only at one level—the level of the lawyer concerned with the working of the 'ordinary' law. This requires supplementation in order to accommodate the important deployment of the language of rights by the constitutional lawyer and the individualistic critic of the law, for whom the core of the notion of rights is neither individual choice nor individual benefit but basic or fundamental individual needs. This result may be felt as distressingly untidy by some, and they may be tempted to combine the perspectives which I have distinguished of the ordinary lawyer, the constitutional lawyer, and the individualistic critic of the law in some general formula embracing all three. Such a general formula is suggested by Hohfeld's statement that the generic sense of a right means 'any legal advantage'.[98] But I fear that, behind the comfortable appearance of generality, we would have only an unilluminating combination or mere juxtaposition of the choice theory together with the benefit theory; and this would fail to be sensitive to the important reasons for describing only some legally secured benefits, only in some contexts, as legal rights.

[98] Op. cit., pp. 42, 71. Cf. also Bentham's discussion in *O.L.G.*, pp. 55–9 of the inclusion in the idea of a 'party favoured by the law' of two kinds of favour: favour in 'point of interest' and 'in point of agency'. A party is 'favoured in point of agency' when he has an *exceptional* liberty, i.e. a liberty to do some act generally prohibited.

VIII
Taking Rights Seriously[1]

RONALD DWORKIN

I. THE RIGHTS OF CITIZENS

THE language of rights now dominates political debate in the United States. Does the Government respect the moral and political rights of its citizens? Or does the Government's war policy, or its race policy, fly in the face of these rights? Do the minorities whose rights have been violated have the right to violate the law in return? Or does the silent majority itself have rights, including the right that those who break the law be punished? It is not surprising that these questions are now prominent. The concept of rights, and particularly the concept of rights against the Government, has its most natural use when a political society is divided, and appeals to co-operation or a common goal are pointless.

The debate does not include the issue of whether citizens have *some* moral rights against their Government. It seems accepted on all sides that they do. Conventional lawyers and politicians take it as a point of pride that our legal system recognizes, for example, individual rights of free speech, equality, and due process. They base their claim that our law deserves respect, at least in part, on that fact, for they would not claim that totalitarian systems deserve the same loyalty.

Some philosophers, of course, reject the idea that citizens have rights apart from what the law happens to give them. Bentham thought that the idea of moral rights was 'nonsense on stilts'. But that view has never been part of our orthodox political theory, and politicians of both parties appeal to the rights of the people to justify a great part of what they want to do. I shall not be concerned, in this essay, to defend the thesis that citizens have moral rights against their governments; I want instead to explore the implications of that thesis for those,

[1] First published in the *New York Review of Books*, 18 December 1970.

including the present United States Government, who profess to accept it.

It is much in dispute, of course, what *particular* rights citizens have. Does the acknowledged right to free speech, for example, include the right to participate in nuisance demonstrations? In practice the Government will have the last word on what an individual's rights are, because its police will do what its officials and courts say. But that does not mean that the Government's view is necessarily the correct view; anyone who thinks it does must believe that men and women have only such moral rights as Government chooses to grant, which means that they have no moral rights at all.

All this is sometimes obscured in the United States by the constitutional system. The American Constitution provides a set of individual *legal* rights in the First Amendment, and in the due process, equal protection, and similar clauses. Under present legal practice the Supreme Court has the power to declare an act of Congress or of a state legislature void if the Court finds that the act offends these provisions. This practice has led some commentators to suppose that individual moral rights are fully protected by this system, but that is hardly so, nor could it be so.

The Constitition fuses legal and moral issues, by making the validity of a law depend on the answer to complex moral problems, like the problem of whether a particular statute respects the inherent equality of all men. This fusion has important consequences for the debates about civil disobedience; I have described these elsewhere[2] and I shall refer to them later. But it leaves open two prominent questions. It does not tell us whether the Constitution, even properly interpreted, recognizes all the moral rights that citizens have, and it does not tell us whether, as many suppose, citizens would have a duty to obey the law even if it did invade their moral rights.

Both questions become crucial when some minority claims moral rights which the law denies, like the right to run its local school system, and which lawyers agree are not protected by the Constitution. The second question becomes crucial when, as now, the majority is sufficiently aroused so that Constitutional amendments to eliminate rights, like the right against

[2] 'On Not Prosecuting Civil Disobedience', *NYR*, 6 June 1968.

self-incrimination, are seriously proposed. It is also crucial in nations, like the United Kingdom, that have no constitution of a comparable nature.

Even if the Constitution were perfect, of course, and the majority left it alone, it would not follow that the Supreme Court could guarantee the individual rights of citizens. A Supreme Court decision is still a legal decision, and it must take into account precedent and institutional considerations like relations between the Court and Congress, as well as morality. And no judicial decision is necessarily the right decision. Judges stand for different positions on controversial issues of law and morals and, as the fights over Nixon's Supreme Court nominations showed, a President is entitled to appoint judges of his own persuasion, provided that they are honest and capable.

So, though the constitutional system adds something to the protection of moral rights against the Government, it falls far short of guaranteeing these rights, or even establishing what they are. It means that, on some occasions, a department other than the legislature has the last word on these issues, which can hardly satisfy someone who thinks such a department profoundly wrong.

It is of course inevitable that some department of government will have the final say on what law will be enforced. When men disagree about moral rights, there will be no way for either side to prove its case, and some decision must stand if there is not to be anarchy. But that piece of orthodox wisdom must be the beginning and not the end of a philosophy of legislation and enforcement. If we cannot insist that the Government reach the right answers about the rights of its citizens, we can insist at least that it try. We can insist that it take rights seriously, follow a coherent theory of what these rights are, and act consistently with its own professions. I shall try to show what that means, and now it bears on the present political debates.

II. RIGHTS AND THE RIGHT TO BREAK THE LAW

I shall start with the most violently argued issue. Does an American ever have the moral right to break a law? Suppose someone admits a law is valid; does he therefore have a duty to obey it? Those who try to give an answer seem to fall into two camps. The conservatives, as I shall call them, seem to disapprove of any act of disobedience; they appear satisfied when such acts are prosecuted, and disappointed when convictions are reversed. The other group, the liberals, are much more sympathetic to at least some cases of disobedience; they sometimes disapprove of prosecutions and celebrate acquittals. If we look beyond these emotional reactions, however, and pay attention to the arguments the two parties use, we discover an astounding fact. Both groups give essentially the same answer to the question of principle that supposedly divides them.

The answer that both parties give is this. In a democracy, or at least a democracy that in principle respects individual rights, each citizen has a general moral duty to obey all the laws, even though he would like some of them changed. He owes that duty to his fellow citizens, who obey laws that they do not like, to his benefit. But this general duty cannot be an absolute duty, because even a society that is in principle just may produce unjust laws and policies, and a man has duties other than his duties to the State. A man must honour his duties to his God and to his conscience, and if these conflict with his duty to the State, then he is entitled, in the end, to do what he judges to be right. If he decides that he must break the law, however, then he must submit to the judgment and punishment that the State imposes, in recognition of the fact that his duty to his fellow citizens was overwhelmed but not extinguished by his religious or moral obligation.

Of course this common answer can be elaborated in very different ways. Some would describe the duty to the State as fundamental, and picture the dissenter as a religious or moral fanatic. Others would describe the duty to the State in grudging terms, and picture those who oppose it as moral heroes. But these are differences in tone, and the position I described represents, I think, the view of most of those who find themselves arguing either for or against civil disobedience in particular cases.

I do not claim that it is everyone's view. There must be some who put the duty to the State so high that they do not grant that it can ever be overcome. There are certainly some who would deny that a man ever has a moral duty to obey the law, at least in the United States today. But these two extreme positions are the slender tails of a bell curve, and all those who fall in between hold the orthodox position I described—that men have a duty to obey the law but have the right to follow their consciences when it conflicts with that duty.

But if that is so, then we have a paradox in the fact that men who give the same answer to a question of principle should seem to disagree so much, and to divide so fiercely, in particular cases. The paradox goes even deeper, for each party, in at least some cases, takes a position that seems flatly inconsistent with the theoretical position they both accept. This position is tested, for example, when someone evades the draft on grounds of conscience, or encourages others to commit this crime. Conservatives argue that such men must be prosecuted, even though they are sincere. Why must they be prosecuted? Because society cannot tolerate the decline in respect for the law that their act constitutes and encourages. They must be prosecuted, in short, to discourage them and others like them from doing what they have done.

But there seems to be a monstrous contradiction here. If a man has a right to do what his conscience tells him he must, then how can the State be justified in discouraging him from doing it? Is it not wicked for a state to forbid and punish what it acknowledges that men have a right to do?

Moreover, it is not just conservatives who argue that those who break the law out of moral conviction should be prosecuted. The liberal is notoriously opposed to allowing Southern school officials to go slow on segregation, even though he acknowledges that these school officials think they have a moral right to do what the law forbids. The liberal does not often argue, it is true, that the desegregation laws must be enforced to encourage general respect for law. He argues instead that the desegregation laws must be enforced because they are right. But his position also seems inconsistent: can it be right to prosecute men for doing what their conscience requires, when we acknowledge their right to follow their conscience?

We are therefore left with two puzzles. How can two parties to an issue of principle, each of which thinks it is in profound disagreement with the other, embrace the same position on that issue? How can it be that each side urges solutions to particular problems which seem flatly to contradict the position of principle that both accept? One possible answer is that some or all of those who accept the common position are hypocrites, paying lip service to rights of conscience which in fact they do not grant.

There is some plausibility in this charge. A sort of hypocrisy must be involved when public officials who claim to respect conscience deny Muhammad Ali the right to box in their states. If Ali, in spite of his religious scruples, had joined the Army, he would have been allowed to box even though, on the principles these officials say they honour, he would have been a worse human being for having done so. But there are few cases that seem so straightforward as this one, and even here the officials do not seem to recognize the contradiction between their acts and their principles. So we must search for some explanation beyond the truth that men often do not mean what they say.

The deeper explanation lies in a set of confusions that often embarrass arguments about rights. These confusions have clouded all the issues I mentioned at the outset and have crippled attempts to develop a coherent theory of how a government that respects rights must behave.

In order to explain this, I must call attention to the fact, familiar to philosophers but often ignored in political debate, that the word 'right' has different force in different contexts. In most cases when we say that someone has a 'right' to do something, we imply that it would be wrong to interfere with his doing it, or at least that some special grounds are needed for justifying any interference. I use this strong sense of right when I say that you have the right to spend your money gambling, if you wish, though you ought to spend it in a more worthwhile way. I mean that it would be wrong for anyone to interfere with you even though you propose to spend your money in a way that I think is wrong.

There is a clear difference between saying that someone has a right to do something in this sense and saying that it is the 'right' thing for him to do, or that he does no 'wrong' in doing it. Someone may have the right to do something that is the wrong thing for him to do, as might be the case with gambling. Conversely, something may be the right thing for him to do and yet he may have no right to do it, in the sense that it would not be wrong for someone to interfere with his trying. If our army captures an enemy soldier, we might say that the right thing for him to do is to try to escape, but it would not follow that it is wrong of us to try to stop him. We might admire him for trying to escape, and perhaps even think less of him if he did not. But there is no suggestion here that it is wrong of us to stand in his way; on the contrary, if we think our cause is just, we think it right for us to do all we can to stop him.

Ordinarily this distinction, between the issues of whether a man has a right to do something and whether it is the right thing for him to do, causes no trouble. But sometimes it does, because sometimes we say that a man has a right to do something when we mean only to deny that it is the wrong thing for him to do. Thus we say that the captured soldier has a 'right' to try to escape when we mean, not that we do wrong to stop him, but that he has no duty not to make the attempt. We use 'right' this way when we speak of someone having the 'right' to act on his own principles, or the 'right' to follow his own conscience. We mean that he does no wrong to proceed on his honest convictions, even though we disagree with these convictions, and even though, for policy or other reasons, we must force him to act contrary to them.

Suppose a man believes that welfare payments to the poor are profoundly wrong, because they sap enterprise, and so declares his full income-tax each year but declines to pay half of it. We might say that he has a right to refuse to pay, if he wishes, but that the Government has a right to proceed against him for the full tax, and to fine or jail him for late payment if that is necessary to keep the collection system working efficiently. We do not take this line in most cases; we do not say that the ordinary thief has a right to steal, if he wishes, so long as he pays the penalty. We say a man has the right to break the law, even though the State has a right to punish him, only when we think that, because of his convictions, he does no wrong in doing so.[3]

These distinctions enable us to see an ambiguity in the ortho-

[3] It is not surprising that we sometimes use the concept of having a right to say that others must not interfere with an act and sometimes to say that the act is not the wrong thing to do. Often, when someone has *no* right to do something, like attacking another man physically, it is true *both* that it is the wrong thing to do and that others are entitled to stop it, by demand, if not by force. It is therefore natural to say that someone has a right when we mean to deny *either* of these consequences, as well as when we mean to deny both.

dox question: Does a man ever have a right to break the law? Does that question mean to ask whether he ever has a right to break the law in the strong sense, so that the Government would do wrong to stop him, by arresting and prosecuting him? Or does it mean to ask whether he ever does the right thing to break the law, so that we should all respect him even though the Government should jail him?

If we take the orthodox position to be an answer to the first—and most important—question, then the paradoxes I described arise. But if we take it as an answer to the second, they do not. Conservatives and liberals do agree that sometimes a man does not do the wrong thing to break a law, when his conscience so requires. They disagree, when they do, over the different issue of what the State's response should be. Both parties do think that sometimes the State should prosecute. But this is not inconsistent with the proposition that the man prosecuted did the right thing in breaking the law.

The paradoxes seem genuine because the two questions are not usually distinguished, and the orthodox position is presented as a general solution to the problem of civil disobedience. But once the distinction is made, it is apparent that the position has been so widely accepted only because, when it is applied, it is treated as an answer to the second question but not the first. The crucial distinction is obscured by the troublesome idea of a right to conscience; this idea has been at the centre of most recent discussions of political obligation, but it is a red herring drawing us away from the crucial political questions. The state of a man's conscience may be decisive, or central, when the issue is whether he does something morally wrong in breaking the law; but it need not be decisive or even central when the issue is whether he has a right, in the strong sense of that term, to do so. A man does not have the right, in that sense, to do whatever his conscience demands, but he may have the right, in that sense, to do something even though his conscience does not demand it.

If that is true, then there has been almost no serious attempt to answer the questions that almost everyone means to ask. We can make a fresh start by stating these questions more clearly. Does an American ever have the right, in a strong sense, to do something which is against the law? If so, when? In order to answer these questions put in that way, we must try to become clearer about the implications of the idea, mentioned earlier, that citizens have at least some rights against their government.

I said that in the United States citizens are supposed to have certain fundamental rights against their Government, certain moral rights made into legal rights by the Constitution. If this idea is significant, and worth bragging about, then these rights must be rights in the strong sense I just described. The claim that citizens have a right to free speech must imply that it would be wrong for the Government to stop them from speaking, even when the Government believes that what they will say will cause more harm than good. The claim cannot mean, on the prisoner-of-war analogy, only that citizens do no wrong in speaking their minds, though the Government reserves the right to prevent them from doing so.

This is a crucial point, and I want to labour it. Of course a responsible government must be ready to justify anything it does, particularly when it limits the liberty of its citizens. But normally it is a sufficient justification, even for an act that limits liberty, that the act is calculated to increase what the philosophers call general utility—that it is calculated to produce more over-all benefit than harm. So, though the New York City government needs a justification for forbidding motorists to drive up Lexington Avenue, it is sufficient justification if the proper officials believe, on sound evidence, that the gain to the many will outweigh the inconvenience to the few. When individual citizens are said to have rights against the Government, however, like the right of free speech, that must mean that this sort of justification is not enough. Otherwise the claim would not argue that individuals have special protection against the law when their rights are in play, and that is just the point of the claim.

Not all legal rights, or even Constitutional rights, represent moral rights against the Government. I now have the legal right to drive either way on Fifty-seventh Street, but the Government would do no wrong to make that street one-way if it thought it in the general interest to do so. I have a Constitutional right to vote for a congressman every two years, but the national and state governments would do no wrong if, following the amendment procedure, they made a congressman's term four years instead of two, again on the basis of a judgment that this would be for the general good.

But those Constitutional rights that we call fundamental, like the right of free speech, are supposed to represent rights against the Government in the strong sense; that is the point of the boast that our legal system respects the fundamental rights of the citizen. If citizens have a moral right of free speech, then governments would do wrong to repeal the First Amendment that guarantees it, even if they were persuaded that the majority would be better off if speech were curtailed.

I must not overstate the point. Someone who claims that citizens have a right against the Government need not go so far as to say that the State is *never* justified in overriding that right. He might say, for example, that although citizens have a right to free speech, the Government may override that right when necessary to protect the rights of others, or to prevent a catastrophe, or even to obtain a clear and major public benefit (though if he acknowledged this last as a possible justification he would be treating the right in question as not among the most important or fundamental). What he cannot do is to say that the Government is justified in overriding a right on the minimal grounds that would be sufficient if no such right existed. He cannot say that the Government is entitled to act on no more than a judgment that its act is likely to produce, overall, a benefit to the community. That admission would make his claim of a right pointless, and would show him to be using some sense of 'right' other than the strong sense necessary to give his claim the political importance it is normally taken to have.

But then the answers to our two questions about disobedience seem plain, if unorthodox. In our society a man does sometimes have the right, in the strong sense, to disobey a law. He has that right whenever that law wrongly invades his rights against the Government. If he has a moral right to free speech, that is, then he has a moral right to break any law that the Government, by virtue of his right, had no right to adopt. The right to disobey the law is not a separate right, having something to do with conscience, additional to other rights against the Government. It is simply a feature of these rights against the Government, and it cannot be denied in principle without denying that any such rights exist.

These answers seem obvious once we take rights against the Government to be rights in the strong sense I described. If I have a right to speak my mind on political issues, then the Government does wrong to make it illegal for me to do so, even if it thinks this is in the general interest. If, nevertheless, the Government does make my act illegal, then it does a further wrong to enforce that law against me. My right against the Government means that it is wrong for the Government to stop me from speaking; the Government cannot make it right to stop me just by taking the first step.

This does not, of course, tell us exactly what rights men do have against the Government. It does not tell us whether the right of free speech includes the right of demonstration. But it does mean that passing a law cannot affect such rights as men do have, and that is of crucial importance, because it dictates the attitude that an individual is entitled to take toward his personal decision when civil disobedience is in question.

Both conservatives and liberals suppose that in a society which is generally decent everyone has a duty to obey the law, whatever it is. That is the source of the 'general duty' clause in the orthodox position, and though liberals believe that this duty can sometimes be 'overridden', even they suppose, as the orthodox position maintains, that the duty of obedience remains in some submerged form, so that a man does well to accept punishment in recognition of that duty. But this general duty is almost incoherent in a society that recognizes rights. If a man believes he has a right to demonstrate, then he must believe that it would be wrong for the Government to stop him, with or without benefit of a law. If he is entitled to believe that, then it is silly to speak of a duty to obey the law as such, or of a duty to accept the punishment that the State has no right to give.

Conservatives will object to the short work I have made of their point. They will argue that even if the Government was wrong to adopt some law, like a law limiting speech, there are independent reasons why the Government is justified in enforcing the law once adopted. When the law forbids demonstration, then, so they argue, some principle more important than the individual's right to speak is brought into play, namely the principle of respect for law. If a law, even a bad law, is left unenforced, then respect for law is weakened, and society as a whole suffers. So an individual loses his moral right to speak when speech is made criminal, and the Government must, for the common good and for the general benefit, enforce the law against him.

But this argument, though popular, is plausible only if we forget what it means to say that an individual has a right against the State. It is far from plain that civil disobedience lowers respect for law, but even if we suppose that it does, this fact is irrelevant. The prospect of utilitarian gains cannot justify preventing a man from doing what he has a right to do, and the supposed gains in respect for law are simply utilitarian gains. There would be no point in the boast that we respect individual rights unless that involved some sacrifice, and the sacrifice in question must be that we give up whatever marginal benefits our country would receive from overriding these rights when they prove inconvenient. So the general benefit cannot be a good ground for abridging rights, even when the benefit in question is a heightened respect for law.

But perhaps I do wrong to assume that the argument about respect for law is only an appeal to general utility. I said that a state may be justified in overriding or limiting rights on other grounds, and we must ask, before rejecting the conservative position, whether any of these apply. The most important—and least well understood—of these other grounds invokes the notion of *competing rights* that would be jeopardized if the right in question were not limited. Citizens have personal rights to the State's protection as well as personal rights to be free from the State's interference, and it may be necessary for the Government to choose between these two sorts of rights. The law of defamation, for example, limits the personal right of any man to say what he thinks, because it requires him to have good grounds for what he says. But this law is justified, even for those who think that it does invade a personal right, by the fact that it protects the right of others not to have their reputations ruined by a careless statement.

The individual rights that our society acknowledges often conflict in this way, and when they do it is the job of government to discriminate. If the Government makes the right choice, and protects the more important at the cost of the less, then it has not weakened or cheapened the notion of a right; on the contrary it would have done so had it failed to protect the more important of the two. So we must acknowledge that the Government has a reason for limiting rights if it plausibly believes that a competing right is more important.

May the conservative seize on this fact? He might argue that I did wrong to characterize his argument as one that appeals to the general benefit, because it appeals instead to competing rights, namely the moral right of the majority to have its laws enforced, or the right of society to maintain the degree of order and security it wishes. These are the rights, he would say, that must be weighed against the individual's right to do what the wrongful law prohibits.

But this new argument is confused, because it depends on yet another ambiguity in the language of rights. It is true that we speak of the 'right' of society to do what it wants, but this cannot be a 'competing right' of the sort that may justify the invasion of a right against the Government. The existence of rights against the Government would be jeopardized if the Government were able to defeat such a right by appealing to the right of a democratic majority to work its will. A right against the Government must be a right to do something even when the majority thinks it would be wrong to do it, and even when the majority would be worse off for having it done. If we now say that society has a right to do whatever is in the general benefit, or the right to preserve whatever sort of environment the majority wishes to live in, and we mean that these are the sort of rights that provide justification for overruling any rights against the Government that may conflict, then we have annihilated the latter rights.

In order to save them, we must recognize as competing rights only the rights of other members of the society as individuals. We must distinguish the 'rights' of the majority as such, which cannot count as a justification for overruling individual rights, and the personal rights of members of a majority, which might well count. The test we must use is this. Someone has a competing right to protection, which must be weighed against an individual right to act, if that person would be entitled to demand that protection from his government on his own title, as an individual, without regard to whether a majority of his fellow citizens joined in the demand.

It cannot be true, on this test, that anyone has a right to have all the laws of the nation enforced. He has a right to have enforced only those criminal laws, for example, that he would have a right to have enacted if they were not already law. The laws against personal assault may well fall into that class. If the physically vulnerable members of the community—those who need police protection against personal violence—were only a small minority, it would still seem plausible to say that they were entitled to that protection. But the laws that provide a certain level of quiet in public places, or that authorize and finance a foreign war, cannot be thought to rest on individual rights. The timid lady on the streets of Chicago is not entitled to just the degree of quiet that now obtains, nor is she entitled to have boys drafted to fight in wars she approves. There are laws—perhaps desirable laws—that provide these advantages for her, but the justification for these laws, if they can be justified at all, is the common desire of a large majority, not her personal right. If, therefore, these laws do abridge someone else's moral right to protest, or his right to personal security, she cannot urge a competing right to justify the abridgement. She has no personal right to have such laws passed, and she has no competing right to have them enforced either.

So the conservative cannot advance his argument much on the ground of competing rights, but he may want to use another ground. A government, he may argue, may be justified in abridging the personal rights of its citizens in an emergency, or when a very great loss may be prevented, or, perhaps, when some major benefit can clearly be secured. If the nation is at war, a policy of censorship may be justified even though it invades the right to say what one thinks on matters of political controversy. But the emergency must be genuine. There must be what Oliver Wendell Holmes described as a clear and present danger, and the danger must be one of magnitude.

Can the conservative argue that when any law is passed, even a wrongful law, this sort of justification is available for enforcing it? His argument might be something of this sort. If the Government once acknowledges that it may be wrong—that the legislature might have adopted, the executive approved, and the courts left standing, a law that in fact abridges important rights—then this admission will lead not simply to a marginal decline in respect for law, but to a crisis of order. Citizens may decide to obey only those laws they personally approve, and that is anarchy. So the Government must insist that whatever a citizen's rights may be before a law is passed and upheld by the courts, his rights thereafter are determined by that law.

But this argument ignores the primitive distinction between what may happen and what will happen. If we allow speculation to support the justification of emergency or decisive benefit, then, again, we have annihilated rights. We must, as Learned Hand said, discount the gravity of the evil threatened by the likelihood of reaching that evil. I know of no genuine evidence to the effect that tolerating some civil disobedience, out of respect for the moral position of its authors, will increase such disobedience, let alone crime in general. The case that it will must be based on vague assumptions about the contagion of ordinary crimes, assumptions that are themselves unproved, and that are in any event largely irrelevant. It seems at least as plausible to argue that tolerance will increase respect for officials and for the bulk of the laws they promulgate, or at least retard the rate of growing disrespect.

If the issue were simply the question whether the community would be marginally better off under strict law enforcement, then the Government would have to decide on the evidence we have, and it might not be unreasonable to decide, on balance, that it would. But since rights are at stake, the issue is the very different one of whether tolerance would destroy the community or threaten it with great harm, and it seems to me simply mindless to suppose that the evidence makes that probable or even conceivable.

The argument from emergency is confused in another way as well. It assumes that the Government must take the position either that a man never has the right to break the law, or that he always does. I said that any society that claims to recognize rights at all must abandon the notion of a general duty to obey the law that holds in all cases. This is important, because it shows that there are no short cuts to meeting a citizen's claim of right. If a citizen argues that he has a moral right not to serve in the Army, or to protest in a way he finds effective, then an official who wants to answer him, and not simply bludgeon him into obedience, must respond to the particular point he makes, and cannot point to the draft law or a Supreme Court decision as having even special, let alone decisive, weight. Sometimes an official who considers the citizen's moral arguments in good faith will be persuaded that the citizen's claim is plausible, or even right. It does not follow, however, that he will always be persuaded or that he always should be.

I must emphasize that all these propositions concern the strong sense of right, and they therefore leave open important questions about the right thing to do. If a man believes he has the right to break the law, he must then ask whether he does the right thing to exercise that right. He must remember that reasonable men can differ about whether he has a right against the Government, and therefore the right to break the law, that he thinks he has; and therefore that reasonable men can oppose him in good faith. He must take into account the various consequences his acts will have, whether they involve violence, and such other considerations as the context makes relevant; he must not go beyond the rights he can in good faith claim, to acts that violate the rights of others.

On the other hand, if some official, like a prosecutor, believes that the citizen does *not* have the right to break the law, then *he* must ask whether he does the right thing to enforce it. In the article I mentioned earlier I argued that certain features of our legal system, and in particular the fusion of legal and moral issues in our Constitution, mean that citizens often do the right thing in exercising what they take to be moral rights to break the law, and that prosecutors often do the right thing in failing to prosecute them for it. I will not repeat those arguments here; instead I want to ask whether the requirement that Government take its citizens' rights seriously has anything to do with the crucial question of what these rights are.

III. CONTROVERSIAL RIGHTS

The argument so far has been hypothetical: if a man has a particular moral right against the Government, that right survives contrary legislation or adjudication. But this does not tell us what rights he has, and it is notorious that reasonable men disagree about that. There is wide agreement on certain clear-cut cases; almost everyone who believes in rights at all would admit, for example, that a man has a moral right to speak his mind in a non-provocative way on matters of political concern, and that this is an important right that the State must go to great pains to protect. But there is great controversy as to the limits of such paradigm rights, and the so-called 'anti-riot' law involved in the Chicago Seven trial is a case in point.

The defendants were accused of conspiring to cross state lines with the intention of causing a riot. This charge is vague—perhaps unconstitutionally vague—but the law apparently defines as criminal emotional speeches which argue that violence is justified in order to secure political equality. Does the right of free speech protect this sort of speech? That, of course, is a legal issue, because it invokes the free-speech clause of the First Amendment of the Constitution. But it is also a moral issue, because, as I said, we must treat the First Amendment as an attempt to protect a moral right. It is part of the job of governing to 'define' moral rights through statutes and judicial decisions, that is, to declare officially the extent that moral rights will be taken to have in law. Congress faced this task in voting on the anti-riot bill, and the Supreme Court will face it if the Chicago Seven case goes that far. How should the different departments of government go about defining moral rights?

They should begin with a sense that whatever they decide might be wrong. History and their descendants may judge that they acted unjustly when they thought they were right. If they take their duty seriously, they must try to limit their mistakes, and they must therefore try to discover where the dangers of mistake lie.

They might choose one of two very different models for this purpose. The first model recommends striking a balance between the rights of the individual and the demands of society at large. If the Government *infringes* on a moral right (for example, by defining the right of free speech more narrowly than justice requires), then it has done the individual a wrong. On the other hand, if the Government *inflates* a right (by defining it more broadly than justice requires) then it cheats society of some general benefit, like safe streets, that it is perfectly entitled to have. So a mistake on one side is as serious as a mistake on the other. The course of government is to steer to the middle, to balance the general good and personal rights, giving to each its due.

When the Government, or any of its branches, defines a right, it must bear in mind, according to the first model, the social cost of different proposals and make the necessary adjustments. It must not grant the same freedom to noisy demonstrations as it grants to calm political discussion, for example, because the former causes much more trouble than the latter. Once it decides how much of a right to recognize, it must enforce its decision to the full. That means permitting an individual to act within his rights, as the Government has defined them, but not beyond, so that if anyone breaks the law, even on grounds of conscience, he must be punished. No doubt any government will make mistakes, and will regret decisions once taken. That is inevitable. But this middle policy will ensure that errors on one side will balance out errors on the other over the long run.

The first model, described in this way, has great plausibility, and most laymen and lawyers, I think, would respond to it warmly. The metaphor of balancing the public interest against personal claims is established in our political and judicial rhetoric, and this metaphor gives the model both familiarity and appeal. Nevertheless, the first model is a false one, certainly in the case of rights generally regarded as important, and the metaphor is the heart of its error.

The institution of rights against the Government is not a gift of God, or an ancient ritual, or a national sport. It is a complex and troublesome practice that makes the Government's job of securing the general benefit more difficult and more expensive, and it would be a frivolous and wrongful practice unless it served some point. Anyone who professes to take rights seriously, and who praises our Government for respecting them, must have some sense of what that point is. He must accept, at the minimum, one or both of two important ideas. The first is the vague but powerful idea of human dignity. This idea, associated with Kant, but defended by philosophers of different schools, supposes that there are ways of treating a man that are inconsistent with recognizing him as a full member of the human community, and holds that such treatment is profoundly unjust.

The second is the more familiar idea of political equality. This supposes that the weaker members of a political community are entitled to the same concern and respect of their government as the more powerful members have secured for themselves, so that if some men have freedom of decision whatever the effect on the general good, then all men must have the same freedom. I do not want to defend or elaborate these ideas here, but only to insist that anyone who claims that citizens have rights must accept ideas very close to these.[4]

It makes sense to say that a man has a fundamental right against the Government, in the strong sense, like free speech, if that right is necessary to protect his dignity, or his standing as equally entitled to concern and respect, or some other personal value of like consequence. It does not make sense otherwise.

So if rights make sense at all, then the invasion of a relatively important right must be a very serious matter. It means treating a man as less than a man, or as less worthy of concern than other men. The institution of rights rests on the conviction that this is a grave injustice, and that it is worth paying the incremental cost in social policy or efficiency that is necessary to prevent it. But then it must be wrong to say that inflating rights is as serious as invading them. If the Government errs on the side of the individual, then it simply pays a little more in social efficiency than it has to pay; it pays a little more, that is, of the same coin that it has already decided must be spent. But if it errs against the individual it inflicts an insult upon him that, on its own reckoning, it is worth a great deal of that coin to avoid.

[4] He need not consider these ideas to be axiomatic. He may, that is, have reasons for insisting that dignity or equality are important values, and these reasons may be utilitarian. He may believe, for example, that the general good will be advanced, *in the long run*, only if we treat indignity or inequality as very great injustices, and never allow our *opinions* about the general good to justify them. I do not know of any good arguments for or against this sort of 'institutional' utilitarianism, but it is consistent with my point, because it argues that we must treat violations of dignity and equality as special moral crimes, beyond the reach of ordinary utilitarian justification.

So the first model is indefensible. It rests, in fact, on a mistake I discussed earlier, namely the confusion of society's rights with the rights of members of society. 'Balancing' is appropriate when the Government must choose between competing claims of right—between the Southerner's claim to freedom of association, for example, and the black man's claim to an equal education. Then the Government can do nothing but estimate the merits of the competing claims, and act on its estimate. The first model assumes that the 'right' of the majority is a competing right that must be balanced in this way; but that, as I argued before, is a confusion that threatens to destroy the concept of individual rights. It is worth noticing that the community rejects the first model in that area where the stakes for the individual are highest, the criminal process. We say that it is better that a great many guilty men go free than that one innocent man be punished, and that homily rests on the choice of the second model for government.

The second model treats abridging a right as much more serious than inflating one, and its recommendations follow from that judgment. It stipulates that once a right is recognized in clear-cut cases, then the Government should act to cut off that right only when some compelling reason is presented, some reason that is consistent with the suppositions on which the original right must be based. It cannot be an argument for curtailing a right, once granted, simply that society would pay a further price in extending it. There must be something special about that further cost, or there must be some other feature of the case, that makes it sensible to say that although great social cost is warranted to protect the original right, this particular cost is not necessary. Otherwise, the Government's failure to extend the right will show that its recognition of the right in the original case is a sham, a promise that it intends to keep only until that becomes inconvenient.

How can we show that a particular cost is not worth paying without taking back the initial recognition of a right? I can think of only three sorts of grounds that can consistently be used to limit the definition of a particular right. First, the Government might show that the values protected by the original right are not really at stake in the marginal case, or are at stake only in some attenuated form. Second, it might show that if the right is defined to include the marginal case, then some competing right, in the strong sense I described earlier, would be abridged. Third, it might show that if the right were so defined, then the cost to society would not be simply incremental, but would be of a degree far beyond the cost paid to grant the original right, a degree great enough to justify whatever assault on dignity or equality might be involved.

It is fairly easy to apply these grounds to one problem the Supreme Court has recently faced, and must face soon again. The draft law provides an exemption for conscientious objectors, but this exemption, as interpreted by the draft boards, has been limited to those who object to *all* wars on *religious* grounds. If we suppose that the exemption is justified on the ground that an individual has a moral right not to kill in violation of his own principles, then the question is raised whether it is proper to exclude those whose morality is not based on religion, or whose morality is sufficiently complex to distinguish among wars. The Court has just held that the draft boards are wrong to exclude the former, and it will soon be asked to decide whether they are wrong to exclude the latter as well.

None of the three grounds I listed can justify either of these exclusions. The invasion of personality in forcing men to kill when they believe killing immoral is just as great when these beliefs are based on secular grounds, or take account of the fact that wars differ in morally relevant ways, and there is no pertinent difference in competing rights or in national emergency. There are differences among the cases, of course, but they are insufficient to justify the distinction. A government that is secular on principle cannot prefer a religious to a non-religious morality as such. There are utilitarian arguments in favour of limiting the exception to religious or universal grounds—an exemption so limited may be less expensive to administer, and may allow easier discrimination between sincere and insincere applicants. But these utilitarian reasons are irrelevant, because they cannot count as grounds for limiting a right.

What about the anti-riot law, as applied in the Chicago trial? Does that law represent an improper limitation of the right to free speech, supposedly protected by the First Amendment? If we were to apply the first model for government to this issue, the argument for the anti-riot law would look strong. But if we set aside talk of balancing as inappropriate, and turn to the proper grounds for limiting a right, then the argument becomes a great deal weaker. The original right of free speech must suppose that it is an assault on human personality to stop a man from expressing what he honestly believes, particularly on issues affecting how he is governed. Surely the assault is greater, and not less, when he is stopped from expressing those principles of political morality that he holds most passionately, in the face of what he takes to be outrageous violations of these principles.

It may be said that the anti-riot law leaves him free to express these principles in a non-provocative way. But that misses the point of the connection between expression and dignity. A man cannot express himself freely when he cannot match his rhetoric to his outrage, or when he must trim his sails to protect values he counts as nothing next to those he is trying to vindicate. It is true that some political dissenters speak in ways that shock the majority, but it is arrogant for the majority to suppose that the orthodox methods of expression are the proper ways to speak, for this is a denial of equal concern and respect. If the point of the right is to protect the dignity of dissenters, then we must make judgments about appropriate speech with the personalities of the dissenters in mind, not the personality of the 'silent' majority for whom the anti-riot law is no restraint at all.

So the argument fails, that the personal values protected by the original right are less at stake in this marginal case. We must consider whether competing rights, or some grave threat to society, nevertheless justify the anti-riot law. We can consider these two grounds together, because the only plausible competing rights are rights to be free from violence, and violence is the only plausible threat to society that the context provides.

I have no right to burn your house, or stone you or your car, or swing a bicycle chain against your skull, even if I find these to be natural means of expression. But the defendants in the Chicago trial were not accused of direct violence; the argument runs that the acts of speech they planned made it likely that others would do acts of violence, either in support of or out of hostility to what they said. Does this provide a justification?

The question would be different if we could say with any confidence how much and what sort of violence the anti-riot law might be expected to prevent. Will it save two lives a year, or two hundred, or two thousand? Two thousand dollars of property, or two hundred thousand, or two million? No one can say, not simply because prediction is next to impossible, but because we have no firm understanding of the process by which demonstration disintegrates into riot, and in particular of the part played by inflammatory speech, as distinct from poverty, police brutality, blood lust, and all the rest of human and economic failure. The Government must try, of course, to reduce the violent waste of lives and property, but it must recognize that any attempt to locate and remove a cause of riot, short of a reorganization of society, must be an exercise in speculation, trial, and error. It must make its decisions under conditions of high uncertainty, and the institution of rights, taken seriously, limits its freedom to experiment under such conditions.

It forces the Government to bear in mind that preventing a man from speaking or demonstrating offers him a certain and profound insult, in return for a speculative benefit that may in any event be achieved in other if more expensive ways. When lawyers say that rights may be limited to protect other rights, or to prevent catastrophe, they have in mind cases in which cause and effect are relatively clear, like the familiar example of a man falsely crying 'Fire!' in a crowded theatre.

But the Chicago story shows how obscure the causal connections can become. Were the speeches of Hoffman or Rubin necessary conditions of the riot? Or had thousands of people come to Chicago for the purposes of rioting anyway, as the Government also argues? Were they in any case sufficient conditions? Or could the police have contained the violence if they had not been so busy contributing to it, as the staff of the President's Commission on Violence said they were?

These are not easy questions, but if rights mean anything, then the Government cannot simply assume answers that justify its conduct. If a man has a right to speak, if the reasons that support that right extend to provocative political speech, and if the effects of such speech on violence are unclear, then the Government is not entitled to make its first attack on that problem by denying that right. It may be that abridging the right to speak is the least expensive course, or the least damaging to police morale, or the most popular politically. But these are utilitarian arguments in favour of starting one place rather than another, and such arguments are ruled out by the concept of rights.

This point may be obscured by the popular belief that political activists look forward to violence and 'ask for trouble' in what they say. They can hardly complain, in the general view, if they are taken to be the authors of the violence they expect, and treated accordingly. But this repeats the confusion I tried to explain earlier between having a right and doing the right thing. The speaker's motives may be relevant in deciding whether he does the right thing in speaking passionately about issues that may inflame or enrage the audience. But if he has a right to speak, because the danger in allowing him to speak is speculative, his motives cannot count as independent evidence in the argument that justifies stopping him.

But what of the individual rights of those who will be destroyed by a riot, of the passer-by who will be killed by a sniper's bullet or the shopkeeper who will be ruined by looting? To put the issue in this way, as a question of competing rights, suggests a principle that would undercut the effect of uncertainty. Shall we say that some rights to protection are so important that the Government is justified in doing all it can to maintain them? Shall we therefore say that the Government may abridge the rights of others to act when their acts might simply increase the risk, by however slight or speculative a margin, that some person's right to life or property will be violated?

Some such principle is relied on by those who oppose the Supreme Court's recent liberal rulings on police procedure. These rulings increase the chance that a guilty man will go free, and therefore marginally increase the risk that any particular member of the community will be murdered, raped, or robbed. Some critics believe that the Court's decisions must therefore be wrong.

But no society that purports to recognize a variety of rights, on the ground that a man's dignity or equality may be invaded in a variety of ways, can accept such a principle. If forcing a man to testify against himself, or forbidding him to speak, does the damage that the rights against self-incrimination and the right of free speech assume, then it would be contemptuous for the State to tell a man that he must suffer this damage against the possibility that other men's risk of loss may be marginally reduced. If rights make sense, then the degrees of their importance cannot be so different that some count not at all when others are mentioned.

Of course the Government may discriminate and may stop a man from exercising his right to speak when there is a clear and substantial risk that his speech will do great damage to the person or property of others, and no other means of preventing this are at hand, as in the case of the man shouting 'Fire!' in a theatre. But we must reject the suggested principle that the Government can simply ignore rights to speak when life and property are in question. So long as the impact of speech on these other rights remains speculative and marginal, it must look elsewhere for levers to pull.

IV. WHY TAKE RIGHTS SERIOUSLY?

I said at the beginning of this essay that I wanted to show what a government must do that professes to recognize individual rights. It must dispense with the claim that citizens never have a right to break its law, and it must not define citizens' rights so that these are cut off for supposed reasons of the general good. The present Government's policy towards civil disobedience, and its campaign against vocal protest, may therefore be thought to count against its sincerity.

One might well ask, however, whether it is wise to take rights all that seriously after all. America's genius, at least in her own legend, lies in not taking any abstract doctrine to its logical extreme. It may be time to ignore abstractions, and concentrate instead on giving the majority of our citizens a new sense of their Government's concern for their welfare, and of their title to rule.

That, in any event, is what Vice-President Agnew seems to believe. In a recent policy statement on the issue of 'weirdos' and social misfits, he said that the liberals' concern for individual rights was a headwind blowing in the face of the ship of state. That is a poor metaphor, but the philosophical point it expresses is very well taken. He recognizes, as many liberals do not, that the majority cannot travel as fast or as far as it would like if it recognizes the rights of individuals to do what, in the majority's terms, is the wrong thing to do.

The Vice-President supposes that rights are divisive, and that national unity and a new respect for law may be developed by taking them more sceptically. But he is wrong. America will continue to be divided by its social and foreign policy, and if the economy grows weaker the divisions will become more bitter. If we want our laws and our legal institutions to provide the ground rules within which these issues will be contested, then these ground rules must not be the conqueror's law that the dominant class imposes on the weaker, as Marx supposed the law of a capitalist society must be. The bulk of the law—that part which defines and implements social, economic, and foreign policy—cannot be neutral. It must state, in its greatest part, the majority's view of the common good. The institution of rights is therefore crucial, because it represents the majority's promise to the minorities that their dignity and equality will be respected. When the divisions among the groups are most violent, then this gesture, if law is to work, must be most sincere.

The institution requires an act of faith on the part of the minorities, because the scope of their rights will be controversial whenever they are important, and because the officers of the majority will act on their own notions of what these rights really are. Of course these officials will disagree with many of the claims that a minority makes. That makes it all the more important that they take their decisions gravely. They must show that they understand what rights are, and they must not cheat on the full implications of the doctrine. The Government will not re-establish respect for law without giving the law some claim to respect. It cannot do that if it neglects the one feature that distinguishes law from ordered brutality. If the Government does not take rights seriously, then it does not take law seriously either.

11

Rights in Legislation

D. N. MACCORMICK*

THERE must be many for whom the beginnings of wisdom in the understanding and analysis of legal systems and legal concepts have been found in the lectures and the writings of H. L. A. Hart. Being one of whom that is true, I take particular pleasure in joining in the tributes to him in this *Festschrift* by presenting an essay on the subject of 'Rights', upon which subject he has had so many illuminating things to say during his career.[1] While I shall here advance a thesis which is fundamentally at variance with Hart's own account of rights, I cannot claim to be doing more than applying techniques learned from Hart in criticizing and (I hope) transcending that account of his.

I

The first point to be made about legal rights must seem, when made, to be of breath-taking banality. The point is that legal rights are conferred by legal rules, or (if you will) by laws.[2] What could be more obvious? Obvious as it may be, the point is one which has not been given sufficient weight in much of what has been written by legal theorists. The point being made that legal rights are conferred by legal rules, it should at once lead any jurist of the school of Hart to ask the question: 'What are the general characteristics of those legal rules which confer rights upon individuals—as distinct from imposing duties, granting powers, or whatever?' (In *The Concept of Law*, for example, Hart quite rightly contends that to expound the meaning of

* Regius Professor of Public Law, University of Edinburgh.

[1] Hart's most interesting contributions on this subject in my opinion are: 'Definition and Theory in Jurisprudence', 70 *Law Quarterly Review* 37 (1954) at 47 f.; 'Bentham', *Proceedings of the British Academy* 48 (1962), 297; 'Are There Any Natural Rights', reprinted in *Political Philosophy*, ed. A. M. Quinton (Oxford, 1968); 'Bentham on Legal Rights' (herinafter cited as 'B.L.R.') in *Oxford Essays in Jurisprudence*, 2nd series, ed. A. W. B. Simpson (Oxford, 1973).

[2] Cf. J. Raz, *The Concept of a Legal System* (Oxford, 1970), pp. 175–83.

terms such as 'duty' and 'obligation' one must first show that any particular obligation or duty arises in virtue of some legal rule, and one must then complete one's exposition by elucidating the general characteristics of those rules which impose duties or obligations.)[3]

That question which ought to be asked has not been asked and answered with clarity, partly indeed because of a false trail laid by the master himself in 'Definition and Theory in Jurisprudence', in which he based a famous account of the meaning and use of the term 'right' upon the supposition that the term was standardly used in sentences such as '*x* has a legal right to . . .' which, as he put it, express 'conclusions of law'. The meaning of the phrase was thus best elucidated by explaining the conditions in which the statement '*x* has a legal right' can be appropriately used as expressing a *true* conclusion of law. Such conditions are presupposed by, though not expressed in, the statement itself.[4]

All that depended upon a view which Hart used to state in his (unpublished) lectures on 'Legal Rights and Duties', delivered in Oxford in the early 1960s, the view that 'right' is a term used in discourse *about* the law, used for making statements *about* individual's positions as seen in terms of the law, rather than a term used *in* the law itself. 'Right' in this view is a term or concept used by the jurist or the commentator upon the law, used discursively, but not used dispositively in the law. The derivation from that view of the theory that 'expressing conclusions of law' is the *standard* use of the term is obvious enough.

At a quite simple empirical level, these assumptions underlying the early Hartian analysis can be falsified completely. The term 'right' and its congeners is in fact used regularly and frequently in dispositive legal utterances and documents. Consider for example section 2(1) of the Succession (Scotland) Act 1964:

Subject to the following provisions of this Part of this Act—
(a) where an intestate is survived by children, they shall have right to the whole of the intestate estate.
(b) . . .

Of that Act, indeed, the first eight sections alone, comprising Part I of the Act, use the word 'right' twenty-four times, a tally which would be greatly swollen were one to incur the labour of counting its appearances throughout the whole Act. And if it were desired to

[3] H. L. A. Hart, *The Concept of Law* (Oxford, 1961), esp. at pp. 82–6.
[4] 'Definition and Theory in Jurisprudence', pp. 49 f.

demonstrate that this is by no means an entirely Caledonian eccentricity of the Scottish draftsman, one might cite a plethora of examples from the English property legislation of 1925, such as section 96(1) of the Law of Property Act 1925 which indeed piles entitlement *expressis verbis* on top of no less explicit 'right'.

A mortgagor, so long as his right to redeem subsists, shall be entitled from time to time, at reasonable times, on his request, and at his own cost, and on payment of the mortgagee's costs and expenses in this behalf, to inspect and make copies or abstracts of or extracts from the documents of title relating to the mortgaged property in the custody or power of the mortgagee . . .

There is no need for further multiplication of examples such as these; they show conclusively that the language of 'rights' and of being 'entitled' is as well adapted to stating general premisses of law (and indeed to establishing them by legislation) as it is to expressing particular conclusions of law. In fact to establish the conclusion that *A* (a Scotsman) has the right to a certain 'intestate estate' or that *B* (an Englishman) is entitled to make copies of certain documents of title held by a Building Society as mortgagee, one would have to refer to the rules of law in s.2(1) of the Succession (Scotland) Act and s.96(1) of the Law of Property Act. If the 'investitive facts' as set out in these and related provisions are satisfied in *A*'s or in *B*'s case, then each has indeed the right in question. But the premisses from which the conclusions as to individual rights follow are rules which expressly purport to confer the postulated right on persons in general whenever the relevant investitive facts are realized. An inquiry into the nature of rights must therefore be an inquiry into the nature and character of the legal rules which concern the conferment of legal rights.

One characteristic which it would be a mistake to postulate as a necessary distinguishing feature of rules which confer rights would be that of expressly using the term 'right'. Consider section 46(ii) of the Administration of Estates Act 1925, which is in the following terms:

The residuary estate of an intestate shall be distributed in the manner or be held on the trusts mentioned in this section, namely:

. . . .

(ii) If the intestate leaves issue but no husband or wife, the residuary estate of the intestate shall be held on the statutory trusts for the issue of the intestate.

The effect of that provision is very broadly similar to the effect of section 2(1)(a) of the Succession (Scotland) Act quoted above. But in this case the statute confers a right without saying so *expressis verbis*. While it is wrong to suppose that legislative provisions never speak of 'rights', it would be equally wrong to suppose that they always do whenever rights are being conferred.

II

Legal theorists have traditionally divided into two camps on the issue of the proper explanation of rights.[5] One line of thought, which may be called the 'will theory', asserts that an individual's having a right of some kind depends upon the legal (or, *mutatis mutandis*, moral) recognition of his will, his choice, as being preeminent over that of others in relation to a given subject matter and within a given relationship. The 'interest theory', by contrast, contends that what is essential to the constitution of a right is the legal (or moral) protection or promotion of one person's interests as against some other person or the world at large, by the imposition on the latter of duties, disabilities, or liabilities in respect of the party favoured. It is against the background of this clash of theories that we must pursue the question announced as to the general characteristics of those rules which confer legal rights. Are these to be conceived primarily in terms of giving a special status to the choice of one individual over others in relation to a given subject matter, or primarily in terms of the protection of the interests of individuals against possible forms of intrusion (or the advancement in other ways of individuals' interests)?

The answer which I shall offer to that question will be that the 'interest theory' is the more acceptable, though not to be accepted without modification. The essential feature of rules which confer rights is that they have as a specific aim the protection or advancement of individual interests or goods. The reasons for holding that view, and the necessary refinements of the view itself, can best be set out by showing the defects of the rival view, and so I shall proceed to expound, and criticize, what seems to me the strongest version of the

[5] For a review of opposed theories see, e.g., G. W. Paton, *A Text-Book of Jurisprudence*, 4th edn. (Oxford, 1972, ed. G. W. Paton and D. P. Derham), at pp. 285–90. Cf. also W. J. Kamba, 'Legal Theory and Hohfeld's Analysis of a Legal Right', [1974] *Juridical Review* 249–62.

In 'B.L.R.' Hart expounds Bentham's theory as an instance of 'interest theory' or (*per* Hart) 'benefit theory'; and he asserts the preferability of his own version of 'will theory' or, as he prefers to call it, 'choice theory'.

'will theory', that advanced by Professor Hart[6] (appropriately enough to the present occasion).

(i) One class of rights is the class of rights which have correlative duties. Duties exist when there exist legal or social rules of a particular kind, in virtue of which individuals in certain circumstances are required to act or abstain from acting in certain ways. For any individual whose circumstances are an instance of those specified in the rule, it is true to say that he has a duty to act or abstain from acting as specified.

Of those rules which impose duties, some provide that the performance of the duty-act is to be conditional upon some other person's choice, either in the sense that it is to be performed only if and when he so requests, or in the sense that the other person can waive the requirement, and, if he does, the act (or abstention) need not be performed. When *A*'s duty is in either sense made conditional upon *B*'s choice, *B* may properly be said to have a right against *A*, a right that *A* act or abstain in the manner laid down in the rule. So also, when it is the case that in the event of *A*'s breach of duty *B* has the power to take appropriate remedial action at law, at least if *B* has a discretion as to the use or non-use of that power.

Thus, for this class of right (sometimes called 'claim rights'[7] or 'rights of recipience'[8]) the 'will theory' asserts that what is constitutive of rights is the way in which the law confers on certain individuals or classes of individuals power to waive or enforce the duties of other individuals, or other classes of individuals.

(ii) There are other classes of rights, for example liberty rights and power rights, in case of which the right-holder is, so to say, the active rather than the passive subject of the law. In so far as the law imposes no duty on me not to do so, I have a right to speak my mind (and you have no right that I should hold my tongue) – and that is a 'liberty right', a right constituted by freedom from legal duty to act or abstain in some specified way. What is more, it is sometimes the case that my acting in a certain way is not merely not impeded by the law, but is indeed recognized by law as achieving a certain change in the legal position of myself, or others, or both; for example, when an utterance of mine (intended as such) is recognized as a declaration of

[6] Variously in the works cited in n.1 above.

[7] Cf. W. N. Hohfeld, *Fundamental Legal Conceptions* (New Haven, 1919; 3rd reprint, 1964); for variants of nomenclature, see W. J. Kamba, op. cit.

[8] The term favoured by D. D. Raphael, in *Problems of Political Philosophy* (London, 1970), pp. 68–71.

trust in favour of some other person over certain property. Such is a case of 'power right'.

In both these cases, yet more obviously than in the case of 'claim right' it is the law's recognition of the freedom or the legal efficacity of the choices of individuals which is central to the notion of 'a right'.

(iii) A further class of 'right', the so-called 'immunity right' presents on the face of it more difficulty for the will theory. This is the right which corresponds to lack of power in others. It may be the case not only that I have a (liberty) right to enter my place of work and to do my job, and a (claim) right to be paid for it, but also that I have a right not to be dismissed save on certain specified grounds proven by certain stipulated processes, and that because my employer cannot *validly* dismiss me from my job, because he has a disability to sack me. And so by way of general characterization of immunity rights we may say that whenever *A*'s legal position is in certain respects protected from change by any act of *B*, in the sense that *B* lacks power to change it, *A* has an immunity (as against *B*) from having his legal position changed in that respect.

Professor Hart admits to a certain difficulty in accommodating 'immunity rights' within his over-all theory.[9] But he suggests that the characteristic manifestation of immunity rights within the law is their manifestation in constitutionally entrenched 'Bills of Rights' which protect various claims and freedoms against derogation or abrogation even by acts of legislation. He therefore regards these as being beyond the ordinary interests of the lawyer and belonging more to the province of the political or moral theorist. While some theory of rights other than that given by will theorists might be necessary to account for such entrenched immunities, the fact (it is alleged) remains that the specific terminology of 'rights' is of peculiar utility to lawyers only when restricted to those instances of 'small-scale sovereignty' which the will theory takes to be constitutive of the notion of 'a right'—and to be the unifying thread among various types of right.

(iv) Subject to that qualification, it is asserted that what gives the concept 'right' its particular function and utility in legal language is that it draws attention to those relationships in which rules of law confer on one individual special recognition of his will or choice as

[9] See 'B.L.R.', pp. 198-200.

predominating over that of others in the relationship. Such are the outlines of the theory which in the succeeding sections of the present essay I intend to refute.

III

There is something, on the face of it, odd about Hart's concession that immunities cannot be properly taken into account within the four corners of the 'will theory' as propounded by himself. For it is often the case that *A*'s immunity is waivable by *A*'s choice. If *A* owns a car, *B* cannot divest him of ownership by any unilateral act (if *B* is another private citizen); in other words, *A*'s rights over the car are in this respect protected by (or do they simply include?) an immunity against *B*. But, of course, *A*'s immunity from being divested of ownership in favour of *B* is not absolute, but conditional on his own choice to transfer or not transfer the property — otherwise sale, exchange, and gift would be impossible.

That being so, it follows that there is a class of immunities which could comfortably be brought within the Hartian version of the will theory, namely, the whole class of those immunities in relation to which the immunity-holder has a power of waiver. Looked at from the other party's point of view, from the point of view of the party *B* who is under a disability to alter *A*'s legal position in some respect, such a disability may be absolute (*B* cannot enslave *A*, even if *A* should consent to be enslaved); or it may be conditional upon *A*'s will; *A* has a right not to be assaulted by *B*, and *B* can't take that away from *A*, unless *A* agrees — for example, in a boxing match.

In the light of those facts, the reasonable extrapolation to make from Hart's thesis in relation to claims, liberties, and powers would be along the lines of including within the genus 'rights' only those immunities which lie within the immunity-holder's own power, those which he can waive or assert at will. Such would be 'immunity rights' (a species of the genus 'rights'): unwaivable immunities would belong outside of the genus 'rights'.

But surely the moment we make that extrapolation we hit upon the fundamental implausibility of the 'will theory'. It seems to me unproblematic to say that I have (legally and morally) a right not to be deprived of my personal freedom and a right not to be deprived of my property. The two rights seem to me to be on all fours with each other, at any rate when we are concerned with the propriety of using the noun 'right' in the statement of such propositions of law (or of morals); in my view, which I believe to be widely held, the former right is of greater importance than the latter—I would rather, if it came to the bit, be propertyless than be a slave. The laws of the U.K. certainly place a higher value on the right of freedom than on the right of property in a certain highly important respect: the former is regarded as absolute in the sense that no person can enslave any other, not even a person willing to be enslaved; whereas the latter is conditional upon the property-holder's will—no person can deprive another of his property *without his consent*.

Let us take note of the point. *A*'s right to personal freedom involves *B* in having (a) a duty not to reduce *A* to a servile condition, e.g. by clapping him in irons; and (b) a disability to impose upon *A* the status of a slave; and (c) a disability to change the relation (a) and (b) *even with A's consent*. *A* does not himself have power to waive his immunities in these respects—he too is under disability here, though it may well be said that the disability is to his own advantage in preventing him ever from bartering away his freedom, whatever the temptation. That, indeed, is one of the grounds upon which untutored common sense would found the assertion that the right to personal freedom is yet more securely protected in our law than any right of property.

But there's the rub, there, for the 'will theory', the paradox. For it appears that this legal dispensation, be it ever so advantageous from the point of view of securing liberty, is so forceful as to thrust liberty beyond the realm of 'right' altogether. If there be no power to waive or assert the immunity, the claim, or whatever, upon some matter, upon that matter there is, *by definition*, no right either. In the matter of non-enslavement no person in any contemporary western legal system can *de jure* waive his immunity; the same is true of other interests characteristically protected by Bills of Rights (whence, perhaps, Hart's embarrassment over these in connection with the notion of 'immunity'). Are we really to conclude that here the terminology of 'rights' is inapposite? Really to conclude that the language of the practical lawyer does such violence to common understanding as to extrude such protections of human interests, when arguably at their most efficacious, from the category which it is interesting or useful to describe as 'rights'? The paradox would seem to me altogether too violent; the ascription of concerns to the practical lawyer, unconvincingly ethnocentric.

Admittedly, we are to some extent in the realms of stipulative definition when we enter into contention over the essential characteristics of the concept 'right'. Yet we are entitled to ask somebody who stipulates that there shall be held to be 'rights' only where there are choices, whether that stipulation does not go wholly against common understanding, and whether there is any profit derived from it.

What seems to me strangest is the way in which the will theory seems to cut off the use of 'rights'-language at a predetermined point on the scale of protection which the law may confer upon people's interests. To take a somewhat trivial case: the law relating to assault prohibits any person from offering or inflicting physical interference or harm on another. *A* has a duty not to interfere with *B*. So far as concerns the 'will theory', *B* has a 'right not to be harmed' *only* if and in so far as he, *B*, can in some way regulate *A*'s duty not to interfere with him. That seems all very well: in relation to minor interference, or manly sports, or bona-fide surgical operations, *B* can waive *A*'s duty. So, for the 'will theory', *B* has a right not to be trivially assaulted, or assaulted in the course of manly sports, or assaulted by a surgeon conducting an operation. Yet in relation to serious assaults, or 'unmanly' pastimes (e.g. flagellation by or of a prostitute),[10] or operations by unqualified persons, no valid consent can be given which releases the assaulting party from the duty of non-interference.[11] It is rather bewildering to suppose that none of us has a right not to be thus grievously assaulted, simply because for various reasons of policy the law denies us the power to consent to these graver interferences with our physical security.

Students of Dicey's *Law and Opinion* will recall his ill-disguised disapproval of those collectivist measures which were introduced in the later nineteenth century in order to protect various elements in the poorer sections of the population.[12] The technique which he deplored was as follows: first, the legislature conferred protection on people which they could have conferred on themselves by contract, e.g. in matters of safety at work; secondly, the legislators, discovering that too many of the protected class exercised the power 'voluntarily' to contract out of the protection, removed the matter from the option

[10] See *R.* v. *Donovan* [1934] 2 K.B. 498 for discussion of this instance, and of consent generally.

[11] G. H. Gordon, *Criminal Law* (Edinburgh, 1967), pp. 773–6; J. C. Smith and B. Hogan, *Criminal Law*, 3rd edn. (London, 1973), pp. 287–90.

[12] A. V. Dicey, *Law and Opinion in England during the Nineteenth Century*, 2nd edn. (London, 1924), pp. 260–9.

of the protected party altogether by depriving of legal effect such waivers of the statutory protection. Perhaps such legislation was as disgracefully paternalistic as Dicey so evidently thought it (though it cannot be said that this century has seen any reversal of its increase, far from it) but can it really be said that the second stage of protection is a stage at which a 'right' disappears? At stage one, the employer is obliged to take certain steps to protect his employee's safety, unless his employee 'contracts out' – here, for the 'will theory' is a classic case of 'right'. At stage two, the employer's duty is made unconditional upon the employee's will, and that with a view to protecting better the interests of employees individually and as a class—and now, for the will theory, the 'right' has gone. How odd that, as the protection is strengthened, the right disappears![13]

There is no point in multiplying such examples, of which there is certainly an abundance; the ones here given reinforce the particular case of the legal and moral protections of children which I have discussed in my recent paper on 'Children's Rights'.[14] If I may immodestly quote, and adopt from, that argument, I should like to repeat what I said in relation to what I conceive to be a child's (legal and moral) right to care and nurture:

> We are put . . . to our election. Either we abstain from ascribing to children a right to care and nurture [on the ground that no one has discretion to waive the responsible adult's duty of care and nurture] or we abandon the will theory. For my part I have no inhibitions about abandoning the latter. It causes me no conceptual shock or mental cramp to say that children have that right. What is more, I will aver that it is *because* children have that right that it is good that legal provision should be made in the first instance to encourage and assist parents to fulfil their duty of care and nurture, and secondarily to provide for its performance by alternative foster parents when natural parents are disqualified by death, incapacity, or wilful and persistent neglect. *Ubi ius, ibi remedium.* So far from its being the case that the remedial provision is constitutive of the right, the fact is rather that recognition of the right justifies the imposition of the remedial provision.

We are all accustomed to talking and thinking about some rights

[13] But note that in 'B.L.R.' at p. 192 Hart shows that the 'fullest measure of control' by one person over another's duty need not be present in every case of a right; there are several distinguishable elements in that 'fullest measure' of which powers of waiver or enforcement are only one (remedial powers and powers of waiver of remedial rights being others). But it must be at least embarrassing to him if measures conceived of as strengthening rights standardly involve derogation from the fullest forms of control.

[14] A paper read to the conference of the Association of Legal and Social Philosophy in Cambridge, April 1975, to be published in 1976 *Archiv für Rechts und sozial Philosophie*.

as 'inalienable'. But if the will theory is correct, the more they are inalienable, the less they are rights. So far at least as concerns claim rights and immunities, I find the paradoxes with which the will theory is faced so great that, rather than swallow them, I am driven to seek an alternative. As a first step towards doing so, I should like to probe some of the grounds which have been suggested as foundations for the will theory with a view to showing that they are not as sound as they sound. In doing so I shall resume consideration of the statutory provisions referred to in my opening section.

IV

> The principal advocates of benefit or 'interest' theories of rights correlative to obligations have shown themselves sensitive to the criticism that, if to say that an individual has such a right means no more than that he is the intended beneficiary of a duty, then 'a right' in this sense may be an unnecessary, and perhaps confusing, term in the description of the law; since all that can be said in a terminology of such rights can be and indeed is, best said in the indispensable terminology of duty.[15]

In that statement we find one of the principal grounds of Hart's case in favour of this theory, and against any version of interest theory. By introducing 'the idea . . . of one individual being given by the law exclusive control, more or less extensive, over another person's duty so that in the area of conduct covered by that duty the individual who has the right is a small-scale sovereign to whom the duty is owed', Hart claims to have shown us an idea by reference to which the 'terminology of . . . rights' can be used without redundancy to say things which cannot be said in the 'indispensable terminology of duty' by itself.[16]

This argument of Hart's perhaps has a certain force as against Bentham's account of rights—even in the brilliantly polished version of it expounded by Hart in his essay thereon. To rest an account of claim rights *solely* on the notion that they exist whenever a legal duty is imposed by a law intended to benefit assignable individuals (in which case all the beneficiaries of the law have rights as against all the duty bearers) is to treat rights as being simply the 'reflex' of logically prior duties. Accordingly, for any statement about rights there could always be substituted a statement about duties which would be at a more fundamental level analytically and which yet would say just the same as the 'rights statement'.

[15] 'B.L.R.', p. 190. [16] Ibid.

It is however no part of my intention here to advance a theory according to which even 'claim rights' are conceived as being merely the reflex of duties,[17] as though the latter must always be understood as being in every way prior to rights. Here I return to the importance of my introductory point, that legal rights are conferred by laws, and that scrutiny of those laws which confer rights must therefore be profitable, not to say essential, for understanding rights. In relation to the point in hand, let me refer again to section 2(1) of the Succession (Scotland) Act 1964: '(a) Where an intestate is survived by children, they shall have right to the whole of the intestate estate.'

It is worth taking a few moments (and repeating a point which I have made elsewhere)[18] in explaining the context and effects of that provision. Under it, whenever a person domiciled in Scotland dies intestate leaving children, there automatically vests in those children a right to the whole of that part of his estate statutorily entitled 'the intestate estate' (i.e. the residue after certain statutorily established prior claims have been satisfied). At the moment at which the right vests, it is not a 'real right' involving ownership of the estate or any particular assets included in it. Rather, each child's right is a right to receive in due course an equal share in the assets remaining in the executor's hands after satisfaction of prior claims. So it seems that we have a normal right–duty relationship, which could as well have been stated in the 'indispensable terminology of duty' as in the terminology which commended itself to the draftsman.

The problem, however, is that whereas the right vests at the moment of the intestate's death, there is not at that moment an executor to bear a correlative duty. Vesting of the right is temporally prior to the vesting in any other individual of the correlative duty, which can occur only when an executor has in due course been judicially confirmed or appointed. The executor dative has then the duty to wind up the estate and to transfer appropriate shares in the intestate estate to those having right thereto. What is more, when the question of confirmation of an executor dative is raised before the relevant court, a person who has beneficial rights in the estate is normally *on that ground* to be preferred to other parties, at least if the

[17] To this extent disagreeing with Geoffrey Marshall 'Rights, Options, and Entitlements' (in Simpson, ed., op. cit., pp. 228–41) with which otherwise I substantially agree. Cf. A. M. Honoré, 'Rights of Exclusion and Immunities against Divesting', 34 *Tulane Law Review* 453 (1959–60).

[18] Op. cit. For a general account of the matters sketched here, see M. C. Meston, *The Succession (Scotland) Act 1964*, 2nd edn. (Edinburgh, 1970).

estate appears to be solvent. So one of the intestate's children may, *because of this right conferred on him by the Act*, have a resultant preferential right to be confirmed as executor. His confirmation as such will in turn result in his incurring the duties of executor, including the duty of distributing the intestate estate to those (including himself) who have right thereto under section 2(1)(*a*) of the 1964 Act.

In this case, therefore, it is not only the case that the vesting of a given right is temporally prior to the vesting of the correlative duty, but it is also the case that the vesting of the right in a given individual is a ground for confirming him in that office to which is attached the duty correlative to the like rights of his brothers and sisters; so that in this context right is logically prior to duty as well. Here then we have a concrete instance of a 'right of recipience' which correlates with 'duty' indeed, but in a much more interesting way than as being a mere 'reflex' of a duty which the legislator might have as readily imposed in simpler and more straightforward terms. An 'interest theory' of rights which can take account of such subtleties as this may well avoid the reproach of redundancy, as well as escaping the paradoxes in which (as the last section showed) the will theory is inevitably drawn.

In drafting a law to deal with intestate succession, a legislator might indeed be very likely to regard the crucial and primary question, as being who is to take the benefit of the estate left by the intestate, and to treat as secondary the means (appointment of executors or administrators, and imposition of appropriate duties upon them) of securing that the benefit in view should actually reach the hands of the intended beneficiary. It is the end which makes sense of the means, not vice versa. This is as obvious in relation to section 46 of the (English) Administration of Estates Act 1925, which likewise confers rights of succession on intestacy though without saying so expressly, as in relation to Section 2 of the Succession (Scotland) Act 1964.

In such a case, given that the legal system recognizes and establishes a system of private property, there is necessarily a vacant 'estate' whenever somebody dies possessed of property. The system must make *some* provision as to the destination of that estate. Whoever gets it, to him will be owed all the duties which are owed to property owners, and to him will ensue also the various liberties, powers, and immunities which accrue to property owners, but *that* person gets all that only because—only if—the law has already vested in him the right of ownership of the property in question. And the step before that is the conferment on some generically identified type of person(s) of the right to have ownership of some part of or share of the property comprising the estate invested in him. What is essentially at stake is, who is to get the more or less substantial advantage of inheriting what share of what part of the estate. It is a quite secondary question to settle by what precise means (imposition of duties and disabilities on *whom*?) that advantage shall be secured to him.

It seems obviously—even trivially—true that at least one function, and that a prominent one, of such laws as those concerning succession, is that they are concerned with the conferment and securing of advantages to individuals; or, rather, to members of given classes severally.[19] To explain the idea of 'members of given classes severally': section 2(1)(*a*) of the Succession (Scotland) Act protects and promotes the interests of a certain class, the class of children of a parent who has died intestate but possessed of some property. But the protection is not of the interests of the class indiscriminately, taking them all together as a group—as, perhaps, aircraft-noise-control legislation indiscriminately protects everybody living or working or doing anything else in the near vicinity of airports. The protection, in the succession case, is rather of each and every individual who is within that class each in respect of some separate share of an identified estate.

It is not necessarily the case that each individual acquiring a right under the law should experience it as a benefit, an advantage, an advancement or protection of his interests. Perhaps there are some people who have been more harmed than benefited by an inheritance. Perhaps in some cases property inherited—e.g. slum properties subject to statutory tenancies at controlled rents—are literally more trouble than they are worth, and, besides, something of an embarrassment to their proprietor. None of that is in any way inconsistent with the proposition that the function of the law is to confer what is considered to be normally an advantage on a certain class by granting to each of its members a certain legal right.

The case of the mortgagor's entitlement (under s.96(1) of the Law of Property Act 1925) to inspect and make copies of title-deeds, also quoted as an example in the introductory section of the present paper,

[19] For Hart's account of an essentially similar view of Bentham's see 'B.L.R.', pp. 186–8. For another similar account, see John Austin on 'absolute' and 'relative' duties in the seventeenth chapter of *Lectures in Jurisprudence* (London, 1862).

further indicates the way in which a legislator's concern with protecting what are conceived to be legitimate interests of the members of a given class of individuals leads naturally to the framing of legislation in terms of the rights or entitlements of the given class rather than in terms of the correlative obligations of the mortgagee. In just this sense, what is essential to a clear and comprehensible law relating to mortgages is that the relevant legislation should make clear the respective advantages, protections, and powers accruing to each of the parties to any mortgage. Judicial enforcement of the legislation may then proceed by elucidation and enforcement of duties etc. as necessarily consequential upon conferment of the relevant rights.

By contrast with this branch of the law, the criminal law is no doubt primarily concerned with duties,[20] with laying down in clear and precise terms the prohibitions infraction of which may expose the citizen to prosecution and punishment. This of course follows from a respect for the right of individuals to freedom from interference by the state save for breach of clear rules of the criminal law. Thus, in so far as it is an important function of the criminal law to protect important individual rights—to freedom, to physical and mental security, and so on—it is nevertheless not surprising that the law is not expressly framed in terms of rights, but rather in terms of duties, or through the imposition of duties by the denomination of offences. Even at that, however, there is a large part of the criminal law which deals with crimes against property, and which therefore necessarily presupposes the existence of that elaborate and interlocking set of laws which define and regulate the institution of property and the many and various rights in relation thereto which the law confers. Rights of, and rights in relation to, property—e.g. a mortgagor's right to redeem, a child's right of intestate succession—are on the face of it much too complex to be dissoluble into a set of bare reflexes of correlative duties. But that is not an objection to the thesis that right-conferring laws are best understood in terms of a standard intention to confer some form of benefit or advantage or protection of interests upon the members of a class severally rather than collectively. There may indeed be simple cases in which some general duty—e.g. a duty not to assault—is imposed upon everyone at large with a view to protecting the physical security of each and every person in society, and where the 'right not to be assaulted' is simply the correlative of the duty not to assault; no doubt in such simple

[20] Cf. 'B.L.R.', pp. 191–5.

cases the 'terminology of rights' does not enable us to say very much more than can be said in the terminology of duty. But it may be well adapted even in this simple case to expressing a reason why people aggrieved by breaches of certain duties *should* be empowered to take various measures and actions at law to secure remedies therefor, and why they *should* be permitted, at least when there are no strong countervailing reasons of policy, to waive other people's duties in this respect. If I'm allowed to be the best judge of my own good, and if such laws (being right-conferring) are aimed at securing what's good for me, why should I not be allowed to have a say over their operation when only my own protection is at stake?

What is more, there are other, more complex, cases in which the legislative decision to confer certain benefits on individuals who satisfy certain generic qualifications ('institutive' or 'investitive' facts) is logically prior to the vesting or the enforcement of a correlative duty. Taken as a whole, there is no reason to suppose that an 'interest theory' so defines 'rights' as to make the term redundant.

In another context, I have expressed as follows the conclusion which follows from arguments such as the foregoing:[21]

> To ascribe to all members of a class C a right to treatment T is to presuppose that T is, in all normal circumstances, a good for every member of C, and that T is a good of such importance that it would be wrong to deny it to or withhold it from any member of C. That as for moral rights; as for legal rights, I should say this: when a right to T is conferred by law on all members of C, the law is envisaged as advancing the interests of each and every member of C, and the law has the effect of making it legally wrongful to withhold T from any member of C.

That is certainly not a perfect or watertight formulation, nor am I sure that I can at present make it so. But it does bring out the three features which must be included in any characterization of rules which confer rights.

First, they concern 'goods' (or 'advantages', or 'benefit', or 'interests', or however we may express the point). Whatever *x* may be, the idea of anyone's having a right to *x* would be absurd unless it were presupposed that *x* is normally a good for human beings, at any rate for those people who qualify as having the 'right' in question. That does not mean that in every case the *x* which is subject matter of a right need be beneficial to a particular potential right-holder, or be thought so by him. Some *hereditates* may be *damnosae*, but our

[21] Op. cit.

general view of the law of succession as conceding '*rights*' of succession is founded on the firm supposition that most are not.

Secondly, they concern the enjoyment of goods by individuals separately, not simply as members of a collectivity enjoying a diffuse common benefit in which all participate in indistinguishable and unassignable shares. But since necessarily the qualifications and conditions which must be satisfied for the application of such a rule of law in favour of any given individual have to be expressible and expressed in generic terms, it is therefore correct to say that such rules of law must be concerned with classes of individuals, but the benefit secured is secured to each and every individual severally upon satisfaction of the 'institutive' or 'investitive' conditions.

Thirdly, benefits are secured to individuals in that the law provides normative protection for individuals in their enjoyment of them. No doubt it is too narrow to envisage such protection purely in terms of its being 'legally wrongful to withhold T from any member of C'. 'Normative protection' may be understood as involving any or all of the various modes identified by Hohfeld and others. Thus an individual *A* may in the relevant sense be 'protected' in his enjoyment of *x* if

(a) some or all other people are under a duty not to interfere with him in relation to *x* or his enjoyment of *x*,

or (b) he is himself not under any duty to abstain from enjoyment of, or avoid or desist from *x* (being therefore protected from any complaint as to alleged wrongful use, enjoyment, etc. of *x*),

or (c) some or all other individuals lack legal power to change the legal situation to the prejudice of *A*'s advantage in respect of *x* (the case of disability/immunity),

or (d) *A* himself is in some respect enabled by law to bring about changes in legal relations concerning *x* in pursuit of whatever he conceives to be his advantage.

Not every right entails protection at all these levels or in all these modes simultaneously, though more than one may be and all sometimes are (this being contrary to the Hohfeldian picture of rights as atomic relations between paired individuals). Consider section 5(1) of the Trade Union and Labour Relations Act 1974: '. . . [E]very worker shall have the right not to be (a) excluded from membership (b) expelled from membership, of a trade union . . . by way of arbitrary or unreasonable discrimination.' That confers protection of at least the first three kinds; it being presumed that membership of a union is beneficial to any worker in normal circumstances (a) people at large are put under a duty not to injure any worker by getting him excluded or expelled from a trade union, (b) every worker is in law free to apply for membership of a union of his choice, and (c) any act of purported expulsion of a worker from his union lacks legal effect if it is judged to be 'by way of arbitrary or unreasonable discrimination'. Consequentially, of course, *A* has various legal remedies which he may pursue for alleged infractions of the primary right conferred by the Act.

Thus using the terminology (in my view indispensable) of 'rights' the legislature can in short and simple words achieve complex legal protections for the several members of a given class. What is more, it can do so in a way which draws attention to the end in view, the protection of those people in relation to a supposedly advantageous condition of things. This serves better than would any alternative formulation the function of conveying to the population in general and to the judiciary in particular the intended aim and object of the measure.

The example most recently used can be used to show why we should not accept the Hohfeldian view of 'rights' as being reducible without residue to atomic relationships (belonging to one or other of his four types) between pairs of identified individuals; or even to sets of such relations. During the whole period when the 1974 Act was in force, any individual who was a worker had the right conferred by Section 5(1) of the Act. For any worker at any moment of time his having that right would have entailed a large set of Hohfeld-type atomic relationships with other individuals in a position to affect his membership (actual or projected) of some union. But although such individual atomic relationships are derivable from the existence of the right conferred by the Act, the converse is not true. The legislature can establish that vast myriad of atomic relationships by establishing the right to non-exclusion and non-expulsion. It could not establish the latter by establishing the former. (Of course, the legislature could establish a whole set of such 'atomic' relationships, but no particular set would be equivalent to the right actually established, which, depending on the circumstances which emerge, results in a variable set of claims, powers, etc.).

Rights, in short, may be more or less simple or complex and might be ranged on a scale of relative complexity. The more complex they are, the more it is necessary, at least for practical understanding, to envisage them as 'institutional' concepts, as I have elsewhere analysed that term.[22] For any given right, e.g. a right of real security, it is (at least for practical comprehension) necessary to distinguish 'institutive' (*per* Bentham, 'investitive') provisions which establish the conditions upon which the right in question vests in qualified individuals; 'consequential' provisions establishing the various normative protections enjoyed by 'right-holders' as such; and 'terminative' or 'divestitive' provisions establishing the conditions in which the 'right' is 'lost' or 'transferred'. In the case of complex provisions of this kind, the concept of 'right' is for practical purposes indispensable. Even if it were theoretically the case that the whole set of rules comprising a developed legal system could be restated purely in terms of the imposition of duties and the conferment of powers, which I doubt, it would be of no advantage for the practical comprehension of the law were anyone to do so. (The difficulties can be gleaned from a scrutiny of Bentham's heroic attempt to show, by way of prolegomenon to a codification project, how it might in principle be done.)

Even in the case of very simple legal provisions expressed in the duty-imposing mode, the interpretation of such rules as also conferring rights is not wholly without point. First of all, if it be supposed that the law was made with a view to protecting the good of individuals severally, so that every qualified individual has a correlative right to the duty (a Hohfeldian 'claim right'), that would supply at least a prima facie reason for supposing that individuals adversely affected by anybody's breach of the duty imposed ought to be entitled to seek a private law remedy, 'Ubi ius, ibi remedium'; to interpret a law as right-conferring is to give a justifying reason why there should be a remedy at private law for its breach. Secondly, and by a similar line of argument, it would appear that when such a law is conceived as conferring individual rights, individuals ought normally to have the power of waiving the duty in particular cases affecting only themselves.

If it be accepted that the identifying feature of right-conferring laws is to secure certain goods to individuals, and if it be accepted (as liberals accept it) that people should have free choice as to the pursuit or not of their own good, that constitutes a reason why, when the law confers rights on people, they *ought* to have the kind of choice which the will theory conceives to be analytically entailed by

22 D. N. MacCormick, 'Law as Institutional Fact', 90 *Law Quarterly Review* 102 (1974).

the term 'right'. But surely it is better to conceive of such 'powers of waiver', like remedial powers, not as being essential to the definition of, but as being consequential on the recognition or conferment of, rights. Paternalistic legislation which seeks to protect people's rights by preventing them from waiving them may be objectionable, but that is for argument. Surely it cannot be the case that, by definition, it destroys as 'rights' the rights which it seeks better to protect? Freedom of choice is a good, but it is not necessarily the only good.

The more one considers the matter, and the more one looks at rights in legislation, the more implausible become the contentions of the 'will theory' as to the definition and elucidation of rights. Rights must be understood in terms of the type of 'interest theory' advanced in this essay. From that it may be seen that there are powerful reasons why people should be free to exercise or not exercise their rights. But these reasons are points of moral and political substance, not analytic truths about rights. What is more, the experience of the past century suggests that in contexts of economic inequality the value of freedom of choice (in its guise as freedom of contract) may justifiably be overridden by other values, at least sometimes. That gives a further reason for not erecting the liberal principle about freedom of choice into an analytic truth following from the definition of 'right'. To follow Hart's example by seeking to elucidate the character not of 'rights' directly, but of the laws that confer them, is to find grounds for rejecting his own theory of rights.

ENDNOTE: *Ius quaesitum tertio*

Of the arguments adduced by Hart against the 'benefit theory', the only one not dealt with here is that which concerns contracts in favour of third parties.[23] If *A* and *B* make a contract which has a provision for the benefit of *C*, it follows that there is a duty under the contract, which is intended to be for the benefit of *C*. Therefore, if the benefit theory is true, *C* has a right under the contract, but in some (indeed most) legal systems the existence of third-party rights under contract is not recognized, so the benefit theory cannot be true.

Observe that the argument proves too much, for with an obvious modification it applies to the will theory too. If *A* and *B* make a contract containing a provision in favour of *C*, to be carried out by

[23] 'B.L.R.', pp. 195-6.

B if *C* requests, but not if *C* does not request, is there a right in favour of *C*? Not under English law, even though that duty of *B*'s has been set up so that its performance is at *C*'s option.

The point in both cases is that under English law (unlike Scots law in either case) *A* and *B* retain the power to alter the provisions of their contract without *C*'s consent. Since the term in *C*'s favour remains precarious until performed, it is not called a 'right'. What is crucial is the presence or absence of immunity. That embarrasses the will theory, but not the interest theory here propounded.

Legal rights

By Carl Wellman

Any adequate theory of legal rights must begin with Wesley Hohfeld's fundamental legal conceptions. He quoted numerous passages in and about the law to show how the expression "a right" is used indiscriminately to refer to any kind of legal advantage. He went on to argue that this established usage fails to distinguish between four very different legal conceptions — a claim, a liberty, a power, and an immunity.

(1) A legal claim. One party x has a legal claim against some second party y that y do some action A if and only if y has a legal duty to x to do A. Thus John Doe has a legal claim against Ace Roofing Company, with whom he has contracted to replace the roofing on his house for an agreed sum, that Ace Roofing Company replace the roofing on his house as specified; upon completion of this work, the Ace Roofing Company has a legal claim against John Doe that he pay the agreed sum. John Doe also has a legal claim against Richard Roe, whoever Richard Roe may be, that he not break into his house or trespass on his land.

(2) A legal liberty. One party x has a legal liberty in face of some second party y to do some action A if and only if x has no duty to y to refrain from doing A. For example, I have the legal liberty in face of Professor Alf Ross of burning my copy of his *On Law and Justice;* I do not, however, have the legal liberty in face of The Royal Library in Copenhagen of burning its copy of this book. Again, if Jones assaults Smith so as to endanger his life or limb, then Smith has the legal liberty in face of Jones of striking Jones in self-defence, although under normal circumstances Smith would have no legal liberty of striking Jones at all.

(3) A legal power. One party x has a legal power over some second party y to bring about some specific legal consequence C for y if and only if some voluntary action of x would be legally recognized as having this consequence for y. Thus I have the legal power of making my wife the beneficiary of my life insurance policy because my act of specifying my wife as beneficiary in my contract with the life insurance company will have this legal consequence for my wife. Similarly, a landowner has the legal power over some neighbor of conferring upon him the legal liberty of walking across his land without trespass simply by giving him permission to do so.

(4) A legal immunity. One party x has a legal immunity against some second party y from some specified legal consequence C if and only if y lacks the legal power to do any action whatsoever that would be recognized by the law as having the consequence C for x. A homeowner is immune against the seizure of his home by a creditor in satisfaction for an unpaid debt, but he is not immune against some officer of the court selling his home at public auction and using the proceeds to liquidate this same debt. Again, a Communist party worker is immune

against any act of an indignant citizen that would pretend to deprive him of his United States citizenship on the grounds that his political activity constitutes treason.

It is imperative, I believe, that we think of legal rights in these terms. Hohfeld's fundamental legal conceptions have tremendous advantages for any theory of legal rights. First, they resolve the modal ambiguity in the language of rights. Imagine that I pay the owner of a parking lot near Washington University for "the right to park my car" on his lot. I now find the lot filled every morning when I drive to my office. Is my legal right violated? It is if I have acquired a legal claim against the lot owner that he make available to me a space in which to park my car, but it is not if I have acquired merely a legal liberty vis-à-vis the owner to park on his lot. Again, does a fence have a legal right to sell a stolen television set? He does if by "a legal right to sell" one means a legal power to sell, for the law in Missouri will recognize such a transaction as legally valid provided the buyer was acting in good faith; he does not if "a legal right to sell" means a legal liberty, for the law forbids anyone knowingly to sell any stolen property. The distinctions marked by Hohfeld's fundamental legal conceptions are genuine and important ones. Any theory that ignores them cannot hope to deal adequately with the reality of legal rights.

Second, these fundamental conceptions show the practical significance of legal rights and of statements about them. I mean the expression "practical significance" to be taken literally; an analysis of rights in Hohfeld's terms shows their significance for practice. This is because the complete description of any instance of these fundamental legal conceptions necessarily includes the specification of some human action. Every legal liberty or power is the liberty or power to do some specific action. Every legal claim is a claim that some second party perform or refrain from some specific action. And any legal immunity is an immunity from any and all actions with specific legal consequences. Thus, to conceive of legal rights in terms of legal liberties, claims, powers and immunities is to think of them in practical terms. This is obviously an advantage for anyone who wishes his legal theory to have practical applications, either to legal cases arising from human actions or to the creation and reform of law designed to regulate human action.

Less obviously, this is a necessary condition for rendering the language of legal rights intelligible. Although we often use sentences in which the content of some legal right is characterized by a noun of noun phrase, I suggest that we do not understand what such sentences mean until we translate them into sentences containing a verb or verb phrase. My legal right to life might be my legal liberty of living, or my legal liberty of defending my life when attacked, or my legal claim upon some second party (presumably my parents or the state) that it provide me with the minimal means of sustaining my life. It might be any of these or all of these or something of the same sort. But suppose that some speaker insists that the content of what he means by "the right to life" is purely and simply *life* and that no action whatsoever is essentially involved. This would be like saying that my property right in my car is to be understood quite independently of the legal facts that I may drive my car without the permission of any second party, that anyone else may drive my car only with my permission, that only I have the legal power to sell that particular car, that I may even destroy that car if I so choose, that anyone else who destroys or damages that car is liable to legal action by me, etc. Take away all connection with human actions and legal rights make no sense at all. This is why it is essential for any theory of legal rights to show their practical significance. Hohfeld's fundamental legal conceptions are valuable theoretical instruments because they do precisely that.

Third, these legal conceptions also reveal the hidden complexity in legal rights. We typically describe the content of any legal right with a single word or a short phrase. Thus, we speak of the legal rights to "life," "liberty," "free speech," "due process" or "the equal protection of the laws." Anyone familiar only with the language of rights might imagine that legal rights are very simple in reality and easy to characterize. Philosophers, like myself, are especially prone to this error. But jurists and practicing lawyers are under no such illusion. They realize that one cannot guess the real nature of any legal right from its mere name but must learn its precise content from a detailed and painstaking study of the legal code and a variety of judicial decisions. They also realize that a single legal right may be relevant to a variety of court cases in very different ways by virtue of its many facets. When statements about legal rights are translated into sentences describing legal claims, liberties, powers and immunities, the legal complexity implicit in the nicknames by which we call them is made explicit and revealed for all to see. Only when the content of any legal right is spelled out in terms of Hohfeld's fundamental legal conceptions is its full legal reality adequately characterized in detail and with precision.

Just because Hohfeld recognized the complexity of the legal phenomena to which I have been referring, he wished to deny all complexity to the concept of a legal right. He proposed that we reform our legal language in order to make our analysis of such complex legal situations more clear and accurate. It is confusing, he argued, to use the expression "a right" to refer ambiguously to every sort of legal advantage. He refused to admit that legal liberties, powers or immunities are rights in the strict sense because they imply no correlative legal duties. It is inaccurate, he thought, to treat a complex of legal claims (what he called "paucital rights" or "multital rights") as a single legal right. He argued that any complex of legal claims is really an aggregate of distinct and independent rights, not *a* legal right. Accordingly, he identified a legal right in the strictest sense with a single unanalyzable legal claim.

There are at least three strong reasons to reject Hohfeld's theory in which a legal right is simply a single legal claim. First, Hohfeld's proposed redefinition of "a right" does not improve our legal or philosophical language. He did not pretend that his definition accurately captures established linguistic usage. Quite the contrary; he proposed to reform our language in order to avoid modal ambiguity and to reveal the internal structure of complex legal situations. These are admirable purposes, but they can be achieved by adopting and using his fundamental legal conceptions as I have done. There is no advantage in going one step further and defining "a legal right" as a single legal claim. We already have the expression "a legal claim" to refer to this legal reality. It is a sheer waste of our limited linguistic resources to use two expressions to refer to this one legal reality and to express a single legal concept. Moreover, it leaves us with no established expression to use when we want to refer to the sort of legal complex we ordinarily call "a right." Finally, to define a legal right as a single legal claim is to rule out of court all those legal theories that refuse to identify legal rights with any sort of claim. Thomas Hobbes and Herbert Hart have constructed theories of rights in which the central concept is that of a legal liberty. Thomas Holland and Hans Kelsen have emphasized the concept of a legal power. And Rudolf von Ihering and John Salmond have identified legal rights with legally protected interests. Surely these theories have some claim upon our attention and are to be rejected only on the basis of rational argument. It is highhanded to dismiss them with an arbitrary stipulative definition.

Second, Hohfeld explained only half the relation between rights and duties. Legal rights are necessarily connected with legal duties, for every legal right imposes one or more legal duties upon one or more second parties. This truth is often reflected in one version of the doctrine of the correlation between rights and duties, the thesis that for every legal right there is a correlative legal duty. Hohfeld accepted this thesis without question and defined a legal right as a legal claim precisely because in his system of fundamental conceptions a legal claim of x against y is the logical correlative of a corresponding legal duty of y to x. Let us also accept this thesis, at least for the sake of the argument, and concede that Hohfeld's theory does explain how it is that rights impose duties. Still, this is only half the story. Not only are legal rights connected with legal duties; they are also contrasted with them. A citizen has a legal right to vote, but a legal duty to pay taxes. A landowner has the legal right to walk in his own fields, but a legal duty not to trespass on his neighbor's fields. The difference seems to be that while legal rights are permissive, legal duties are mandatory; one may exercise one's rights if one wishes, but one must fulfill one's duties whether or not one wishes to do so. Thus, the creditor is permitted to exact payment, but the debtor is required to pay. Hohfeld completely fails to explain this essential feature of legal rights. The identification of a legal right with a single legal claim may explain the connection between rights and duties, but it ignores the essential contrast between them.

Third, Hohfeld's own analysis fails to explain away the complexity of legal rights. He defined a legal right as a single legal claim because he wanted to identify a legal right with a legal atom, with some ultimate and unanalyzable legal relation. He refused to identify a legal right with any complex legal reality because anything complex is composed of logically distinguishable and legally separable parts; any legal complex ultimately lacks unity, he imagined, because one or more of its parts could exist without the others. Therefore, he concluded that it must constitute, not *a* right, but a number of separate rights. In his system, the concept of a legal claim is a "fundamental" conception. Just because it is logically fundamental, he assumed that the expression "a legal claim" is indefinable and that the legal reality to which it refers is indivisible. As it turns out, however, a legal claim is not as simple as he imagined. A legal claim of x against y is the logical correlative of a corresponding legal duty of y to x. Difficulties arise as soon as one begins to ask precisely what it is that makes any legal duty a duty *to* some second party. Although several answers have been proposed to this question, the correct answer, I believe, is that a legal duty is a duty *to* the party who can take legal action to enforce that duty. The debtor's duty to repay the debt is a duty to the creditor because it is the creditor who has the legal power to sue should the debtor fail or refuse to perform this duty. If I am correct, then the concept of a legal duty of y to x is complex: it is to be analyzed in terms of two more fundamental legal conceptions, that of a legal duty of y and that of a legal power of x. Since a legal claim of x against y is the logical correlative of a legal duty of y to x, the concept of a legal claim is similarly complex. Thus it is that although Hohfeld explicitly refused to identify a legal right with any complex legal reality, his own theory implicitly concedes the complexity of legal rights.

Alf Ross also recognizes the complexity of legal phenomena and the ambiguity of legal language. This is precisely why he adopts Hohfeld's fundamental legal conceptions and uses them in his own theory of legal rights. But unlike Hohfeld, who tried to deny all complexity to the concept of a legal right in order to use that concept in analyzing complex legal situations into their ultimate constituents, Ross affirms that the concept of a legal right is itself complex. In his theory, the expression "a legal right" reflects and refers to a certain sort of structure or pattern in the law, a structure that contains much more than a single legal claim. I believe that Ross is correct in maintaining the complexity of legal rights.

Granted that legal rights are complex, the question remains as to what sort of unity they have. Alf Ross holds that a legal right is essentially a logical and conceptual complex. We use the linguistic expression "a right" in the law as a conceptual shorthand or linguistic abbreviation for a very complicated set of legal rules. Each of these rules connects some operative fact with some specified legal consequence. For example, "if one has purchased Blackacre, then one has the legal liberty to use the land as one wishes"; "if one has inherited Blackacre, then one has the legal power to sell Blackacre"; "if one has been given Blackacre, then one has the legal power to permit others to use its land if one wishes"; etc. The total import of such a complex of legal rules is that any *one* of a set of operative facts implies *all* of a set of legal consequences. Thus, "If one has purchased Blackacre, then one has the legal liberty to use the land as one wishes, and one has the legal power to sell Blackacre, and one has the legal power to permit others to use its land if one wishes, etc.; *and* if one has inherited Blackacre, then one has the legal liberty to use the land as one wishes, and one has the legal power to sell Blackacre, and one has the legal power to permit others to use its land if one wishes, etc.; . . . etc." The concept of a legal right is simply a conceptual device for summing up such combinations of legal rules and facilitating the logical inference from operative fact to legal consequence.

This analysis seems to fit ownership, Ross' paradigm case, very well. I suspect, however, that ownership is not a typical legal right. It is much more like citizenship, a status that confers a variety of rights, than like such typical rights as the right to free speech, to due process, or to performance of contract. When one acquires the status of citizenship, one acquires a number of distinct rights, such as the right to vote, the right to police protection within the state, and the right to diplomatic protection abroad. Similarly, when one acquires ownership in something, one acquires the right to exclusive use of that thing, the right to dispose of that thing, and the right to lend it to another. Thus ownership would appear to be a legal status rather than a paradigm case of a legal right.

Although I do not adamantly deny that ownership is a complex legal right, I do insist that Alf Ross has neglected the real unity in any legal right. On his theory, we employ the concept of a legal right just in case the rules of a legal system are such that any one of a variety of operative facts implies *all* of a set of legal consequences. Ross seems never to have asked, and certainly does not answer, the question of why it is that this totality of legal consequences goes together in the law. Why does a legal system connect the liberty to use a piece of land, a claim against its use by others, the power to permit others to use the land, the power to dispose of the land, etc. together? The answer, I believe, is that this set of legal consequences, this complex of legal advantages, has a functional unity ignored by Ross. It is this functional unity that is the key to any adequate theory of legal rights because this explains the meaning of the expression "a legal right" and the nature of the legal reality to which it refers.

A legal right is a cluster of legal elements. It consists of a collection of legal claims, liberties, powers, immunities and duties. Since the legal realities that together make up any legal right are best thought of in terms of Hohfeld's fundamental legal conceptions, I call them "Hohfeld elements." Just because a right is a legal advantage, most of its constituents are themselves legal advantages — legal claims, liberties, powers or immunities. Often, however, one or more of these legal advantages is protected by legal duties arising from the criminal law and to which no constituent claims correspond. The complexity of legal rights arises from the variety and multiplicity of these Hohfeld elements that together constitute the right.

A legal right is no mere random aggregate of legal claims, liberties, powers, immunities and duties, however; it is a unified and structured system of Hohfeld elements. At the center of every legal right stands a defining core. Thus, the core of my right to free speech is my legal liberty of speaking out on controversial issues and the core of the creditor's right to repayment is his legal claim against the debtor that the debtor repay him the agreed sum at the agreed time. This core is of crucial importance in at least three ways. First, it unifies the right by providing a single Hohfeld element or logically connected set of elements to which every other constituent in the right is tied. Much as a number of planets constitute a single right because of the way in which they all relate to a single central sun, so a number of legal claims, liberties, powers, immunities and duties constitute a single right because of the way in which they all relate to a single core. Second, the core defines the essential content of the right. Legal rights are not monolithic creations of the law that spring into existence in complete and final form to persist unchanged until they disappear from the legal system *in toto*. Legal rights grow, diminish, and change as the processes of legislation and adjudication add or subtract associated Hohfeld elements. As long as the core persists, however, these changes in the law leave the right essentially unchanged, for it is the core that makes any right the right it is — the right to free speech or to repayment. Third, the core determines the modality of the right as a whole. The right to free speech is a liberty-right, in spite of containing other sorts of Hohfeld elements, because at its core is a legal liberty. Although the legal right to be repaid contains several legal liberties, it is, by contrast, a claim-right because its core is a legal claim.

Around the defining core of any legal right revolve a set of associated legal claims, liberties, powers, immunities and duties. What ties each of these associated Hohfeld elements to the central core is the way in which it contributes some kind of freedom or control over this core to the possessor of the legal right. Thus, the creditor's legal power of waiving repayment confers upon him considerable control over his claim to repayment, the core of his legal right to be repaid; and his bilateral legal liberty to exercise or refrain from exercising this power gives him freedom of choice in this regard. The two sorts of string that bind together a number of Hohfeld elements into a single legal right are freedom and control.

Freedom and control are essentially related. One cannot be really free if one is under the control of others, and one is fully free only if one has control over those who would interfere with one's action. Conversely, one has control over some thing or in some area of action only if one is free to act in relation to that thing or in that area. Perhaps the best word to capture this two-sided freedom-control is "autonomy," in the sense of self-government, for whether the possessor of a right exercises or enjoys his right is governed primarily by his own will rather than that of any alien will. Here we have discovered the functional unity that Alf Ross neglected. The various legal claims, liberties, powers, immunities and duties that make up a legal right function together to allocate some specific legal autonomy to its possessor. Accordingly, a legal right is best thought of as a system of legal autonomy.

A good example is my legal right to free speech. This right does not consist in a single legal claim, or liberty, but in a complex structure of Hohfeld elements. Its core is my legal liberty of speaking out on controversial issues. It is this core that defines what it is that I have a legal right to, to speak freely. Around this core liberty cluster a number of associated legal elements, including at least the following:

(1) I also have the legal liberty of refraining from speaking out on controversial issues. This liberty gives me freedom of choice with respect to the core liberty of speaking out, for together they imply that I am legally permitted but not legally required to speak out on any given issue.

(2) I also have a legal claim against others that they not interfere with by speaking out on controversial issues by using force or the threat of force against me. Although this associated legal claim leaves newspapers free to refuse to print my letter to the editor and radio stations free to refuse to sell me radio time, it does offer some measure of protection to my core liberty because it forbids some actions that might prevent me from exercizing it.

(3) I also have the legal power to take legal action to protect my core liberty of speaking out. If I have evidence that some political opponent has hired thugs to beat me up when I next address a political rally, I can go to court and petition for a restraining injunction to prevent this interference with my speaking; if I have evidence that my political opponent has taken such action against me in the past, I can sue him for judicial remedy. Presumably this legal power affords me some freedom of speech by giving me some measure of control over those who would prevent me from speaking when and as I wish.

(4) I also have a Constitutional immunity against laws limiting or extinguishing my legal liberty of speaking out on controversial issues. This immunity protects my core liberty from those who would deprive me of it by legislation. Disparate as these associated legal liberties, claims, powers and immunities may be, they all belong to this single right by virtue of the various ways in which they confer freedom or control over its core to me. Taken as a whole, this complex structure of Hohfeld elements constitutes a system of legal autonomy with respect to speaking out on controversial issues.

Legal rights must be complex because only a combination of legal liberties, claims, powers and immunities could perform their essential function of allocating autonomy. Ross recognized the complexity of legal rights but ignored their functional unity; Hohfeld denied their complexity because he reduced their function to that of deciding claims in court. Consider, however, the creditor's legal right to repayment. Imagine a primitive legal system in which the creditor has only a single legal claim to repayment against the debtor, as stipulated in Hohfeld's theory. Would this be sufficient to give autonomy, freedom and control, with respect to the act of repayment to the creditor when confronted with a debtor who chooses not to repay the amount due on the due date? Well, the debtor does have a legal duty to repay and the creditor does have a legal power to sue should the debtor fail to fulfill this duty: this is precisely what a legal claim amounts to in Hohfeldian terms. We can imagine, however, that the possessor of this legal claim lacks the legal power to waive his claim and so cancel the debt. Surely this is a serious lack of freedom and control with respect to repayment, for legally the creditor must then be repaid whether he wishes it or not, and he is unable to do anything to change this legal situation. Again, imagine that the creditor has both the legal power to cancel the debt and the legal power to sue a reluctant debtor *but* that he lacks the legal liberty to exercise either of these powers. Surely this greatly reduces his freedom with respect to repayment. Finally, let us imagine that the creditor has a legal claim to repayment against the debtor but that the debtor has the legal power to extinguish this legal claim simply by signifying to the creditor in writing his firm intention not to repay the debt. Without some sort of legal immunity against the loss of his legal claim at the mere whim of the debtor, the legal claim in and of itself hardly allocates autonomy with respect to repayment to the creditor vis-à-vis the debtor. Only a complex structure of Hohfeld elements could constitute a genuine system of legal autonomy, a real legal right.

Notice that legal autonomy is necessarily relational. To give autonomy with respect to repayment to the creditor is to deny autonomy in this respect to the debtor; to extend freedom and control over the act of speaking out to one party is to withdraw some measure of freedom and control over his speaking to all those who might wish to silence him. Thus, any legal right allocates some sort of autonomy to its possessor in face of one or more second parties. Taken collectively, the legal rights existing in a given legal system determine the distribution of freedom and control to the several parties subject to that legal system. This is why legal rights become relevant precisely when the choice of one party is incompatible with the choice of some second party, when there is a confrontation between opposed wills. If nobody cares whether I speak out or not, my legal right to free speech hardly matters. My autonomy with respect to speaking out on controversial issues becomes legally relevant and practically important just when I want to speak out against a political opponent who wants to deprive me of every opportunity to speak in public or when I choose to criticize my government and my government chooses to silence me. In allocating autonomy to one party vis-à-vis another in such actual or potential confrontations, legal rights determine legally which of two conflicting wills is to prevail. This is the practical import of legal rights; this is the reality of legal rights in the functioning of any legal system.

Such, in essence, is my conception of a legal right. I have not dreamed it up all by myself, and I would hardly dare reveal it to you were it not suggested by previous theories of jurisprudence. Wesley Hohfeld has given us the fundamental legal conceptions in which to articulate the content of any legal right. Alf Ross has shown us the complexity of legal rights. My footnote is to point out the functional unity that Ross ignored and Hohfeld rejected. Each legal right is a system of legal autonomy, an allocation of freedom and control to one party in face of one or more second parties in an actual or potential conflict of wills. The instrument that any legal system uses in allocating is a cluster of legal claims, liberties, powers, immunities and duties. Such a complex system of Hohfeld elements constitutes a legal right.

On the Nature of Rights

J. RAZ

The nature of rights is one of the perennial topics of practical philosophy. One would have expected that interest in it would grow in times when rights are perceived to be central to morality or to political theory. This article is motivated by an interest in the importance of rights in morality and political theory. But that interest will here be kept in the background. My present purpose is to offer an outline of an account of the nature of rights and to leave the examination of its moral consequences for another occasion.[1]

The first section outlines an account of rights. The others explain it. Sections 2–5 are concerned with relatively technical points. Sections 6–9 touch on the philosophically significant aspects of the account here offered: the capacity to have rights and the relations between rights, duties and interests.

1. The outline of an account of rights

Is the 'ulterior' purpose of assessing the importance of rights in morality and politics in danger of infecting an account of the nature of rights with an illegitimate bias? One danger of prefacing a discussion of the importance of rights with a definition of rights is that one may end with a definition according to which rights are not important, but which is not acceptable to those who claim that they are.

An opposite danger is of proving the importance of rights by calling anything of value a right. Both dangers exemplify the vice of spuriously arguing for a moral or a political view by surreptitious verbal legislation. Both dangers result from the fact that a philosophical definition of 'a right' like those of many other terms, is not an explanation of the ordinary meaning of a term. It follows rather the usage of writers on law, politics and morality who typically use the term to refer to a sub-class of all the cases to which it can be applied with linguistic propriety.

1 I have pursued some aspects of this question in 'Right-based moralities' in R. Frey (ed.), *Rights and Utility*, forthcoming.

Philosophical definitions of rights[1] attempt to capture the way the term is used in legal, political and moral writing and discourse. They both explain the existing tradition of moral and political debate and declare the author's intention to carry on the debate within the boundaries of that tradition. At the same time they further that debate by singling out certain features of rights, as traditionally understood, for special attention, on the grounds that they are the features which best explain the role of rights in moral, political, and legal discourse. It follows that while a philosophical definition may well be based on a particular moral or political theory (the theory dictates which features of rights, traditionally understood, best explain their role in political, legal and moral discourse), it should not make that theory the only one which recognizes rights.[2] To do so is to try to win by verbal legislation. A successful philosophical definition of rights illuminates a tradition of political and moral discourse in which different theories offer incompatible views as to what rights there are and why. The definition may advance the case of one such theory but if successful it explains and illuminates all. In this spirit, I shall first propose a definition of rights and then explain various features of the definition and criticize some alternative definitions.

Definition: 'x has a right' if and only if x can have rights, and other things being equal, an aspect of x's well-being (his interest) is a sufficient reason for holding some other person(s) to be under a duty.[3]

The Principle of Capacity to have Rights: An individual is capable of having rights if and only if either his well-being is of ultimate value or he is an 'artificial person' (e.g. a corporation).

1 I refer of course to what philosophers most commonly do, whether they know this or not. I do not wish to deny that some understand their enterprise in other ways.

2 Though a consideration of notions such as 'chastity', 'honour', 'chivalry' shows that not all political or moral theories have room for all normative concepts. Some theories may not recognise rights. For an argument that utilitarianism is incompatible with the existence of rights see D. Lyons, 'Utility and Rights', *Nomos* **24** (1982).

3 The definition draws on several elements of analyses of rights which stem from Bentham's beneficiary theory. It has much in common with R. M. Dworkin's explanation in *Taking Rights Seriously* (London: Duckworth, 1977), p. 100 (but not with his more well known 'trump' theory), and with D. N. MacCormick's 'Rights in Legislation' in P. M. S. Hacker and J. Raz (eds.), *Law, Morality and Society* (Oxford, 1977). Most of all I have been influenced by K. Campbell's ideas in his *The Concept of Rights*, 1979, an Oxford D.Phil. thesis.

Note that since 'a right' is a very general term, one rarely asserts that someone has a right without specifying what rights he has, just as one does not normally mention that a person is subject to a duty without saying something more about what duty it is. Sometimes one may state of another that he has rights in order to indicate that he is the kind of creature who is capable of having rights. For example, one may say that slaves have (legal or moral) rights, or that partnerships have rights, or that foetuses have them. (Similarly one may say that the monarch has duties, etc.) The fact that assertions of rights *tout court* are rare does not invalidate the definition, nor does it detract from its value as the key to the explanation of all rights. It is true that there is much about statements of rights which cannot be learned from my definition alone. One needs to distinguish a right to act from a right in an object, and that from a right to an object, and that from a right to a service or a facility, and that again from 'a right to . . .' where the dots stand for an abstract noun. A right to use the highway, for example, is a liberty right to use the highway or a right to have that liberty. A right in a car may be a right of ownership in the car, or some other right in it. Detailed explanations of rights are in part linguistic explanations (a right to a car differs from a right in a car) but in part they depend on political, legal, or moral argument (does a right to free speech include access to the mass media or to private premises?) The proposed definition is meant to be neutral concerning all such detailed questions. At the same time, it aims to encapsulate the common core of all rights, and thus to help to explain their special role in practical thought.

The definition is of rights *simpliciter*. Some discourse of rights is of rights as viewed from the point of view of a certain system of thought, as when one compares Kantian rights with Utilitarian rights. Prefixing an adjective to 'rights' is one way to indicate that the speaker does not necessarily accept the existence of the right and is merely considering the implications of a system of thought. (On other occasions such adjectives identify the contents of the rights, e.g., economic rights, or their source, e.g., promissory rights, or both.)

Rights are grounds of duties in others. The duties grounded in a right may be conditional.[1] Consider the duty of an employee to

1 Throughout this essay I draw no distinction between duties and obligations. Nor will I indicate how to distinguish a future duty which will exist if a condition is satisfied (If . . then one has a duty to . . .) from a presently existing conditional duty (One has a duty to . . . if . . .). I will assume that only conditional duties can be conditioned on the exercise of powers to impose them.

obey his employer's instructions concerning the execution of his job. It is grounded in the employer's right to instruct his employees. But it is a conditional duty, i.e. a duty (in matters connected with one's employment) to perform an action if instructed by the employer to do so. When the condition which activates the duty is an action of some person, and when the duty is conditional on it because it is in the right-holder's interest to make that person able to activate the duty at will, then the right confers a power on the person on whose behaviour the duty depends.[1] Thus the employer's right over the employees is a ground for his power to instruct them. This power is one aspect or one consequence of his right. But the very same right also endows him with a power to delegate his authority to others. It can, if he chooses to delegate authority, become the source of a power in one of his subordinates. In that case the employee will have a duty to obey the person in whom power was vested and that duty as well as the power of the delegated authority are grounded in the right of the employer. To simplify I shall not dwell specifically on rights as the grounds of powers.

2. *Core and derivative rights*

Some rights derive from others. Just as rights are grounds for duties and powers so they can be for other rights. I shall call a right which is grounded in another right a derivative right. Non-derivative rights are core rights. The relation between a derivative right and the core right (or any other right) from which it derives is a justificatory one. The statement that the derivative right exists must be a conclusion of a sound argument (non-redundantly) including a statement entailing the existence of the core right. But not every right thus entailed is a derivative one. The premises must also provide a justification for the existence of the derivative right (and not merely evidence or even proof of its existence). To do so their truth must be capable of being established without relying on the truth of the conclusion. An example may illustrate the point.

Let us assume that I own a whole street because I bought (in separate transactions) all its houses. My ownership of a house in the street does not derive from my ownership of the street as a whole,

1 For a clarification of the notion of a normative power cf. my *Practical Reason and Norms* (London: Hutchinson, 1975), sec. 3.2. By extending the same reasoning rights can be shown to be grounds of immunities and liberties: they are reasons for not subjecting individuals to duties or to the power of others.

even though the statement that I own a house in the street is entailed by the statement that I own the street. For in attempting to provide a normative justification for my rights I have to refer to the individual transactions by which I acquired the houses. Therefore my right in the street derives from my rights in the houses and not the other way round. Had I inherited the whole street from my grandfather the situation would have been reversed.

Without grasping the relation between core and derivative rights one is liable to fall into confusion. My right to walk on my hands is not directly based on an interest served either by doing so or by others having duties not to stop me. It is based on my interest in being free to do as I wish, on which the general right to personal liberty is directly based. The right to walk on my hands is one instance of my general right to personal liberty. The right to personal liberty is the core right from which the other derives. Similarly with my right to make the previous statement, which is a derivative of the core right of free speech, and my right to spoil the cigarette I am holding at the moment, which derives from my ownership in it, and so on. Often right-holders have direct interest in that to which they have derivative rights. But those do not always ground their rights. A right is based on the interest which figures essentially in the justification of the statement that the right exists. The interest relates directly to the core right and indirectly to its derivatives. The relation of core and derivative rights is not that of entailment, but of the order of justification. The fact that a statement that everyone has a right to freedom of expression appears to entail the statement that everyone has a right to free political expression does not establish that the first is the core right and the second its derivative. It may well be that freedom of political speech is justified by considerations which do not apply to other kinds of speech. If it is also the case that, while separate independent considerations justify freedom of commercial speech and others still freedom of artistic expression, scientific and academic communications, etc., there are no general considerations which apply to all of the protected areas of speech, then the general right to freedom of expression is a derivative right. It is a mere generalization from the existence of several independent core rights.

Furthermore, a general right statement does not entail those statements of particular rights which are instances of it. I may have a right to free speech without having a right to libel people. In matters of libel, the right to free expression may be completely defeated by the interests of people in their reputation. I will return to this point later.

3. The correlativity of rights and duties

It is sometimes argued that to every duty there is a corresponding right. It is evident from the proposed definition that there are no conceptual reasons for upholding such a view. Some moral theories may yield such a correlativity thesis as a result of their moral principles, but this possibility cannot be explored here. A more popular thesis maintains that to every right there is a correlative duty. Since a right is a ground for duties there is a good deal of truth in this kind of correlativity thesis. Yet most of its common formulations are very misleading. R. Brandt's definition can serve as an example of many: 'x has an absolute right to enjoy, have or be secured in y' means the same as 'It is someone's objective overall obligation to secure x in, or in the possession of, or in the enjoyment of y, if y wishes it.'[1] He proceeds to define *prima facie* rights in terms of *prima facie* obligations. First, note that Brandt misleadingly suggests that to every right there corresponds one duty, that that duty is to guarantee the enjoyment or possession of the object of the right, and that it is conditional on the desire of the right-holder. All three points are mistaken. A right to education grounds a duty to provide educational opportunities to each individual, whether he wishes it or not. Many rights ground duties which fall short of securing their object, and they may ground many duties not one. A right to personal security does not require others to protect a person from all accidents or injury. The right is, however, the foundation of several duties, such as the duty not to assault, rape or imprison the right-holder.

Secondly, and more importantly, Brandt fails to notice that the right is the ground of the duty. It is wrong to translate statements of rights into statements of 'the corresponding' duties. A right of one person is not a duty on another. It is the ground of a duty, a ground which, if not counteracted by conflicting considerations, justifies holding that other person to have the duty.

Thirdly, there is no closed list of duties which correspond to the right. The existence of a right often leads to holding another to have

1 Richard Brandt, *Ethical Theory* (Englewood Cliffs, N.J.: Prentice Hall, 1959), p. 438.

a duty because of the existence of certain facts peculiar to the parties or general to the society in which they live. A change of circumstances may lead to the creation of new duties based on the old right. The right to political participation is not new, but only in modern states with their enormously complex bureaucracies does this right justify, as I think it does, a duty on the government to make public its plans and proposals before a decision on them is reached, as well as a duty to publish its reasons for a decision once reached (except in special categories of cases such as those involving defence secrets). This dynamic aspect of rights, their ability to create new duties, is fundamental to any understanding of their nature and function in practical thought. Unfortunately, most if not all formulations of the correlativity thesis disregard the dynamic aspects of rights. They all assume that a right can be exhaustively stated by stating those duties which it has already established.[1] This objection to the reduction of rights to duties does not rule out the possibility of holding that 'A has a right to x' is reducible to 'There is a duty to secure A in x'. But since this duty can be based on grounds other than A's interest, the two statements are not equivalent.

4. *Holding individuals to be under a duty*

The proposed definition states that if an individual has a right then a certain aspect of his well-being is a reason for holding others to be under a duty. I used this phrase advisedly to preserve the ambiguity between saying that rights are a reason for judging a person to have a duty, and saying that they are reasons for imposing duties on him. They are in fact reasons of both kinds, but primarily of the first. Let me explain. Rights are (part of) the justification of many duties. They justify the view that people have those duties. But, as has already been noted, they justify such a view only to the extent that there are no conflicting considerations of greater weight. Within certain institutional settings, there are weighty reasons not so much against allowing rights to generate new duties as against allowing official action on the basis of new duties unless they are recognised by the appropriate institutions. Institutions such as universities, states, trade unions and football clubs are based on a concentration of power in certain bodies and a division of labour between officials whose duties are the execution of the institutions' policies and rules,

1 Needless to say core rights can lead also to new derivative rights.

and those who make and change those policies and rules. In such an institution it may be proper to say that rights are grounds not so much for judging that certain duties exist as for imposing them.

The right to political participation is a legal right in English law. But though in contemporary societies this right justifies holding the government to be under a duty to publicize its plans and the reasons for its decisions, there is no such legal duty on the government in English law. The duty is a purely moral duty. But the existence of the legal right to political participation, i.e. the fact that this right is given legal recognition and is already defended by some legal duties, is a ground for the authorised institutions (Parliament or the courts) to impose such a duty on government officials. If and when they do so, they will be making new law. But they will do so on the ground that this is justified and required by existing law. By the same token the legal right to political participation is a reason for investing people with a legal right to free information. It cannot be used to establish that they already have such a right.

5. *Promises and agreements*

Some of the points made in the previous sections can be illustrated and clarified by using them to explain the rights involved in promises and agreements. These are two. There is the right to promise which a promisor must have if his promise is to be binding. And there is the right conferred on the promisee by the promise. I will examine them in that order.

The right to promise is based on the promisor's interest to be able to forge special bonds with other people.[1] The right is qualified. Not every person has it. Small children and some mentally deranged people lack it. Furthermore, if it is not permissible to have bonds based on immorality, one's right to promise does not include the right to promise to perform immoral acts. The right to promise is no doubt further qualified. Since we are not here concerned with any of these qualifications I will from now on disregard them.

Those who assign sufficient importance to the interest people have in being able to impose on themselves obligations to other people as a means of creating special bonds with other people

1 I am here summarizing some of the points made in my 'Promises and Obligations', in P. M. S. Hacker and J. Raz (eds.), *Law, Morality and Society*; and in 'Promises in Morality and Law', *Harvard Law Rev.* Vol. 95 (February 1982), p. 916.

believe in a right to promise. But why is it a right? The interest on which it is based validates the promising principle, namely:

> If a person communicates an intention to undertake by that very act of communication a certain obligation then he has that obligation.

The promising principle establishes that if we promise we are obligated to act as we promised. It also establishes a present obligation to keep our promises, i.e. we are obligated to perform action x, if we promise to perform x. This is a conditional obligation. The condition is an action of the promisor and his obligation is conditioned on his action because it is desirable that he should be able to bind himself if he so wishes. It follows that people's interest in being able to bind themselves is the basis of a power to promise which they possess and of an obligation to keep promises imposed on them. But neither the power nor the obligation point to a right to promise. The right exists because the very same interest on which the power to promise and the duty to keep promises are based is also the ground to hold others to be subject to a duty not to interfere with one's promising. The duty requires one not to prevent a person from promising (e.g. by denying him the means of communicating an intention to undertake by that very communication an obligation, or by stopping others from receiving such communications). It also requires one not to force people to promise nor to induce them improperly to promise or not to promise. (Again I avoid examining the way these duties are qualified.) Violation of the duty not to interfere with a person's promising will frustrate his right to promise and the interest on which it is based either by preventing the person from exercising his rights or by perverting the considerations on which he decides whether to promise or not. The fact that such interferences with the right are infrequent is reflected by the fact that the right to promise is rarely invoked in ordinary practical discourse. To conclude, the power to promise and the right to promise are distinct notions. But both stem from a common core, i.e. the interest of persons to be able to forge normative bonds with others. That is why they co-exist, and one has the power to promise if and only if one has a right to do so.

The right to make a particular promise (e.g., to visit my aunt next weekend) is a derivative of the general right to promise. One such derivative right is the right to make a conditional promise. Two kinds of conditional promises are of interest here:

First a promise made conditional on an action by the promisee (e.g., 'I will give you 10 pounds if you give me the books'). Second (which is in fact a special case of the above), a promise made conditional on a promise to be given by the promisee (e.g., 'I will give you 10 pounds if you promise to give me the book').

Whenever such a promise is made and the condition is fulfilled, there is an agreement between the promisor and the promisee. The right to make such promises is therefore a right to enter into agreements. There are other ways of making agreements but their analysis does not matter to our purpose.

So far we have discussed the right to promise. The right which the promise creates in *the promisee* does not derive from the right to promise which is a right of *the promisor*. Many writers on promises insist that the promised act must be or at least must be thought to be in the interest of the promisee. Elsewhere I have challenged the view and I will not return to this controversy here.[1] But it is interesting to relate this issue to the question of the promisee's right created by the promise.

One view regards the promisee's right under any particular promise as a core-right based on his interest in the promised act (and the intention of the promisor to be obligated to perform the act). On this view if there could be binding promises which do not benefit the promisee (and are not intended to do so) then there are promises which do not create rights in the promisee.

Such a consequence seems at odds with the conventions of discourse concerning promises. I therefore favour a second view (which complements the first) according to which each person has an interest that promises made to him will be kept. Of course, he might lose interest in the specific content of some promises and keeping some of them may even work against his overall interest. But invariably he has a *pro tanto* interest that promises given to him be kept. This interest is the very one which is reflected in his right to promise. Namely, it is the interest to have voluntary special bonds with other people. We should remind ourselves that while the promisee may not be the initiator of the bond of which the promise is the whole or a part, he is not entirely passive either. It is always up to him to waive his right under the promise and thus terminate the binding force of the promise. It is this general interest which

1 See 'Promises and Obligations', ibid

explains why every promise, and not only those performance of which are to the specific advantage of the promisee, creates a right in the promisee.

6. *Capacity for rights*

The definition of rights itself does not settle the issue of who is capable of having rights beyond requiring that right-holders are creatures who have interests. What other features qualify a creature to be a potential right-holder is a question bound up with substantive moral issues. It cannot be fully debated here. But the special role of statements of rights in practical thought cannot be elucidated and the significance of the definition cannot be evaluated without a brief explanation of the conditions for the capacity for having rights.

There is little that needs be said here of the capacity of corporations and other 'artificial persons' to have rights. Whatever explains and accounts for the existence of such persons, who can act, be subject to duties, etc. also accounts for their capacity to have rights. Whether certain groups, such as families or nations, are artificial or natural persons is important for determining the conditions under which they may have rights. But we need not settle such matters here.

There is a view, which I shall call the reciprocity thesis, that only members of 'the same moral community' can have rights. This is narrowly interpreted when the same moral community is a community of interacting individuals whose obligations to each other are thought to derive from a social contract or to represent the outcome of a fair bargaining process or if morality is conceived of in some other way to be a system for the mutual advantage of all members of the community. Wider conceptions of the moral community extend it to all moral agents and regard anyone who is subject to duties as being capable of rights.

The principle of capacity for rights stated above is not committed to the reciprocity thesis but is consistent with it. Since by definition rights are nothing but grounds of duties, if duties observe a reciprocity condition and can be had only towards members of the (same) moral community then the same is true of rights. Alternatively, the reciprocity thesis obtains even if one can have duties towards non-members of the (same) moral community provided those are not based on the interests of the beneficiaries of those duties. For example, if my duties to animals are based on considerations of my own character (I should not be a person who can tolerate causing pain, etc.) and not on the interests of animals then animals do not have rights despite the fact that I have duties regarding them.

The merits of the reciprocity thesis will not be examined here. The problem to which the principle of capacity for rights is addressed is different. Often we ought or even have duties to act in ways that benefit certain things, and often we ought so to act because of the benefit our action will bring those things. For example, I have a duty to preserve certain plants because I promised their owners to do so while they are away on holiday. My gardener has a duty to look after my garden because his contract of employment says so. Some scientists have a duty to preserve certain rare species of plants because they are the only source of a medicine for a rare and fatal disease. In all these cases the people who have duties to act in certain ways have them because it benefits plants. Yet in none of these cases is it true that the plants have a right to the benefits. The reason is that in all these cases the benefit is to be conferred on a thing whose existence and prosperity are not of ultimate value.

Being of ultimate, i.e. non-derivative[1] value is being intrinsically valuable, i.e. being valuable independently of one's instrumental value. Something is instrumentally valuable to the extent that it derives its value from the value of its consequences, or from the value of the consequences it is likely to have, or from the value of the consequences it can be used to produce. Being of ultimate value is being valuable even apart from one's instrumental value. But not everything which is intrinsically valuable is also of ultimate value. Consider a person who has a deep attachment to his dog. I share many people's feeling in thinking of the relationship as valuable and of the man's life as richer and better because of it. Many feel that the relationship is intrinsically valuable. Its value is not just that of a cause of a feeling of security and comfort in the man. Such feelings may be produced by some tranquillizers. The relationship is not valued just as a tranquillizer. Its value is in its being a constitutive part of a valuable form of life. For all who share these views the existence of the dog is intrinsically valuable. It is a logically

1 To say that something is of ultimate value is not to claim that one cannot justify the statement that that thing is valuable. It merely indicates that its value does not derive from its contribution to the value of something else.

necessary condition of the relationship and one which contributes to its value (it is the more valuable for being a relationship to a living—rather than a dead—dog). But so far as the story goes the intrinsic value of the dog is not ultimate for it derives from the dog's contribution to the well-being of the man. The man's well-being is here taken as the ultimate value. The dog non-instrumentally contributes to it. Hence his existence is intrinsically but derivatively valuable.

Some people are willing to go further and to hold that the value of the relationship between the man and the dog derives equally from its contribution to the well-being of the dog and that the dog's well-being is not merely derivatively important because of its contribution to the man's well-being. They hold it to be ultimately valuable. They regard the relationship between man and dog in the same way as they and most others regard a relationship between two persons.

My proposed principle of capacity for rights entails that those who regard the existence and well-being of (some) dogs as derivatively valuable (even if they believe them to be intrinsically valuable) are committed to the view that dogs can have no rights though we may well have duties to protect or promote their well-being. For such people dogs have the same moral standing that many ascribe to works of art. Their existence is intrinsically valuable in as much as the appreciation of art is intrinsically valuable. But their value is derivative and not ultimate. It derives from its contribution to the well-being of persons.

It seems plausible to suppose[1] that just as only those whose well-being is of ultimate value can have rights so only interests which are considered of ultimate value can be the basis of rights. But there are plenty of counter-examples demonstrating that some rights protect interests which are considered as of merely instrumental value. All the rights of corporations are justified by the need to protect the interests of these corporations but these are merely of instrumental value. But the counter-instances are not confined to the rights of 'artificial persons'. Consider the rights (however qualified) of journalists to protect their sources (i.e. not to disclose their sources). Those who believe that journalists have such a right base it on the interest of journalists in being able to collect information which is valued because it enables them to inform the public. That

1 Something like this supposition is made by K. Campbell, ibid.

is, the journalists' interest is valued because of its usefulness to members of the public at large. The rights of priests, doctors and lawyers to preserve the confidentiality of their professional contacts are likewise justified ultimately by their value to members of the community at large.

Furthermore, some people, and this seems to be the general view of the English Common Law, regard the interests on which a right as fundamental as freedom of speech is based as instrumentally valuable. Scanlon[1] distinguishes between three kinds of interest on which the right of free speech is based: (1) speaker's interest, (2) audience interest, and (3) third party interest. Only the first is the interest of the right-holder, the interest of a person to be able to communicate with others. The second (the interest of persons that others will be free to communicate with them) and third (the interest of people to live in a society in which communication is free—even if they personally do not wish to communicate with others) are interests of people other than the right-holder in his right. In the Common Law freedom of expression is regularly defended, where it is defended, on grounds of the public interest, that is on the interest of third parties. The right-holder's interest itself conceived independently of its contribution to the public interest is deemed insufficient to justify holding others to be subject to the extensive duties and disabilities commonly derived from the right to free speech.[2]

We must conclude that (apart from artificial persons) only those whose well-being is intrinsically valuable can have rights. But that rights can be based on the instrumental value of the interests of such people.

7. *Rights and interests*

According to the definition, rights-discourse indicates a kind of ground for a requirement of action. To say that a person ought to behave in a certain way is to assert a requirement for action without indicating its ground. To assert that an individual has a right is to indicate a ground for a requirement for action of a certain kind, i.e. that an aspect of his well-being is a ground for a duty on another

1 See T. M. Scanlon, Jr., 'Freedom of Expression and Categories of Freedom', *U. of Pittsburgh L.R.* (1979), p. 519.

2 Two typical English cases are: A.-G. v. Jonathan Cape Ltd. [1976] *Q.B.* 752; Home Office v. Harman [1982] 1 *All E.R.* 532.

person. The specific role of rights in practical thinking is, therefore, the grounding of duties in the interests of other beings.

Rights ground requirements for action in the interest of other beings. They therefore assume special importance in individualistic moral thinking. But belief in the existence of rights does not commit one to individualism. States, corporations and groups may be right-holders. Banks have legal and moral rights. Nations are commonly believed to have a right of self-determination and so on.

Though rights are based on the interests of the right-holders, an individual may have rights which it is against his interest to have. A person may have property which is more trouble than it is worth. It may be in a person's interest to be imprisoned, even while he has a right to freedom. The explanation of this puzzle is that rights are vested in right-holders because they possess certain general characteristics: they are the beneficiaries of a promise, nationals of a certain state, etc. Their rights serve their interests as individuals with those characteristics, but they may be against their interests overall.

Some rights are held by persons as the agents, or organs of others. Thus company directors have rights as directors of the company. In such cases it is the interest of the principal which the right reflects. The same applies to rights held by persons *qua* guardians, trustees and the like.

The proposed definition of rights identified the interest on which the right is based as the reason for holding that some persons have certain duties. Later on I referred to the rights themselves as being the grounds for those duties. The explanation is simple: the interests are part of the justification of the rights which are part of the justification of the duties. Rights are intermediate conclusions in arguments from ultimate values to duties. They are, so to speak, points in the argument where many considerations intersect and where their results are summarized to be used with additional premises when need be. Such intermediate conclusions are used and referred to as if they are themselves complete reasons. The fact that practical arguments proceed through the mediation of intermediate stages so that not every time a practical question arises does one refer to ultimate values for an answer is of crucial importance in making social life possible, not only because they save time and tediousness, but primarily because they enable a common culture to be formed round shared intermediate conclusions, in spite of a great degree of haziness and disagreement concerning ultimate values.

For example, many who agree that people have a right to promise will disagree with my view, expressed above, of the interest on which it is based and will justify it only by reference to some other interests of the right-holders. The importance of intermediate steps like rights, duties, rules of conduct and the like to a common culture explains and justifies the practice of referring to them as reasons in their own right, albeit not ultimate reasons.

An interest is sufficient to base a right on if and only if there is a sound argument of which the conclusion is that a certain right exists and among its non-redundant premises is a statement of some interest of the right-holder, the other premises supplying grounds for attributing to it the required importance, or for holding it to be relevant to a particular person or class of persons so that they rather than others are obligated to the right-holder. These premises must be sufficient by themselves to entail that if there are no contrary considerations then the individuals concerned have the right. To these premises one needs to add others stating or establishing that these grounds are not altogether outweighed by conflicting reasons.[1] Together they establish the existence of the right.

One result of the fact that a right exists where the interests of the right-holders are sufficient to hold another to be obligated should be noted. Sometimes the fact that an action will serve someone's interest, while being a reason for doing it, is not sufficient to establish a duty to do it. Different moral theories differ on this point. Some utilitarian theories deny that there is a useful difference between moral reasons for action and duties. Some moral views confine duties to matters affecting human needs, or human dignity, etc. Be that as it may, it is in principle possible that a person should not have a right that others shall behave to promote a certain interest of his simply on account of the fact that while they should do so, while it is praiseworthy or virtuous of them if they do, they have no obligation so to act.

These considerations help to explain how it is that even if a person has a right, not everyone is necessarily under an obligation to do whatever will promote the interest on which it is based. Rights

1 One case deserves special attention: If B's interest does not justify holding A to be under a duty to ϕ then B has no right that A shall ϕ even if A has a duty to ϕ based on the fact that ϕ-ing will serve the interest of a class of individuals of whom B is one. Thus a government may have a duty to try to improve the standard of living of all the inhabitants of the country even though no single inhabitant has a right that the government shall try to improve his standard of living.

are held against certain persons. Some rights are held against the world at large, i.e. against all persons or against all with certain specified exceptions. Thus the right to personal security is the ground of a duty on everyone not to assault, imprison or rape a person. Other rights are held against certain persons in virtue of a special relation they have to the right-holder. Thus children have a right to be maintained by their parents. The reasons many rights are against some definite people are varied. Sometimes the interests on which they are based can be satisfied only by some people and not by others. For example, since contractual rights are based on an interest in being able to create special relations, they give rise to rights against other parties to the agreement as they are the only ones who can satisfy that interest on that occasion. In other cases, even though many can satisfy the interests of the right-holder, these interests may be sufficient to establish a duty on some people and not on others.[1]

Just as rights may impose duties on some persons and not on others, so they can impose a duty to do certain things but not others. The right to live may impose a duty not to kill or endanger the life of another without imposing a duty to take whatever action is necessary to keep him alive. Which duties a right gives rise to depends partly on the basis of that right, on the considerations justifying its existence. It also depends on the absence of conflicting considerations. If conflicting considerations show that the basis of the would-be right is not enough to justify holding anyone subject to any duty, then the right does not exist. But often such conflicting considerations, while sufficient to show that some actions cannot be required as a duty on the basis of the would-be right, do not affect the case for requiring other actions as a matter of duty. In such cases, the right exists, but it successfully grounds duties only for some of the actions which could promote the interest on which it is based.

8. *Rights and duties*

Rights are the grounds of duties in the sense that one way of justifying holding a person to be subject to a duty is that this serves

1 The fact that rights may hold against some persons only is compatible with the principle that everyone ought to respect everyone's rights. That principle asserts that all persons have a reason (not necessarily a conclusive one) to avoid action which will make it more difficult for those subject to duties towards right-holders to fulfil their obligations.

the interest on which another's right is based. Naturally there may be other grounds for not holding a person to be subject to such a duty. The definition requires that the right is a sufficient reason for a duty. Hence, as we saw, where the conflicting considerations altogether outweigh the interests of the would-be right-holder, and no one could justifiably be held to be obligated on account of those interests, then there is no right. Where the conflicting considerations override those on which the right is based on some but not on all occasions, the general core right exists but the conflicting considerations may show that some of its possible derivations do not. There is a necessary conflict between free speech on the one hand and the protection of one's reputation or the need to suppress criticism of the authorities in time of a major national emergency on the other. (I assume that in both cases the reasons for suppressing libellous or critical expression are also reasons for not holding individuals to have a duty to protect the freedom to express such views.) If in these circumstances the reasons against free expression by their nature override those in favour of free expression, then while it is true that one has a right to free expression, one does not have a right to libel or to criticize the government in an emergency. A general right is, therefore, only a *prima facie* ground for the existence of a particular right in circumstances to which it applies. Rights can conflict with other rights or with other duties, but if the conflicting considerations defeat the right they cannot be necessarily coextensive in their scope.[1]

These remarks help explain one sense in which rights ground duties. Two further points are, however, crucial to the understanding of the priority of rights to the duties which are based on them (and not all duties are based on rights). First, one may know of the existence of a right without knowing who is bound by duties based on it or what precisely are these duties. A person may know that every child has a right to education. He will, therefore, know that there are duties, conditional or unconditional, to provide children with education. But he may have no view who has the duty. This question involves principles of responsibility. It is part of the function of such principles to determine the order of responsibility

1 Conflicts of rights are possible if conflicts of duties are. If the considerations against requiring an action defeat the right-based reasons for requiring it on all the occasions to which they apply, then the right does not create a duty for that action. If, however, they defend the right based reasons on some occasions only, then the right-based reasons create a duty which is sometimes defeated.

of different persons to the right-holder. Does the primary responsibility rest with the parents, with the community stepping in only if they can't or won't meet their obligations? Or does the primary responsibility rest with the community? The issue is of great importance. If it is the parents' duty then there is no duty on the community to provide free education to all. And yet one may be in a position to assert that there is a right to education without knowing the answer to such a problem, or to whether the communal responsibility is local or national, whether it extends only to primary education or beyond and so on and so forth.

In a sense such ignorance shows that the person's knowledge of the precise content of the right to education is incomplete. But this merely means that he does not know all the implications of the right to education (given other true premises). It does not mean that he does not understand the statement that every child has a right to education. Furthermore it is reflection on the right to education, its point and the reasons for it which helps, together with other premises, to establish such implications.

The second point to bear in mind is that the implications of a right, such as the right to education, and the duties it grounds, depend on additional premises and these cannot in principle be wholly determined in advance. At least if it is true in principle that the future cannot be entirely known in advance then there may be future circumstances which were not predicted and which, given the right to education, give rise to a new duty which was not predicted in advance. Even if no such duty is unpredictable, the total implications of the right to education are in principle unpredictable.

Because of this rights can be ascribed a dynamic character. They are not merely the grounds of existing duties. With changing circumstances they can generate new duties.

9. *The importance of rights*

The main purpose of this article was to state and explain a coherent account of rights which is within a recognisable philosophical tradition while hoping to improve on previous definitions in the details of the account. The argument for my account is in its use in moral, political and legal thought and in its success in avoiding the shortcomings of its alternatives. These are matters for other occasions. I will conclude by commenting briefly on the main feature of my account, its view of rights as intermediate between individual interests and people's duties.

Rights ground duties. To say this is not to endorse the thesis that all duties derive from rights or that morality is right-based. It merely highlights the precedence of rights over some duties and the dynamic aspect of rights, their capacity to generate new duties with changing circumstances. Notice that precisely because duties can be based on considerations other than someone's rights the statement (1) 'Children have a right to education' does not mean the same as the statement (2) 'There is a duty to provide education for children.' (1) entails (2) but not the other way round. (1) informs us that the duty stated in (2) is based on the interests of the children. This information is not included in (2) by itself.

It may be claimed that by defining rights as based on the well-being of individuals I have ruled out of court the view that morality is right-based. By definition rights are not fundamental but derive from interests. If true this is a damaging criticism. As explained in the first section the account of rights aims to make sense rather than nonsense of rival theories about the role of rights in morality. I think, however, that the view that rights are fundamental can be explained in terms of the proposed account.

All rights are based on interests. Some rights may be based on an interest in having those same rights.[1] No vicious circularity is involved in the claim that x has a certain right because it is in his interest to have it. It is no more circular than the statement that Jack loves Jill because she needs his love. In many cases an individual's interest in a right does not justify holding him to have it unless it serves some other worth-while interest of his (or of others). My son's interest in a right to education justifies holding him to have it only because the right will serve his interest in education.

If school places were saleable I would have had an interest in having a right to education even if further education is not in my interest, because such a right would serve my interest in my economic welfare since it would add to my disposable assets. Such

1 One may think that one's right to x always derives from one's interest in x. If so then one's interest in having a right to x yields at best a right to have a right to x. It does not yield the right to x itself. This objection is based on a misunderstanding. While rights are based on the interests of the right-holder, these need not be his interests in the object of the right. They can be any interests which can be served by the possession of the right. Since an interest in having a right can be served by having it, it can be the foundation of such a right.

an interest would not, of course, justify holding me to have the right.

A right is a morally fundamental right if it is justified on the ground that it serves the right-holder's interest in having that right in as much as that interest is considered to be of ultimate value, i.e. in as much as the value of that interest does not derive from some other interest of the right-holder or of other persons.

Thus the proposed account of rights allows for the existence of fundamental moral rights. It has to be admitted that this account makes it highly unlikely that morality is right-based. If morality is right-based then all rights have to be either fundamental rights or be derivable from fundamental rights. It is highly unlikely that no one has any right which does not derive from the ultimate value of his interest in having that right. It seems plausible to suppose that people have rights which derive from other interests. The right to education seems, e.g., to derive from the interest in education. The fact that my account of rights makes the view that morality is right-based improbable is not, however, an argument against it. As mentioned at the beginning of the article it is part of the function of a philosophical account of a concept to use it to advance some controversial thesis. There are in any case independent arguments against the view that morality is right-based.[1]

BALLIOL COLLEGE,
OXFORD, OX1 3BJ

1 See my 'Right-based Moralities', ibid. I am grateful to K. Campbell, Wayne Summer and to Jeremy Waldron for helpful criticism of an earlier draft of this article.

3 · *Self-Defense and Rights*

1. Suppose Agressor has got hold of a tank. He had told Victim that if he gets a tank, he's going to get in it and run Victim down. Victim sees Aggressor get in his tank and start towards Victim. It is open country, and Victim can see that there is no place to hide, and nothing he can put between himself and Aggressor which Aggressor cannot circle round. Fortunately, Victim happens to have an anti-tank gun with him, and it is in good working order, so he can use it to blow up the tank, thereby saving his life, but of course thereby also killing Aggressor. I think that most people would say that it is morally permissible for Victim to use that anti-tank gun: surely it is permissible to kill a man if that is the only way in which you can prevent him from killing you!

On the other hand, one of the things we are firmly wedded to is the belief that human beings have a right to life, and this presumably includes the right to not be killed. Aggressor is a human being; so he, like the rest of us, has a right to life, and presumably, therefore, the right to not be killed. So how *can* Victim kill him? Precisely *why* is it permissible for Victim to use that anti-tank gun on Aggressor? I propose we look at three replies which I think come fairly readily to mind.

2. The first reply I am going to call "forfeit," and it goes like this. "We good folk all do have a right to life, and that does include the right to not be killed. But there is such a thing as forfeiting a right. We say such things as that the right to life, liberty, and the pursuit of happiness are 'natural rights,' and therefore unconditionally possessed by all people; but that is just so much high-minded rhetoric.

What has happened in the case described is that Aggressor, by virtue of his attack on Victim, has forfeited his right to not be killed, and therefore his right to life. And *that* is why Victim may use his anti-tank gun on Aggressor, thereby killing him: he violates no right of Aggressor's in doing so."

But this very natural first reply is not at all satisfactory. Suppose that as Victim raises his anti-tank gun to fire it, Aggressor's tank stalls. Aggressor gets out to examine the engine, but falls and breaks both ankles in the process. Victim (let us suppose) now has time to get away from Aggressor, and is in no danger. I take it you will not think that Victim may all the same go ahead and kill Aggressor. But why not?—if Aggressor really has forfeited his right to not be killed by virtue of his attack on Victim.[1]

It could, of course, be said that at this point utilitarian considerations come into play. That is, it could be said that yes, Aggressor has forfeited his right to life, but no, Victim cannot now kill him, and that this latter is true because Victim now has no need to kill Aggressor—indeed, because killing Aggressor would mean the loss of a life, whereas not killing Aggressor would mean no loss at all.

But I think this cannot be right. Suppose Victim is a great transplant surgeon. There is Aggressor, lying helpless next to his tank, with two broken ankles—but the rest of him physically fine and healthy. Can Victim now cart Aggressor off to surgery, cut him up, and give his one heart, two kidneys, and two lungs to five who need the parts? If Aggressor now has no right to not be killed (having forfeited it by his attack on Victim), so that utilitarian considerations are all we have to weigh here, it is hard to see why not. After all, five lives would be saved at a cost of only one. Yet surely Victim cannot do this.

I am inclined to think that it would no more be permissible for Victim to cut Aggressor up and parcel out his parts to save five than it would be for Victim to cut *you* up and parcel out *your* parts to save five. He cannot do this to you; and it is often said that the reason why he cannot (despite the fact that utilities might be maximized by doing so) is the fact that you have a right to life, and thus, presumably, the right to not be killed.[2] I should imagine that the very same thing makes it impermissible for Victim to do this to Aggressor, namely,

1. This question is asked by Sanford H. Kadish, in "Respect for Life and Regard for Rights in the Criminal Law," *California Law Review* 64 (July 1976).

2. But it is not at all obvious that this is what explains the fact that Victim cannot cut you up and parcel out your parts to save five. See footnote 6 below.

the fact that Aggressor, now helpless and no danger to anyone, has a right to life, and thus, presumably, the right not to be killed.

There are, of course, those who think it permissible for a state to impose death, as a penalty, on one who commits one or another very serious crime. If any one of them is a friend of the reply I am calling "forfeit," he will no doubt say that what makes it permissible is the fact that one who commits such a crime has forfeited his right to not be killed. But in the first place, I doubt that those who think of death as an acceptable penalty would think it an acceptable penalty for an (unsuccessful) attempt on the life of another, and it will be remembered that an (unsuccessful) attempt is all that Aggressor is guilty of. More important, even if it could be made out that it *will* be permissible, after trial and conviction, for an agent of the state to kill Aggressor, no agent of the state can kill him *now* (prior to trial and conviction). And Victim not only cannot kill him now, Victim—unless he is himself an agent of the state—is not going to be able to kill him at any time. So while it is (I suppose) open to those who regard death as an acceptable penalty for Aggressor's crime to say that he *will* (after trial and conviction) have no right to not be killed by an agent of the state, he at any rate *now* has a right to not be killed by Victim, indeed a right to not be killed by anybody at all, and thus a right to not be killed.

There are two moves open to a friend of "forfeit." He can say (1) that the fact that the tank stalled and Aggressor broke both ankles shows that it never was necessary for Victim to kill Aggressor, so that Aggressor never did forfeit his right to not be killed. Or he can say (2) that Aggressor did forfeit his right to not be killed when he launched his attack on Victim, but that he regained this right at the moment at which he ceased to pose a threat to Victim's life.

Alternative (1) would be an unfortunate choice for the purpose of "forfeit." For surely Victim could, permissibly, have killed Aggressor at any time between the launching of Aggressor's attack and the stall of the tank. (Who in such circumstances could be expected to know that the tank would stall? Who in such circumstances could be expected to wait in hopes of so freakish an accident?) That indeed was where we began: i.e., with the fact that it was then permissible for Victim to shoot. "Forfeit" proposed to explain this fact by saying that Aggressor forfeited a right; yet (1) denies that he did.

For the purpose of this reply (2) seems preferable. If Aggressor did forfeit his right to not be killed when he launched the attack, that would explain why, between the launching of it and the stall of the tank, Victim could shoot; and if Aggressor re-acquired that right when he ceased to pose a threat to Victim, that would explain why, after the stall of the tank, Victim could no longer shoot.

But it is a far from happy choice. If it were by virtue just of the launching of that attack that Aggressor forfeited his right, then it would seem possible to say that when the attack ceases, Aggressor re-acquires his right—the right being, as it were, in abeyance throughout the time of the attack. But it surely cannot be said to have been by virtue *just* of the launching of that attack that Aggressor forfeited his right. Compare a second aggressor and a second victim. Suppose that Second Aggressor launches a similar attack on Second Victim, but that Second Aggressor (by contrast with Aggressor) is innocent. Second Aggressor, let us suppose, is a schizophrenic, and he is under a hallucination that Second Victim is in a tank of his own, driving towards Second Aggressor's home and family, so that, as Second Aggressor sees it, he is merely trying to ward off an attack. Morality may not protect us from getting run down by lunatics in tanks, but it does permit our protecting ourselves from such a fate; and it seems plain that poor Second Victim, who is himself innocent, may permissibly use his anti-tank gun on Second Aggressor. Why is this permissible? It is an excellent question. But presumably "forfeit" would be a most implausible reply in this case.[3] Perhaps Aggressor, being a villain, can be thought to have forfeited a right; Second Aggressor, however, being himself innocent, cannot. But then it is not by virtue *just* of launching an attack on Victim that Aggressor forfeits his right; Aggressor's bad intention figures too. Yet Aggressor's bad intention may be supposed to remain even after he becomes helpless—we may imagine him continuing to plot as he is carried off to jail—and if that remains, how can he be thought to have re-acquired the right he forfeited at least in part because of that bad intention?

There is room for maneuver here. It could be said that the point is this: both Aggressor and Second Aggressor simply cease to have a right to not be killed when they launch their attacks on their victims, and both of them re-acquire that right when their tanks stall. (On this view, while Aggressor is guilty and Second Aggressor is not, this does not matter: launching an attack by itself—whether guilty or not—is what makes one lose the right to not be killed.) I shall

3. See Kadish, "Respect for Life . . ."

come back to this idea later. For the moment, it should be noted that saying that Aggressor simply ceased to have the right is not the same as saying that Aggressor has forfeited the right. That is, *this* reply is entailed by the reply I am calling "forfeit," but is not identical with it.

3. The second reply I am going to call "specification." Actually I mean to use the term "specification" so as to cover two connected replies. Both begin in the same way. "You only think there's a problem here because you think that 'Aggressor has a right to life' entails 'Aggressor has a right to not be killed.' But it doesn't. We all do have a right to life, but that right to life is a more complicated business than it at first may appear to be. In particular, having a right to life *doesn't* include having a right to not be killed. Indeed, *nobody* has a right to not be killed: all you have is—" and here there are two ways in which the speaker may go on. I will call the first "moral specification": ". . . all you have is the right to not be wrongly, unjustly killed." I will call the second "factual specification": ". . . all you have is the right to not be killed if you are not in process of trying to kill a person, where that person has every reason to believe he can preserve his life only by killing you." There is what seems to me a serious objection, which bears against both of these equally. But first let us look at difficulties specific to each.

I used to think that the reply I have called "moral specification" was the right reply to make in the case I described, as in other, similar, cases. That is, I used to think it just a mistake to suppose that anyone has a right to not be killed. It is so obvious that there are cases in which it is permissible, and therefore no violation of anyone's rights, to kill a person that it seems right to say that the most we can plausibly be thought to have is a right to not be wrongly or unjustly killed. But if so, then it is hard to see how appeal to rights which we do or do not have can *explain* why it is or is not permissible for a person to kill. Consider Victim. We were asked to explain why it is permissible for Victim to use his anti-tank gun on Aggressor, thereby killing him; and consider the following answer: "The reason why it is permissible for Victim to kill Aggressor is that Aggressor has no right to not be killed—he only has a right to not be killed wrongly or unjustly—and in killing Aggressor, Victim would not be killing Aggressor wrongly or unjustly." One does not mind all circles, but this circle is too small. For it to be permissible for Victim to kill Aggressor *is* for it to be the case that in killing Aggressor, Victim does not act wrongly or unjustly;

and we cannot say that the reason *why* Victim is not acting wrongly or unjustly in killing Aggressor is the fact that in killing Aggressor, Victim is not acting wrongly or unjustly.

The reply I have called "factual specification" is, I think, even less satisfactory. Let us look at it again. "Nobody has a right to not be killed: all you have is a right to not be killed if you are not in process of trying to kill a person, where that person has every reason to believe he can preserve his life only by killing you." Hence Victim can kill Aggressor. For Victim violates no right of Aggressor's in killing him, for Aggressor *is* in process of trying to kill Victim, where Victim has every reason to believe he can preserve his life only by killing Aggressor.

But the fact is that there are a great many other cases in which it is permissible to kill a man—defense of your life against a villain is by no means the only one. Consider Second Aggressor again. Second Aggressor is no villain; yet Second Victim can shoot to kill.

Again, consider a case which involves what Robert Nozick calls an "innocent shield of a threat."[4] Third Aggressor is driving his tank at you. But he has taken care to arrange that a baby is strapped to the front of the tank, so that if you use your anti-tank gun, you will not only kill Third Aggressor, you will kill the baby. Now Third Aggressor, admittedly, is in process of trying to kill you; but that baby isn't. Yet you can presumably go ahead and use the gun, even though this involves killing the baby as well as Third Aggressor.

It would, of course, be consistent to opt for "factual specification" in the original case of Aggressor and Victim, and yet not opt for a similar reply in these other cases. Yet it is hard to see what reason there could be for distinguishing. And if a similar reply is opted for in these other cases, we shall find ourselves having to say, not only that nobody has a right to not be killed, but also that you do not even have a right to not be killed if you are not in process of trying to kill a person, where that person has every reason to believe he can preserve his life only by killing you. We shall find ourselves having to say that the most you have is a right to not be killed if (a) you are not a villain who is trying to kill a person, and (b) you are not a schizophrenic who is trying to (as he sees it) ward off an attack on his home and family, and (c) you are not tied to a tank which will kill a person—where the threatened person in (a), (b), and (c) has

4. See his *Anarchy, State, and Utopia* (New York: Basic Books, 1974), p. 35.

every reason to believe he can preserve his life only by killing you.

And this is obviously not the end of it. Consider a case of a quite different kind, which I borrow from Philippa Foot.[5] You are the driver of a trolley. On the track ahead of you are five track workmen. The banks are very steep at that point, and the men are not able to get off the track. Well, it is plain enough: you had better put on your brakes. Alas, the brakes do not work. You notice just then that there is a spur of track leading off to the right, and you can turn off onto it. But again alas, you can see that there is one track workman on that spur, and he too cannot get off the track. If you do nothing, you kill five; if you turn off to the right, you kill one. Presumably it is morally permissible—some would even say it was morally required—that you turn the trolley off to the right, thereby killing one. But *why* is it permissible to kill that one? Does he not have a right to life?[6] Notice that *he* is not threatening anybody at all; nor is he an innocent shield of a threat. A friend of "factual specification" will then presumably have to expand still further his list of conditions under which killing is permissible, and thus make still more complicated the right which—as he says—is the most we have in respect of life.

Where is this to end? Is there anybody who knows what right it is which (it is here suggested) is the most we have in respect of life?

Moreover, it is worth noticing that a kind of circle is going to turn up here too. What the friend of factual specification has to do is to figure out when it is permissible to kill, and then tailor, accordingly, his account of what right it is which is the most we have in respect of life. But, if that is the only way anyone can have of finding out what right it is we have in respect of life, how can anyone then *explain* its being permissible to kill in such and such circumstances by appeal to the fact that killing in those circumstances does not violate the right which is the most the victim has in respect of life?

But I think there is a still more serious objection, which bears equally against both moral specification and factual specification. What I have in mind is that both replies issue from what I think is an incorrect

5. See her "Abortion and the Doctrine of the Double Effect," *Oxford Review* 5 (1967).

6. If the workman on the right-hand track has a right to life (and it seems plain that if we do, he does), then we cannot explain the fact that a surgeon cannot cut you up and parcel out your parts to save five by appeal to the fact that you have a right to life. For so does the workman, yet the driver *can* turn the trolley onto him to save five. Mrs. Foot (ibid.) has an explanation; others may be found in Essays 6 and 7 of this volume.

view of rights: neither would be opted for by anyone who did not take the view that rights are, in a certain sense, *absolute.* What this sense is may best be brought out if we make a terminological distinction. Suppose a man has a right that something or other shall be the case; let us say he has a right that p, where p is some statement or other, and now suppose that we make p false. So, for example, if his right is the right that he is not punched in the nose, we make that false, that is, we bring about that he *is* punched in the nose. Then, as I shall say, we *infringe* his right. But I shall say that we *violate* his right if and only if we do not merely infringe his right, but more, are acting wrongly, unjustly in doing so. Now the view that rights are absolute in the sense I have in mind is the view that every infringing of a right is a violating of a right.

This view of rights seems to me, as I said, to be incorrect. That it is comes out in the following case. You are rich, and therefore own lots of steak, which you keep in a locked freezer on your back porch. Here is a child with a terrible protein deficiency: he will die if I do not get some protein into him fast. I have none myself at the moment. I call you to see if you will lend or sell me a steak, but your answering service says you are out of town for the weekend, and they do not know where. The only way in which I can get some protein for that child is to break into your freezer and take a steak. Now most people would say it is okay, I can go ahead. But why? Don't you have a right that people will not break into your freezer and take a steak? If anyone thinks that rights are absolute, then he is committed to saying that you do not after all have a right that people will not break into your freezer and take a steak, and this on the ground that I do not act wrongly or unjustly if I do so—and I surely do not act wrongly or unjustly if I do so, since it is permissible for me to do so. This is not to say he has to deny you have *any* rights over your freezer and your steak. We are all familiar by now with the kind of right he can say you have. He can engage in moral specification: he can say that although you do not have a right that people will not break into your freezer and take a steak, you do have a right that people will not do this wrongly or unjustly. Or, alternatively, he can engage in factual specification: he can say that the right you do have is that people will not do this except where they have in hand a child with a protein deficiency, who will die if it is not done. But the point, I think, is that the wrong move was made from the start. Surely you *do* have a right that people will not break into your freezer and take a steak. If you had no such right, why would I have to compensate you later for having done so? And surely I do have to compensate you: I have to pay for the damage I caused to the freezer, and I have to replace, or pay you for, the steak I took.

If all you had was a right that I not wrongly or unjustly break into the freezer and take a steak, then I would have done nothing at all you have a right I not do; in which case, why would I owe you anything for what I did? Similarly, if all you had was a right that I not break into the freezer and take a steak when I do not have a starving child to feed, then since I did have a starving child to feed, I would have done nothing at all you had a right I not do; so once again, no compensation would be owing. The fact that compensation *is* owing shows (and it seems to me, shows conclusively) that I did do something you had a right that I not do. How are we to square this fact with the fact that I did not act wrongly or unjustly in doing so? I think we had better allow that there are cases in which a right may be infringed without being violated—i.e., cases in which one does a thing another has a right he not do, and yet in which one does not violate a right.

Now I do not suppose that if Victim kills Aggressor in the circumstances I described at the outset, then Victim must pay compensation to Aggressor's heirs. I do not suppose that if the trolley driver turns off to the right, killing the one, then he must pay compensation to the one's heirs. But there surely are cases in which it is permissible to kill, and in which compensation *is* owed. If you are an "innocent threat"[7] to my life (you threaten it through no fault of your own), and I can save my life only by killing you, and therefore do kill you, I think I do owe compensation, for I take your life to save mine. If so, I infringe a right of yours but do not violate it. And this means that at least some rights in respect of life—as well as at least some rights in respect of property—are not absolute.

It could, of course, be insisted that Victim (supposing he killed Aggressor) not only violated no right of Aggressor's, but also infringed no right of Aggressor's. And as I said, there is no need for Victim to compensate Aggressor's heirs, so there is not available *that* ground for saying that Victim infringed a right of Aggressor's. On the other hand, if we do say that Victim infringed a right of Aggressor's (and that the trolley driver infringed a right of the one on the

7. The term is Robert Nozick's: see *Anarchy, State, and Utopia*, p. 34.

right-hand track, and . . .), then it is open to us to say—what had certainly seemed plausible at the outset—that we all of us do have a right to not be killed. Quite simply: a right to not be killed. Not an absolute right to not be killed, of course, only a nonabsolute right to not be killed. And saying this would be entirely consistent with saying that we also have the (absolute) right to not be killed wrongly or unjustly, which the moral specifier attributes to us, and the (absolute) right to not be killed if (a) we are not a villain who is trying to kill a person, and (b) we are not a schizophrenic who . . . , which the factual specifier will attribute to us if and when he ever finishes specifying it.

It is not surprising that people are inclined to opt for the view that rights are absolute: if a person has a *right* to such and such how can it be that anyone may, permissibly, deprive him of it? Isn't a right something one can positively *demand* accordance with? But the fact is that there are occasions on which a right is infringed but not violated; and a moral philosopher has to find some way of explaining what makes this be the case when it is. A move which is familiar enough is to say that what makes this be the case when it is is the fact that the right in question is "overridden." It is a natural idea, then, that we should make the same move in respect of Victim and Aggressor. Ths brings us to the third of the three replies to the question I asked: for obvious reasons, I will call it "overriding."

4. An overrider begins as follows. "Yes, Aggressor does, like the rest of us, have a right to not be killed. A nonabsolute right is all it is, however. And the reason why it is permissible for Victim to kill Aggressor is the fact that, the circumstances being what they are, Aggressor's right to not be killed is overridden." But what does "His right is overridden" mean? If it means only "It is permissible to infringe his right," then—so far as explanatory force is concerned—the overrider might as well have instead said "And the reason why it is permissible for Victim to kill Aggressor is the fact that, the circumstances being what they are, it is permissible for Victim to kill Aggressor."

Moreover, by what is Aggressor's right supposed to be overridden? That is (as I take it), what in the circumstances makes it permissible for Victim to kill Aggressor? An overrider may be expected to answer in one or another of two ways. He may say "Aggressor's right to not be killed is overridden by the fact that a great lot of utility will get produced if Victim kills Aggressor—much more utility than if Victim does not kill Aggressor." Or he may instead say "Aggressor's right to not be killed is overridden by a more stringent right of Victim's." I find the first of these two answers uninteresting: it is easy enough to add details to the story which, *prima facie*, at any rate, suggest that the utilities are not as the answer claims they are, and I think that a dispute as to whether or not they really do is not theoretically fruitful. So I shall attend only to the second of the two answers.

The answer obviously invites a question: "What makes one right be more stringent than another?" If what makes Victim's right (whatever it is) be more stringent than Aggressor's right to not be killed is merely the very fact that it is permissible for Victim to kill Aggressor, then it is hard to see how we can explain the fact that it is permissible for Victim to kill Aggressor by appeal to a right in Victim which is more stringent than Aggressor's right to not be killed. I do not say that no independent account of relative stringency among rights can be given; I say only that an overrider plainly needs one.

Moreover, there is a second question which the answer invites, and which we should take note of, namely the question "*What* right is it which Victim has, and which is more stringent than Aggressor's right to not be killed, and which is such that, the circumstances containing the fact that that right of Victim's is more stringent than Aggressor's right to not be killed, it is permissible for Victim to kill Aggressor?" It is a good question, I think.

We might begin with this: the right which Victim has, and which meets those further conditions, is the right to preserve his life. But *is* Victim's right to preserve his life more stringent than Aggressor's right to not be killed? Certainly it just is not the case, quite generally, that one person's right to preserve his life is more stringent than another person's right to not be killed. Suppose I am starving, and need food or else I die. Suppose further that the only available food is *you*. I should imagine I do have a right to preserve my life; but surely your right to not be killed is more stringent than my right to preserve my life—surely it is not permissible for me to kill you to preserve my life!

Well, perhaps we simply fastened on the wrong right; perhaps we should instead have said that the right which Victim has, and which meets those further conditions, is the right to self-defense—more precisely, perhaps, the right to preserve his life against an attack on it. (Your being the only available food does not make it be the case that you are *attacking* me.) But *is* Victim's right to preserve his life against an attack on it more stringent than Aggressor's right to not be killed? Certainly it just is not the case, quite generally, that one person's right to preserve his life against an attack on it is more stringent than another person's right to not be killed. Suppose I am being threatened with a gun, and the only way in which I can preserve my life against that attack on it is by grabbing some innocent bystander and shoving him in front of me. I should imagine I do have a right to preserve my life against an attack on it; but surely the innocent bystander's right to not be killed is more stringent than my right to preserve my life against an attack on it—surely it is not permissible for me to shove the innocent bystander in front of me!

I suppose it could be said that Aggressor's right to not be killed is less stringent than yours is, and than the innocent bystander's is, and that that is why Victim may act though I may not. Aggressor is a villain, after all, and neither you nor the innocent bystander is.

But then are we to suppose that after the stall of the tank, and Aggressor's breaking of his ankles, Aggressor's right to not be killed sweeps back to being just as stringent as yours is, and as the innocent bystander's is? For after that time, Victim may not kill Aggressor on any weaker grounds than would permit of his killing you or an innocent bystander.

The right to not be killed (as well as the right to preserve one's life, the right to preserve one's life against an attack on it, and the right to life itself) is traditionally thought to be a natural right, that is, a right a human being has simply by virtue of being a human being.[8] Now if a right is a right which we have simply by virtue of being human beings, it is not possible that some human beings possess it and others do not. Moreover, it is not possible that a human being possesses it at one time and not at another, so long as he remains a human being throughout.

Suppose the time now is after the start of Aggressor's attack on Victim, but before the time at which Aggressor ceases to pose a threat to Victim. If the right to not be killed is a natural right, so defined (henceforth I shall take this qualification to be understood), then we plainly cannot say

8. See H. L. A. Hart's definition of "natural right" in "Are There Any Natural Rights?" *The Philosophical Review* 64 (April 1955). See also Joel Feinberg's definition of what he calls "human rights" in *Social Philosophy* (Englewood Cliffs, N.J.: Prentice-Hall, 1973).

(1) Aggressor had (before launching his attack) and will again have (after breaking his ankles) a right to not be killed, but he does not have this right now. *That* is why Victim may now kill him.

But *is* the right to not be killed a natural right? It is by no means obvious that it is. Perhaps the right to not be killed is forfeitable. Hobbes thought that the right to not be killed is inalienable, but perhaps even this is wrong. Could one not voluntarily relinquish one's right to not be killed? Suppose I am terminally ill, and want to be able to provide for my children. Here is a rich man, who likes to kill. I say "For so and so much, to be given to my children, you may kill me now." Suppose, then, that he accepts my offer, and kills me. No doubt he does not act *well.* Perhaps he does what it is impermissible for him to do. But I think it arguable that he violates—even that he infringes—no right of mine, and that if he does act impermissibly, it is nothing to do with my rights that makes this so.

Moreover, even if the right to not be killed is a natural right, this does not settle what we are to say about the case in hand. Of course we may not say (1). I should imagine also that we cannot say

(2) Aggressor has (at all times) a right to not be killed, but Aggressor's right to not be killed is (at all times) less stringent than any innocent person's is—so much less stringent as to be less stringent than Victim's right to preserve his life against an attack on it. *That* is why Victim may now kill him.

It is not inconsistent to suppose that a certain right is a right which we all have by virtue of being human beings, and nevertheless that it varies in stringency between human beings—in particular, between the innocent and the villains. We do of course say about natural rights that they are "equal" in both of the following two senses: every human being has them, and no one human being's are any more stringent than any other human being's. But only the first follows from the definition of "natural right" which I gave above. So taking the right to not be killed to be a natural right does not rule out opting for (2). But I take it that what I drew attention to a moment ago *does* rule out opting for (2). What I have in mind is the fact that after the stall of the tank, and Aggressor's breaking of his ankles, Aggressor's right to not be killed is surely just as stringent as yours is, and as the innocent bystander's is—for after that time, Victim may not kill Aggressor on any weaker grounds than would permit of his killing you or an innocent bystander.

This points, however, to a further possibility. It is not inconsistent to suppose that a certain right is a right which we all have by virtue of being human beings, and nevertheless that it sweeps back and forth from one degree of stringency to another in one human being—according as he is or is not threatening another. I do not think it is as commonly said that natural rights are also equal in the following (third) sense: no one human being's are any more stringent at one time than they are at any other time. That they are equal in this sense certainly does not follow from the definition of "natural right" I gave, or even from their being equal in either of the two senses I pointed to. So it would be consistent to say that the right to not be killed is a natural right, and yet also opt for

(3) Aggressor has (at all times) a right to not be killed, and Aggressor's right to not be killed was (before launching his attack) and will again be (after breaking his ankles) as stringent as any innocent person's is, but it is less stringent now—so much less stringent now as to be less stringent than Victim's right to preserve his life against an attack on it. *That* is why Victim may now kill him.

So far as I can see, nothing in the case rules this out.

But there is plainly yet another alternative. Don't we all of us have a right to kill a person who is currently giving us every reason to believe that he will kill us unless we kill him? And isn't this right as good a candidate for the status of natural right as the right to not be killed is? And isn't it, moreover, *always* more stringent than the right to not be killed? If so, there is a fourth alternative:

(4) Aggressor has (at all times) an equally stringent right to not be killed, but that right is (always) less stringent than the right—possessed by Victim—to kill a person who is currently giving every reason to believe that he will kill Victim unless Victim kills him. *That* is why Victim may now kill him.

Is there any principled ground for choosing between (3) and (4)? Indeed, between (1), (3), and (4)?—since, as I said, it is by no means obvious that the right to not be killed is a natural right.

The other side of the same coin is that (1), (3), and (4) are marvelously *ad hoc*. Consider the appeal in (1) to loss of, and then re-acquisition of, the right to not be killed; is there any reason to opt for (1) other than the fact that if we do, we seem to have in hand an explanation of why Victim may kill Aggressor? Similarly for the appeal in (3) to difference in stringency in one person across time. And what of that right to kill a person who is currently giving every reason to believe that he will kill you unless you kill him? Can there be any reason to suppose we have such a right other than the fact that it is permissible for a victim to kill an aggressor who is currently giving every reason to believe that he will kill the victim unless the victim kills him? Notice how carefully tailored to its explanatory purpose this right is.

Notice, moreover, how difficult it would be to find a lesson in any of this in respect of permitted killings generally. Take the case of the trolley driver I mentioned earlier. Surely the trolley driver may turn his trolley, to save five at a cost of one. Does it seem at all plausible to say that the reason why he may is that the one has ceased to have a right to not be killed, or that his right to not be killed is now less stringent than it was before he started work on that particular stretch of track? Of course we could say that the reason why the trolley driver may turn the trolley is that he has a right to turn his trolley onto one to save five, and that that right is always more stringent than the right to not be killed—compare (4) above. But you might as well say: Leave me alone, I'm too busy to do moral philosophy this afternoon.

5. Many people who do moral philosophy these days appeal to rights to *explain* why this or that piece of behavior is or is not permissible. For example, it is common to say that the reason why you cannot maximize utility in such and such a case is the fact that the utility-maximizing course of action would involve infringing a right—indeed, violating a right, since the right in question is a stringent one, and the utility to be got not sufficiently great to override the right. But when we say that, in that case, the utility-maximizing course of action would involve violating a right, *are* we saying anything more than that, in that case, it is not permissible to take the utility-maximizing course of action? If not, then we can hardly take ourselves to have explained why it is not permissible, in that case, to take the utility-maximizing course of action. It is arguable that if there is to be any point at all in appealing to rights in such discussions, there had better be something independent of permissibilities and impermissibilities which fixes their existence and degree of stringency. It is not obvious that this is true. It might be that to attribute a right is only

to talk about permissibilities and impermissibilities, but in a way that groups or collects them, and brings whole clusters of cases to bear on each other. I do not for a moment think it a novel idea that we stand in need of an account of just how an appeal to a right may be thought to function in ethical discussion. What strikes me as of interest, however, is that the need for such an account shows itself even in a case which might have been thought to be transparent.[9]

9. I am indebted to the students and faculty of the Department of Philosophy at the University of Kansas, and to the members of the Society for Ethical and Legal Philosophy, for criticisms of earlier versions of this essay.

II

WHAT MAKES RIGHT ACTS RIGHT?

THE real point at issue between hedonism and utilitarianism on the one hand and their opponents on the other is not whether 'right' means 'productive of so and so'; for it cannot with any plausibility be maintained that it does. The point at issue is that to which we now pass, viz. whether there is any general character which makes right acts right, and if so, what it is. Among the main historical attempts to state a single characteristic of all right actions which is the foundation of their rightness are those made by egoism and utilitarianism. But I do not propose to discuss these, not because the subject is unimportant, but because it has been dealt with so often and so well already, and because there has come to be so much agreement among moral philosophers that neither of these theories is satisfactory. A much more attractive theory has been put forward by Professor Moore: that what makes actions right is that they are productive of more *good* than could have been produced by any other action open to the agent.[1]

This theory is in fact the culmination of all the attempts to base rightness on productivity of some sort of result. The first form this attempt takes is the attempt to base rightness on conduciveness to the advantage or pleasure of the agent. This theory comes to grief over the fact, which stares us in the face, that a great part of duty consists in an observance of the rights and a furtherance of the interests of others, whatever the cost to ourselves may be. Plato and others may be right in holding that a regard for the rights of others never in the long run involves a loss of happiness for the agent, that 'the just life profits a man'. But this, even if true, is irrelevant to the rightness of the act. As soon as a man does an action *because* he thinks he will promote his own interests thereby, he is acting not from a sense of its rightness but from self-interest.

[1] I take the theory which, as I have tried to show, seems to be put forward in *Ethics* rather than the earlier and less plausible theory put forward in *Principia Ethica*. For the difference, cf. my pp. 8-11.

To the egoistic theory hedonistic utilitarianism supplies a much-needed amendment. It points out correctly that the fact that a certain pleasure will be enjoyed by the agent is no reason why he *ought* to bring it into being rather than an equal or greater pleasure to be enjoyed by another, though, human nature being what it is, it makes it not unlikely that he *will* try to bring it into being. But hedonistic utilitarianism in its turn needs a correction. On reflection it seems clear that pleasure is not the only thing in life that we think good in itself, that for instance we think the possession of a good character, or an intelligent understanding of the world, as good or better. A great advance is made by the substitution of 'productive of the greatest good' for 'productive of the greatest pleasure'.

Not only is this theory more attractive than hedonistic utilitarianism, but its logical relation to that theory is such that the latter could not be true unless *it* were true, while it might be true though hedonistic utilitarianism were not. It is in fact one of the logical bases of hedonistic utilitarianism. For the view that what produces the maximum pleasure is right has for its bases the views (1) that what produces the maximum good is right, and (2) that pleasure is the only thing good in itself. If they were not assuming that what produces the maximum *good* is right, the utilitarians' attempt to show that pleasure is the only thing good in itself, which is in fact the point they take most pains to establish, would have been quite irrelevant to their attempt to prove that only what produces the maximum *pleasure* is right. If, therefore, it can be shown that productivity of the maximum good is not what makes all right actions right, we shall *a fortiori* have refuted hedonistic utilitarianism.

When a plain man fulfils a promise because he thinks he ought to do so, it seems clear that he does so with no thought of its total consequences, still less with any opinion that these are likely to be the best possible. He thinks in fact much more of the past than of the future. What makes him think it right to act in a certain way is the fact that he has promised to do so —that and, usually, nothing more. That his act will produce the best possible consequences is not his reason for calling it right. What lends colour to the theory we are examining, then, is not the actions (which form probably a great majority of our actions) in which some such reflection as 'I have promised' is the only reason we give ourselves for thinking a certain action right, but the exceptional cases in which the consequences of fulfilling a promise (for instance) would be so disastrous to others that we judge it right not to do so. It must of course be admitted that such cases exist. If I have promised to meet a friend at a particular time for some trivial purpose, I should certainly think myself justified in breaking my engagement if by doing so I could prevent a serious accident or bring relief to the victims of one. And the supporters of the view we are examining hold that my thinking so is due to my thinking that I shall bring more good into existence by the one action than by the other. A different account may, however, be given of the matter, an account which will, I believe, show itself to be the true one. It may be said that besides the duty of fulfilling promises I have and recognize a duty of relieving distress,[1] and that when I think it right to do the latter at the cost of not doing the former, it is not because I think I shall produce more good thereby but because I think it the duty which is in the circumstances more of a duty. This account surely corresponds much more closely with what we really think in such a situation. If, so far as I can see, I could bring equal amounts of good into being by fulfilling my promise and by helping some one to whom I had made no promise, I should not hesitate to regard the former as my duty. Yet on the view that what is right is right because it is productive of the most good I should not so regard it.

There are two theories, each in its way simple, that offer a solution of such cases of conscience. One is the view of Kant, that there are certain duties of perfect obligation, such as those of fulfilling promises, of paying debts, of telling the truth, which admit of no exception whatever in favour of duties of imperfect obligation, such as that of relieving distress. The other is the view of, for instance, Professor Moore and Dr. Rashdall, that there is only the duty of producing good, and

[1] These are not strictly speaking duties, but things that tend to be our duty, or *prima facie* duties. Cf. pp. 19–20.

that all 'conflicts of duties' should be resolved by asking 'by which action will most good be produced?' But it is more important that our theory fit the facts than that it be simple, and the account we have given above corresponds (it seems to me) better than either of the simpler theories with what we really think, viz. that normally promise-keeping, for example, should come before benevolence, but that when and only when the good to be produced by the benevolent act is very great and the promise comparatively trivial, the act of benevolence becomes our duty.

In fact the theory of 'ideal utilitarianism', if I may for brevity refer so to the theory of Professor Moore, seems to simplify unduly our relations to our fellows. It says, in effect, that the only morally significant relation in which my neighbours stand to me is that of being possible beneficiaries by my action.[1] They do stand in this relation to me, and this relation is morally significant. But they may also stand to me in the relation of promisee to promiser, of creditor to debtor, of wife to husband, of child to parent, of friend to friend, of fellow countryman to fellow countryman, and the like; and each of these relations is the foundation of a *prima facie* duty, which is more or less incumbent on me according to the circumstances of the case. When I am in a situation, as perhaps I always am, in which more than one of these *prima facie* duties is incumbent on me, what I have to do is to study the situation as fully as I can until I form the considered opinion (it is never more) that in the circumstances one of them is more incumbent than any other; then I am bound to think that to do this *prima facie* duty is my duty *sans phrase* in the situation.

I suggest '*prima facie* duty' or 'conditional duty' as a brief way of referring to the characteristic (quite distinct from that of being a duty proper) which an act has, in virtue of being of a certain kind (e.g. the keeping of a promise), of being an act which would be a duty proper if it were not at the same time of another kind which is morally significant. Whether an act

[1] Some will think it, apart from other considerations, a sufficient refutation of this view to point out that I also stand in that relation to myself, so that for this view the distinction of oneself from others is morally insignificant.

is a duty proper or actual duty depends on *all* the morally significant kinds it is an instance of. The phrase '*prima facie* duty' must be apologized for, since (1) it suggests that what we are speaking of is a certain kind of duty, whereas it is in fact not a duty, but something related in a special way to duty. Strictly speaking, we want not a phrase in which duty is qualified by an adjective, but a separate noun. (2) '*Prima*' *facie* suggests that one is speaking only of an appearance which a moral situation presents at first sight, and which may turn out to be illusory; whereas what I am speaking of is an objective fact involved in the nature of the situation, or more strictly in an element of its nature, though not, as duty proper does, arising from its *whole* nature. I can, however, think of no term which fully meets the case. 'Claim' has been suggested by Professor Prichard. The word 'claim' has the advantage of being quite a familiar one in this connexion, and it seems to cover much of the ground. It would be quite natural to say, 'a person to whom I have made a promise has a claim on me', and also, 'a person whose distress I could relieve (at the cost of breaking the promise) has a claim on me'. But (1) while 'claim' is appropriate from *their* point of view, we want a word to express the corresponding fact from the agent's point of view—the fact of his being subject to claims that can be made against him; and ordinary language provides us with no such correlative to 'claim'. And (2) (what is more important) 'claim' seems inevitably to suggest two persons, one of whom might make a claim on the other; and while this covers the ground of social duty, it is inappropriate in the case of that important part of duty which is the duty of cultivating a certain kind of character in oneself. It would be artificial, I think, and at any rate metaphorical, to say that one's character has a claim on oneself.

There is nothing arbitrary about these *prima facie* duties. Each rests on a definite circumstance which cannot seriously be held to be without moral significance. Of *prima facie* duties I suggest, without claiming completeness or finality for it, the following division.[1]

[1] I should make it plain at this stage that I am *assuming* the correctness of some of our main convictions as to *prima facie* duties, or, more strictly, am claiming that we

(1) Some duties rest on previous acts of my own. These duties seem to include two kinds, (*a*) those resting on a promise or what may fairly be called an implicit promise, such as the implicit undertaking not to tell lies which seems to be implied in the act of entering into conversation (at any rate by civilized men), or of writing books that purport to be history and not fiction. These may be called the duties of fidelity. (*b*) Those resting on a previous wrongful act. These may be called the duties of reparation. (2) Some rest on previous acts of other men, i.e. services done by them to me. These may be loosely described as the duties of gratitude.[1] (3) Some rest on the fact or possibility of a distribution of pleasure or happiness (or of the means thereto) which is not in accordance with the merit of the persons concerned; in such cases there arises a duty to upset or prevent such a distribution. These are the duties of justice. (4) Some rest on the mere fact that there are other beings in the world whose condition we can make better in respect of virtue, or of intelligence, or of pleasure. These are the duties of beneficence. (5) Some rest on the fact that we can improve our own condition in respect of virtue or of intelligence. These are the duties of self-improvement. (6) I think that we should distinguish from (4) the duties that may be summed up under the title of 'not injuring others'. No doubt to injure others is incidentally to fail to do them good; but it seems to me clear that non-maleficence is apprehended as a duty distinct from that of beneficence, and as a duty of a more stringent character. It will be noticed that this alone among the types of duty has been stated in a negative way. An attempt might no doubt be made to state this duty, like the others, in a positive way. It might be said that it is really the duty to

know them to be true. To me it seems as self-evident as anything could be, that to make a promise, for instance, is to create a moral claim on us in someone else. Many readers will perhaps say that they do *not* know this to be true. If so, I certainly cannot prove it to them; I can only ask them to reflect again, in the hope that they will ultimately agree that they also know it to be true. The main moral convictions of the plain man seem to me to be, not opinions which it is for philosophy to prove or disprove, but knowledge from the start; and in my own case I seem to find little difficulty in distinguishing these essential convictions from other moral convictions which I also have, which are merely fallible opinions based on an imperfect study of the working for good or evil of certain institutions or types of action.

[1] For a needed correction of this statement, cf. pp. 22–3.

prevent ourselves from acting either from an inclination to harm others or from an inclination to seek our own pleasure, in doing which we should incidentally harm them. But on reflection it seems clear that the primary duty here is the duty not to harm others, this being a duty whether or not we have an inclination that if followed would lead to our harming them; and that when we have such an inclination the primary duty not to harm others gives rise to a consequential duty to resist the inclination. The recognition of this duty of non-maleficence is the first step on the way to the recognition of the duty of beneficence; and that accounts for the prominence of the commands 'thou shalt not kill', 'thou shalt not commit adultery', 'thou shalt not steal', 'thou shalt not bear false witness', in so early a code as the Decalogue. But even when we have come to recognize the duty of beneficence, it appears to me that the duty of non-maleficence is recognized as a distinct one, and as *prima facie* more binding. We should not in general consider it justifiable to kill one person in order to keep another alive, or to steal from one in order to give alms to another.

The essential defect of the 'ideal utilitarian' theory is that it ignores, or at least does not do full justice to, the highly personal character of duty. If the only duty is to produce the maximum of good, the question who is to have the good—whether it is myself, or my benefactor, or a person to whom I have made a promise to confer that good on him, or a mere fellow man to whom I stand in no such special relation—should make no difference to my having a duty to produce that good. But we are all in fact sure that it makes a vast difference.

One or two other comments must be made on this provisional list of the divisions of duty. (1) The nomenclature is not strictly correct. For by 'fidelity' or 'gratitude' we mean, strictly, certain states of motivation; and, as I have urged, it is not our duty to have certain motives, but to do certain acts. By 'fidelity', for instance, is meant, strictly, the disposition to fulfil promises and implicit promises *because we have made them.* We have no general word to cover the actual fulfilment of promises and implicit promises *irrespective of motive*; and I use 'fidelity', loosely but perhaps conveniently, to fill this gap. So too I use 'gratitude' for the returning of services, irrespective of motive. The term 'justice' is not so much confined, in ordinary usage, to a certain state of motivation, for we should often talk of a man as acting justly even when we did not think his motive was the wish to do what was just simply for the sake of doing so. Less apology is therefore needed for our use of 'justice' in this sense. And I have used the word 'beneficence' rather than 'benevolence', in order to emphasize the fact that it is our duty to do certain things, and not to do them from certain motives.

(2) If the objection be made, that this catalogue of the main types of duty is an unsystematic one resting on no logical principle, it may be replied, first, that it makes no claim to being ultimate. It is a *prima facie* classification of the duties which reflection on our moral convictions seems actually to reveal. And if these convictions are, as I would claim that they are, of the nature of knowledge, and if I have not misstated them, the list will be a list of authentic conditional duties, correct as far as it goes though not necessarily complete. The list of *goods* put forward by the rival theory is reached by exactly the same method—the only sound one in the circumstances—viz. that of direct reflection on what we really think. Loyalty to the facts is worth more than a symmetrical architectonic or a hastily reached simplicity. If further reflection discovers a perfect logical basis for this or for a better classification, so much the better.

(3) It may, again, be objected that our theory that there are these various and often conflicting types of *prima facie* duty leaves us with no principle upon which to discern what is our actual duty in particular circumstances. But this objection is not one which the rival theory is in a position to bring forward. For when we have to choose between the production of two heterogeneous goods, say knowledge and pleasure, the 'ideal utilitarian' theory can only fall back on an opinion, for which no logical basis can be offered, that one of the goods is the greater; and this is no better than a similar opinion that one of two duties is the more urgent. And again, when we consider the infinite variety of the effects of our actions in the way of

pleasure, it must surely be admitted that the claim which *hedonism* sometimes makes, that it offers a readily applicable criterion of right conduct, is quite illusory.

I am unwilling, however, to content myself with an *argumentum ad hominem*, and I would contend that in principle there is no reason to anticipate that every act that is our duty is so for one and the same reason. Why should two sets of circumstances, or one set of circumstances, *not* possess different characteristics, any one of which makes a certain act our *prima facie* duty? When I ask what it is that makes me in certain cases sure that I have a *prima facie* duty to do so and so, I find that it lies in the fact that I have made a promise; when I ask the same question in another case, I find the answer lies in the fact that I have done a wrong. And if on reflection I find (as I think I do) that neither of these reasons is reducible to the other, I must not on any *a priori* ground assume that such a reduction is possible.

An attempt may be made to arrange in a more systematic way the main types of duty which we have indicated. In the first place it seems self-evident that if there are things that are intrinsically good, it is *prima facie* a duty to bring them into existence rather than not to do so, and to bring as much of them into existence as possible. It will be argued in our fifth chapter that there are three main things that are intrinsically good—virtue, knowledge, and, with certain limitations, pleasure. And since a given virtuous disposition, for instance, is equally good whether it is realized in myself or in another, it seems to be my duty to bring it into existence whether in myself or in another. So too with a given piece of knowledge.

The case of pleasure is difficult; for while we clearly recognize a duty to produce pleasure for others, it is by no means so clear that we recognize a duty to produce pleasure for ourselves. This appears to arise from the following facts. The thought of an act as our duty is one that presupposes a certain amount of reflection about the act; and for that reason does not normally arise in connexion with acts towards which we are already impelled by another strong impulse. So far, the cause of our not thinking of the promotion of our own pleasure as a duty is analogous to the cause which usually prevents a highly sympathetic person from thinking of the promotion of the pleasure of others as a duty. He is impelled so strongly by direct interest in the well-being of others towards promoting their pleasure that he does not stop to ask whether it is his duty to promote it; and we are all impelled so strongly towards the promotion of our own pleasure that we do not stop to ask whether it is a duty or not. But there is a further reason why even when we stop to think about the matter it does not usually present itself as a duty: viz. that, since the performance of most of our duties involves the giving up of some pleasure that we desire, the doing of duty and the getting of pleasure for ourselves come by a natural association of ideas to be thought of as incompatible things. This association of ideas is in the main salutary in its operation, since it puts a check on what but for it would be much too strong, the tendency to pursue one's own pleasure without thought of other considerations. Yet if pleasure is good, it seems in the long run clear that it is right to get it for ourselves as well as to produce it for others, when this does not involve the failure to discharge some more stringent *prima facie* duty. The question is a very difficult one, but it seems that this conclusion can be denied only on one or other of three grounds: (1) that pleasure is not *prima facie* good (i.e. good when it is neither the actualization of a bad disposition nor undeserved), (2) that there is no *prima facie* duty to produce as much that is good as we can, or (3) that though there is a *prima facie* duty to produce other things that are good, there is no *prima facie* duty to produce pleasure which will be enjoyed by ourselves. I give reasons later[1] for not accepting the first contention. The second hardly admits of argument but seems to me plainly false. The third seems plausible only if we hold that an act that is pleasant or brings pleasure to ourselves must for that reason not be a duty; and this would lead to paradoxical consequences, such as that if a man enjoys giving pleasure to others or working for their moral improvement, it cannot be his duty to do so. Yet it seems to be a very stubborn fact, that in our ordinary consciousness we are not aware

[1] pp. 135–8.

of a duty to get pleasure for ourselves; and by way of partial explanation of this I may add that though, as I think, one's own pleasure is a good and there is a duty to produce it, it is only if we *think* of our own pleasure not as simply our own pleasure, but as an objective good, something that an impartial spectator would approve, that we can think of the getting it as a duty; and we do not habitually think of it in this way.

If these contentions are right, what we have called the duty of beneficence and the duty of self-improvement rest on the same ground. No different principles of duty are involved in the two cases. If we feel a special responsibility for improving our own character rather than that of others, it is not because a special principle is involved, but because we are aware that the one is more under our control than the other. It was on this ground that Kant expressed the practical law of duty in the form 'seek to make yourself good and other people happy'. He was so persuaded of the internality of virtue that he regarded any attempt by one person to produce virtue in another as bound to produce, at most, only a counterfeit of virtue, the doing of externally right acts not from the true principle of virtuous action but out of regard to another person. It must be admitted that one man cannot compel another to be virtuous; compulsory virtue would just not be virtue. But experience clearly shows that Kant overshoots the mark when he contends that one man cannot do anything to *promote* virtue in another, to bring such influences to bear upon him that his own response to them is more likely to be virtuous than his response to other influences would have been. And our duty to do this is not different in kind from our duty to improve our own characters.

It is equally clear, and clear at an earlier stage of moral development, that if there are things that are bad in themselves we ought, *prima facie*, not to bring them upon others; and on this fact rests the duty of non-maleficence.

The duty of justice is particularly complicated, and the word is used to cover things which are really very different—things such as the payment of debts, the reparation of injuries done by oneself to another, and the bringing about of a distribution of happiness between other people in proportion to merit. I use the word to denote only the last of these three. In the fifth chapter I shall try to show that besides the three (comparatively) simple goods, virtue, knowledge, and pleasure, there is a more complex good, not reducible to these, consisting in the proportionment of happiness to virtue. The bringing of this about is a duty which we owe to all men alike, though it may be reinforced by special responsibilities that we have undertaken to particular men. This, therefore, with beneficence and self-improvement, comes under the general principle that we should produce as much good as possible, though the good here involved is different in kind from any other.

But besides this general obligation, there are special obligations. These may arise, in the first place, incidentally, from acts which were not essentially meant to create such an obligation, but which nevertheless create it. From the nature of the case such acts may be of two kinds—the infliction of injuries on others, and the acceptance of benefits from them. It seems clear that these put us under a special obligation to other men, and that only these acts can do so incidentally. From these arise the twin duties of reparation and gratitude.

And finally there are special obligations arising from acts the very intention of which, when they were done, was to put us under such an obligation. The name for such acts is 'promises'; the name is wide enough if we are willing to include under it implicit promises, i.e. modes of behaviour in which without explicit verbal promise we intentionally create an expectation that we can be counted on to behave in a certain way in the interest of another person.

These seem to be, in principle, all the ways in which *prima facie* duties arise. In actual experience they are compounded together in highly complex ways. Thus, for example, the duty of obeying the laws of one's country arises partly (as Socrates contends in the *Crito*) from the duty of gratitude for the benefits one has received from it; partly from the implicit promise to obey which seems to be involved in permanent residence in a country whose laws we know we are *expected* to obey, and still more clearly involved when we ourselves invoke the protection of its laws (this is the truth underlying the doctrine of the social contract); and partly (if we are fortunate in our country) from the fact that its laws are potent instruments for the general good.

Or again, the sense of a general obligation to bring about (so far as we can) a just apportionment of happiness to merit is often greatly reinforced by the fact that many of the existing injustices are due to a social and economic system which we have, not indeed created, but taken part in and assented to; the duty of justice is then reinforced by the duty of reparation.

It is necessary to say something by way of clearing up the relation between *prima facie* duties and the actual or absolute duty to do one particular act in particular circumstances. If, as almost all moralists except Kant are agreed, and as most plain men think, it is sometimes right to tell a lie or to break a promise, it must be maintained that there is a difference between *prima facie* duty and actual or absolute duty. When we think ourselves justified in breaking, and indeed morally obliged to break, a promise in order to relieve some one's distress, we do not for a moment cease to recognize a *prima facie* duty to keep our promise, and this leads us to feel, not indeed shame or repentance, but certainly compunction, for behaving as we do; we recognize, further, that it is our duty to make up somehow to the promisee for the breaking of the promise. We have to distinguish from the characteristic of being our duty that of tending to be our duty. Any act that we do contains various elements in virtue of which it falls under various categories. In virtue of being the breaking of a promise, for instance, it tends to be wrong; in virtue of being an instance of relieving distress it tends to be right. Tendency to be one's duty may be called a parti-resultant attribute, i.e. one which belongs to an act in virtue of some one component in its nature. *Being* one's duty is a toti-resultant attribute, one which belongs to an act in virtue of its whole nature and of nothing less than this.[1] This distinction between parti-resultant and toti-resultant attributes is one which we shall meet in another context also.[2]

Another instance of the same distinction may be found in the operation of natural laws. *Qua* subject to the force of

[1] But cf. the qualification in p. 33, n. 2. [2] Cf. pp. 122-3.

gravitation towards some other body, each body tends to move in a particular direction with a particular velocity; but its actual movement depends on *all* the forces to which it is subject. It is only by recognizing this distinction that we can preserve the absoluteness of laws of nature, and only by recognizing a corresponding distinction that we can preserve the absoluteness of the general principles of morality. But an important difference between the two cases must be pointed out. When we say that in virtue of gravitation a body tends to move in a certain way, we are referring to a causal influence actually exercised on it by another body or other bodies. When we say that in virtue of being deliberately untrue a certain remark tends to be wrong, we are referring to no causal relation, to no relation that involves succession in time, but to such a relation as connects the various attributes of a mathematical figure. And if the word 'tendency' is thought to suggest too much a causal relation, it is better to talk of certain types of act as being *prima facie* right or wrong (or of different persons as having different and possibly conflicting claims upon us), than of their tending to be right or wrong.

Something should be said of the relation between our apprehension of the *prima facie* rightness of certain types of act and our mental attitude towards particular acts. It is proper to use the word 'apprehension' in the former case and not in the latter. That an act, *qua* fulfilling a promise, or *qua* effecting a just distribution of good, or *qua* returning services rendered, or *qua* promoting the good of others, or *qua* promoting the virtue or insight of the agent, is *prima facie* right, is self-evident; not in the sense that it is evident from the beginning of our lives, or as soon as we attend to the proposition for the first time, but in the sense that when we have reached sufficient mental maturity and have given sufficient attention to the proposition it is evident without any need of proof, or of evidence beyond itself. It is self-evident just as a mathematical axiom, or the validity of a form of inference, is evident. The moral order expressed in these propositions is just as much part of the fundamental nature of the universe (and, we may add, of any possible universe in which there were moral agents at all) as is the spatial or numerical structure expressed in the axioms of geometry or arithmetic. In our confidence that these propositions are true there is involved the same trust in our reason that is involved in our confidence in mathematics; and we should have no justification for trusting it in the latter sphere and distrusting it in the former. In both cases we are dealing with propositions that cannot be proved, but that just as certainly need no proof.

Some of these general principles of *prima facie* duty may appear to be open to criticism. It may be thought, for example, that the principle of returning good for good is a falling off from the Christian principle, generally and rightly recognized as expressing the highest morality, of returning good for evil. To this it may be replied that I do not suggest that there is a principle commanding us to return good for good and forbidding us to return good for evil, and that I do suggest that there is a positive duty to seek the good of all men. What I maintain is that an act in which good is returned for good is recognized as *specially* binding on us just because it is of that character, and that *ceteris paribus* any one would think it his duty to help his benefactors rather than his enemies, if he could not do both; just as it is generally recognized that *ceteris paribus* we should pay our debts rather than give our money in charity, when we cannot do both. A benefactor is not only a man, calling for our effort on his behalf on that ground, but also our benefactor, calling for our *special* effort on *that* ground.

Our judgements about our actual duty in concrete situations have none of the certainty that attaches to our recognition of the general principles of duty. A statement is certain, i.e. is an expression of knowledge, only in one or other of two cases: when it is either self-evident, or a valid conclusion from self-evident premisses. And our judgements about our particular duties have neither of these characters. (1) They are not self-evident. Where a possible act is seen to have two characteristics, in virtue of one of which it is *prima facie* right, and in virtue of the other *prima facie* wrong, we are (I think) well aware that we are not certain whether we ought or ought not to do it; that whether we do it or not, we are taking a moral risk. We come in the long run, after consideration, to think one duty more pressing than the other, but we do not feel certain that it is so. And though we do not always recognize that a possible act has two such characteristics, and though there *may* be cases in which it has not, we are never certain that any particular possible act has not, and therefore never certain that it is right, nor certain that it is wrong. For, to go no further in the analysis, it is enough to point out that any particular act will in all probability in the course of time contribute to the bringing about of good or of evil for many human beings, and thus have a *prima facie* rightness or wrongness of which we know nothing. (2) Again, our judgements about our particular duties are not logical conclusions from self-evident premisses. The only possible premisses would be the general principles stating their *prima facie* rightness or wrongness *qua* having the different characteristics they do have; and even if we could (as we cannot) apprehend the extent to which an act will tend on the one hand, for example, to bring about advantages for our benefactors, and on the other hand to bring about disadvantages for fellow men who are not our benefactors, there is no principle by which we can draw the conclusion that it is on the whole right or on the whole wrong. In this respect the judgement as to the rightness of a particular act is just like the judgement as to the beauty of a particular natural object or work of art. A poem is, for instance, in respect of certain qualities beautiful and in respect of certain others not beautiful; and our judgement as to the degree of beauty it possesses on the whole is never reached by logical reasoning from the apprehension of its particular beauties or particular defects. Both in this and in the moral case we have more or less probable opinions which are not logically justified conclusions from the general principles that are recognized as self-evident.

There is therefore much truth in the description of the right act as a fortunate act. If we cannot be certain that it is right, it is our good fortune if the act we do is the right act. This consideration does not, however, make the doing of our duty a mere matter of chance. There is a parallel here between the doing of duty and the doing of what will be to our personal advantage. We never *know* what act will in the long run be to our advantage. Yet it is certain that we are more likely in general to secure our advantage if we estimate to the best of our ability the probable tendencies of our actions in this respect, than if we act on caprice. And similarly we are more likely to do our duty if we reflect to the best of our ability on the *prima facie* rightness or wrongness of various possible acts in virtue of the characteristics we perceive them to have, than if we act without reflection. With this greater likelihood we must be content.

Many people would be inclined to say that the right act for me is not that whose general nature I have been describing, viz. that which if I were omniscient I should see to be my duty, but that which on all the evidence available to me I should think to be my duty. But suppose that from the state of partial knowledge in which I think act *A* to be my duty, I could pass to a state of perfect knowledge in which I saw act *B* to be my duty, should I not say 'act *B* was the right act for me to do'? I should no doubt add 'though I am not to be blamed for doing act *A*'. But in adding this, am I not passing from the question 'what is right' to the question 'what is morally good'? At the same time I am not making the *full* passage from the one notion to the other; for in order that the act should be morally good, or an act I am not to be blamed for doing, it must not merely be the act which it is reasonable for me to think my duty; it must also be done for that reason, or from some other morally good motive. Thus the conception of the right act as the act which it is reasonable for me to think my duty is an unsatisfactory compromise between the true notion of the right act and the notion of the morally good action.

The general principles of duty are obviously not self-evident from the beginning of our lives. How do they come to be so? The answer is, that they come to be self-evident to us just as mathematical axioms do. We find by experience that this couple of matches and that couple make four matches, that this couple of balls on a wire and that couple make four balls: and by reflection on these and similar discoveries we come to see that it is of the nature of two and two to make four. In a precisely similar way, we see the *prima facie* rightness of an act which would be the fulfilment of a particular promise, and of another which would be the fulfilment of another promise, and when we have reached sufficient maturity to think in general terms, we apprehend *prima facie* rightness to belong to the nature of any fulfilment of promise. What comes first in time is the apprehension of the self-evident *prima facie* rightness of an individual act of a particular type. From this we come by reflection to apprehend the self-evident general principle of *prima facie* duty. From this, too, perhaps along with the apprehension of the self-evident *prima facie* rightness of the same act in virtue of its having another characteristic as well, and perhaps in spite of the apprehension of its *prima facie* wrongness in virtue of its having some third characteristic, we come to believe something not self-evident at all, but an object of probable opinion, viz. that this particular act is (not *prima facie* but) actually right.

In this respect there is an important difference between rightness and mathematical properties. A triangle which is isosceles necessarily has two of its angles equal, whatever other characteristics the triangle may have—whatever, for instance, be its area, or the size of its third angle. The equality of the two angles is a parti-resultant attribute.[1] And the same is true of all mathematical attributes. It is true, I may add, of *prima facie* rightness. But no act is ever, in virtue of falling under some general description, necessarily actually right; its rightness depends on its whole nature[2] and not on any element in it. The reason is that no mathematical object (no figure, for instance, or angle) ever has two characteristics that tend to give it opposite resultant characteristics, while moral acts often (as every one knows) and indeed always (as on reflection we must admit) have different characteristics that tend to make them at the same time *prima facie* right and *prima facie* wrong; there is

[1] Cf. pp. 28, 122–3.

[2] To avoid complicating unduly the statement of the general view I am putting forward, I have here rather overstated it. Any act is the origination of a great variety of things many of which make no difference to its rightness or wrongness. But there are always many elements in its nature (i.e. in what it is the origination of) that make a difference to its rightness or wrongness, and no element in its nature can be dismissed without consideration as indifferent.

3738 D

probably no act, for instance, which does good to any one without doing harm to some one else, and *vice versa.*

Supposing it to be agreed, as I think on reflection it must, that no one *means* by 'right' just 'productive of the best possible consequences', or 'optimific', the attributes 'right' and 'optimific' might stand in either of two kinds of relation to each other. (1) They might be so related that we could apprehend *a priori*, either immediately or deductively, that any act that is optimific is right and any act that is right is optimific, as we can apprehend that any triangle that is equilateral is equiangular and *vice versa.* Professor Moore's view is, I think, that the coextensiveness of 'right' and 'optimific' is apprehended immediately.[1] He rejects the possibility of any proof of it. Or (2) the two attributes might be such that the question whether they are invariably connected had to be answered by means of an inductive inquiry. Now at first sight it might seem as if the constant connexion of the two attributes could be immediately apprehended. It might seem absurd to suggest that it could be right for any one to do an act which would produce consequences less good than those which would be produced by some other act in his power. Yet a little thought will convince us that this is not absurd. The type of case in which it is easiest to see that this is so is, perhaps, that in which one has made a promise. In such a case we all think that *prima facie* it is our duty to fulfil the promise irrespective of the precise goodness of the total consequences. And though we do not think it is necessarily our actual or absolute duty to do so, we are far from thinking that any, even the slightest, gain in the value of the total consequences will necessarily justify us in doing something else instead. Suppose, to simplify the case by abstraction, that the fulfilment of a promise to *A* would produce 1,000 units of good[2] for him, but that by doing some other act I could produce 1,001 units of good for *B*, to whom I have made no

[1] *Ethics*, 181.

[2] I am assuming that good is objectively quantitative (cf. pp. 142–4), but not that we can accurately assign an exact quantitative measure to it. Since it is of a definite amount, we can make the *supposition* that its amount is so-and-so, though we cannot with any confidence *assert* that it is.

promise, the other consequences of the two acts being of equal value; should we really think it self-evident that it was our duty to do the second act and not the first? I think not. We should, I fancy, hold that only a much greater disparity of value between the total consequences would justify us in failing to discharge our *prima facie* duty to *A*. After all, a promise is a promise, and is not to be treated so lightly as the theory we are examining would imply. What, exactly, a promise is, is not so easy to determine, but we are surely agreed that it constitutes a serious moral limitation to our freedom of action. To produce the 1,001 units of good for *B* rather than fulfil our promise to *A* would be to take, not perhaps our duty as philanthropists too seriously, but certainly our duty as makers of promises too lightly.

Or consider another phase of the same problem. If I have promised to confer on *A* a particular benefit containing 1,000 units of good, is it self-evident that if by doing some different act I could produce 1,001 units of good for *A* himself (the other consequences of the two acts being supposed equal in value), it would be right for me to do so? Again, I think not. Apart from my general *prima facie* duty to do *A* what good I can, I have another *prima facie* duty to do him the particular service I have promised to do him, and this is not to be set aside in consequence of a disparity of good of the order of 1,001 to 1,000, though a much greater disparity might justify me in so doing.

Or again, suppose that *A* is a very good and *B* a very bad man, should I then, even when I have made no promise, think it self-evidently right to produce 1,001 units of good for *B* rather than 1,000 for *A*? Surely not. I should be sensible of a *prima facie* duty of justice, i.e. of producing a distribution of goods in proportion to merit, which is not outweighed by such a slight disparity in the total goods to be produced.

Such instances—and they might easily be added to—make it clear that there is no self-evident connexion between the attributes 'right' and 'optimific'. The theory we are examining has a certain attractiveness when applied to our decision that a particular act is our duty (though I have tried to show that it does not agree with our actual moral judgements even here). But it is not even plausible when applied to our recognition of *prima facie* duty. For if it were self-evident that the right coincides with the optimific, it should be self-evident that what is *prima facie* right is *prima facie* optimific. But whereas we are certain that keeping a promise is *prima facie* right, we are not certain that it is *prima facie* optimific (though we are perhaps certain that it is *prima facie* bonific). Our certainty that it is *prima facie* right depends not on its consequences but on its being the fulfilment of a promise. The theory we are examining involves too much difference between the evident ground of our conviction about *prima facie* duty and the alleged ground of our conviction about actual duty.

The coextensiveness of the right and the optimific is, then, not self-evident. And I can see no way of proving it deductively; nor, so far as I know, has any one tried to do so. There remains the question whether it can be established inductively. Such an inquiry, to be conclusive, would have to be very thorough and extensive. We should have to take a large variety of the acts which we, to the best of our ability, judge to be right. We should have to trace as far as possible their consequences, not only for the persons directly affected but also for those indirectly affected, and to these no limit can be set. To make our inquiry thoroughly conclusive, we should have to do what we cannot do, viz. trace these consequences into an unending future. And even to make it reasonably conclusive, we should have to trace them far into the future. It is clear that the most we could possibly say is that a large variety of typical acts that are judged right appear, so far as we can trace their consequences, to produce more good than any other acts possible to the agents in the circumstances. And such a result falls far short of proving the constant connexion of the two attributes. But it is surely clear that no inductive inquiry justifying even this result has ever been carried through. The advocates of utilitarian systems have been so much persuaded either of the identity or of the self-evident connexion of the attributes 'right' and 'optimific' (or 'felicific') that they have not attempted even such an inductive inquiry as is possible.

And in view of the enormous complexity of the task and the inevitable inconclusiveness of the result, it is worth no one's while to make the attempt. What, after all, would be gained by it? If, as I have tried to show, for an act to be right and to be optimific are not the same thing, and an act's being optimific is not even the ground of its being right, then if we could ask ourselves (though the question is really unmeaning) which we ought to do, right acts because they are right or optimific acts because they are optimific, our answer must be 'the former'. If they are optimific as well as right, that is interesting but not morally important; if not, we still ought to do them (which is only another way of saying that they *are* the right acts), and the question whether they are optimific has no importance for moral theory.

There is one direction in which a fairly serious attempt has been made to show the connexion of the attributes 'right' and 'optimific'. One of the most evident facts of our moral consciousness is the sense which we have of the sanctity of promises, a sense which does not, on the face of it, involve the thought that one will be bringing more good into existence by fulfilling the promise than by breaking it. It is plain, I think, that in our normal thought we consider that the fact that we have made a promise is in itself sufficient to create a duty of keeping it, the sense of duty resting on remembrance of the past promise and not on thoughts of the future consequences of its fulfilment. Utilitarianism tries to show that this is not so, that the sanctity of promises rests on the good consequences of the fulfilment of them and the bad consequences of their non-fulfilment. It does so in this way: it points out that when you break a promise you not only fail to confer a certain advantage on your promisee but you diminish his confidence, and indirectly the confidence of others, in the fulfilment of promises. You thus strike a blow at one of the devices that have been found most useful in the relations between man and man—the device on which, for example, the whole system of commercial credit rests—and you tend to bring about a state of things wherein each man, being entirely unable to rely on the keeping of promises by others, will have to do everything for himself, to the enormous impoverishment of human well-being.

To put the matter otherwise, utilitarians say that when a promise ought to be kept it is because the total good to be produced by keeping it is greater than the total good to be produced by breaking it, the former including as its main element the maintenance and strengthening of general mutual confidence, and the latter being greatly diminished by a weakening of this confidence. They say, in fact, that the case I put some pages back[1] never arises—the case in which by fulfilling a promise I shall bring into being 1,000 units of good for my promisee, and by breaking it 1,001 units of good for some one else, the other effects of the two acts being of equal value. The other effects, they say, never are of equal value. By keeping my promise I am helping to strengthen the system of mutual confidence; by breaking it I am helping to weaken this; so that really the first act produces $1{,}000+x$ units of good, and the second $1{,}001-y$ units, and the difference between $+x$ and $-y$ is enough to outweigh the slight superiority in the *immediate* effects of the second act. In answer to this it may be pointed out that there must be *some* amount of good that exceeds the difference between $+x$ and $-y$ (i.e. exceeds $x+y$); say, $x+y+z$. Let us suppose the *immediate* good effects of the second act to be assessed not at 1,001 but at $1{,}000+x+y+z$. Then its *net* good effects are $1{,}000+x+z$, i.e. greater than those of the fulfilment of the promise; and the utilitarian is bound to say forthwith that the promise should be broken. Now, we may ask whether that is really the way we think about promises? Do we really think that the production of the slightest balance of good, no matter who will enjoy it, by the breach of a promise frees us from the obligation to keep our promise? We need not doubt that a system by which promises are made and kept is one that has great advantages for the general well-being. But that is not the whole truth. To make a promise is not merely to adapt an ingenious device for promoting the general well-being; it is to put oneself in a new relation to one person in particular, a relation which creates a specifically new *prima facie* duty to him, not reducible to the duty of promoting the general well-being of society. By all

[1] p. 34.

means let us try to foresee the net good effects of keeping one's promise and the net good effects of breaking it, but even if we assess the first at $1,000+x$ and the second at $1,000+x+z$, the question still remains whether it is not our duty to fulfil the promise. It may be suspected, too, that the effect of a single keeping or breaking of a promise in strengthening or weakening the fabric of mutual confidence is greatly exaggerated by the theory we are examining. And if we suppose two men dying together alone, do we think that the duty of one to fulfil before he dies a promise he has made to the other would be extinguished by the fact that neither act would have any effect on the general confidence? Any one who holds this may be suspected of not having reflected on what a promise is.

I conclude that the attributes 'right' and 'optimific' are not identical, and that we do not know either by intuition, by deduction, or by induction that they coincide in their application, still less that the latter is the foundation of the former. It must be added, however, that if we are ever under no special obligation such as that of fidelity to a promisee or of gratitude to a benefactor, we ought to do what will produce most good; and that even when we are under a special obligation the tendency of acts to promote general good is one of the main factors in determining whether they are right.

In what has preceded, a good deal of use has been made of 'what we really think' about moral questions; a certain theory has been rejected because it does not agree with what we really think. It might be said that this is in principle wrong; that we should not be content to expound what our present moral consciousness tells us but should aim at a criticism of our existing moral consciousness in the light of theory. Now I do not doubt that the moral consciousness of men has in detail undergone a good deal of modification as regards the things we think right, at the hands of moral theory. But if we are told, for instance, that we should give up our view that there is a special obligatoriness attaching to the keeping of promises because it is self-evident that the only duty is to produce as much good as possible, we have to ask ourselves whether we really, when we reflect, *are* convinced that this is self-evident, and whether we really *can* get rid of our view that promise-keeping has a bindingness independent of productiveness of maximum good. In my own experience I find that I cannot, in spite of a very genuine attempt to do so; and I venture to think that most people will find the same, and that just because they cannot lose the sense of special obligation, they cannot accept as self-evident, or even as true, the theory which would require them to do so. In fact it seems, on reflection, self-evident that a promise, simply as such, is something that *prima facie* ought to be kept, and it does *not*, on reflection, seem self-evident that production of maximum good is the only thing that makes an act obligatory. And to ask us to give up at the bidding of a theory our actual apprehension of what is right and what is wrong seems like asking people to repudiate their actual experience of beauty, at the bidding of a theory which says 'only that which satisfies such and such conditions can be beautiful'. If what I have called our actual apprehension is (as I would maintain that it is) truly an apprehension, i.e. an instance of knowledge, the request is nothing less than absurd.

I would maintain, in fact, that what we are apt to describe as 'what we think' about moral questions contains a considerable amount that we do not think but know, and that this forms the standard by reference to which the truth of any moral theory has to be tested, instead of having itself to be tested by reference to any theory. I hope that I have in what precedes indicated what in my view these elements of knowledge are that are involved in our ordinary moral consciousness.

It would be a mistake to found a natural science on 'what we really think', i.e. on what reasonably thoughtful and well-educated people think about the subjects of the science before they have studied them scientifically. For such opinions are interpretations, and often misinterpretations, of sense-experience; and the man of science must appeal from these to sense-experience itself, which furnishes his real data. In ethics no such appeal is possible. We have no more direct way of access to the facts about rightness and goodness and about what things are right or good, than by thinking about them;

the moral convictions of thoughtful and well-educated people are the data of ethics just as sense-perceptions are the data of a natural science. Just as some of the latter have to be rejected as illusory, so have some of the former; but as the latter are rejected only when they are in conflict with other more accurate sense-perceptions, the former are rejected only when they are in conflict with other convictions which stand better the test of reflection. The existing body of moral convictions of the best people is the cumulative product of the moral reflection of many generations, which has developed an extremely delicate power of appreciation of moral distinctions; and this the theorist cannot afford to treat with anything other than the greatest respect. The verdicts of the moral consciousness of the best people are the foundation on which he must build; though he must first compare them with one another and eliminate any contradictions they may contain.

It is worth while to try to state more definitely the nature of the acts that are right. We may try to state first what (if anything) is the universal nature of *all* acts that are right. It is obvious that any of the acts that we do has countless effects, directly or indirectly, on countless people, and the probability is that any act, however right it be, will have adverse effects (though these may be very trivial) on some innocent people. Similarly, any wrong act will probably have beneficial effects on some deserving people. Every act therefore, viewed in some aspects, will be *prima facie* right, and viewed in others, *prima facie* wrong, and right acts can be distinguished from wrong acts only as being those which, of all those possible for the agent in the circumstances, have the greatest balance of *prima facie* rightness, in those respects in which they are *prima facie* right, over their *prima facie* wrongness, in those respects in which they are *prima facie* wrong—*prima facie* rightness and wrongness being understood in the sense previously explained. For the estimation of the comparative stringency of these *prima facie* obligations no general rules can, so far as I can see, be laid down. We can only say that a great deal of stringency belongs to the duties of 'perfect obligation'—the duties of keeping our promises, of repairing wrongs we have done, and of returning the equivalent of services we have received. For the rest, ἐν τῇ αἰσθήσει ἡ κρίσις.[1] This sense of our particular duty in particular circumstances, preceded and informed by the fullest reflection we can bestow on the act in all its bearings, is highly fallible, but it is the only guide we have to our duty.

When we turn to consider the nature of individual right acts, the first point to which attention should be called is that any act may be correctly described in an indefinite, and in principle infinite, number of ways. An act is the production of a change in the state of affairs (if we ignore, for simplicity's sake, the comparatively few cases in which it is the maintenance of an existing state of affairs; cases which, I think, raise no special difficulty). Now the only changes we can *directly* produce are changes in our own bodies or in our own minds. But these are not, as such, what as a rule we think it our duty to produce. Consider some comparatively simple act, such as telling the truth or fulfilling a promise. In the first case what I produce directly is movements of my vocal organs. But what I think it my duty to produce is a true view in some one else's mind about some fact, and between my movement of my vocal organs and this result there intervenes a series of physical events and events in his mind. Again, in the second case, I may have promised, for instance, to return a book to a friend. I may be able, by a series of movements of my legs and hands, to place it in his hands. But what I am just as likely to do, and to think I have done my duty in doing, is to send it by a messenger or to hand it to his servant or to send it by post; and in each of these cases what I *do* directly is worthless in itself and is connected by a series of intermediate links with what I do think it is my duty to bring about, viz. his receiving what I have promised to return to him. This being so, it *seems* as if what I *do* has no obligatoriness in itself and as if one or other of three accounts should be given of the matter, each of which makes rightness not belong to what I do, considered in its own nature.

(1) One of them would be that what is obligatory is not *doing* anything in the natural sense of producing any change

[1] 'The decision rests with perception'. Arist. *Nic. Eth.* 1109 b 23, 1126 b 4.

in the state of affairs, but *aiming at* something—at, for instance, my friend's reception of the book. But this account will not do. For (*a*) to aim at something is to act from a motive consisting of the wish to bring that thing about. But we have seen[1] that motive never forms part of the content of our duty; if anything is certain about morals, that, I think, is certain. And (*b*) if I have promised to return the book to my friend, I obviously do not fulfil my promise and do my duty merely by aiming at his receiving the book; I must see that he actually receives it. (2) A more plausible account is that which says I must do that which is likely to produce the result. But this account is open to the second of these objections, and probably also to the first. For in the first place, however likely my act may seem, even on careful consideration, and even however likely it may in fact be, to produce the result, if it does not produce it I have not done what I promised to do, i.e. have not done my duty. And secondly, when it is said that I ought to do what is likely to produce the result, what is *probably* meant is that I ought to do a certain thing as a result of the wish to produce a certain result, and of the thought that my act is likely to produce it; and this again introduces motive into the content of duty. (3) Much the most plausible of the three accounts is that which says, 'I ought to do that which will actually produce a certain result.' This escapes objection (*b*). Whether it escapes objection (*a*) or not depends on what exactly is meant. If it is meant that I ought to do a certain thing from the wish to produce a certain result and the thought that it will do so, the account is still open to objection (*a*). But if it is meant simply that I ought to do a certain thing, and that the reason why I ought to do it is that it will produce a certain result, objection (*a*) is avoided. Now this account in its second form is that which utilitarianism gives. It says what is right is certain acts, not certain acts motivated in a certain way; and it says that acts are never right by their own nature but by virtue of the goodness of their actual results. And this account is, I think, clearly nearer the truth than one which makes the rightness of an act depend on the goodness of either the *intended* or the *likely* results.

[1] pp. 5–6.

Nevertheless, this account appears not to be the true one. For it implies that what we consider right or our duty is what we do *directly*. It is this, e.g. the packing up and posting of the book, that derives its moral significance not from its own nature but from its consequences. But this is *not* what we should describe, strictly, as our duty; our duty is to fulfil our promise, i.e. to put the book into our friend's possession. This we consider obligatory in its own nature, just because it is a fulfilment of promise, and not because of *its* consequences. But, it might be replied by the utilitarian, I do not do this; I only do something that leads up to this, and what I do has no moral significance in itself but only because of its consequences. In answer to this, however, we may point out that a cause produces not only its immediate, but also its remote consequences, and the latter no less than the former. I, therefore, not only produce the immediate movements of parts of my body but also my friend's reception of the book, which results from these. Or, if this be objected to on the grounds that I can hardly be said to have produced my friend's reception of the book when I have packed and posted it, owing to the time that has still to elapse before he receives it, and that to say I have produced the result hardly does justice to the part played by the Post Office, we may at least say that I have *secured* my friend's reception of the book. What I do is as truly describable in this way as by saying that it is the packing and posting of a book. (It is equally truly describable in many other ways; e.g. I have provided a few moments' employment for Post Office officials. But this is irrelevant to the argument.) And if we ask ourselves whether it is *qua* the packing and posting of a book, or *qua* the securing of my friend's getting what I have promised to return to him, that my action is right, it is clear that it is in the second capacity that it is right; and in this capacity, the only capacity in which it is right, it is right by its own nature and not because of its consequences.

This account may no doubt be objected to, on the ground that we are ignoring the freedom of will of the other agents—the sorter and the postman, for instance—who are equally responsible for the result. Society, it may be said, is not like a machine, in which event follows event by rigorous necessity. Some one may, for instance, in the exercise of his freedom of will, steal the book on the way. But it is to be observed that I have excluded that case, and any similar case. I am dealing with the case in which I secure my friend's receiving the book; and if he does not receive it I have not secured his receiving it. If on the other hand the book reaches its destination, that alone shows that, the system of things being what it is, the trains by which the book travels and the railway lines along which it travels being such as they are and subject to the laws they are subject to, the postal officials who handle it being such as they are, having the motives they have and being subject to the psychological laws they are subject to, my posting the book was the one further thing which was sufficient to procure my friend's receiving it. If it had not been sufficient, the result would not have followed. The attainment of the result proves the sufficiency of the means. The objection in fact rests on the supposition that there can be unmotived action, i.e. an event without a cause, and may be refuted by reflection on the universality of the law of causation.

It is equally true that non-attainment of the result proves the insufficiency of the means. If the book had been destroyed in a railway accident or stolen by a dishonest postman, that would prove that my immediate act was not sufficient to produce the desired result. We get the curious consequence that however carelessly I pack or dispatch the book, if it comes to hand I have done my duty, and however carefully I have acted, if the book does not come to hand I have not done my duty. Success and failure are the only test, and a sufficient test, of the performance of duty. Of course, I should deserve more praise in the second case than in the first; but that is an entirely different question; we must not mix up the question of right and wrong with that of the morally good and the morally bad. And that our conclusion is not as strange as at first sight it might seem is shown by the fact that if the carelessly dispatched book comes to hand, it is not my duty to send another copy, while if the carefully dispatched book does not come to hand I must send another copy to replace it. In the first case I have not my duty still to do, which shows that I have done it; in the second I have it still to do, which shows that I have not done it.

We have reached the result that my act is right *qua* being an ensuring of one of the particular states of affairs of which it is an ensuring, viz., in the case we have taken, of my friend's receiving the book I have promised to return to him. But this answer requires some correction; for it refers only to the *prima facie* rightness of my act. If to be a fulfilment of promise were a sufficient ground of the rightness of an act, all fulfilments of promises would be right, whereas it seems clear that there are cases in which some other *prima facie* duty overrides the *prima facie* duty of fulfilling a promise. The more correct answer would be that the ground of the actual rightness of the act is that, of all acts possible for the agent in the circumstances, it is that whose *prima facie* rightness in the respects in which it is *prima facie* right most outweighs its *prima facie* wrongness in any respects in which it is *prima facie* wrong. But since its *prima facie* rightness is mainly due to its being a fulfilment of promise, we may call its being so the salient element in the ground of its rightness.

Subject to this qualification, then, it is as being the production (or if we prefer the word, the securing or ensuring) of the reception by my friend of what I have promised him (or in other words as the fulfilment of my promise) that my act is right. It is not right as a packing and posting of a book. The packing and posting of the book is only incidentally right, right only because it is a fulfilment of promise, which is what is directly or essentially right.

Our duty, then, is not to do certain things which will produce certain results. Our acts, at any rate our acts of special obligation, are not right because they will produce certain results—which is the view common to all forms of utilitarianism. To say that is to say that in the case in question what is essentially right is to pack and post a book, whereas what is essentially right is to secure the possession by my friend of what I have promised to return to him. An act is not right because it, being one thing, produces good results different from itself; it is right because it is itself the production of a certain state of affairs. Such production is right in itself, apart from any consequence.

But, it might be said, this analysis applies only to acts of special obligation; the utilitarian account still holds good for the acts in which we are not under a special obligation to any person or set of persons but only under that of augmenting the general good. Now merely to have established that there *are* special obligations to do certain things irrespective of their consequences would be already to have made a considerable breach in the utilitarian walls; for according to utilitarianism there is no such thing, there is only the single obligation to promote the general good. But, further, on reflection it is clear that just as (in the case we have taken) my act is not only the packing and posting of a book but the fulfilling of a promise, and just as it is in the latter capacity and not in the former that it is my duty, so an act whereby I augment the general good is not only, let us say, the writing of a begging letter on behalf of a hospital, but the producing (or ensuring) of whatever good ensues therefrom, and it is in the latter capacity and not in the former that it is right, if it *is* right. That which is right is right not because it is an act, one thing, which will produce another thing, an increase of the general welfare, but because it is itself the producing of an increase in the general welfare. Or, to qualify this in the necessary way, its being the production of an increase in the general welfare is the salient element in the ground of its rightness. Just as before we were led to recognize the *prima facie* rightness of the fulfilment of promises, we are now led to recognize the *prima facie* rightness of promoting the general welfare. In both cases we have to recognize the *intrinsic* rightness of a certain type of act, not depending on its consequences but on its own nature.

H. L. A. HART

Legal and Moral Obligation

Moral philosophers in both England and America have long spoken and written as if the phenomenon under investigation was primarily, if not exclusively, moral *obligation* or moral *duty;* very few have questioned the suitability of the expressions "obligation" and "duty" to describe the principal subject of their study. Yet, as their examples show, these philosophers have been very much concerned with such actions as the gratuitous infliction of pain on children or animals, the killing of human beings, the heartless abandonment of friends, lying and other forms of deception. Something more, I hope, than a blind wish to adhere to our common speech prompts the protest that it is absurd to speak of having a moral *duty* not to kill another human being, or an *obligation* not to torture a child. Surely when we are moved by moral repugnance and shrink from some squalid action the situation is ill-conveyed by saying that here we are acknowledging a *duty;* and surely it is at least misleading to say that we have acknowledged (or recognized) an *obligation* when in difficult circumstances, not provided for by anything that could reasonably be called a rule, we think out the consequences of alternative lines of conduct and decide what on the whole is best to do.

82

The point of such a protest is not, or at any rate not merely, that "duty" or "obligation" are too weak, too feeble in condemnatory force, for the blacker moral offenses. "Obligation" and "duty" are not inappropriate here because they are reserved for the relatively minor matters on a single moral scale to which belong also more serious elements (moral crimes). The point, rather, is that they do not belong to the same scale and the extension of these terms to the whole field of morality blinds us to its variety and complexity.

Two considerations might perhaps alert us to this fact. The first is that among the examples used by moral philosophers there are certainly some where the expressions "obligation" and "duty" sit quite happily. Moral obligations do arise from promises, from the position of parent, and there may be a moral obligation to obey the law. So, too, moral duties do spring from positions of trust like that of a confidential servant, or from recognized positions or roles in a social group such as that of being a host or a neighbor, a husband or a father. Such cases where the terminology of obligation and duty is so obviously appropriate have, I think, discernible common or related features, and these contrast with the kind of thing at stake when we insist that we ought not to inflict gratuitous pain. What tends to obscure the difference is that "ought" (and in some contexts both "must" and "should") may be used in urging others to abstain both from breaking their promises and from torturing children, and in moral criticism of these offenses when committed. Yet this is no better ground for the identification of what are disparate, though of course related, segments of morality than is the fact that, given appropriate contexts, "ought," "must," and "should" may be used when it is patent that nothing moral is at stake. You ought to, you should, you must change your wet clothes.

Second, and more important, there is a whole world where duties and obligations are really at home. This is the legal world: for here both expressions are almost always appropriate for whatever the rules of an actually existing legal system forbid. If a statute forbids cruelty to children or animals, then we have a legal duty to forbear from such cruelty. In speaking of the legal obligation to do what we have bound ourselves by contract to do, we make no more felicitous use of the word "obligation" than when we speak of the legal obligation to keep off other people's land, or to refrain from assaulting or libeling them; but in ordinary nonlegal discourse and in morals it is different. So in the succeeding sections of this paper I propose first to inquire into the character of legal obligation and then to determine why in referring to certain moral situations we naturally make use of the legally colored concepts of obligation and duty.

I

It may perhaps help with the understanding of legal obligation and duty if we begin, not with an onslaught on definition, but by noting some of the remarkable things that can, in any developed legal system, be done about them, and hence be said about them. First and foremost, it is the case (and perhaps more obviously true of obligations than of many other features of a legal system) that legal obligations are very often (though not always) human artifacts in the sense that they may be deliberately created by the appropriate action of human beings and subjected to various modes of change and manipulation. Their status as obligations may be independent of their content for we not only may *have* legal duties and obligations, but we may *create,* or *impose* them (e.g., by legislation), or *incur* or *assume* them (e.g., by making contracts). They may be *varied* and *modified* and *extinguished;* and persons may (notably where obligations are created by contract) be *released* from them.

Of course, in any developed legal system, not only obligations or duties but other legal entities (rights, powers, immunities, and disabilities) may be similarly created, modified, or extinguished; and rights may be transferred, e.g., when property is alienated upon a sale. The most prominent and important example of the deliberate *creation* of legal duties and obligations is the creation of a legal obligation by legislative enactment. In any modern society legislation is a very complex operation. The legislative process involves not only the cooperation of numerous persons qualified under existing legal rules to take part, but also their compliance with a complex procedure determined by legal rules, which exist and are accepted as governing the process. Normally, the crucial step is a vote for or against a legislative proposal usually presented in written form. Given such circumstances, the upshot of the vote and of certain subsequent formalities (assent by the Queen, or signature by the President, or lapse of a certain time without notice of disapproval) is that a law is *made* or *enacted*, introducing, say, two years of military service for all males between the ages of twenty-one and thirty-five, or prohibiting the sale of intoxicating liquors. In this manner legislators create obligations and impose them on others (and on themselves in their personal capacity) who are thenceforth legally bound to do or forbear doing certain things. Subordinate authorities may also by enactment be given a derivative legal *power* to create further obligations and duties within a certain area.

It is perhaps useful to compare and contrast these legislative operations with those operations whereby a person also creates obligations but imposes them, not on others, but only upon himself. The most notable example of this is, of course, the bilateral or consensual contract which is the legal analogue of the promise where, e.g., one man binds himself to deliver a ton of bricks to another by a certain date in consideration of the other's binding himself to pay £100 for them. But there are other forms of self-imposition of obligation: both in the

English and in the American systems a person may declare himself a trustee of property perhaps for persons yet unborn, and immediately thereupon is under obligation or duty not to deal with it in certain ways which were open to him up to that point.

How are the creation, imposition, modification, and extinction of obligations and other operations on other legal entities such as rights possible? How can such things be done? This Kantian-sounding question can only be answered by describing in detail how in fact they are done. The lawyer, so used to this kind of thing, would reply in his own terminology, "These things can be done because the law confers *powers* upon persons to do these things: they do them in the exercise of legal powers." But the philosopher may well inquire: What are these powers? What is it for a law to confer a power and for someone to exercise such a power? "Power" here does not mean capacity to bring about observable physical change, and certainly to some these operations have appeared a sort of legal (and moral) alchemy, not susceptible of any explanation. Hagerström,[1] faced with the difficulties of analyzing the simplest one of such operations, namely, the transfer of ownership, concluded that the character of all such operations could only be elucidated by reference to a widespread belief in the magical powers of words to bring about changes in a suprasensible world of legal rights and duties. He developed his theories mainly in relation to Roman law, starting from the acute observation that the crucial words used by the purchaser in the *mancipatio*, the Roman formal transfer of property ("I say this slave is mine according to the law"), could not be intended as a statement of ordinary fact since the words, if treated as a statement, would be false at the time

[1] See Axel Hagerström, *Inquiry into the Nature of Law and Morals*, ed. Karl Olivecrona, trans. C. D. Broad (Stockholm: Almqvist & Wiksell, 1953), and the present writer's review in *Philosophy*, XXX (1955), 369–73.

they were spoken, for the ownership did not "pass" to the purchaser till later.

This certainly was a flash of insight, but Hagerström's approach suffered badly from the failure to notice that the theory that the creation, transfer, or modification of obligations and rights was "magical" had just as much (so just as little) force in relation to the central operative words used in the enactment of a modern statute imposing obligations, or the operative words (words of grant) in a private document such as conveyance or will. The modern legislative formulas ("Now it is hereby enacted") and the operative words ("X hereby conveys unto Y," "I hereby bequeath to B") taken as statements of facts are also false, for the "acts," "deeds," or "instruments" in which they appear do not "take effect" until further formalities (signing, sealing, witnessing, delivery, and so forth) are completed or often until some later event happens, such as the testator's death in the case of a will.

So Hagerström leaves us with the residual problem: How can words have legal effects, and what are the effects that they have? Our concern is only with a special part of his question: How can words create legal obligations, and what are the legal obligations they create? But even this necessarily involves consideration of the foundation of any legal system, and of part of what is involved in the assertion that a legal system exists; for any answer that stops short of this will leave the original problem on our hands. Thus we might, indeed, we must, begin by saying that, if words are to be used to create legal obligations, rules of the system must exist providing that if they are used (by the appropriate persons in the appropriate circumstances) these persons designated by these words shall be legally bound or have a legal obligation to do or to abstain from certain actions. It is easy to see that both behind the words used by a municipal corporation enacting a bylaw imposing an obligation on occupiers of land to drain or to fence it in from the highway, and behind the words used in a lease under which the tenant has an obligation to pay rent, there must be rules of the system providing that if certain words are used in this way then the occupiers of land in the one case and the tenant in the other case shall have these obligations. But what does it mean to say of those rules that they exist and that they provide that persons shall have such obligations? In the case of subordinate rules of the system, such as the statutes conferring legislative powers on a municipal corporation, the assertion that the rules exist means that they belong to a class of rules marked off as valid rules of the particular system by criteria specified in the fundamental rules of the system, such as the English rule that what the Queen in Parliament enacts is law, or in the United States the rule of the Constitution that (subject to certain restrictions) what Congress enacts is law in certain fields. But to say of these fundamental rules (which provide and specify the legislative competence of the legislative authority) that they *exist* is to say something different. "Exist" here cannot mean "valid, given the system's criteria of validity" as, roughly, it does in the case of subordinate rule of the system. In this case "exists" must refer to the *actual practice* of the particular social group whose legal system is under consideration. Even in the case of the simplest imaginable legal system where a monarch has unrestricted legislative authority to enact law imposing legal obligations by pronouncing or writing down what he requires to be done, the actual practice of the group presupposed by the assertion that he has this authority is complex and not shortly describable. It was too shortly described by Austin[2] as a general habit of obedience to a person or persons not in a like habit of obedience to others. Kelsen,[3] seeing the in-

[2] See John Austin, *The Province of Jurisprudence Determined*, ed. H. L. A. Hart (London: Weidenfeld & Nicolson, 1954), Lecture VI, pp. 198–205.

[3] See Hans Kelsen, *General Theory of Law and State* (Cambridge, Mass.: Harvard University Press, 1949): ". . . a juristic hypothesis—that is, a basic norm, to be established by a logical analysis of actual

adequacies of this formulation, divorced the "basic norm" of a legal system from any actual practice by misleadingly characterizing it as a fundamental "hypothesis" or "postulate" made by the jurist examining the system. The inadequacies of both these extremes have led others to insist that what is at the root of every legal system is a general recognition of a *moral* obligation to obey the law so that there is a necessary[4] or analytic connection and not merely an empirical one between the statement that a legal system exists and the statement that most of the population recognizes a moral obligation to obey the law.

To steer between these aberrations of juristic theory it is necessary first to see why "habit" and "obedience" are not enough to characterize the situation in which we say legal obligations are created by legislation. If members of a group merely have a *habit* of obeying an individual, X, who threatens them and is able to harm them in the event of disobedience, this situation might be described by saying they are *obliged* or *compelled* to obey him or to do what he says, but not by saying that they have or recognize an *obligation* to do what

---

juristic thinking" (p. xv); "The basic norm of a legal order is the postulated ultimate rule according to which the norms of this order are established and annulled, receive and lose their validity" (p. 113); "That the basic norm really exists in the juristic consciousness is the result of a simple analysis of actual juristic statements" (p. 116).

[4] See, for example, A. L. Goodhart, *English Law and the Moral Law* (London: Stevens & Sons, 1953): "By blandly suggesting that this basic norm must be 'presupposed to be binding' Kelsen avoids the most important problem in legal philosophy" (p. 18); "If . . . we regard the law as a rule which is recognised as obligatory then the element of force becomes of minor importance. We then realise that the obligatory nature of these rules is based on other grounds, and that one of the most important of these is that of moral law. It is for this reason that the moral sense is one of the dominant forces not only in establishing the efficacy of law, but also in its very existence. The jurist cannot ignore the moral law as irrelevant to his subject because if he does so then he will be ignoring one of the grounds on which the basic idea of obligation is based" (p. 28).

X says. If we are to speak of their having or recognizing an obligation to do what X says, their attitude to X's words must be more than habitual obedience. The minimum required in *addition* to general obedience, if we are to speak of the group's recognizing or having a legal obligation to do something specified by X, is (1) that X's words should generally be accepted as constituting a standard of behavior so that deviations from it (unlike the mere failure to follow a mere habit current in the society, such as that of drinking tea or coffee) are treated as occasions for criticism of various sorts; (2) that references to X's words are generally made as *reasons* for doing or having done what X says, as supporting *demands* that others should do what he says, and as rendering at least permissible the application of coercive repressive measures to persons who deviate from the standard constituted by X's words.

How many of the social group (subjects or officials) must do these things, how continuously, and how long to constitute "general" obedience and "general" use of X's words in this way admits of no determinate answer, just as we are not called on to say exactly how old a man must be to be middle-aged. But in any social group where obligations are created by legislation, and the expressions "I have a legal obligation to do this" and "He has a legal obligation to do that" have their present force, there must be a social practice at least as complex as I have described and not merely habitual obedience on the part of the members of the group. Anyone who uses such forms of expression as "I (you) have an obligation to" implies that his own attitude to the legislator's words is that described, for these statements of obligation are used to draw conclusions from legal rules on the footing that the rules are authoritative for the speaker. One who repudiated the authority altogether might of course recognize that he would be made to suffer if he disobeyed the rules, but the natural expression for this point of view would be not "I (you) have an obligation to" but "I am (you are) obliged to" or "under this system I (you) will suffer if I (you) do not."

The foregoing perhaps sufficiently shows the inadequacies of the characterization of the root of a legal system in terms of a *habit* of obedience. Kelsen was right in insisting that there must be more than habits or regularities of behavior in the narrow sense of regularly doing what the authority says. Yet his conception of the basic norm as a rule, "hypothesis," or "axiom," the "validity" of which is "assumed" or "postulated" [5] brings in a set of quite inappropriate quasi-mathematical expressions that we might indeed adopt if those were the only alternatives to describing the relevant facts in terms of "habits of obedience." But there is a third alternative, and this is to describe the relevant facts in terms not of habits but of the rules actually accepted by a social group. The question whether a group does accept a given rule is different in the ways already indicated from the question whether it habitually obeys a person, though the two questions are alike in that both are questions of fact and Austin is to be preferred to Kelsen for seeing that a statement of fact and not an "assumption of validity" is presupposed in any statement that someone has a legal obligation. If a group of persons behaves in the way we have distinguished as accepting what a legislator says as constituting a standard of behavior, then they accept the rule that he is to be obeyed, and then the rule that his word is law exists. The rule that what the Queen in Parliament enacts is law exists in this way. Once such a rule is thus found to exist in the actual practice of a group, it is absurd to speak of it as a *valid* rule, equally absurd to speak of it as *invalid* or of *assuming* or *postulating* its *validity*. We

[5] See Kelsen, *General Theory of Law and State*, as cited above and as follows: "The validity of this first constitution is the last presupposition, the final postulate, upon which the validity of all the norms of our legal order depends" (p. 115); "The basic norm is an indispensable assumption because, without it, the normative character of the basic historical event could not be established" (p. 396).

might as well speak of postulating or assuming the validity of an actually existing social rule that we take hats off on entering a house. Of course we can raise a number of different questions about such rules, e.g., whether it is a good or desirable thing that members of a group should accept them or have a moral obligation to go on with them, but it is most confusing to discuss this question in terms of "validity."

The third misconception, namely, that if a legal system exists there must (logically) be a general recognition of a *moral* obligation to obey the law, is an excessive reaction to Kelsen's geometrical characterization of the basic norm. Of course it is probably true that unless a majority voluntarily cooperated in obeying the rules of a coercive legal system it could not endure; it may even be true that unless a great number conceived themselves and others morally bound to obey, the system might be quite unstable. But this is insufficient to demonstrate the alleged *logical* connection between "There is a legal system in England" and "In England there is a general recognition of a moral obligation to obey the law," though the first of these is certainly true and the second is probably true. Equally irrelevant to the precise point are the undoubted facts that the development of the law by courts and legislature has been powerfully influenced by the moral convictions of the population and always will be. This does not show that no legal system exists unless obedience is motivated by a conviction that there is a moral obligation to obey. The assertion that there is a legal system in England (or anywhere else) does entail that there is in fact general acceptance of a fundamental rule such as the rule that what the Queen in Parliament enacts is law, though its form may be far more complex than this: general acceptance of such a rule does consist in more than habitual obedience for it includes the further use of, and attitude to, the enacted law which I have described. But both this general obedience and the further use of and attitudes to the law may be motivated by fear, inertia, admiration of tradition, or long-sighted calculation of selfish interests as well as by recognition of moral obligation. As long as the general complex practice is there, this is enough to answer affirmatively the inquiry whether a legal system exists. The question of what motivates the practice, though important, is an independent inquiry.

Once the complex social practice is established whereby a person's words are accepted as constituting a standard of behavior to the group, the legislative authority thereby constituted need not (though it may) be limited to the simple case of direct creation of obligation by legislation enjoining or forbidding specific actions or classes of action. The legislator may have authority to enact further rules conferring authority on others similar to his own for the regulation of limited areas of conduct (subordinate legislation) or rules empowering private individuals to create obligations for themselves, e.g., by contract. But the obligations created in those derivative ways under enacted rules owe their status as obligations ultimately to the underlying practice of the social group in accepting the legislative enactments as constituting standards of behavior and can be understood only if we understand the simple fundamental case of the creation of obligation by direct enactment and its dependence on the complex social practice that constitutes this basic authority.

We now can consider shortly those cases where legal obligations are not *created* at all but arise directly not under rules that have been deliberately introduced by legislation but under customary rules, and also those obligations that are created by the exercise of power conferred by such customary rules. Hitherto we have concentrated attention on those legal obligations that are brought into existence by deliberate legislation in order to demonstrate certain important features; it is, however, true that in most legal systems many rules under which obligations arise are not deliberately created but are customary in origin. "Custom" is usually a subordinate criterion of validity in modern legal systems in the sense that such customary rules may be deprived of their validity by legislative enactment while the converse in most cases is not true; but there is no *logical* reason (though every practical reason) why a legal system should not have as its sole criterion of validity the rule that only those rules are valid which represent the customary long-established practice of the group in certain matters or the practice of some subgroup. In such cases authority is not attributed to the holder of any office and obligations are not conceived as created by deliberate acts but as owing their status to the fact of traditional practice: *this practice* is taken as the standard. Sometimes even the degree of generalization involved in the recognition of "custom" as a general criterion of validity may not be achieved. There may be no recognition of any general principle as rendering actions legally obligatory but only a discrete set of rules may exist, which means that the social group simply accepts certain distinct types of conduct as standards of behavior and for the criterion of behavior in the way described. This plainly would be near the vanishing point of legal *system*.

It remains only to draw attention to the fact that, even where legal rules are customary, powers to create obligations may arise under such rules. The power to create obligations by simple contract in many Anglo-American jurisdictions arises under common law rules that were not introduced by deliberate legislation, but are conceived of as representing the long-established customary practice of the courts. Of course where a legal system exists containing among its criteria of validity a rule of precedent, i.e., that those rules are valid which are extracted from past cases by loosely defined rules of interpretation, the line between those rules that owe their validity to an authority's deliberate act and those that do not becomes blurred though not (as some Realists have argued) nonexistent.

II

We have yet to discuss in detail what most people would regard as *the* salient feature of an obligation and to some extent of duties: this is the important connection between obligation and coercion or compulsion. If we have an obligation to do something there is some sense in which we are bound to do it, and where we are bound there is some sense in which we are or may be compelled to do it. To probe these notions it is important to distinguish three things: (1) being physically compelled to do something, (2) being obliged to do something, (3) having an obligation to do something. The difficulty of the topic is that of stating without exaggeration the relation between the third member of this trio and the others, and Austin, who made in the introductory sections of *The Province of Jurisprudence Determined* the most painstaking effort to understand the notion of obligation, did fatally exaggerate this relation. He perceived correctly that when a man is dragged to prison, and so in some sense compelled to enter it, this is not a case of having an obligation or duty to go there. But, though he avoided this mistake, Austin defined obligation and duty in terms of the sanction or evil which one who commands (signifies his desire to another that he should do something) threatens to inflict in the event of disobedience.[6] To have a duty or an obligation, according

[6] See Austin, *The Province of Jurisprudence Determined*: "Being liable to evil from you if I comply not with a wish which you signify, I am *bound* or *obliged* by your command, or I lie under a *duty* to obey it" (p. 14); ". . . wherever a duty lies, a command has been signified; and whenever a command is signified, a duty is imposed" (p. 14); "The evil which will probably be incurred in case a command be disobeyed or (to use an equivalent expression) in case a duty be broken, is frequently called a *sanction*, or an *enforcement of obedience*. Or (varying the phrase) the command or duty is said to be *sanctioned* or *enforced* by the chance of incurring the evil" (p. 15); "When I am talking *directly* of the chance of incurring the evil, or (changing the expression) of the liability or obnoxiousness to the evil, I employ the term *duty*, or the term *obligation* . . ." (p. 18).

to Austin, is to be liable or obnoxious to an evil so threatened where "liable" or "obnoxious" means "likely to incur." The most obvious defect of this definition is that it would be satisfied by the case of a gunman's ordering me to hand over my purse at the point of a gun, where we would *not* say, "I had an obligation to hand over my purse"; what encourages the mistake is that we *would* say in such a case, "I was *obliged* to hand over my purse." So at first sight Austin's account looks like a fairly accurate definition of "being obliged" to do something and a very poor definition of "having an obligation" to do something. But we must take into account Austin's additions to and refinements upon his starting point. His account of specifically *legal* obligation differs from the primitive example of the gunman in a number of respects. Instead of the gunman, we have the sovereign defined as the person or persons whom the bulk of society generally obey, and who is himself not in a like habit of obedience to anyone else; further, commands of the sovereign are to follow "general" [7] courses of conduct and are addressed usually to numbers of persons. Apart from these qualifications for the special case of legal obligation, Austin also insists that his definition would be satisfied even if the chance of incurring the threatened evil was very small, and the evil itself was very small: "the slightest chance of the slightest evil" is enough to constitute obligation or duty.[8] Lastly, Austin, albeit with hesitation, suggests that if a person has an obligation or duty he must have the threatened evil "in prospect," i.e., fear it,[9] though certainly this psychological element is little stressed.

[7] *Ibid.*: "Now where it obliges *generally* to acts or forbearances of a *class*, a command is a law or rule" (p. 19).

[8] *Ibid.*: "But where there is the smallest chance of incurring the smallest evil, the expression of a wish amounts to a command, and, therefore, imposes a duty. The sanction, if you will, is feeble or insufficient; but still there *is* a sanction, and, therefore, a duty and a command" (p. 16).

[9] *Ibid.*: "If, in spite of that evil in prospect, I comply not with the

Unfortunately these additions and refinements cause Austin's analysis to fall between two stools. It ceases to be a plausible analysis of "being obliged" to do something and remains an inadequate analysis of "having an obligation." To see precisely where it fails we must concede something which may be disputed: Austin would not allow any system of rules to count as a legal system unless its rules provided for the infliction of evil in the case of disobedience. We may for the purpose of the argument concede this as a part of the definition of "legal," though it was deduced by Austin from propositions that we might wish to reject: he thought laws were commands, and he thought commands were significations of desire by one who had the intention and some ability to inflict some evil in the event of disobedience. But, even if we concede the analytical connection between the notion of a legal system and that of a sanction in the form of evil or harm, the definition of having an obligation in terms of the *chance* of incurring the threatened evil, and of the individual's having this evil in prospect, leads to absurdities.

We may deal first with the psychological element (prospect of evil), which Austin only very uncertainly uses. The statement that a thief has a legal obligation not to take the purse is not a psychological statement about him. He may have no fear at all of the threatened evil, and yet his obligation remains. If he is deterred by fear we may say, rather oddly, that he was obliged to leave it alone. Second, the statement that a person has an obligation on a particular occasion is quite independent of any assessment of the chances of his incurring the evil though these may be very important in considering where he could be said to be obliged to do something

---

wish which you signify, I am said to disobey your command, or to violate the duty which it imposes" (p. 14); ". . . *superiority* signifies *might:* the power of affecting others with evil or pain, and of forcing them, through fear of that evil, to fashion their conduct to one's wishes" (p. 24).

that he did on a particular occasion. There is no contradiction or even oddity in saying, "It's your duty to report for military service, but, since you're living in Monte Carlo and there's no extradition treaty, there's not the slightest chance of their getting you."

Third, there is something quite ludicrous in Austin's first stressing the importance of the threatened evil and then reducing it to "the slightest chance of the slightest evil." This ruins his analysis as an analysis even of being obliged to do something. Only where a choice is made less eligible by some substantial disadvantage do we speak of being obliged.

The most general criticism of Austin's analysis of obligation is that his inadequate notions of chance of incurring evil, prospect of threatened evil, are misleading because they obscure a central element, and this is simply the existence of rules of the appropriate kind. The most charitable view of Austin's talk of the chances of incurring evil is to regard it as expressing in inappropriate predictive terminology the following two facts: (1) if a legal system is to exist under which obligations are created there must at its root be the complex social practice we have already described; (2) the system must contain rules providing for the application of sanctions in the event of disobedience though not all rules need have sanctions "annexed" to them. Without the notion of a system of rules resting on that complex social practice, the difference between "obliging" and "imposing or creating an obligation" cannot be made clear.

Hence the important connection between the concept of coercion and obligation cannot be clearly stated in Austinian terms with its impoverished vocabulary of habit and its inadequate analysis of a command in terms of the expression of a wish that people should act in certain ways made by one who intends and has some power to visit disobedience with some evil. The coercion in question may indeed take the form of the infliction of evil as it does in the case of a municipal legal system, but if it does the application of the evil must be something for which the rules of the system itself provide. However clear the actual power of a legislator was to visit certain conduct with pains, his threat and even use of force to coerce people to obey him would not constitute an obligation unless these were provided for by means of the appropriate legislative forms. At the most people would be obliged to do what he said. So the essential element of coercion is not the fact (the chance or the prospect) that evil will follow disobedience, but there should be an existing system of rules conferring authority on persons to prohibit behavior and to visit breaches of the prohibition with the appropriate coercive, repressive, or punitory techniques of the system.

Some qualification though not abandonment must be made of this last point. In all municipal legal systems there are some cases where there is no provision for sanctions in the event of a breach of a rule. Though perhaps no logical vice or infinite regress would attach to a self-referring rule that all officials should exact sanctions for all offenses including any breach of this rule itself, it is quite common for legal rules to require officials to do certain things and for the system to provide no sanction in the case of their breach. This is for example the case with the obligation imposed by the United States Constitution on the President to take care for the due execution of the laws. Yet we do not hesitate to refer to such cases as cases of official duty or obligation. They show that even within a legal system the complex features that characterize the standard case of obligation may come apart. This is reflected in juristic terminology, such as that of "duties of imperfect obligation," which the Romans invented for just such cases; and it helps to generate part of the skeptical doubts whether international law is "really" law or better classified as a branch of morality.

III

Within the vaguely bounded field of morality, there is certainly a sector (no doubt also vaguely bounded) in which we make use of a concept characterized by three salient features distinctive of the concept of a legal obligation. These features I shall refer to by terms that I hope will be found self-explanatory: (1) dependence on the actual practice of a social group, (2) possible independence of content, and (3) coercion. Outside philosophy, the expressions "obligation" and "duty" are used mainly for the appraisal or criticism of conduct by standards that have these three features and are not used indifferently for all forms of moral judgment. But certainly even nonphilosophical usage sometimes extends beyond this, and my concern is not to legislate in favor of a more restricted use of these expressions but only to determine the differences between different sorts of moral phenomena obscured by this extension. This is worth doing for perhaps two reasons: first, there is undoubtedly a standing temptation in philosophy to assimilate all types of moral judgment to a single type; second, we can best understand other areas of morality if we *first* focus clearly on the three salient features of obligation as they appear in the actual morality of a social group. To characterize morality (as, e.g., R. M. Hare does in his illuminating book, *The Language of Morals* [10]) as *primarily* a matter of the application to conduct of those ultimate principles which the individual accepts or to which he commits himself for the conduct of his life seems to me an excessively Protestant approach. Important as this aspect or kind of moral judgment is, we need to understand it as a development from the primary phenomenon of the morality of a social group.

In suggesting that we distinguish one type of moral judgment from another, I do not in the least wish to deny that

[10] R. M. Hare, *The Language of Morals* (Oxford: Clarendon Press, 1952).

the conduct that they require may often be identical. It is often the case that one and the same particular action is required by different moral principles. If I promise to look after and protect a neighbor's child I have an obligation to do this which arises from my promise; but I may also think it inconsistent with my moral principles to permit unnecessary suffering of this as of any other child though I should not naturally phrase my recognition of this latter principle in terms of recognizing an obligation. Here is one way in which different principles of moral conduct overlap. But they may also coincide in a different and more important way. It may be that the social group in which we live and accept the institution of a promise as breeding obligations also endorses the different and wider principle that it is wrong to inflict gratuitous suffering. Even here, so long as we think that the force of this wider principle does not depend on its actual acceptance by the social group (but is something by which we may judge the actual morality of social groups), we have again to distinguish two different kinds of principle requiring the same action on a particular occasion. The area of morality I am attempting to delineate is that of principles which would lose their moral force unless they were widely accepted in a particular social group.

Promises constitute the obvious case of moral obligation, and here certainly we have all the three salient features that we have noticed. If we are to incur such obligations there must be some established procedure generally accepted by some specific social group whereby the utterance or writing of a certain range of expressions is sufficient to render actions specified by them obligatory for the speaker or writer. If no such procedures exist, promising is logically impossible, just as saluting would be logically impossible if there were no accepted conventions specifying the gestures of formal recognition within a military group. When we promise we make use of specified procedures in order to change the moral situation; in lawyer's language we exercise a "power" conferred by rules to change moral relations.

Promises have pre-eminently the feature I have called independence of content: the obligation springs not from the nature of the promised action but from the use of the procedure by the appropriate person in the appropriate circumstances. This independence is further manifested by the fact that the obligation thus deliberately created may also be deliberately extinguished by the promisee. This independence of content does not, however, entail that there is no restriction whatsoever upon the classes of action that a person may make obligatory for himself by promising to do them. Morals like law may have principles of "public policy" and render "void" a promise that from the start involved doing something patently immoral; but we should distinguish from such cases those where we subsequently discover moral reasons (perhaps in changed circumstances) against doing what we have promised to do. In these latter cases we have a moral obligation arising from the promise, but one that we consider in the light of other principles we ought not to carry out.

The third element of *coercion* needs careful scrutiny in this and other cases of moral obligation. In the case of legal obligation, rules typically provide that, in the event of failure or threatened failure to do what other primary rules require, there must be some official determination of the fact of this failure (judgment of a court) and then a variety of official steps taken to punish the failure or, in civil cases, to secure performance or its nearest equivalent. These steps include imprisonment used as punishment or used differently as a means of inducing obedience in a particular case or the forcible seizure of money or goods (execution) for compensation —and there are many other variants. By contrast (and this is one major distinction between moral and legal obligation), the coercion characteristic of moral obligation takes the form not of the infliction of harm or the use of force but primarily of the exposure of the individual to reminders that he has failed to comply with rules regarded by the social group as a matter of serious importance and to demand that he should comply. The typical moral pressure takes the form of an appeal not to fear of harmful consequences or to the futility of refusing to do what in the end one will be forced to do but to the delinquent's presumed respect for the rules he has broken. "You have broken your promise." "That would involve breaking your promise." The assumption inherent in such criticism is that what is most needed is a reminder of what the rules require and that the guilt or shame engendered by the contemplation of their breach will suffice or at least tend to inhibit future or continued failure to comply. Of course there are ancillary techniques: blame, praise, exhortation, severance of social relations, temporary exclusion from the group may be used, and these may shade off into something very like threats of harm and punishment. Yet, as soon as an appeal is made primarily to fear even of unorganized "sanctions," we are on the way from moral to legal obligation. The fact that moral pressure is characteristically exerted through an appeal to the delinquent's assumed respect for the institution violated, together with the fact that the plea, "I could not help it," is, if substantiated, always an excuse, jointly constitute the "internality" of morals as compared with the "externality" of law. This has sometimes been grossly misrepresented by the contention that whereas laws require us to do certain actions morals only require us to be in certain states of mind (or soul).

If we now consider not promises but the moral duties attached to an office or role in social life, these differ most notably in that the particular duties attached to these roles (a husband's duty to support his wife, the father's to look after his children) are not conceived of as truly created by the deliberate choice of the individual. The independence of content that these duties have is therefore rather different in that they are conceived of as *assumed* by entry upon the particular role so that one who takes up the role is thereby specially committed to discharging these duties. They are not principles of universal application to all societies alike but are conceived of as something that may vary from society to society together with a whole mass of associated institutions. Hence the obligation to maintain wife or children may not attach to husband or father in societies that think of it as normal for the wife to work and for children to be provided with support at the public expense. As noted above, though wider principles of morality may require a man to look after any child in need of care, the *duty* on a parent to do this springs from the fact that this particular society attaches moral importance to persons occupying such a position doing this.

If we consider the notion of a moral obligation to obey the law, we find that there are a number of issues requiring separation. One of them we have already discussed: viz., the claim that if a legal system exists then it follows that there must logically be a general recognition of moral obligation to obey the law so that if there is no such general recognition of a moral obligation to obey the law it would be a mistake to say that a legal system existed. Apart from this, however, there is some ambiguity in the notion of an obligation to obey *the law*. Presumably, if we consider that we should obey only those laws whose effects are likely to be (morally) good or the lesser of two (moral) evils, this would not be the recognition of a moral obligation to obey the law but only the application of some general principle that we should maximize good and minimize evil. The recognition of an obligation to obey *the law* must as a minimum imply that there is at least some area of conduct regulated by law in which we are not free to judge the moral merits of particular laws and to make our obedience conditional on this judgment. In a modern state it seems most plausible to suggest that this area is that which includes matters of defense and economic welfare but excludes, say, matters of religion or esthetic taste. Do we in fact recognize that we are bound within some such area to obey the law as such? There is at least a plausible argument that we do not in fact recognize any such obligation to obey the law as such but that our moral scruples against disobeying those laws whose effects we may think bad is due to the consideration that our disobedience might encourage general disorder and would therefore be the greater of two evils. Yet, though plausible, this is not convincing: it ignores, first, the fact that if we are ready to go to prison rather than obey our attitudes might very well strengthen the system as a whole and not weaken it; second, it ignores the very important fact that obedience often appears to most not as something required by a general principle that we should not harm human beings unnecessarily but as something required by the consideration that the particular members of our own society have obeyed the law and expect it to be obeyed. Where obedience to the law is motivated by such considerations, there is recognition of a moral obligation to obey with the three salient features that characterize it.

IV

In conclusion, I shall shortly consider certain motives for extending the use of "obligation" or "duty" to a much wider field so as to include those principles by reference to which we criticize adherence to or departures from the accepted morality of a social group. In the little-read second and third chapters of *The Province of Jurisprudence Determined*, Austin described the area of morality with which I have been concerned as that of "positive morality"; [11] with it he contrasted the Law of God, which constituted in his view the proper standard for the criticism of both positive law and positive morality and to which the principles of general utility

[11] Austin, *The Province of Jurisprudence Determined*, pp. 12 and 125–29.

are our "index." On such a view the ultimate principles of morality are the commands of God, and on this view we shall have no difficulty in conceiving of all the actions that they require as obligations. This is so because of the strength of the analogy between fundamental principles so conceived and the three salient features of obligation. For, first, fundamental moral principles on this view will be independent of content since they will owe their status not to what they require but to their being the commands of God. Second, God has every power and, on some accounts, every intention to punish disobedience or render it futile. But God's authority is not on such a view constituted by the actual practice of a social group, and it is this which renders the analogy imperfect so that the claim that "I have a moral obligation to do X" means the same as "God has commanded me to do X" may be a source of confusion even among those who share this view.

A very different motive for the extension of the concept of obligation is to be found in J. S. Mill's *Utilitarianism* [12] and probably still inspires most of those who wish to use the term widely. Mill says that

> . . . the idea of penal sanction, which is the essence of law, enters not only into the conception of injustice, but into that of any kind of wrong. We do not call anything wrong, unless we mean to imply that a person ought to be punished in some way or other for doing it; if not by law, by the opinion of his fellow-creatures; if not by opinion, by the reproaches of his own conscience. This seems the real turning point of the distinction between morality and simple expediency. It is a part of the notion of Duty in every one of its forms, that a person may rightfully be compelled to fulfil it.

Here, it seems to me, Mill very accurately fastens on the notion of coercion as essential to both legal and moral obligation, but this is accurate where coercion refers to the at-

[12] See J. S. Mill, *Utilitarianism* (Everyman's Library ed.; New York: E. P. Dutton & Co., 1910), chap. v, p. 45.

titudes or actions of other human beings and where compulsion has a similar meaning. There is, however, a step of some magnitude from the notion of being punished or compelled by "the law and the opinion of fellow creatures" to the notion of "punishment or compulsion by the reproaches of conscience." Some analogy there is; yet it may well be felt that its utility is limited, and that the line between all "morality" and "simple expediency" is far too complex to be drawn in this way.

V.—THE CONCEPTS OF OBLIGATION AND DUTY

By R. B. Brandt

Philosophers often use the following expressions as approximate equivalents: "It is X's duty to do *A*"; "It is obligatory for X to do *A*"; "It would be wrong for X not to do *A*"; and "X ought to do *A*". Some statements in Moore are a good example of this; see *Principia Ethica*, 1929, p. 148 (but also pp. 168-70).

Other philosophers, however, have protested that this practice obscures important differences among "wrong", "obligation", "duty", and "ought". Language, it is said, does not proliferate forms without corresponding functions. The philosopher who lumps these words all together is at least ignoring distinctions ordinary language makes; much worse, he may be led by his lack of discrimination into confusions and oversights of substance. H. L. A. Hart, for instance, has charged this practice with being "one factor obscuring the nature of a right" (*Phil. Rev.* lxiv, p. 179). It is, of course, one thing to criticize, another to supply an adequate substitute theory of one's own, and the critics differ among themselves in their accounts of the ordinary, nonphilosophical use of these words. C. H. Whiteley, for instance, while he does not propose any explicit definitions, says that "duty" and "obligation" are approximate synonyms and that "a duty or obligation is a consequence of a contract or undertaking, either explicit or implicit. My duty is that which I am engaged or committed to do, and which other people can therefore expect and require me to do."[1] A much fuller account by H. L. A. Hart is along different lines. Hart contrasts "duty" and "obligation" with each other, and both with "right" and "ought". According to him,[2] duty and obligation are jointly distinctive in that their content depends on the practice and code of the agent's group (*e.g.* duties to parents depending on local practices); moreover, what conduct is one's duty or obligation need not be fixed by the *nature* of the act in question (past facts

[1] "On Duties", *Proceedings of the Aristotelian Society* (1952-53), p. 96. For a very similar view see D. Kading, "Are there Really 'No Duties to Oneself'?", *Ethics*, lxx (1960), 155.

[2] "Legal and Moral Obligation" in A. I. Melden (ed.), *Essays in Moral Philosophy* (Seattle: University of Washington Press, 1958); and in "Are There any Natural Rights?" *Philos. Review*, lxiv (1955), 175-191. It is not clear that Hart is any longer defending all these points in *The Concept of Law* (Oxford: Clarendon Press, 1961). *Cf.* pp. 79-89, 163-180.

like promises, or special relations, may be decisive); and the force of duty-obligation is coercive. What distinguishes obligations from duties is that "they may be voluntarily incurred or created" (whereas duties arise from position, status, role), and that "they are *owed to* special persons (who have rights)". Hart wisely claims for these generalizations only that they represent major tendencies in ordinary usage.

The aim of the present paper is to take further steps toward an accurate description of the ordinary use of the "obligation" and "duty" families. I propose to say relatively little about the more exciting problem about what (possibly) is common to these various concepts, and how this common element should be analyzed; I shall have nothing at all to say about naturalist, noncognitive (etc.) accounts of "morally ought" or "ought, from a moral point of view" or "ought, on moral grounds." The conclusions we reach may have some implications for the more exciting problems, but I shall aim my discussion at marking the differences and similarities among the various terms I have listed.

We are naturally concerned about *present* usage. Both "duty" and "obligation" have an honourable history; both appear in written documents of the thirteenth century. It would be foolish not to take historical "texts" into account in considering what present usage is. But conversely it would be a great mistake to forget that language is continuously accommodating itself to new problems. The concept of "rights" in John Locke's day was narrower than the concept as it appears in the United Nations Declaration of Rights—nor is there good reason to think that the latter document misuses the term, or stretches its meaning beyond its ordinary use at present. Similarly, some of the following contemporary uses of our words *may* need to be regarded as fairly recent developments of the language: On 23rd March 1961, *The New York Times* reported Mr. Nkrumah as saying that it is "the *duty* of all nations in the world to bring pressure to bear on South Africa to abandon her *apartheid* system". The same source reports President Kennedy as having said at a recent news conference: "I would conceive it to be the *duty* of the United States . . . to defend the Charter of the United Nations by opposing any attempt by any government to intervene unilaterally in the Congo." On 8th April 1961, the writer heard a business man say that it is a person's "*moral duty*" to report cruelty to birds to the S.P.C.A. One evening recently the writer heard a recital of a particularly vicious teen-age "prank"—the tossing of a "Molotov-cocktail" through a window, with the result that all the windows in the room were blown out, although no one was injured—and of its victim wondering whether she should report the incident to the police. Someone commented: "It isn't a matter of choice in a case like this; it's an *obligation* to report an incident of that kind." The historian Merle Curti, in a lecture in October 1960, said that "Jane Addams thought that people are *under an obligation* to affirm their own vision of truth". Some students at Swarthmore College recently arranged a debate on the question "whether students are *morally obligated* to report infractions of college rules which they observe". I propose to offer a theory which takes these contemporary uses into account.

1. *Grammar*

In the case of "obligation" there is a family of words to be kept in mind: the verbs "oblige" and "obligate", their passives, "obliged" and "obligated"; the adjective "obligatory". All members can be combined with "moral" in some way or other; we speak of "moral obligation", "being morally obligated" (which in the U.S.A. is more familiar than what is said to be the more frequent British form, "being morally obliged"), and "morally obligatory". "Obligatory", like "right" and "wrong", applies to actions; doing a certain thing is what is obligatory, whereas it is people who are obligated, and who "have" obligations.

The "duty" family is simpler. "Duty" is the only word, a noun; there is no corresponding verb or adjective. There are, however, "dutiful" and "duty-bound".

I shall now review the grammar of these terms. On the first five of the points to be mentioned, at least one of our terms differs from either "wrong" or "ought" or both. And there are interesting similarities and differences between "duty" and "obligation".

1. We can "have" both obligations and duties: "The president of a college inevitably *has* a good many outside obligations" and "The chairman of a department *has* many time-consuming duties".

2. Both terms may be followed by "to" succeeded by a term referring to a person or persons. For instance, we may say that an elected official "has an obligation to" the ones who elected him. The Girl Scout pledges that "on my honour I will try to do my duty to God and my country". It is not so clear that we speak of "*a* duty *to*" anybody, although *O.E.D.* cites someone as saying that the New Testament "enlarges upon duties to

inferiors ". We can also say we are " *under* obligation to " someone ; but there is no parallel expression with " duty ". A very familiar form of the " obligation to " construction is the following : If I have promised to play tennis with someone on a certain date and am then invited to play tennis with someone else on the same day, I can say " I have a prior obligation to someone else for that day " or " I am already obligated to someone for that date ". Another familiar type of remark is likely to be made by one's wife : " We are obligated [have an obligation, are under obligation] to the Joneses, having been there for dinner three times last autumn." (Note that we can use " obligated to " or " an obligation to " without indication of anything specific we must do.)

3. There is a slightly different construction. When Anthony Eden resigned as premier he issued a statement pointing out his inability, because of health, to " do my full duty *by* my Sovereign and the country ". This remark illustrates a " duty by " construction which has no parallel with " obligation " : it also shows there is a use of " duty " in which a man may be *unable* to do what is still his duty, so that " is my duty " does not always imply " can ". Note that the Girl Scout promises only to *try* to do her duty to God and country. (We are also sometimes unable to discharge our obligations.)

4. Another grammatical difference between the terms is that we often say " I have *some* obligation to go to the lecture " or " I feel *some* obligation to him " ; but we never say " I have *some* duty to . . . " The " some " construction with " obligation " we can call an *explicit prima facie use*, because the obligation is asserted at the same time it is suggested there may well be considerations which will make it right not to meet the obligation. There is some plausibility, however, despite the absence of a " some duty " construction, in recognizing an explicit *prima facie* use of " duty ", either when we say " One of his duties is to . . . " or " His duty, as secretary, is to . . . ". In either case, because of the *many* duties suggested, and our knowledge that duties may conflict, there is some approximation to the suggestion of " some obligation ". However this may be, the terms are identical in *allowing* for the possibility of over-riding considerations, at least in most instances, even without these special constructions. Not in all, for we can specifically exclude it, as in " Everything considered, my obligation—or duty—is to . . . ". Furthermore, it is implied, or perhaps even asserted, that there are no countervailing considerations when we say, without qualification, " My duty is to . . . " or " My obligation is to . . . ".

(There is a marked difference between these words when preceded, say, by " my " or " your " and when preceded by " a " or " an ", or " one of your ".) But if I say it is my duty to king and country to do so-and-so, I do not exclude the possibility that a higher allegiance, to God, may require doing something different—and I need not retract the former statement if later, in view of duty to God, I say I am not free to do my duty to my country. And roughly the same with " obligation ".

On this matter, " duty " and " obligation " are like " ought " which can be countered by conflicting " oughts " (etc.), although there is, I think, no simple grammatical construction which must be classified as an explicit *prima facie* use. All of these words, however, differ from " wrong " and " right " which permit no *prima facie* use at all. I say this with some hesitation, in view of the fact it has been suggested to me that we can say " I know it is wrong to lie, but in the present circumstances this is the best thing to do ". People *do* sometimes say this, but I am inclined to think that doing so is a misuse of English, an improper ellipsis for " it is *normally* wrong to lie ". If one disagrees with my judgment, one will then say that these terms too can, in some contexts, have a *prima facie* use; but I believe one must say they clearly never have an explicit *prima facie* use.

Incidentally, if there are two conflicting obligations, recognized as such, and a decision must be made what should be done, we do not normally say, " What then really is my obligation ?" To ask this is somewhat odd, since it is already clear that there are two obligations, which conflict. We can ask, of course, which obligation is stronger or more pressing. But the preferred phrasing in this situation is, " What *ought* I to do ?"

5. We " do " or " perform " our duty but not our obligations; the parallel verbs proper for use with " obligation " are not easy to identify, but we seem to " meet ", " fulfill ", or " discharge " it. An obligation thus sounds a bit like a payment due on a debt, which we are able to meet; whereas our duty is more like a job or chore which we can do or perform.

6. Other persons can obligate us: my son, by accepting hospitality in a far-off city, may obligate me to take his hosts sight-seeing when they come my way. There is no comparable " duty " verb. Another person or group can *make* something my duty: *e.g.* Congress can make it the duty of the President to appoint a commission to review tariffs, but only by what amounts to making a change in the definition of the office of the presidency. Moreover, of course, I can obligate myself, *e.g.* by a promise. I cannot " duty " myself. Indeed, it even sounds

queer to say that I have " made " something my duty ; what is more natural is to say that, through my acceptance of a certain post, certain things have " become " my duties. Tennyson said, " The path of duty is the way to glory." It would sound odd to say the same of " the path of obligation ", perhaps for the reason that the path of obligation is too much a matter of our own doing.

7. It has been doubted that there are obligations to *do* something, except as obligations *to* some person or persons ; this contrasts with " duty ", about which a parallel claim would be much less plausible. It is important to see that this is not true, at least for current usage. It is not true, I believe, of obligation-statements reported earlier : the one about the Molotov-cocktail, Curti's statement, and the topic of the student debate. Moreover, we say " Citizens have an obligation to observe the laws of their country " ; " Citizens in a democratic country have an obligation to vote " ; " Mentally gifted people are under an obligation to develop their capacities." To go back to earlier times, *O.E.D.* cites Burke as saying, " What obligations lay on me to be popular ?" And it gives an 1859 example, " You are obligated to vindicate yourself." In most of these cases it seems hardly sensible to attempt to identify any individual to whom obligation is owed. On the other hand if we had the authors of these statements before us, and more context were filled in, possibly in some instances it would be natural to pick out such an individual. We must conclude, however, that there are uses of " obligated " and " obligation " in connection with which it would be absurd to identify an individual to whom the obligation is owed.

Nevertheless some people feel that there must be someone to whom one is obligated if one is obligated at all ; otherwise, one would be talking as senselessly as if one talked of a debt not owed to anybody. Moreover, an implicit assumption to this effect may lie behind the way a good many persons *talk*. For there is widespread talk of " obligations to oneself "—an expression used sometimes, I think, to refer to a person's obligation to protect his own interests when it would be easier to allow aggressive persons to impose on him, but used more often, probably, in affirming one's right to live up to one's own moral standards, when one has convictions one feels should be respected by others, particularly by persons with less rigid standards who encourage participation in activities one considers wrong. Such talk is understandable if there is an implicit assumption to the effect that obligations are always *to* someone. For, given such a tendency, in case no *other* person is identifiable as the one to whom an obligation is owed, it is not surprising that the " to X " blank is filled in as " to myself ". But why should anyone think, or talk as if, obligations are always owed *to* someone ? This is a puzzle. We shall see later that, in what I shall call " paradigm " (and apparently historically earliest) uses, " obligations " *are* always owed *to* someone. This fact has doubtless influenced how people talk and think, and may be the solution to the puzzle.

I shall be making use of some, but not all, of the foregoing points in constructing a proposal about the logical relations of our two concepts to each other, and to related concepts.

It may be objected to some of the above statements about " grammar " (and to any use of them for making further points) that they are misleading because the moral and the non-moral senses of our words are not carefully distinguished. It is true that they are not, despite the fact I should concede that some mentioned phrases hardly have a moral use. The main reason they are not is that it is dubious whether there *are* sharply distinct moral and non-moral *senses.* It may be that " obligation " and " duty " preserve an identical core of meaning throughout moral and non-moral uses. This, in fact, is the view of the matter best supported by the evidence.

The question merits consideration, and I propose to digress and set forth the reasons for the above judgment of the matter, although the theory to be presented in Sections III and IV is independent of my conclusion.

2. *Moral and Non-moral Uses*

Both " obligation " and " duty " are sometimes used in statements which make no moral point. As extreme examples, consider " The duty on that coat is $25 " and " I have an obligation at the bank ". Moreover, we often speak of social obligations, outside obligations, and family obligations, not to mention legal obligations and military duty. When we do, we are not *saying* something about moral obligation or duty. Moreover, presumably " moral obligation " and " moral duty " have a use precisely because there is a contrast with obligations and duties that are not moral. *Prima facie* it seems that " duty " and " obligation " often make non-moral points, and that we can say properly that there are many non-moral duties and obligations.

One possible philosophical construction of these facts is the supposition that there are sharply differing *senses* of our terms, and that these can be exhaustively grouped into two types : the ethical sense or senses, and the descriptive senses in which our words are used in statements which can be confirmed by ordinary observation and inductive inference. Statements of legal duty, for instance, may be construed as descriptive statements to the effect that, if a person fails to do a certain thing, legal machinery may be used to coerce him. Another quite different possibility is to ignore " moral obligation " and " moral duty " as meaningless vestiges of outworn theology which should be dropped from our vocabulary.

In contrast to both these views I think we must hold that, with the exception of some extreme instances, each of our words has one generic sense among its various uses: " obligation " and " duty " mean the same throughout their many uses, as much as any genus is identical throughout its species. At the same time we must acknowledge different species: the complex predicate " moral obligation " does a job different from that of " social obligation ". And, in context, when just " obligation " is *said*, " moral obligation " may properly be understood. (I am not, of course, assuming either that these terms do, or that they do not, designate a property.)

It would probably be agreed that, in view of the obvious continuities of force and flavour of the moral and at least many of the non-moral uses of these terms, there is reason to avoid a sharp division between moral and non-moral *senses* of " duty " and " obligation "—provided it is possible to give a tolerably clear and convincing account of the common core, as well as of what happens when modifiers like " moral ", " legal ", and " social " are added. I shall now attempt a very brief sketch along this line.

It is helpful to begin with the modifier " moral ". What must we suppose about a duty or obligation in order to speak properly of it as a " moral " one? (1) It must be a matter of conscience. That is, in part, failure to perform will, unless there is adequate justification or excuse, arouse guilt feelings in the agent and moral disapproval in observers, if they know the facts and are sensitive. (This condition may be more dependent conceptually on condition no. 3, than at first appears.) (2) The requirement must command roughly community-wide support, not merely that of some class or caste, as would be the case for certain " codes of honour ". (3) Failure to perform, without excuse, will reflect on *character*—this being spelled out by reference to traits like honesty, respect for the rights of others, and so on. (4) The requirement is not one just of prudence or convenience, but a matter of principle. (5) The requirement must be construed (if the question is raised) to have stringency superior to that of claims of manners, custom, taste, law, and courtesy. Admittedly these conditions are vague and may need supplement.

Let us now concentrate on " duty "-statements, adding a word about the parallel with " obligation "-statements at the end. I shall offer some examples of non-moral " duty "-statements, which we can use for drawing out the core-meaning of " duty " and at the same time for contrasting moral duty with other kinds of duty. These exemplar " duty "-statements will be felt to be very close to statements of moral duty ; hence our very first job is to see that they are not really statements of moral duty.

Consider : (1) A soldier, having been given a legal order by a superior—say an order to commit suicide if necessary in order to avoid capture—may say it is his " duty " to do that thing. (2) Many people say it is a man's " duty to defend his country, right or wrong ". (3) It is traditional to speak of " duty to king and country ". (4) The manager of a firm may say it is his " painful duty " (doubtless to the firm) to discharge an inefficient employee. I think it will be conceded that the force and flavour of all these statements is very like that of statements of " moral duty "—as when Regulus might have said he considered it his moral duty to return to Carthage. So that, if there is reason to view moral statements as nondescriptive, there is equal reason to regard these statements as nondescriptive.

Are these statements covertly statements of *moral* duty ? We need not deny that, possibly, it is the moral duty of the soldier to do what he here calls his " duty ", of a citizen to do his duty to king and country, or of an executive to discharge his duty to his firm. All the same it is not an analytic proposition that this is so. The above numbered statements are not, and do not entail, statements of moral duty. For apply Moore's open-question test. Might not the soldier be in doubt if asked whether, everything considered, it was morally right for him to do what had been ordered ? Could " moral duty " require one to be loyal to king and country, right or wrong ? Might a man not concede that something was his duty as stated, and then go on to say it was his moral duty not to do it—a pious man, for instance, citing higher allegiances ? It has been suggested to me that the above statements are after all statements of moral duty, only statements of *prima facie* duty in Ross's sense. But it is not convincing to suppose that a soldier who says it is his duty to advance is saying that he has a moral duty to do that thing unless overriding moral considerations of some sort arise. When a soldier is awarded a medal for actions " over and above the call of *duty* ", moral duty is surely not what anybody has in mind.

Yet how can this be? Are there features of non-moral duties which are different from those of moral duties (thereby explaining how the compounds "moral duty" and say "military duty" can have different roles), and is there something identical in all (thereby explaining how "duty" can have a core meaning identical in all these contexts)? Let us probe both some similarities and differences.

First, while failure to do moral duty will, unless there is an excuse, reflect on one's character in some way, failure to do one's duty in one of the non-moral contexts will reflect on one in other ways, not exactly in respect of features of character but in respect of closely-related traits which a man will be anxious to claim himself to have in connection with certain organizations or relationships. The soldier who fails to commit suicide according to orders is a coward by army standards. Failure in duty to king and country may not show a defective character; but, unless there is an excuse, it reflects on loyalty and patriotism. How would a manager's colleagues describe him, if he failed in his "duty" to discharge the employee? Given no suitable justification, as a weakling, without the will necessary for executive office. Second, if failure to do one's non-moral duty does not arouse moral disapproval (this is a complex concept) in others it will still arouse critical reactions (*e.g.* contempt), doubtless not in every sensitive and informed person, but in some—perhaps those who belong to the organization in which the "duty" has a place, such as fellow-soldiers. Moreover, if such failure does not arouse feelings of what is properly called "guilt" (again a complex concept), it will arouse pangs of anxiety and self-reproach. We must notice that there are kinds of blame different from moral blame. For instance, Lord Ismay in his recent *Memoirs* (1960, pp. 122-123) talks of the blame that would have attached to his government, if a decision for a direct attack on Trondheim had been made. It is clear that the sort of blame he had in mind is connected with the defensibility of a policy before the country. Defensible *morally?* Not at all. Defensible as sound military strategy, as judicious policy encouraging reliance on its framers as fitted to lead England to victory in a desperate war. For these purposes, disastrous policy, however well-intentioned, is a ground for blame, except for excuses of a sort to indicate no repetition need be expected from the leadership. It is clear that Ismay would have felt pangs of self-reproach, if he had thought his policies blameworthy in this way.

I shall not attempt to sketch further parallels with "moral" duty, such as the claims of non-moral duties usually having precedence over personal preferences in the direction of conduct. It is enough if I have shown that the structure of a soldier's situation when he speaks of " his duty " in view of an order, and that of other non-moral situations where we use " duty "-talk, are both similar to and different from the structure of situations where we speak of " moral duty ", so that it is not surprising that " duty " serves for all.

The same sort of thing is true for " obligation ". Take the giving of a wedding present. A person may explain his sending a gift by saying, " I felt some obligation to send a present ". Is the obligation moral ? It could be, if failure to meet it would cause real hurt. But very often we should not claim this. Wha kind of obligation is it, then ? Most people would say it is a matter of custom, courtesy, friendliness, and the like.

Obligations of this sort have similarities to, and differences from, moral obligations, parallel to the case of " duty ". Failure to make a gift is some reflection, not on character, but on a person's friendliness or concern for family ties. Furthermore, if the man fails to make the gift he will feel some discomfort, though hardly guilt-feelings ; and other persons may slightly cool toward him.

We do not, then—except for some extreme examples—need to postulate quite different *senses* of " obligation " and " duty " in moral and non-moral contexts. There are differences between the moral and the non-moral uses, and the modifiers—" moral ", " legal ", " social "—give some expression to these. But there are common features : failure involving reflection on the agent, justifiably critical attitudes on the part of others, and so on. These common features make it plausible to claim a common core of meaning for our words, throughout these varied contexts.

3. *Paradigm Uses*

The job of marking out the logical relations between " duty " and " obligation ", and between these and " ought " and " wrong ", still lies before us. Insisting on the continuity of uses of " duty " and " obligation " has, of course, not advanced us with this task. Nor do our conclusions about " grammar " take us far. Some of the differences, *e.g.* the fact of a " duty by " construction which has no parallels with other words, may well be a mere accident of idiom. The same may be true of differences arising from the fact that " duty " and " obligation " are nouns ; it may still be that " it is X's duty to do *Y* " is identical in substance with " It would be wrong for X not to do

Y". The "grammatical" evidence, then, needs interpretation; if it is important, it is so as a symptom of something deeper.

At the outset I alluded to two different traditions among philosophers: the one emphasizing the substantial identity of the above four concepts, the other (*e.g.* Whiteley and Hart) emphasizing their difference. I wish now to propose that *both* these traditions are in large part correct, provided one of them is construed as a theory only about a specifiable class of the uses of our terms. Correspondingly, I wish to urge a distinction between *paradigm* and *extended* uses of our two words. My point is that the Hart-Whiteley tradition is not far off as an account of the paradigm uses, and the Moore tradition not far off as an account of what is common to *all* uses. Both views, however, are mistaken about some details.

The fact that the paradigm use of these words is what it is will help to make intelligible, I hope, some of the grammatical peculiarities we have noticed.

I must explain what I mean by a "paradigm" use, since I am employing this term in a peculiar way. There is sometimes a sub-class, within the wider class of all correct uses of a term, which has two features. First, members of this subclass are felt to be especially natural uses of the term: there is no better word for the occasion and there are no better occasions for the word. We might express part of what this comes to in another way: there is a class of contexts such that, if speakers were given a choice between phrases incorporating "duty", "obligation", "wrong", "ought", and so on, the vast majority would make the same selection, although for other contexts where one of these words can be applied with perfect correctness, speakers would have no preference for one phrase over another. Second, the contexts in which a given term is felt to be especially appropriate have certain features in common, and the term has come, to some extent, to *suggest* these features; speakers associate the two, to some degree. It seems likely that only relatively few words have paradigm uses in this sense.

There may be both historical and psychological reasons—in the case of our terms, it is probably both—why a word now has paradigm use in a certain context. The historical reason may be that the word has had close associations with that context for a long time; perhaps the principal correct use of the term was, for centuries, in that context. The psychological reason may be that the paradigm context is the setting for the child's first familiarity with the term. "Ontogeny recapitulates phylogeny": the historically earliest use is first learned by the individual speaker. The resulting association between word and context explains the suggestions of the word, and is behind the fact that the word feels especially appropriate in that context.

Let me now make concrete proposals about the paradigm uses of, first, " obligation ", and then " duty ".

The word " obligation " has, I suggest, paradigm use both in the context of talk about promises or agreements, and in the context of talk about acceptance of benefactions. When we wish to talk about what a person ought to do in virtue of his having promised or of his having accepted a benefaction, " obligation " is the word to use. Indeed, to say " I have an obligation " will, unless the context points explicitly in another direction, imply or suggest that I have either promised or accepted a favour.

That the paradigm use should be such is not surprising in view of *O.E.D.*'s indication of the historic roots. All members of the " oblige " family are derived from *ob* plus *ligare,* " to bind ". They were first used in connection with promises, contracts, and oaths, all of which were conceived to bind in some way or other. For instance, in 1297, according to *O.E.D.*, R. Gloucestor wrote : " Ye emperor of rome to him . . . obligede bi his messengers alle ying yat was his." Again : " Ye king . . . bed him . . . and made him obligacion & ostage him gan sende yat he ssold to him come al sauf." In 1330 R. Brunne wrote : " He with scrite and oth mad obligacion. . . . " Whether the authors had in mind primarily a legal or some other kind of tie we probably should not ask ; insistence on such distinctions is anachronistic. Talk of " obligations of gratitude " seems to come later, the earliest reference in *O.E.D.* being 1632 : " She might not see him, to acknowledge the obligation she owed him." Despite the relatively late date, the " under obligation to " grammatical construction seems most naturally used in this type of case—testimony to the depth of the roots. The same may be said of the colloquial expression, " I'm much obliged to you ".

The adoption of a word referring to a physical bond for this nonphysical relation (if we may call it a " relation ") presumably would not have occurred but for the fact that promises and the acceptance of benefactions obviously do initiate a relation rather like a physical bond. The exact nature of the bond, however, might differ from case to case. Sometimes it might be predominantly moral : there is a bond in that failure to perform will reflect on a person, arouse—and properly—guilt feelings in the individual and disapproving attitudes in others, and so on. Sometimes, as suggested in the preceding section, the bond might be predominantly legal, or a matter of manners only.

What features do these paradigm contexts have in common? (*a*) A roughly specifiable service is " required " of one person. (*b*) Two parties are involved: the one who is required to perform a service, and the one for whom, or at the bidding of whom, the service is to be performed. (*c*) A prior transaction, the promise or benefaction, is the source of the relationship.

If the above historical suggestions are well taken, there probably was a time when these three features would have properly been included in a *definition* of " obligation ". They are, however, now only suggested by the word, and they are characteristic of the situations in which the word is most naturally applied. If we confined our attention solely to paradigm uses, they could today with some reason be included in the definition of the term. There is so much justification for their inclusion in contemporary philosophers' characterizations of the word.

There are, however, now perfectly correct uses of " obligation " where these three features are not all present. Various examples of such usage have already been set forth; a familiar example is the fact that I may have an obligation to assist a motorist in trouble on a little-travelled road. It is of course not surprising that it has become correct to use " obligation " for this wider group of situations. For, perhaps as a result of developments in moral standards in the past few centuries or even decades, there are other nonphysical ties on behaviour rather similar to those which promises and acceptance of benefactions institute, but which do not arise from promises and benefactions.

The term "duty ", in contrast, has paradigm use in connection with tasks associated with occupancy of an office or station in some organization in which the office confers rank, rights, or privileges. When we want to talk about what a person is bound to do in virtue of some office (etc.), " duty " is the word to use. A paradigm use of " duty ", then, occurs in statements like " It is your duty *as* housewife [citizen, president of the club, father, servant of God] to do so-and-so ". (This was first suggested to me by remarks by J. L. Austin.)

That " duty " should have this paradigm use is, like the case of " obligation ", not surprising in view of the apparent history of the word, as indicated by *O.E.D.* The word appears to come from " due ", and to refer to services or payments due, not on account of promise or contract, but as a consequence of one's place in a system of stations. " Duty " was paid as a mark of submission to one's feudal lord, or to the church for its services, or as public revenue. So Chaucer: " His maister had not half his duetee " (as cited by *O.E.D.*) Notice that " duty " in the sense of custom's duty still refers to a payment due the public and not to some private individual as a result of contract. (*O.E.D.* gives only one example—1487 : " To defraude ther creditours of their duties "—which suggests construction in terms of contractual debt.) Since God was conceived in the image of a feudal lord, it was natural to speak of duty to him—doubtless eventually a bridge between moral and non-moral conceptions of duty. Note *Ecclesiastes* xii : " Fear God and keep his commandments ; for this is the whole duty of man."

A case might be made out that the antiquity of use of " duty " in this context explains some facts of present grammar. If one's duty is fixed by one's position, we should not expect to find an " enduty " verb parallel to " obligate ". Since jobs associated with positions are fairly definite, we need not expect to find talk of " some duty " parallel to " some obligation ", or talk of " feeling one's duty ". And if one's duty is part of one's job, then it is perhaps not surprising that, along with talk of " doing one's job " we also speak of " doing one's duty ".

Presumably the word " duty " with this application would not have developed had there not been agreement that certain services or payments are, rather like money-debts, " due " from incumbents of certain offices or stations. The sense in which they were " due ", of course, might vary from case to case, as suggested in the preceding section. The force might be moral ; or failure to pay might instigate a review of the fitness of the encumbent for the post ; and so on.

What features are characteristic of the paradigm context ? (*a*) An individual occupies an office or station in an organization or some kind of system. (*b*) A certain job is deemed of some value for the welfare of the organization. (*c*) This job is associated, somehow or other, with the office occupied by the individual. (*d*) Performance is expected and " required " of him.

At one time, if our historical suggestions are correct, these features might properly have been included in a definition of " duty ". At present they are characteristic of the situations in which the word is most naturally applied, and to some extent they are suggested by the word.

" Duty " is correctly used today, however, in non-paradigm contexts which do not have all these features. The remarks by Nkrumah and Kennedy, cited earlier, are probably examples of this ; the statement cited about the duty to report cruelty to animals is certainly one. Possibly Bishop Butler was using the word in a non-paradigm way when he said (as cited by *O.E.D.*) that " economy is the duty of all persons ". A woman once told the writer that she and another woman had considered it their "duty" to complain to the manager of a firm when they observed that some of its workmen were being required to work without adequate safety precautions. People sometimes say that it is a person's duty to keep his promises, that it is one's duty to use one's talents effectively, that it is one's duty to support causes one believes in, that it is one's duty to help others who are in trouble. All of these are "extended" uses of "duty". Presumably "duty" has come to be used in these non-paradigm ways because situations have arisen, or have been supposed to have arisen, in which a person's bonds are more aptly characterized by "duty"-talk than by any other.

There are two factors which, at least today, tend to blur the difference between "duty" and "obligation" when we are talking about offices or roles. First, many positions are held voluntarily and can be relinquished at will. Service in them is thought of as being primarily a quasi-contractual performance in return for a monetary reward. When one thinks of a position in this way, it is natural to speak of its requirements as "obligations". Second, at present we seem to distinguish between the jobs essential to an office, and other chores which are involved in full or meritorious service in the post. Thus giving lectures is essential to a faculty member's job; but giving a lot of time to committee work is not. The term "duties" seems to be reserved for the former, and the term "obligation" for the latter. As a result, "obligation" is used for jobs connected with one's post or office, along with "duty".

4. *Extended Uses*

I have suggested that our words have come in time to be used in non-paradigm but rather "extended" ways. Such uses are paler or abstracter; they connote less, because the situations in which they are applied have fewer features in common, as compared with the historically earlier or paradigm type of use. It is the whole class of uses, both the paradigm and the extended, which fixes the features necessary for "correct" use today. I have further suggested that Moore was not mistaken by much when he was, seemingly, prepared to equate "duty to do", "obligation to do", and "wrong not to do", if we fix attention on the minimum features necessary for correct usage.

The question we must now consider is whether we can identify any elements at all common and necessary to all correct uses of our words (the ones not definitely odd), which may serve to

26

contrast them, to some extent, with " ought " and " wrong " and with each other.

What must we strike from the paradigm use of " obligation " in order to arrive at elements common to correct uses? First, we must strike out the notion that obligation is an obligation *to* someone. In Section I we examined exceptions to this rule, familiar in contemporary use. Second, we must strike out the idea that the bond derives from some prior act or event, such as an agreement or the acceptance of a benefaction. The obligations to give help to one in dire need or to make some contribution to charitable enterprises are sufficient reason for elimination of this restriction. This second move has a corollary: if not all obligations derive from prior events (often acts), then it is not essential to an obligation that it can be brought about by an act of the person obliged or someone else. Some obligations are (to keep a promise), but some are not (to help others in dire need).

But then what is left? Two things. First, what one is obligated to do is always to achieve some positive goal. One's obligation always concerns a state of affairs to be reached, something to be planned for along with one's personal goals. It is a prescribed end, to be taken into account in designing one's behaviour. Like the payment of a debt, it is a goal which may be reached in various ways but is prescribed as a goal to be reached in some way. As such, the obligatory is distinguished from the prohibited. What is prohibited is territory to be avoided in behaviour. Obligations are territory to be reached somehow; they contrast with " no trespassing " areas to be avoided in the course of going where one is to go. Adultery, for instance, is thought wrong and hence as something to be avoided; but there is no such thing as non-adultery which is a goal to be achieved.

This implication of a positive goal to be achieved is the most important distinction of " obligatory " from " wrong not to do ". For " wrong " is a term which can be used to label certain kinds of behaviour as justifiably prohibited, as, everything considered, morally out of bounds. There are lesser differences. " Obligatory ", we saw, normally bears a *prima facie* sense whereas " wrong " at least normally does not.

The contrast here emphasized between " obligatory " and " wrong not to do ", however, is not absolute; it is relative to a point of view. The language properly used can shift from one to another, depending on the agent's slant. Take sexual behaviour. Normally we do not speak of obligations here; one is apt to say: " It is wrong to . . . ". But one may think of the matter in another way. One can think of chastity as a morally required goal of behaviour. In that case, one can say that there is a moral obligation to be chaste. Similarly, injury to other persons is normally spoken of as wrong. But a state of taking-care may be thought of as a demand on one's behaviour. Then one can say that there is a moral obligation to drive carefully. In a similar mood one can say there is an obligation to be careful of the property of others. *If*, then, one can contrive to view not-committing-adultery or not-abandoning-a-friend, to take Hart's examples, as somehow positive goals, then it can be correct to speak of a moral obligation to do these things.

There is a further limitation to the force of our distinction. Suppose someone says a person is obligated not to commit adultery, when there is no special reason for regarding this event as somehow a positive achievement—when, that is, " wrong to do " would be the natural thing to say. Would such a person's statement be meaningless ? Of course not. We understand him to be saying awkwardly what is better said by " wrong "-language. Philosophers are not failing to communicate if they make " is morally obligated to do " serve a great many uses far from the paradigm uses of " obligation " ; such uses are intelligible and for some purposes a helpful simplification. They are harmful only in blurring our sense of how language is ordinarily used.

There is a second distinctive feature, present in paradigm uses of " obligation ", which is common also to all normal uses. It is on account of it that one cannot quite say that for one to have an obligation is for there to be some positive goal one *ought* to bring about. This is the fact that " obligated " in its extended uses retains what we may call the " coercive " flavour of the paradigm uses. There is not necessarily an agreement-like bond to a specific individual, etc., but the suggestion is that there is a *bond as if there were*. " Obligation " is never used just to talk about what ideally ought to be, or even about what ideally someone ought to do. When we say someone has an obligation we mean more than this. For when someone has an obligation to do something, and fails to do it without a suitable excuse or justification, there is a reflection on him as a person, and he is properly subject to sanctions, at least to criticism and disapproval. (As we have seen, the criticism and disapproval need not be " moral " since obligations are not always " moral ".)

The case of " duty " is very similar to that of " obligation ". Its paradigm uses are the most frequent and natural, but these are far from being the only proper uses, as we have seen. In particular, " duty " is sometimes used when we know quite well that what is said to be one's duty is not a task associated with a position or station in life. Much less need the duty be *to* an association or group (or to someone within this group, perhaps the head), for whose organized activity the job is deemed significant.

What then is common to *all* the non-odd uses of " duty " ? " Duty " is very similar to " obligation ". Like " obligation ", one's " duty " is always to do something conceived positively as a goal to be aimed at. We rarely speak of a duty *not* to do so-and-so. Again, like " obligation ", " it is your duty to " typically has more force than " you ought to ". Indeed, in some contexts people feel that " it is your duty " is an even more compelling, solemn, or decisive claim than " it is your obligation ". Failure to do one's duty without suitable justification or excuse is a reflection on one, and is the object of sanctions, at least unfavourable attitudes on the part of the relevant group of people.

Like " obligation ", then, " duty " differs from " ought " primarily in strength and " feel ". It differs from " wrong " mainly in that what is one's duty is the achievement of some positive goal. But, again like " obligation ", what is an achievement of a positive goal depends on one's slant or point of view. And, as in the case of " obligation ", it is not *meaningless* to say it is a person's duty, say, not to treat animals cruelly, although this is an awkward and jarring mode of speech.

Is there then a difference between " obligation " and " duty " ? We have noted a difference of paradigm use : " Obligation " functions in agreement-relations and retributive-relations, where "duty" does not, and "duty" functions in pure organization-role relations, where " obligation " does not. But generalizations about merely *correct* usage are difficult and delicate. We can say something. We may require a circumlocution if we are to use " duty " when an explicit *prima facie* sense is needed, whereas " some obligation " supplies this readily. " Duty " may have a more compelling, serious, life-and-death air about it. Again, " obligation " perhaps ties in a bit more closely with conscience and personal moral standards—as reflected in the fact we speak of " feeling an obligation ". " Duty " is more naturally used when moral demands are backed up by institutional sanctions—as when we say it is one's duty to serve in the armed forces, as both law and conscience may require. But I think the most important thing we can say is that the more a context approximates to the type suitable for a paradigm use, the more we incline to use the corresponding word for speech about what is required, and the more use of the other term strikes us as odd or out of place. But in many cases—where use of either term would be "extended"—either one can replace the other without noticeable jar. And either one *always can* replace the other—sometimes some circumlocution being necessary—and the whole be meaningful.[1]

[1] Preparation of this paper was made possible by a grant from the Rockefeller Foundation.

Swarthmore College

MIND ASSOCIATION

Those who wish to join the Association should communicate with the Hon. Treasurer, Mr. PETER ALEXANDER, Department of Philosophy, The University, Bristol 8, to whom the yearly subscription of Twenty-five Shillings (payable in advance) should be sent. Cheques should be made payable to the Mind Association. Members may pay a Life Composition of £27 instead of the annual subscription. The annual subscription may be paid by Banker's Order; forms for this purpose can be obtained from the Hon. Treasurer.

The Hon. Secretary of the Association is Professor A. R. WHITE, The University, Hull.

Members resident in U.S.A. are requested to pay the subscription ($4.00) to the Hon. Assistant-Treasurer, Professor Alan Anderson, 993 Yale Station New Haven, Conn.

Those who join the Association after previously buying MIND direct from the publishers or through a bookseller are asked to inform the Hon. Treasurer of this (and of the name of the bookseller) when they join.

SPECIAL NOTICE TO CONTRIBUTORS

Contributors of Articles and Discussion Notes should in future always enclose a stamped and addressed envelope. Those from countries outside the United Kingdom should send international stamp coupons to cover return postage.

ANALYSIS 30.2 DECEMBER 1969

'DUTY', 'OBLIGATION' AND 'OUGHT'*

By JAMES K. MISH'ALANI

THIS will be an investigation of 'Duty', 'Obligation', and 'Ought': how they differ from each other and what relations obtain among them.

'Duty'

Two uses of 'duty' must be distinguished: (a) the use we make of it when we say that it is someone's *duty* to do something at a given time, with the implication that he ought to do that thing at that time; and (b) the other use we make of it when we enumerate someone's *duties*, or some of them, with no implication that he ought to be discharging them all the time during which they are truly his.

The latter of these two uses is the one that is distinctive of the word 'duty', the former (as will be explained later) being nothing but a special sort of colouring of the word 'ought'.

The duties of a person are the duties of his office or station; they are his only insofar as he occupies the station in question and only in his capacity as occupant of it.

'Station' must be understood widely enough to cover such diverse things as a person's role (*e.g* , father), status (*e.g.*, company manager), office (*e.g.*, governor), job (*e.g.*, teacher), calling (*e.g.*, minister, priest, physician), position (*e.g.*, chief surgeon). There are differences among these different types of "station": an office is not a calling and a job may involve neither position nor status. But there is something common to all of them—namely, that a given role, job, status, position, office, or calling is definable, at least partly, in terms of the duties it involves. Other defining features may be the powers and privileges it carries (if it carries any).

A person assumes the duties of a given station in coming to occupy that station, and he is not relieved of them until he relinquishes or otherwise loses it. In the meantime, he is to *perform* or *discharge* his duties, and his performing them one day does not relieve him from having to perform them the next. Duties are not met, as debts are met, once and for all. A teacher who performs his teaching duties for the day continues to have them as long as he remains a teacher. It would be, therefore, mistaken to think of the duties of a person as a set of actions that are expected of him. The number and, within certain limits, even the nature of those acts that one must needs do in the course of discharging one's

*A version of this paper was read at the forty-third annual meeting of the American Philosophical Association, Pacific Division, March 27, 1969.

duties cannot be determined at the time one first assumes one's duties, and consequently one's knowledge of what the duties are does not consist in an anticipation of what one's actions will be.[1]

A person is not required to discharge his duties all the time during which they are his; a judge remains a judge and continues to bear the duties of that office, even though he may not be at the bench. With regard to most stations, there is a clear division between the times when a person bears the duties of that station but is not required to perform them and those times when he both bears them and is required to perform them. The words 'off duty' and 'on duty' mark this distinction, although in the case of some stations, as for instance that of a parent, there are no clearly designated times when the occupant of that station is really "off duty".

The times during which one bears one's duties and is also required to perform them usually recur according to a roughly regular pattern; and such times must at each recurrence be of an appreciable enough length to allow for the completion of a significant set of tasks. One's round of duties is quite often suited to the interval of a single day. We, therefore, speak of daily duties or of having finished one's duties for the day; but it is hard to imagine the same being true of an interval of a few seconds.

The duties of station are also called responsibilities; although it may be more accurate to reserve the title 'responsibilities' to those duties for the proper discharge of which one is answerable to someone else. This special relationship of being answerable to someone else for filling a station of one's own may repeat itself from person to person and from station to station, and thus generate, at the farthest extreme of formality, a chain of command, with its corresponding distinctions of rank and degree.

Not every type of conduct required of an occupant of a station is a discharge of some duties of that station. In this regard, the duties of a station must be distinguished from each of the following (wherever the latter are present to be distinguished): (i) conduct becoming an occupant of that station, (ii) the demands of professional ethics, and (iii) the standards governing the proper means of discharging the duties of the station. Thus, initiating an open brawl with a student of one's own in a public tavern over the favours of a lady of pleasure may be conduct unbecoming a professor, but is neither professionally unethical behaviour (as plagiarising the ideas of a colleague would be) nor substandard performance of one's duties (as shoddy preparation of lectures would be).

[1] Some exceptions: (a) There may be some actions associated with a station, and normally considered to be some of its duties, that can be done for once and all; *e.g.*, the president taking the oath of office, or the new king interring his predecessor. (b) Some routine aspects of discharging the duties of a station can be anticipated and clearly specified at the time of assuming one's duties; *e.g.*, gathering the documents and putting them safely away before leaving work every day at 4.30.

Furthermore, a professor's duties do not comprise any such duties as the "duty" *not* to start a public brawl, *not* to plagiarise, or *not* to be careless in preparing lectures (though giving ill-prepared lectures is a bad way of carrying out one's professional duties). There are no duties *not* to do certain sorts of action. 'Do's and 'don't's are determined by rules; the duties of a station are not attached to that station by rules—they rather define the station, and what they are is determined by the definition of it. It is of the nature of a station to be for the purpose of accomplishing certain ends; the types of task that are essential for fulfilling this function are the duties of that station.

In short: the duties of a station are determined by the *definition* of that station, and non-performance of them is *dereliction*; the ethic and demeanour proper to a station are determined by *rules*, and violations of these rules constitute *misbehaviour* (either behaviour unbecoming a person of that station, or unethical conduct); the proper manner of discharging the duties of a station is governed by *standards*, and failures on these standards constitute *incompetence* or *carelessness*.

In those cases where station carries with it rank and degree, the occupant of the station, should his rank place him in a subservient position, will be required to carry out the wishes, commands, or orders of his superiors. The execution of such instructions may come to constitute the major portion of the duties of a given station, or even the only clearly stated duty of it. Thus, kings called their subjects dutiful for no other reason than that they were obedient; and servants are characterized as dutiful when they exhibit those skills and traits of character that make them especially willing and able to follow their masters' directions. Herein lies a connection, presumed by some to be more than merely occasional, between performing one's duties and submitting to higher command. Perhaps, this is why 'duty' comes to evoke reverence.

'Obligation'

The very word 'obligation' does not tolerate some verbal contexts within which 'duty' naturally fits. Thus, there is no such thing as being "on obligation" or "off obligation" in analogy with being on or off duty; we don't expect obligation to call in the same way we expect duty to call; deeds may not be described as being "in line of obligation" or "beyond the call of obligation", although they are often correspondingly described as being in line of duty or beyond the call of duty.

If the key to a proper understanding of duties was found in their being logically bound to stations, the key to obligations must be sought in the fact that they are owed to someone. He to whom an obligation is owed is entitled to that which would be secured to him by the fulfilment of the obligation, and it is in consideration of that title, that right of his, that the obligation to him exists. Thus, an obligation is generated when two parties enter into a special relationship whose nature is such that it invests one party with certain rights and commits the other to honouring them. Examples of such a relationship are the relationships of promisor to promisee, creditor to debtor, employer to employee, trader to customer.

Obligations are commitments. An obligation is *met* or *fulfilled* by the successful completion of a specific undertaking, and once it is met, he who was under obligation is thenceforth free of it. What one needs to do to meet an obligation of his may range from a rather isolated act (such as delivering certain goods to someone at a given place and at a pre-ordained hour of a specific day) to the persistence in a manner of conduct for a protracted period of time specifically so as to fulfil certain pre-determined conditions (such as completing a tenure of service for an employer). Until such things are actually done, one remains under the obligation in question. Thus, unlike duties, of which one cannot rid oneself simply by performing them, obligations are extinguished by their fulfilment.

Whereas concerning duties of office the manner in which they are discharged is subject to evaluation according to certain standards (so that we may be concerned not only with whether a given person can perform such duties but also with how well he can do so), all that matters with regard to obligations is the fact of their fulfilment or non-fulfilment. There is no clear sense in which a lender who has every assurance that the borrower will return his property to him in good repair may yet be concerned as to how well his borrower will do so. There is, without a doubt, a difference between returning something graciously and returning it grudgingly. But a person who does not return debts until he has been reminded, notified, badgered, and threatened is not someone who is particularly unskilled at returning debts; he is rather someone who, left to himself, is not likely to return them at all, and it is for this reason that he is not to be trusted.

Returning a debt is not a task requiring special skills and competences; it is a matter of satisfying certain conditions and fulfilling certain terms, which doubtless may call for the use of some skills, but whatever skills are thus needed (such as the skills to speak, write, and count) are not peculiar to returning debts as such. One may contract with another to do a skilled job for him, such as building him a garage, and in such a case one needs certain competences in order to fulfil the obligation one has thus incurred. But meeting the terms of the agreement as such (*e.g.*, finishing the job on a certain date, using the specific grade of material required by the contract) is not the exercise of a special skill. There is no such skill as that of finishing a job on a given day, although one may need to exercise many other skills to proceed with one's job at a certain rate of progress.

Differences in skill aside, there remains a difference between better and worse ways of meeting an obligation. By returning a hundred-dollar debt in two thousand five-cent pieces a debtor may be working an inconvenience on his creditor, and thus be doing worse than someone who repays a similar debt by cheque; and a person who makes such repayment in ten thousand pennies may be doing worse still. But such means of repayment, eccentric and infelicitous as they may be, do amount in each case to full and unstinted repayment. They are equally adequate to the purpose of meeting the debt, and from that point of view a debtor would not meet his obligation any better by choosing an otherwise better way of doing so than they. In contrast with this, a person who performs the duties of his station badly does less of a job than he who does them well, and the worse he is at them the closer he is to not doing that which his station requires of him.

Some Connections

(i) A common way in which one comes to occupy a station is by contracting with another to fill the station in question, in which case one assumes certain duties by incurring some obligations. Nevertheless, the duties and the obligations remain distinct. When a trainer takes on a job at the racing stables he both incurs obligations to the owner and assumes certain duties. Part of his duties is to exercise the horses, but he is not thereby under an obligation to them. His obligations are solely to his employer, and they are roughly these: commencing to perform the duties of trainer at a given time and continuing in this capacity until certain specified conditions are satisfied. If, after entering into such an agreement, the trainer for no good reason fails to appear for work on the appointed day, he will have failed to meet his obligations to his employer, but he will not be guilty of dereliction of duty, as he might have been had he commenced work but neglected the horses utterly. If, on the other hand, he actively assumes his rôle at the stables and discharges his duties without fault and then of a sudden disappears, leaving his employer in the lurch, we will say that although he performed his duties most satisfactorily he did not meet his obligations.

(ii) The proper discharge of one's duties may on occasion require that one incur certain obligations. Thus, a teacher who in the course of performing the duties of guidance and supervision, posts his office hours, comes thereby under an obligation to his students to be available for private conferences at those times. Failure to honour such obligations counts against a favourable judgment as to how well he performs his duties.

(iii) In order to meet his obligations an agent may find it necessary to institute various offices with their appropriate duties and appoint different people to them. That is how a university meets its obligations to its students.

'Ought'

What obligations a person is under and what duties he bears are matters not of what ought to be the case, but of what is the case—matters of fact. If one actually occupies a certain station, then it logically follows that one as a matter of fact bears certain duties and responsibilities, namely those that define the station in question. And if one has indeed entered into a relationship which by its very nature commits one to satisfying certain conditions, then it also logically follows that one is as a matter of fact under an obligation to someone to satisfy those conditions.

The facts of one's having certain duties and being under certain obligations do, nonetheless, bear on what one ought to do. For there will be things that a person ought to do in view of the duties he bears, although the step from the fact that he bears such-and-such duties to the judgment that he ought here and now to conduct himself thus-and-so is by no means a simple step. At least it is not a step simple enough to allow us to say that since he is trainer at the stables he ought to be taking White Cloud around the tracks right now, for White Cloud may not be the only horse at the stables, or it may be night and the work-day is over, or it may be time to brush down the horses rather than exercise them, or a vast number of other things that would prevent taking White Cloud out from being the proper discharge of his duties as trainer. But that there must be times at which it will be true that he ought to take White Cloud out on the tracks, and that it will be true that he ought to do so then by reason of the duties he bears as trainer, is quite undeniable.

When we make a judgment as to what someone ought to do, and we make it exclusively or mainly on the basis of what we know to be duties of his which he bears in virtue of his occupying a certain station, we often express ourselves by saying, 'It is his duty to do so-and-so'. By using the construction 'It is his duty to do . . .' we both express a judgment as to what he ought to do and at the same time indicate the kind of considerations we would be ready to cite in support of it. When we make a similar judgment specifically on the basis of obligations that we know him to be under, we can express ourselves by saying, 'It is his obligation to do that', or 'He is obligated to do it'.

Morality

There is no such thing as a specifically moral 'ought', although judgments as to what ought or ought not to be done can be, and often are, supported by considerations of a specifically moral nature. The question of what duties a person bears is one consideration of this special sort.

We are indeed horrified by the S.S. officer who pleads that he was only performing the duties of his office at an extermination camp, but we also recognize that his plea is not entirely irrelevant. In fact, the reason why the phenomenon of such a man is a monstrosity lies precisely in this: here is someone who quite accurately notices a moral point in favour of an action against which there exists an enormity of moral censure of which he seems unaware. That he should be morally responsive enough to hear and answer the call of duty and yet be utterly insensible to the crying shame of the hellish suffering of millions of innocents is something that we are not willing to condone or even admit as possible. We had rather think him a monster. Here we feel the point of the philosopher's notion that behind the multiplicity of those moral considerations that we acknowledge, there lies (must lie) a single moral sensibility.

Besides a person's duties, we also acknowledge his obligations as carrying moral weight. But these two do not exhaust all the types of moral considerations that there are. Thus wilful deception is a specifically moral turpitude, but in itself it is not in any clear sense the dereliction of the duties of a station, nor is it a clear-cut case of despising an obligation owed to someone. Of course, it can be either one of these two things. A clerk at an information booth would be abusing his office and not performing his duties properly if he were to deceive someone entitled to his guidance on a point on which it is his duty to dispense information. Again, someone who has promised to tell you where the treasure is if you supplied him with all the rum you carried would be violating a specific obligation to you if, after acquiring your rum, he were to lead you to dig in the wrong spot. But not all deception is of either one of these two kinds. The fact is that wilful deception, whether of these kinds or not, is quite simply wrong, and it would serve on purpose, save that of mere embellishment, to say that it is one of "our duties as moral agents" to tell the truth, or that we are "under obligation to our fellow men" to tell the truth, that somehow we "owe" it to them.

Such embellishments seem to have a profound appeal, however; for in a number of instances they have been transmuted from rhetorical devices to philosophical theories. Philosophers whose sensibilities may have made them responsive particularly and above all to their duties sought to represent the myriad requirements of morality as so many duties of a single station, that of being a human being or a rational being. Thus we have the vast range of philosophical theories that see all of morality as that which would be required for discharging a specifically human function or rôle in the universe.

Other philosophers, enchanted more by obligations than by duties, saw in all morally satisfactory conduct a fulfilment of an unspoken promise implicit in one's original consent to live within human society. For them, to live in society is to have consented to do so, and to have consented to do so is to have become party to an agreement, and hence to have incurred a specific obligation, to abide by certain rules.

Utilitarians, being on the whole empiricists wary of unverifiable claims such as those made by Natural Law theorists (to the effect that nature is a kingdom within which man occupies a distinct station), or by Social Contract theorists (to the effect that the social mode of human existence betokens an unspoken agreement among men), and perhaps tending to be by temperament more susceptible of being moved by the palpable signs of human happiness and misery than by the more formal considerations of duty and obligation, have urged that all the things that morality demands are so many different ways of being kind to one's fellow men.

It remained for the intuitionists, and particularly the deontologists, to remind us of the truism that there are many different sorts of moral considerations relevant to what one ought to do, and that there is no reason in the world to suppose that one of these different types of consideration must be the source of all the others. However, the one question they disparaged the most will continue to bewitch those who seek to understand themselves, namely: What is there in morality for men that they should find it worth their trouble to allow moral considerations to weigh with them?

University of Washington

1

LEGAL AND MORAL OBLIGATION

JOHN LADD

The problem of political and legal obligation is a facet of the more general problem of the relationship of the individual to the political and legal order, for the main function of the concepts of political and legal obligation is to provide an answer to the question: "Why ought one to obey the political authorities and the laws of the state?" The purported obligation, ostensibly a moral obligation, is invoked to explain not only why one ought to obey but also the limits of that obedience. If there is such an obligation, then we would have a pretty good answer to the general question of political and legal obedience.

It should be observed, however, that an alleged obligation to political and legal obedience is not the only possible kind of moral basis of obedience. Indeed, as I shall argue, the use of the concept of *obligation* in this connection has many significant moral implications that, when examined carefully, we might not wish to accept. Inasmuch as the whole question of civil obedience and disobedience has become a critical practical issue, it seems well worthwhile to re-examine the traditional and accepted view that from the moral point of view the question is one of obligation and the limits to that obligation.

The question that I want to discuss in this paper is not the usual question concerning the basis and limits of this alleged obligation or even the question concerning when this obligation, as a prima facie obligation, is overridden by other more pressing obligations. Rather I want to consider the prior question, namely, whether or not the concept of obligation itself is the proper one to use in explaining why we should obey the political and legal order.

Obviously we cannot begin to understand and assess the use of the concept of political and legal obligation until we have a clear idea of what we mean by the term *obligation* and until we have some notion of how it differs from other related concepts, e.g., justice, the common good, political duty, expediency, and the like. Part of our initial task is, of course, fixing on a terminology. Basically, however, we require a detailed logical analysis; for once we have decided on a certain usage for the term "obligation," e.g., the sense in which it is used in ordinary, common talk about obligations, our chief concern will be to explore the logical implications, presuppositions, and consequences of having an obligation in that sense. I shall argue that if we agree to use the word in the ordinary and strict sense, then it will become quite clear that the concept of political obligation or of an obligation to obey the law is not only inapposite but morally objectionable as well.

Since the word "obligation" has several different meanings in English, it will be necessary at the very beginning to settle two matters of terminology. Once we have noted the ambiguities in "obligation" and have made the required distinctions, we may, I hope, avoid unnecessary disputes simply over words and be able to proceed at once to more substantive issues.

Obligation: Abstract vs. Concrete Sense

Like many other words in English ending in "ation," "obligation" is used in both an abstract and a concrete sense. In the abstract sense, it stands for the state or condition a person is in when he has an obligation, i.e., the state or condition of *having* or *being under* an obligation. We use "obligation" in an abstract sense when we speak of the feeling of obligation, the sense of obligation, the grounds of obligation, theories of obligation, and so on. Thus, for instance, the "feeling of obligation" means the feeling of being under an obligation. (In German, obligation in the abstract sense is referred to as *Verpflichtung*.) [1]

In the concrete sense, the word stands for concrete obligations, i.e., the products or results of the condition of obligation (abstract sense). In this sense, "obligation" can be pluralized and given articles. A person can have obligations or an obligation, e.g., to his family, to his employer, or to his country. Here "obligation" is used to refer to particular moral requirements in much the same way grammatically as the word "duty" is used to refer to particular duties. (Again, in German, the concrete sense of "obligation" is captured by a different word, *Pflicht,* often translated "duty.")

The ambiguity of "obligation," as between the abstract and the concrete sense, is reflected when we try to describe kinds of obligation, for when "obligation" is used abstractly "kinds of obligation" means "ways of being under an obligation" or "ways of being bound or tied morally." Thus, when a person refers to kinds of obligation in this sense, he is talking about kinds of ties. For convenience we may call them *forms of obligation.* (German: *Art der Verpflichtung.*) Accordingly, legal, social, and moral obligation represent different forms of obligation.

There is a considerable body of philosophical writing on the nature of obligation (abstract sense) and its forms. It is sometimes held that, for instance, legal obligation and social obligation represent entirely different forms of obligation from moral obligation. Legal obligation, for example, might be said to differ

[1] The distinction referred to here is one adopted by Kant in his philosophy of law, where he uses the terms *Verpflichtung* and *Pflicht* to mark off the two senses of "obligation." See Kant, *The Metaphysical Elements of Justice,* trans. J. Ladd (New York: Bobbs-Merrill, 1965). The term *Verpflichtungsart* is there translated as a "way of being bound to a duty."

in form from moral obligation in that it involves sanctions. Sometimes it is held that there is only one form of obligation, e.g., moral or legal. I shall not discuss these questions.

When "obligation" is taken in the concrete sense, however, kinds of obligation are differentiated in terms of their content rather than their form. In this sense, we speak of family, financial, or military obligations. There are several ways in which kinds of obligation so construed may be specified: by reference to the persons to whom the obligation is owed, e.g., family obligations; by reference to the kind of performance required, e.g., financial obligations; or by reference to the basis of the obligation, e.g., contractual obligations. I shall call these kinds of obligations *varieties of obligation* in order to distinguish them from what I have called *forms of obligation.*[2]

It is clear at once that in speaking of political and legal obligation in the same breath, we are confusing descriptions based on the concrete and the abstract senses of "obligation." For political obligation represents a variety of obligation, namely, an obligation to obey the government; whereas legal obligation represents a form of obligation, i.e., the form of obligation created and enforced by law. Political obligation is contrasted with, say, a family obligation, while legal obligation is contrasted with moral or social obligation.

A great deal of confusion has resulted from the failure to distinguish the forms from the varieties of obligation. Unfortunately the expression "legal obligation" has been used to describe both a form of obligation and a variety of obligation. In this paper, I shall use it only for a form of obligation, to be contrasted, say, with moral obligation.

"Political obligation" will be used for a variety of obligation, namely, the obligation to obey the political authorities and to obey the law of the land. Since our question is one of ethics, the form of obligation with which we shall be concerned is moral obligation. Hence our question becomes: is political obligation one of our moral obligations, i.e., do we have a political moral

[2] It is obvious that many different classifications can be developed by combining ways of describing obligations. Thus, under one form, e.g., of legal obligation, we have many varieties of obligation, e.g., financial, military, and family legal obligations.

obligation? (Henceforth, unless designated otherwise, I intend to use "political obligation" to refer to this alleged kind of moral obligation.)

Obligation: Extended vs. Strict Sense[3]

A second matter of terminology that has to be settled before we begin is to determine whether we shall use "obligation" in an extended sense or in a narrow, strict sense. Moral philosophers are prone to use "obligation" in an extended sense so as to cover almost the whole, if not the whole, of morality. Thus, "moral obligation" is accepted as a synonym for "duty," "right," "wrong not to do," or, in general, "what ought to be done." Obligation is taken to be equivalent to moral oughtness, and ethics is described as the inquiry into the principles of moral obligation.[4]

Philosophically the net effect of adopting the extended usage of "obligation" is to submerge the traditional problem of political obligation in the more general problem of the moral basis of the individual's submission to political authority and to law. The distinctive claims of a theory of political obligation are lost and the theory easily becomes confused with, for instance, utilitarian theories. (Hume's theory of political obligation is a case in point.) In this regard one suspects that proponents of the extended usage are making a philosophical point in the guise of a terminological decision.

There is, of course, a much more restricted use of "obligation" which covers not the whole of morality but only one relatively specific kind of moral requirement. A narrower usage seems more in accord with the way the term is actually used in ethical and political discourse; for when we say that someone has

[3] The distinction discussed in this section has been examined in some detail by R. B. Brandt, "The Concepts of Obligation and Duty," *MIND*, vol. lxxiii, no. 291 (July 1964). The position that I defend here resembles in some important respects the views presented by H. L. A. Hart, "Legal and Moral Obligation," in A. I. Melden, *Essays in Moral Philosophy* (Seattle: University of Washington Press, 1958). As will soon become evident, however, I differ with Hart on many key issues.

[4] I must personally plead guilty to having used "obligation" in this philosophers' sense in my book, *The Structure of a Moral Code* (Cambridge, Mass.: Harvard University Press, 1957), 441 n.l.

an obligation to do *X* we intend something much more specific and perhaps stronger than when we say that someone ought to do *X*. (It makes perfectly good sense to say that Jones ought to do *X* but has no obligation to do so.) Thus obligation in the ordinary sense carries with it certain implications and nuances that specifically differentiate it from other kinds of moral requirements. What these specific features are will be the subject of the main part of this paper. My thesis will be that to ascribe to a person an obligation to do an act is to single out him and his act for special moral consideration, to stress something very special and peculiar about the person and his act, and to call attention to the special stringency of the moral requirement so described. The special character of obligations becomes clear in the case of obligations created by promises, and so we shall take such obligations as paradigmatic of obligations in general, although it will be assumed that there are other kinds of obligation to be considered as well.

In this chapter, I intend to restrict my discussion of political obligation to the narrow and strict sense of "obligation." It should be emphasized that this decision does not rest on any essentialistic presuppositions; rather it is made for purely pragmatic reasons, namely, to help focus our attention on a certain characteristic and traditional kind of answer to the question of political obedience. In order to join the issue with most historical and contemporary theories of political obligation, I therefore propose as a matter of strategy that we adopt the narrow and strict sense of "obligation."

My procedure will be to spell out in some detail what is generally understood and implied by the term "obligation," when used narrowly and strictly, and then to ask with regard to obligation, so construed, whether or not there is such a thing as political obligation. If our answer should turn out to be no, then I submit that the burden of showing what he means by "obligation" will be shifted to anyone who claims that there is such an obligation.

There are, of course, many dangers in following this procedure and, as Aristotle warned us long ago, we should not expect more exactness than the nature of the subject permits. My intent is admittedly speculative and, hopefully, provocative.

The rest of this chapter falls into three parts. In Part I, I shall set forth six formal features of obligations in general that seem to me characteristic of ordinary kinds of obligation, e.g., those resulting from promises. In Part II, I shall illustrate this analysis by showing how these features apply in playing a game. And, finally, in Part III, I shall discuss whether or not the concept of obligation so delineated, and in particular as it is applied to playing a game, is relevant to the issues of obedience to the political and legal order.

In order to forestall any possible misunderstanding of my argument, I want to emphasize once more that I am not concerned with the problem of when and under what conditions political obligations are overridden. Rather, I am interested in the question to whether or not there is such a thing as political obligation, to begin with. Only if it is assumed there is such an obligation, i.e., a prima facie obligation,[5] does the question arise concerning when it must give away to other demands of morality. My object here is to scrutinize this assumption.

I. SIX CHARACTERISTICS FEATURES OF OBLIGATIONS

Wittgenstein and others have taught us not to search for exact definitions of fuzzy and multifunctional concepts. It is clear that the concept of obligation is a kind of family-resemblance or open-textured concept. Hence the six features that I shall present should not be taken to provide the necessary and sufficient conditions of something's being an obligation. They are merely characteristic or typical in a loose sense; they serve as marks or criteria that can help us to decide when it is proper to say that someone has an obligation to do something.

1. The first thing to note about obligations in the strict sense is that they can be created and terminated. They come into being through being assumed or incurred, and they go out of being through being discharged or dissolved. An obligation typically makes an act (or attitude) that was previously morally indifferent or optional into something that one is required to do or not to do. The implication of saying that a person is under an

[5] The subject of prima facie duties and obligations and the question of how they are overridden will be discussed in a forthcoming paper entitled "Moral Dilemmas."

obligation to do or not to do something is that his doing of it is per se neither right nor wrong, but has become right or wrong for him to do solely on account of the obligation that has arisen with respect to it.[6]

This morally creative side of obligations can be easily seen in the case of promises. If I promise to do *A*, e.g., go for a walk, then that act, walking, is no longer something that I may choose to do or not, but has become something that I am required to do, i.e., an action that would be wrong for me not to do.[7] Or if I promise not to tell Jones something, then my act of telling Jones, which was previously morally indifferent or optional, now becomes something wrong for me to do. Insofar as legislative and judicial acts create obligations, the same point obtains, for they make acts that are per se indifferent or optional into acts that are right or wrong.

In sum, in connection with obligations, acts become right or wrong for a person to do by virtue of his having an obligation, rather than becoming obligations for him by virtue of their being right or wrong. It follows that one cannot have a general obligation to do acts that are right in themselves, e.g., to save a life; or to refrain from doing acts that are wrong in themselves, e.g., to refrain from murder or from lying; for these acts are already right or wrong, as the case may be.

Obligations are, in a sense, superadded to the ordinary requirements of morality. This is because they characteristically impose new and special requirements on particular persons in particular circumstances. They make what was previously indifferent or optional for a particular person into something he *must* do. In this sense, they add a new kind of moral reason for doing or refraining from doing something.

[6] Here I am using "right" in a strong sense to mean something like "wrong not to do." It should be noted that there are other moral terms, besides "right" and "wrong," that are weaker, for example, "good to do," "desirable," or "meritorious." The latter are used for what are sometimes called "acts of supererogation," i.e., acts that are good to do but not wrong not to do. Such acts are good but also optional. I do not mean to exclude such acts from becoming the subject matter of an obligation. On acts of supererogation, see my *Structure of a Moral Code*, pp. 125-30. Also, Joel Feinberg, "Supererogation and Rules," *Ethics*, vol. 71 (1961) and R. M. Chisholm, "Supererogation and Offence," *Ratio*, vol. 5 (1963).

[7] *Ceteris paribus*, for there might be some other, unmentioned moral reason for not doing it which overrides the obligation in this case.

2. Every obligation must have come into being through some fact, occurrence or circumstance, specifically related to the agent-obligor.[8] In other words, obligations are attached to particular people on account of particular facts, which are, as it were, unique to them. I shall call this fact the *basis of the obligation.*

Promising provides a good example of this aspect of obligation, for the act of promising, the factual occurrence, provides the basis of the obligation that it creates. The basis explains how the obligor came to have the obligation.

It is often held that the basis of an obligation must be a voluntary act of the obligor, e.g., a promise, a commitment, or an acceptance of a benefit. That is, it is assumed that obligations are always incurred voluntarily and freely.[9] The appeal of this voluntaristic conception of obligation is that it permits us to invoke the principle *volenti non fit injuria* to justify the keeping of obligations that are ostensibly or immediately contrary to our self-interest.

It seems unnecessarily restrictive, however, to limit the basis of obligations in this way. There seems no reason to exclude obligations that are based upon a person's involuntary acts; for instance, the obligation that a person may have to repair the damage he has caused completely involuntarily to another's person or property. We might, indeed, wish also to allow for obligations arising from the acts of others, e.g., servants or children. And, of course, we want to allow for the possibility that legislative and judicial acts can create obligations quite independently of any voluntary acts of our own.

For our purposes, then, all we need assume is that the basis of an obligation be some special fact about the person (the obligor) that places him under an obligation.

It should be observed that the basis of a particular obligation explains not only why there is an obligation in the first place but also why the obligation attaches to one particular person rather than another. This is clear in the case of promising, for Jones has the obligation, rather than Smith, because he, Jones, was the one

[8] Henceforth I shall use the term *obligor* for the person-agent who has the obligation and the term *obligee* for the person-subject to whom it is owed.

[9] Thus Rawls writes: "obligations are normally the consequence of voluntary acts of persons," in "Legal Obligation and the Duty of Fair Play," *Law and Philosophy*, ed. S. Hook (New York: New York University Press, 1964), p. 4.

who made the promise. The basis thus functions as a kind of principle of individuation by putting the person's name, as it were, on the obligation.

Since every obligation must have a basis, we are always justified in asking for the basis of an alleged obligation. We can ask: what special fact is there about the agent-obligor that places him under an obligation? If no basis can be given, we may conclude that the person in question has no such obligation.

We see now why there can be no general obligation binding on everyone to save lives or to refrain from murdering. There could be no basis for such an obligation, i.e., special facts about particular agents that require them to do these things. In contradistinction to obligations, the rightness of saving lives and the wrongness of committing murder arise from facts about the persons affected, e.g., their needs, rather than from facts about the particular persons who might perform these acts.

3. Obligations are interpersonal, that is, they involve not only a particular person who owes the obligation but also a particular person to whom the obligation is owed. Obligations, in other words, involve both an obligor and an obligee. (We may have to admit that collective persons, composed in some way or other of individual persons, can be obligors or obligees; for example, a family may owe an obligation or have an obligation owed to it.)

The existence of an obligee is as essential to an obligation as the existence of an obligor; for the obligee, as it were, holds the other end of the rope and can determine whether or not the performance owed must take place. To begin with, the obligee can release the obligor from his obligation. Moreover, he can refuse the performance owed. The right of refusal is evident when we consider the absurdity of an utterance such as: "I am under an obligation to do this for you, whether you want me to do it or not!" (Such an utterance would make sense only if the obligee were different from the beneficiary, e.g., in a situation in which one has promised parents he would look after their children.) The voluntary acquiescence of the obligee seems necessary to the bindingness of an obligation, for an obligation cannot be performed against his will.

The obligee also has, under certain conditions, the power to require the performance owed and to invoke sanctions or reparations for failure to perform. If the obligee insists, then the obligor must perform or else suffer the consequences.

Other things being equal, then, the will of the obligee is not only necessary but also sufficient for binding the obligor to the performance owed. The obligee is thus in many respects more important than the obligor as far as the obligation itself is concerned.

Here again, the crucial logical function of the basis can be observed. For the basis determines not only who has the obligation but to whom it is owed. Both obligor and obligee are particular persons related to each other through a particular fact that creates the obligation. It follows that we cannot know about a person's obligations or about persons to whom obligations are owed, unless we know something about them personally, i.e., some part of their personal history. This feature is quite evident in the case of obligations arising from promises, because we can know nothing about such obligations without knowing an historical fact about the obligor and the obligee, namely, that the one made a promise to the other.

In this respect, obligations represent a very personal sort of moral requirement, i.e., obligations are always individualized. That is, they attach to persons by virtue of the historical situations they find themselves in, rather than by virtue of, say, a role or office, or even by virtue of simply being a human being. This might be one way of distinguishing obligations from duties, which are often attached to roles or offices. It should be noted, however, that an individual, Mr. Smith, may, through a commitment of some kind, place himself under an obligation to his clients or constituents to fulfill the duties of a certain office.

The fact that obligations are personalized in this sense may explain, in part, why obligations are among the most stringent moral requirements. Since they come with "names on them," they cannot be so easily avoided. They are not like other kinds of moral requirements, which are relatively anonymous.

At this point, it is worthwhile pointing out that there is what might be called a hyperbolic sense of obligation, that is, the concept of obligation is sometimes used in an extended, hyperbolic sense in order to accentuate the extreme stringency of a moral requirement. Thus we find statements like: "We all have a moral obligation to work for peace," or "Everyone has a moral obligation to vote." Such statements receive their forcefulness precisely from the fact that obligations are individualized, for they imply that the obligations referred to attach to every individual as an individual. He, as an individual, no longer has any option. Nevertheless, the use of "obligation" in such contexts is, I submit, hyperbolic, for it is parasitic on the more usual use already noted, which individualizes obligations in a more specific way.

4. Another typical feature of obligations in the strict sense is that they authorized the use of sanctions in the case of nonfulfillment. (By "sanctions" I mean to include not only punishment but also various forms of social condemnation and the so-called "internal sanctions" of conscience.) I have just mentioned the fact that the obligee can require the obligor to perform what is owed. Another way of stating this is to say that obligations confer certain rights on the obligee, not only the right to the performance but also the right to enforce and the right to remedy in case of nonfulfillment. Thus, obligations and rights represent two sides of the same coin.[10]

I want to stress that obligations justify many different kinds of measures that would otherwise be morally objectionable, e.g. (in some cases) the use of force. The reason for this is that where there is an obligation, the nonperformance of the required act is morally wrong and blameworthy. There is no merit in performing one's obligations, only demerit in not performing them. That is why writers like Kant say of obligations that they are "perfect duties."[11]

Because of the intimate logical connection between obligations and sanctions, many philosophers, e.g., Hobbes, Bentham, and Austin, have tried to define "obligation" in terms of sanctions rather than the other way around. Their attempt may partly be explained by the fact that they took "obligation" to mean "being obliged." This identification is, of course, gratuitous, not to say misleading; for one can be obliged to do many things where no

[10] It is no mere coincidence, I submit, that in Roman Law the term *obligatio* refers to "a legal relation between two ascertained persons, in virtue of which the one is entitled to claim an act or forbearance from the other. The one, or creditor, has a right in personam, the other, or debtor, owes to him a relative duty, etc." Quoted from *Imperatoris Iustiniani Institutionum*, edited with commentary by J. B. Moyle (Oxford: The Clarendon Press, 1955), pp. 345–46 *et passim*.

[11] Kant's distinction between perfect and imperfect duties is set forth in his *Metaphysics of Morals:* Part I, *The Metaphysical Elements of Justice* (see note 1) and Part II, *The Metaphysical Principles of Virtue*, trans. J. Ellington (New York: Bobbs-Merrill, 1964). It is also discussed in Paul D. Eisenberg, "Basic Categories in Kant's *Tugendlehre*," *American Philosophical Quarterly*, vol. 3, no. 4 (October 1966).

obligation is involved and vice versa. (One may be obliged to jump off a burning ship, but that does not mean that one is under an obligation to jump.)[12] The positivist reduction of obligation to sanctions can be seen to be mistaken as soon as it is noted that obligations are logically prior to sanctions, for obligations are used to justify the application of sanctions rather than vice versa.

5. Another interesting feature of obligations is that to be morally binding they must conform to the limits set by other general moral principles (and perhaps even positive laws). By this I mean that the moral validity of an obligation is automatically nullified if what it requires conflicts with these principles. Obligations supplement the ordinary requirements of morality but cannot contradict them.

Ordinary practices (including legal practices) relating to promises and contracts illustrate this aspect of obligations, for promises and contracts are considered binding only if they do not require acts that are immoral. One cannot through a promise or contract acquire an obligation to commit murder or even to lie. Such promises and contracts would ipso facto be rendered null and void. This does not simply mean that, e.g., a promise to do something (known to be) wrong is overridden by other moral demands. The question of such an "obligation" being overridden does not arise, since it is not morally binding to begin with. Thus "obligations" to do something immoral are not prima facie obligations; rather they are not moral obligations at all, although they may, of course, be obligations of another kind. One way of seeing the difference between a morally binding obligation and one that is not is to note that in the case of nonfulfillment of an immoral "obligation" the obligee has no moral recourse, i.e., no moral right to enforce or to be compensated, and sanctions are not properly applied for nonfulfillment.

I should hasten to add that what I have said applies only to moral obligations, i.e., morally binding obligations, and not to other forms of obligations. As Plato pointed out, there is honor among thieves. Murderers and thieves often scrupulously honor

[12] As any quick reference to a dictionary will attest, "to be obliged" means to be compelled or forced, including by natural forces. There is, of course, a usage, "to oblige," which means to do a favor or a service of, e.g., "I am obliged to you for helping me." This point is brought out clearly in K. Baier, "Moral Obligation," *American Philosophical Quarterly*, vol. 3, no. 3 (July 1966), 220 n.

their obligations in defiance of the precepts of morality. We all know how strong these obligations can be, especially when they involve keeping promises; witness the Salome story. But such obligations, however powerful, cease to be moral obligations and become institutional obligations of another sort. That is, they no longer can provide moral reasons for doing what is demanded by the obligation. To say that I murdered because I promised is not even an extenuating circumstance!

At this point we face the whole issue of whether or not obligations are part of morality, e.g., whether obligations are moral or, say, only institutional.[13] If it is admitted that there can be immoral obligations, in the same sense of obligation in which one can have a moral obligation, then it would appear that obligation is a nonmoral concept. In that case, it would be of no interest in connection with the moral problem of political obedience. On the other hand, if we want to allow for moral obligations as at least a subspecies of obligation, we would have to adduce moral principles of some kind over and above the principle of honoring one's obligations to substantiate the claim that a particular obligation is a moral obligation. If we choose the latter course, then we will have to accept proposition 5 as a necessary feature of moral obligations.

6. Finally, within the moral limits just pointed out in 5, obligations have what I shall call the qualities of being *opaque* and *totalistic*. In calling them *opaque* I mean that obligations bind us to actions quite independently of the intrinsic nature or other interesting properties of those actions themselves. That is, if a person is under an obligation to do something, then, other things being equal, he should (or must) do it whether or not what is required is in itself a good, desirable, or worthwhile thing for him to do, i.e., apart from the obligation. In other words, an obligor may not inquire into the merits or demerits of the action in question when determining whether or not it should be done; having an obligation is of itself a sufficient reason for performing the action.

Opaqueness is obvious in the case of obligations arising from

[13] I do not intend to imply, however, that obligations cannot be both. The relationship between morality and institutions (conventions, customs) is, in my opinion, a subtle and complicated one. See my article "Custom," the *Encyclopedia of Philosophy*, ed. Paul Edwards (New York: The Free Press, 1967), Vol. 2, pp. 278-80.

promises: if I promise you that I will do something, then I am required to do what is promised and whether or not I want to do it is no longer relevant. Having promised, I can no longer have regard to whether doing what I have promised is unpleasant, tedious, difficult, onerous, disadvantageous for me, or even whether or not there are other things that I could do instead that would be better for you or for others.

In calling an obligation *totalistic* I mean that when one undertakes or is placed under an obligation to do something, one is *eo ipso* required to do the whole of it. In a sense, obligations come as wholes. If one has promised to do *A*, which comprises a set of parts, say, subactions *a,b,c,d,e,* one is bound to do all five of these subactions, i.e., the totality of the parts, and is not permitted to choose which ones he will do. If I am engaged as a gardener, I cannot choose to weed the flowers and neglect the vegetables and cleaning up. I cannot pick and choose which parts of an obligation to perform any more than I can pick and choose which parts of a promise to keep. The obligation has to be taken as applying to the whole.

Both the opaqueness and the totalism of obligations follow from the fact already frequently alluded to, that an obligation creates a new kind of reason for acting that is logically independent of the nature of the acts themselves. An obligation typically provides per se not only a sufficient reason for doing something but also a reason that automatically excludes other considerations not related to the obligation from determining whether the action, or any part of it, should be done. (One must, of course, specify "under normal conditions," in order to allow for those unusual cases in which an obligation is overridden or invalidated.) The opaqueness and totalism of obligations thus explain, in part at least, why obligations have such a high degree of stringency, one of the striking characteristics of obligations already mentioned.

II. APPLICATION TO THE PLAYING OF A GAME

The six characteristic features of obligation that I have just set forth are readily apparent in the kind of mutual obligation that exists between people engaged in playing a game, e.g., softball or chess, for when a group of individuals plays a game together, they mutually bind themselves to obey the rules of the game.

There are several reasons for choosing game-playing to illustrate the points that have been made about obligation. First, the obligations found in connection with game-playing differ in some interesting ways from obligations arising from promises and contracts. Thus I hope to achieve greater generality for the analysis presented here by using a somewhat different type of example from the ones already used.

Second, and more important, the game-playing model has already received considerable attention in political philosophy as an alternative to the older contractual model; for it has many advantages over the latter as a way of analyzing the traditional problems of political obligation. To begin with, the game model makes it possible to avoid having to postulate an *actus contractarius*, which has always been a source of embarrassment to contractarians. Furthermore, it enables us to conceive of the political and legal order as a body of rules, practices, and roles, rather than as a simple personal relationship between a sovereign and his subjects analyzed in terms of commands and obedience. Recent studies of the logic of rules and of the different types of rules provide a much more useful model of analysis than the traditional command model.[14]

Nevertheless, I shall try to show that the game model cannot, in the final analysis, give us a completely satisfactory account of political obligation. Before we can judge the merits or shortcomings of this particular model, we must first see how the six features described earlier appear in the obligation to obey the rules when playing a game. Let us examine each of these features in turn.

1′. Upon entering into a game certain actions that are per se indifferent or optional become for the player actions that are

[14] The literature on rules and games is by now quite extensive. For general discussions involving this type of analysis, see Max Black, *Models and Metaphors* (Ithaca: Cornell University Press, 1962), ch. 6; Newton Garver, "Rules," in *Encyclopedia of Philosophy*, vol. 7, pp. 231–33. The game analogy was used with great skill by Rawls in his well-known essay, "Two Concepts of Rules," *Philosophical Review*, vol. lxiv (1955) and by John Searle in his "How to Derive 'Ought' from 'Is,'" *Philosophical Review*, vol. lxxiii, no. 2 (January 1964) and "What Is a Speech Act?" in *Philosophy in America*, ed. Max Black (Ithaca: Cornell University Press, 1965). The approach has also been adapted for political philosophy by Hannah Pitkin in her "Obligation and Consent," *American Political Science Review*, vol. 59, no. 4 (December 1965) and vol. 60, no. 1 (March 1966).

right or wrong, required or forbidden. For instance, although previously Jones was free to throw the ball to anyone or to arrange the men on the board in any way he chose, once he started to play the game these actions became circumscribed for him: certain actions must be done and others must not be done. The rules of the game now determine what acts are right or wrong for him to do, and the obligation to adhere to the rules now makes what the rules prescribe mandatory for him.

2′. The basis of a person's subjection to the rules is the simple fact of joining the game and continuing to play it. A kind of consent is implied by the mere fact of participation.[15] This fact of participation is what differentiates the agent-obligor from others who are not bound to obey the rules because they are not playing. In this case, as in the earlier ones, we see how the basis determines who does and who does not have the obligation.

3′. Who has the obligation and to whom is it owed? Obviously, both obligor and obligee must be participants in the game. No one outside the game is bound by the rules and no one outside the game has the right to demand that another obey the rules.[16]

It is interesting to observe the role of players as obligees, for it is in this capacity, rather than as obligors, that players are able to abrogate or change the rules or institute new ones. Thus, when playing softball in the backyard, certain special rules have to be agreed upon (e.g., because of the greenhouse next door, every hit in that direction must be counted an out). Since every player is an obligee as well as an obligor, the assent of all the players is considered both a necessary and a sufficient condition for changing the rules, i.e., the content of the obligation (unless the game itself contains some special rule for changing rules).

4′. The obligation to play according to the rules also justifies the application of sanctions in the case of noncompliance with them, i.e., cheating. For game-playing, the usual sanctions are social sanctions, e.g., a reprimand ("That's unfair" or "That's

[15] Rawls writes: "the obligation to obey the law . . . (is) an obligation in the more limited sense that it depends upon our having accepted and our intention to continue accepting the benefits of a just scheme of cooperation. . . ." "Legal Obligation and the Duty of Fair Play," in Hook, *Law and Philosophy*, p. 10.

[16] It is obvious that the basis, i.e., participation, determines who is the obligee as well as who is the obligor. The obligation describes a relation only between players.

cheating") or, in the extreme case, being thrown out of the game altogether.

The punishment involved here is directly related to failure to comply with the rules, i.e., it is for violation of the obligation to heed the rules. As such, it should not be confused with the various penalties provided within the framework of the rules of the game themselves for particular acts, such as for being offside in football or not jumping in checkers. Logically speaking, rules setting forth such penalties can be construed as presenting options, e.g., if you don't do *X*, then *Y* will happen, and, as such, they are a regular part of the game comparable to, for instance, a sacrifice hit.[17]

Penalties, in contrast to sanctions, are part of the game itself; and, in a sense, a person is not indeed hurt by the penalties except in the context of playing the game. Thus, penalties obtain within the system, whereas sanctions obtain with regard to the system (and in this sense are outside the system).

5′. The moral limitations on the obligation to submit to the rules of the game one is playing are obvious. If some act is required by the obligation that is patently immoral, e.g., killing or maiming someone, the obligation is simply dissolved. There is, for instance, no longer any obligation to continue if a player is injured or if someone else's rights are violated. It should be noted that in such cases the obligation is nullified, i.e., extinguished, and not merely overridden.

It is interesting to note that often within games and as long as one is playing them there is a sense in which certain general moral principles are suspended. For example, the Christian precept to turn the other cheek is an inappropriate one to follow if you happen to be boxing, or the precept to help the poor is not a necessary guide for action if you are playing Monopoly. Indeed, lying, cheating, and physical assault are often accepted parts of a game. And generosity, kindness, solicitude, and even courage are often not virtues in games, whereas rational egoism, on the other hand, which is normally frowned upon by moralists, is taken for granted by most interesting competitive games.

[17] It is interesting to observe that lawyers often talk as if the penalties set forth in the law are to be construed as options: you have a choice between doing *X* or paying a penalty Y, e.g., "Walk or pay $2.00" or "File your tax return on time or pay 6 percent interest." The game model has its abuses as well as its proper uses!

The obvious point is that although there are many otherwise morally objectionable actions that are permissible within a game, this permissibility, like the prescriptions and prohibitions of the game, holds only within the bounds of the game. It is a severely limited permissibility, for we usually explain the actions in question as "being done in play" or as "not being serious." The main point of this section still holds, therefore, namely, that the obligation to obey the rules of the game is limited by what is antecedently right or wrong.

6′. The opaqueness and totalism of the obligation to obey the rules while playing a game are obvious. The obligation is opaque because the intrinsic properties of the acts required or proscribed, e.g., even whether they are acts of kindness or of courage, are completely irrelevant to the question of whether or not they should be done *while playing the game.* Indeed, as has often been observed, many acts are quite meaningless apart from the rules of the game, e.g., moving a piece of wood a couple of inches.[18] Acts that are per se insignificant or even meaningless become right or wrong as the result of the obligation to obey the rules.

The obligation is also totalistic, that is, it applies to all the rules; for a player is bound to obey all the rules all the time he is playing. He cannot pick and choose which rules he wants to obey or even which rules he thinks ought to be obeyed. As soon as an individual, for whatever reason, becomes selective about which rules he will obey, he has simply stopped playing the game.[19]

General Comments on the Game-Playing Model

It is hardly necessary to point out the advantage of the game model over the contractual model as a tool for analyzing political obligation. It provides us with a model of consent through participation rather than through contract. It also provides us with a much more satisfactory answer to the question: to whom is the political obligation owed? In determining that the obligees be the other players, i.e., the other participants in the political process, the game philosopher has found a way of

[18] Such rules are called "constitutive rules" by Searle. See footnote 22.

[19] "The notion of somebody breaking the rules constantly but yet playing chess does not make sense," Black, *Models and Metaphors,* p. 123.

relating political obligation to the individual's role as a citizen-subject rather than leaving it hanging as an external, accidental feature, say, of his birth.

Above all, the use of the game model suggests important analogies between rules in games and rules in politics and law. One of the most important of these, at least for democratic theory, is the property of *reversibility,* namely, that every rule applies to a person regardless of whether he is at the giving or receiving end. For when playing a game, a player is committed to abiding by a rule if and when the players' roles are reversed, e.g., the same rule holds when he plays defense as when he plays offense. When it is the other player's turn, then I must grant him the same advantage (benefits, rights) as I have when it is my turn, and when it is my turn, I must do what he has to do when it is his turn.[20]

The reversibility of the rules of a game, or at least of typical competitive games, provides a seductive model for the moral-political concepts of fairness and justice, equality and impartiality. Justice is thought to require that laws be made and applied impartially and equally to everyone alike. This means that they must be accepted and obeyed by each one of us without regard to whether he is, or will be, at the giving or receiving end. To agree

[20] The term "reversibility" is used by K. Baier in *The Moral Point of View* (New York: Random House, 1965), pp. 108, 135. Baier believes that reversibility is essential to rules regarded from the moral point of view. Substantially the same property of rules is stressed by Rawls when he proposes a "procedure . . . to let each person propose the principles upon which he wishes his complaints to be tried with the understanding that, if acknowledged, the complaints of others will be similarly tried . . . (and) no one (will) be given the opportunity to tailor the canons of a legitimate complaint to fit his own conditions and then to discard them when they no longer fit his purpose," in "Justice as Fairness," reprinted in *Philosophy, Politics and Society,* second series, eds. P. Laslett and W. G. Runciman (Oxford: Blackwell, 1962), p. 138. In another article, Rawls secures this reversibility by stipulating that "the initial situation (in which people decide about their conception of justice) one of the significant features of which is that no one knows his position in society, etc. . . . A veil of ignorance prevents anyone from being advantaged or disadvantaged. . ." from "Distributive Justice," in *Philosophy, Politics and Society,* third series, eds. P. Laslett and W. G. Runciman (Oxford: Blackwell, 1967), p. 60. These features, regarded by Baier as descriptive of the moral point of view and by Rawls as part of the procedure for establishing the rules of justice, are, I submit, taken in the first instance from the model of playing games. In their application to morality and politics, they are open to the same criticisms as the game-playing model in general.

to rules of this sort means to be ready and willing to abide by them even if the roles are reversed or, to put it in another way, on the supposition that one does not know whether he, personally, will be at the giving or receiving end.

In the case of games it seems eminently reasonable for an individual to assent to reversible rules of this kind, because it is quite possible that sometime in the course of the game he (or his partners) will be in a position to play the role of the giver as well as that of the receiver: he will have his turn, his innings, and so on. Therefore it is to his long-term advantage, as a player, to accept certain rules even though he knows that they will sometimes work to his disadvantage. As far as games are concerned, we can agree with Rawls that "the system of cooperation consistently followed by everyone else itself produces the advantages generally received."[21]

It should be quite clear that the game analogy provides a nice, plausible rationale for many of the practices and ideals of a democracy like ours. For example, it applies to the relations between the majority and the minority: the majority respects the rights of the minority because the individuals who are in the majority today may be in the minority tomorrow; and the minority accepts and obeys the decrees of the majority because some day those who are in the minority will be in the majority and will want the others to obey them in turn. The possibility, indeed probability, of the roles being reversed sometimes makes it easy to accept reversible rules. Similarly, in judicial proceedings, the adversary system is based on a system of reversible rules that assure to each party that it will have its turn in court, so that he who is the accuser today will play under the same rules when he is the defendant tomorrow. Accordingly, in many of our institutions, we regard it as fair to accept and obey rules granting rights to others because we may sometime be in their position and want them to respect our rights in turn. The question, of course, is whether this is a dream or a reality.

The fact that reversible rules like those found in competitive games are also to be found in political and legal institutions, or if not found there, ought to be there as a requirement of justice (or fairness), still does not prove that the game model provides a

[21] Rawls, "Legal Obligation and the Duty of Fair Play," *op. cit.*, p. 16.

satisfactory answer to the question: why should we obey the law? For, as we shall see, joint acknowledgment of reversible rules is neither a necessary nor a sufficient condition justifying obedience to the political and legal order as a whole.

In addition to reversibility, there are, of course, other properties of rules in a game that are useful in the analysis of political and legal concepts. For example, we find in games what have been called "constitutive rules," that is, rules that define moves, roles, penalties, goals, and even the game itself. Such rules function not so much to tell us what or what not to do as what is to "count as," for instance, a move, a strike, a checkmate.[22] Obviously many laws, or parts of laws, are constitutive in this sense. Perhaps, indeed, the whole political setup or the judicial system can only be defined by reference to the rules under which they operate. Furthermore, the game model may be useful in explaining the function of roles like that of umpire and leader, which find their counterparts in the political and legal order. Finally, of course, the concept of strategies, taken from formal game theory, has many applications within the sphere of politics and law. Thus, even if we reject the game model as a model for understanding political obligation, we may find it useful for other, more limited purposes.

III. APPLICATION TO THE POLITICAL AND LEGAL ORDER

Let us now turn to the question of whether or not there is such a thing as political obligation, that is, a special moral obligation to obey the political authorities and the law, say, under a democratic form of government and constitution. (It would, of course, have to be a prima facie obligation.) I have proposed as one way of answering the question that we examine the individual's relation to the political and legal order and see

[22] See Rawls' definition of "practice" as "any form of activity specified by a system of rules which defines offices, roles, moves, penalties, defences, and so on, and which gives the activity its structure," from "Justice as Fairness," *op. cit.*, p. 132n. The expression "constitutive rule" is used by Searle in the two articles mentioned above in note 14. Searle distinguishes between "regulative rules," which he says can be paraphrased as imperatives, and "constitutive rules," which define moves, and so on, and determine what is to "count as," e.g., a touchdown or checkmate.

whether any or all of the six features that seem to characterize obligations in the ordinary sense are found to be present in that relation. In order to maintain plausibly that the individual does have a political obligation of the sort mentioned, it is not necessary that all six of these features be present. However, if none of these features seems to characterize an individual's political and legal relationships we should hardly be justified in asserting that an obligation exists. It would have to be a very curious kind of obligation indeed, and the burden would be on the proponent of such an obligation to explain what he has in mind in asserting there is such an obligation and to give us some reason for supposing that it exists.

Our next task, then, is to examine each of our six features with a view to finding out whether or not they are to be found in the individual's relation to the political and legal order.

1″. There is no doubt that the political and legal authorities can, through various decrees and legislative acts, make acts that are per se morally neutral or optional into acts that are right or wrong. As in the case of games, therefore, the political and legal order can, through its own rules, create new moral demands and restrictions on our behavior. The acts that are thus made wrong are known as *mala prohibita.*

Mala prohibita and, in general, rights and wrongs created by law constitute only a part of the political and legal order; for a large part of that order is concerned with actions that are already, antecedently, part of morality, e.g., *mala in se.* Without entering into the question of the difference between law and morality, it seems obvious that a considerable part of the law is concerned directly or indirectly with enforcing the standards of morality, taken in the broad sense to include the demands of public interest and justice. Therefore, unlike typical obligations, the requirements proceeding from the political and the legal order follow from the antecedent requirements of morality.[23]

The question therefore naturally arises: does the alleged political obligation apply only to *mala prohibita,* or to *mala in se* as well? The assumption of the state of nature vs. civil society dichotomy made by many traditional contract theories gives aid

[23] I have explained this at greater length in my "Law and Morality: Internalism *vs.* Externalism," in *Law and Philosophy,* ed. S. Hook (New York: New York University Press, 1964).

and comfort to the view that civil (or positive) law creates a new obligation supplemental to the requirements of the natural law. But this position presupposes that a clear-cut and meaningful distinction can be made between *mala prohibita* and *mala in se.* More generally, if, as I have argued, obligations do not apply to actions that are antecedently right or wrong, then, in order to save the notion of political obligation, we would have to assume that positive law and its requirements are in themselves morally neutral (or optional). This seems, on the face of it, a gratuitous assumption and one that it is as difficult to defend as the distinction between *mala prohibita* and *mala in se.*

In any case, the first feature on our list raises some questions about the proper applicability of the concept of obligation with respect to the law.

2″. The question of the basis of political obligation has always been a source of embarrassment to political theorists who believe in political obligation. The older contract theory has given way to the idea of consent through participation. Accordingly, Rawls writes that political obligation "depends upon our having accepted and our intention to continue accepting the benefits of a just scheme of cooperation that the constitution defines. In this sense it depends on our voluntary acts."[24] To someone who is not especially enamored of the contractarian approach, it does not seem that benefits received constitute either a necessary or a sufficient condition for the duty to obey the law.

Apart from the difficult question of determining what kind of facts could serve as the basis of the alleged obligation to obey the law, it will suffice here to point out that the assertion of any sort of basis whatsoever of the alleged obligation is a logical impossibility. It is logically impossible to have such a basis, simply because the logical function of any basis is to tie down an obligation to one particular individual or set of individuals rather than another, whereas the purported intent of the notion of political obligation is to impose a requirement on everyone in the state. Obligations are individual, whereas political obligation, if there were such a thing, would have to be universal.

Another way of putting the same point is to say that the moral requirement that we obey the political order and the state is

[24] Rawls, "Legal Obligation and the Duty of Fair Play," *op. cit.*, p. 10.

contingent not upon benefits received, acts of consent, or other hypothetical facts, but on the nature and intent of the laws and the acts and procedures of the political order itself. Unless benefits and consent are construed so loosely and generally as to make the fact of their occurrence not really an empirical issue at all, it is clear that these "facts" apply only to a restricted segment of the population. Accordingly, it would follow that only a restricted segment of the population has the moral obligation to obey the political authorities and the law. Only the élite is under such an obligation![25]

The obligation theorist is thus presented with a dilemma. If he claims that there is such a thing as political obligation, then he must admit that there is some basis in fact that creates the obligation which is thereby binding only on some, but not all, members of the society. If, on the other hand, he wants to preserve the notion that there is a universal moral requirement binding on everyone in the society to obey the law, then he has to abandon the notion of a general moral obligation to obey the law and the state.

Since the two purposes of the obligation theorist are logically incompatible, the only way for him to save his theory is to move into the realm of mythology, the land of impossible facts, where so much of political philosophy has traditionally found its home.[26]

3″. The traditional answer to the question, to whom is the political obligation owed, is that it is owed to the other members of the society, just as our obligation to play a game according to the rules is an obligation owed to the other players. The consequence is that political obligation, being a kind of moral obligation, is a personal obligation owed to other persons linked together through the factual basis of the obligation.

[25] Some consent theorists do, of course, allow some "shrinkage," i.e., limitation on the class of individuals who are bound by the obligation to obey. See, for example, Joseph Tussman, *Obligation and the Body Politic* (New York: Oxford University Press, 1960), p. 37, "non-consenting adult citizens are, in effect, like minors who are governed without their own consent."

[26] For an illuminating discussion of the function of pictures invented by political philosophers, see Margaret MacDonald, "The Language of Political Theory," in *Logic and Language*, first series, ed. A. Flew (Oxford: Blackwell, 1952).

If the obligation is a kind of mutual obligation where obligors are at the same time obligees, as in games, then it follows that we owe the obligation of political obedience only to that restricted segment of the population who are plausibly considered obligors. We have a kind of in-group élite of individuals who are bound by mutual political obligation; the citizenry, like players in a game, are the only ones bound to observe the rules. Outsiders, i.e., those who have not placed themselves through some act under an obligation, are not bound, nor is anyone bound to them.

It would be absurd to deny that within a society such mutually obligated groups do exist and, indeed, have some validity. It would be perfectly correct to describe moral relations between members of particular political groups in terms of moral obligation. But the positive moral aspects of political obedience and obedience to the laws is not at all adequately described in such terms, at least under a constitutional or democratic regime, for we want also to be able to say that we ought to obey the law for general moral reasons and not for personal reasons, even if the personal reasons are also moral ones. This is what we intend when we say metaphorically that our moral obligation is to the laws or to the constitution, rather than to individuals. (That is not to say, of course, that, e.g., under a totalitarian regime, political obedience cannot be construed as a personal obligation owed to an individual, e.g., the *Führer*.)[27]

4″. It would appear that when we turn to the role of sanctions in the concept of obligation we have at last discovered something that is essential to both obligation and to the political and legal order; for the power of sanctions has always been regarded as one of the perquisites of this order. Nevertheless, when we look closer, we see that the obligation model's way of construing sanctions does not strictly apply to the way that sanctions operate (logically) within a modern political and legal order. The disanalogy is illuminating.

With regard to obligations, sanctions, as we have seen, come into play when a moral obligation is violated, and they may be justified by reference to the obligation alone. Pursuing the analogy in the case of an alleged political obligation, sanctions would

[27] See H. Arendt, *Eichmann in Jerusalem* (New York: Viking Press, 1963) for vivid illustrations of this point.

come into play and be justified solely on the basis of the failure to comply with that obligation, e.g., disobeying the law. In the game model, the analogous condition of a sanction would be cheating.

As was pointed out earlier, sanctions, which hold with regard to observing the rules of a game, must be distinguished from penalties, which are provided for within the rules of the game. Penalties are provided for specific breaches; whereas sanctions, as referred to here, apply to the violation of a rule as a rule. A cheater is, as it were, an outlaw rather than a criminal.

Sanctions, insofar as they are imposed by law and government, are more like penalties for specific breaches than they are like sanctions brought against players who cheat or, more generally, individuals who renege on their obligations. For legal sanctions, i.e., legal punishment and other coercive measures, are provided for and governed by the rules of the legal order itself. They are sanctions within the system rather than sanctions with regard to the system. Legal sanctions are always for specific crimes, specific breaches. There is, as far as I know, no sanction for the general disregard of the law, i.e., for reneging on one's "political obligation."

Once more the basic analogy upon which the notion of political obligation is founded breaks down. The underlying reason for the breakdown is that sanctions, and obligations, for that matter, are part of the legal order, i.e., exist within it, and do not bind the individual to that order from the outside. Thus we cannot have an obligation, say a political obligation, to perform our other obligations, e.g., our legal obligations, which arise out of and are defined by the political and legal order itself.

5″. The principle that moral obligations are limited to what is not incompatible with the moral law is, of course, part of the traditional contract theory; for according to the usual versions of that theory the political contract is limited by the natural law. Political obligations are supplemental to, but not contradictory of, the moral (or natural) law.

The consequences of taking this position on the relation of morality to the political and legal order have already been touched upon under 1″, and will be discussed further later in this chapter. In the meantime, two remarks on the question may be in order here. First, the idea that our moral relationships to the political and legal order are, in some way, supplemental or added to our other moral relationships, say, by means of an obligation, tends to trivialize the moral aspects of the relationship, making them extrinsic rather than intrinsic to the relationship and to the political and legal order itself.

Second, the requirement that obligations are rendered null and void if they conflict with the moral law hardly represents an accurate rendering of the type of moral dilemma that political and legal issues often present us with. If, as Locke would presumably hold, our political obligation is valid only as long as it requires nothing contrary to the natural law and does not exceed the bounds of the powers delegated by the contract, then no great moral issues can arise within the political framework. The moral issues of politics are, as it were, apolitical. Once again, then, it appears that the obligation model requires us to separate politics from morality in the wrong way and at the wrong place.

6″. The distorted picture of the relation of politics and morality forced on us by the obligation model becomes even clearer when we turn to the opaqueness and totalism of obligations.

The opaqueness of an obligation requires us to do the required actions without regard to the intrinsic merits or desirability of the actions themselves, excepting the conditions mentioned under 5. When applied to political obligation this means that we ought to do anything at all that is prescribed by the political authorities and the law, regardless of its content, providing only that it is not incompatible with the moral law. The mere fact that something is prescribed by them is not only a sufficient reason for doing it; it is the only relevant consideration. For obligations as such function logically so as to exclude other considerations. That is the main force of attributing an obligation to a person. Consequently, given such an obligation, it is quite irrelevant to ask whether the decree or law to be obeyed is good or poor, well- or ill-considered, trivial or momentous, foolish, capricious, or simply a nuisance. It is the law, we are bound to obey the law, and so no further questions are in order—excepting, of course, those covered under 5. As far as our obligation is concerned, all laws and decrees of the proper authorities are on the same level. We must be blind to their content.[28]

[28] Sometimes, of course, one must take account of the content and what is the "best thing to do," namely, when the obligation itself specifies what is to be done in those terms. If, e.g., the orders are to solve a problem as

The totalism of the alleged political obligation leads to the same result, for it requires us to do everything that is prescribed by the authorities. We cannot pick and choose which laws to obey and which ones to disregard. Our obligation binds us to the totality of them. Our obligation to obey all the laws is as binding as our obligation to obey any particular law; for, indeed, it is the same obligation.

These are the logical consequences following from the obligation model. Needless to say none of us, even the authorities themselves, would ever contemplate fulfilling them completely and to the letter. There are many well-known cases in which law and order have broken down simply because all the laws on the books were being scrupulously executed. That is why the injunction to obey the law as a whole and "blindly" is more a piece of propaganda than it is a serious moral demand.

The analogy with games, which is so popular these days, makes the consequences just noted quite clear. The game model provides a good illustration of the implicit logic of obligation that is assumed here: through the very act of participating in a game we accept the system of rules of that game *in toto,* and without regard to their content, and are thereby placed under an obligation to obey every particular rule without questioning it.

On closer inspection, it should become obvious that the game model describes the individual's relation to the rules in a way that is exactly opposite to the way in which they are related in the political and legal order. Within a game it makes no sense to challenge a particular rule; for example, I cannot ask "Why should I obey the rule that I have to stop batting when I have three strikes?" The answer is simply "Because that is one of the rules of the game. You have to accept that rule if you want to play." On the other hand, it makes perfectly good sense to challenge the enterprise as a whole: "Why should I play that game?"

When we examine the political and legal order we find that exactly the opposite holds, namely, that it makes sense to challenge a particular rule (decree or law) but not the order as a

---

expeditiously as possible, then one would have to consider the qualities of the alternative acts open to one. But such qualities would be relevant only because they are elements involved in executing the obligation. I am indebted to Oskar Wood for pointing out this difficulty to me.

whole. The difference between games and law is not simply a moral difference but a logical one; for the logical presuppositions that make one set of questions, e.g., with regard to games, meaningful are absent in the case of the political order and law. We cannot challenge the political order and law as a whole simply because we would not know what we are challenging.

Underlying the notion of political obligation is the notion, exemplified in games, that the political and legal order comprises a *system* of rules (laws, norms, and so on). The notion of obligation would make no sense if law could not be conceived as a system. Indeed, it would have to be a system which could provide us with a determinate decision-procedure by means of which it could be determined what falls under the law and what does not. Presumably this condition is what Hart and Kelsen intend by their doctrine of the Rule of Recognition and the Basic Norm, respectively. It hardly needs to be observed that one of the principal objectives of the legal positivists is to reduce law to a system of some kind or other, in order, of course, to be able to define it independently of morality.

The whole notion of a legal system is, however, an obscure one. It is impossible, I submit, to supply the necessary and sufficient conditions for determining whether or not a rule belongs to the system.[29] The legal system and the political system, insofar as they are properly regarded as systems at all, are not closed systems like the systems we find in highly structured games. (The notion of a "dynamic system" presented by Kelsen merely substitutes another way of closing the system, for in principle it provides a decision-procedure for determining what is law.)

Indeed, for reasons that need not be detailed here, the concepts of law and the state are open-textured and multifunctional concepts. At the very least they are "family-resemblance" concepts, in Wittgenstein's terms. They might, indeed, even be what W. B. Gallie calls "essentially contested concepts."[30] For it will suffice to point out that only if they are so regarded will we be able to explain why law and politics provide an arena of controversy and debate quite unlike anything that takes place in

[29] This, I take it, is the underlying issue in the famous Hart-Fuller debate, "Separation of Law and Morals," *Harvard Law Review*, lxxi (1958).

[30] See W. B. Gallie, "Essentially Contested Concepts," *Philosophy and the Historical Understanding* (New York: Schocken Books, 1968), ch. 8.

connection with the rules of a game. (I do not want to deny that some parts of law are systematized or systematizable. Here, however, I am speaking of law and the political order as a whole.)

My point can be put in another way by once more examining the concept of obligation. Obligation, it will be recalled, makes sense as a moral category only if we can contrast an individual's being under an obligation to do something with his not being under that obligation, or with others' not being under the obligation. The logical function of the basis is precisely to explain why one individual does and other individuals do not have an obligation to do a certain thing. It follows that we can make sense out of the notion of a person's having an obligation to do something only if we can make sense out of the notion of his not having the obligation, i.e., its not being wrong for him to do the thing in question if he so desires.

When we come to the alleged obligation to obey the political and legal order as a whole, the condition just mentioned does not seem to obtain; for it is not possible to conceive what it would be like not to accept or not to obey the order as a whole, i.e., in its entirety. The philosophers who invented the concept of a state of nature intended to conceptualize that possibility, but Plato is more likely to be right in holding that any society whatsoever involves a kind of political and legal order, however minimal. Especially today, however, it is impossible to say what it would be like to refrain from accepting the political and legal order as such. (Of course, we can refuse to accept and obey parts of it. But that is a different question and, needless to say, a perfectly legitimate one if we reject the obligation theory.)

The logical point here is that the obligation model and the game model require us to conceive of ourselves as placed outside the political and legal order altogether, as if we were watching a game and deliberating whether or not to join. But, as I have argued, we simply cannot place ourselves outside or even conceive of ourselves as outside these orders.[31]

But perhaps even more important than the logical objections to the notion of political obligation are the moral objections to it. A final word on this aspect may be in order.

[31] I have argued this point in more detail in my "Law and Morality: Internalism *vs.* Externalism," *op. cit.* Theories that I have called "externalist" are those that involve placing or conceiving oneself outside the legal system.

It should not be thought that because I have rejected the notion of political obligation that I deny that we ought to obey the political authorities and the law. For there are many other kinds of moral requirements and moral relations besides those created by obligations.

Whitehead used to ascribe many of the difficulties of modern philosophy to what he called the "fallacy of misplaced concreteness." With apologies to Whitehead, I should like to coin a phrase, the "fallacy of misplaced morality," to stand for a similar source of many of our difficulties in political and legal philosophy. The notion of political obligation provides an exemplary illustration of this fallacy, for what it does is to place the moral emphasis in the wrong place and by implication take it away from the right place.

By placing the moral emphasis on the political and legal order as a whole, e.g., on the constitution, it deflects our attention from the moral aspects of particular decrees, rules, statutes, codes and procedures. It says that, e.g., as long as we have a "just" constitution, then, other things being equal, we must obey all its decrees and laws regardless of their content. By the same token, if the constitution is "unjust," we have no obligation at all to obey the government and the law. In the latter case, we should have regard only to the content and consequences, etc.

This seems an odd way to have to "cut" our moral relations to the law and the state, for it forces us to buy many things wholesale without examining them, as well as to reject other things without examining them. Lest it be thought that the difference between the two approaches, which I have elsewhere labeled externalism (e.g., obligation theory) and internalism, let me point out some practical differences between them.

If we assume that the basis of political obedience is an obligation, then the onus is on an individual who is inclined to disobey a particular legal or judicial prescription to defend his doing so. And he can do so only by showing either that what is required is immoral in itself and therefore the prima facie obligation should be overridden or else that the constitution is unjust.[32] The Establishment, on the other hand, does not *ab initio* have to justify its claim that we ought to obey any particular decree

[32] Or else, of course, that the requirement is not part of the legal system.

issued by it; for the notion of political obligation has, as it were, given it a blank check for our obedience. In sum, if any of its laws are challenged, the burden of proof devolves upon the challenger to show why it should not be obeyed. The net effect of the logic of the situation is that the rulers of a constitutional democracy are invested with a certain kind of immunity to being challenged. This immunity, it is obvious, tends to relieve them of the moral responsibility of making their decrees worthy of being obeyed by the people.[33]

Part of the mythology that justifies this misplacement of morality is the picture of democracy as a kind of game, with reversible rules, umpires, moves, and penalties.[34] Therefore, its procedures are "fair," for "someday we will have our turn. We will be in the majority and they will be in the minority, and they will have to obey us. So let us play according to the rules now." That is a very fine argument for those who have some genuine prospect of being in the majority in the not too distant future. But it is not an argument that has any appeal for individuals who are members of a permanent minority, which in our society comprises not only Negroes but also intellectuals. The liberal mythology should not blind us to the facts about how things work and, as I have argued, the notion of political obligation is based on this mythology.

My conclusion, then, is that the theory of political obligation permits and, indeed, requires the separation of law and morality at precisely the level where they should come together, namely, at the level of the concrete actions and choices of individual people. It is about time, I submit, that we should try to bring law and morality together again.

[33] It is interesting to note that today the contract theory is employed for precisely the opposite purpose from that for which it was originally framed. Under Locke and his followers it was a revolutionary doctrine. Today it represents the position of the Establishment, for the reasons just mentioned.

[34] This model of democratic decision-making is brilliantly portrayed in J. M. Buchanan and G. Tullock, *The Calculus of Consent* (Ann Arbor: University of Michigan Press, 1967).

VI
Sanction Theories of Duty[1]

P. M. S. HACKER

I. INTRODUCTION

THE concept of a sanction plays a dominant role in many philosophical analyses of duty. Any theory which specifies an analytic connection of some sort between failure to perform an obligatory[2] act and a consequent sanction may be called a sanction theory of duty. The specific nature of the nexus is of course a matter of controversy. Three different views may be distinguished. According to one theory the connection is predictive and probabilistic. According to another, the connection is imperatival, i.e. the sanction is commanded in the event of non-performance of the act in question. According to the third view the failure to perform the relevant act is a reason or ground for the sanction.

An alternative kind of analysis of duty approaches the problem from an investigation of the requirement to perform the act which is said to be a duty. Here too at least three distinct kinds of analysis have been suggested to explain the nature of the requirement to act analytically involved in the concept of duty. According to one theory a duty is an act commanded under certain circumstances. Such an account may be termed imperatival. According to an alternative theory a duty is an act the performance of which is required by a rule of a certain kind. This account may be termed normative. A third approach suggests that the requirement to perform the duty act must be explained by reference to certain kinds of justifying reasons (other than a prospective sanction) which support the doing of

[1] I should like to acknowledge my indebtedness and gratitude to Professor H. L. A. Hart and Dr. Joseph Raz.

[2] Like Bentham I shall treat duty and obligation as synonymous. In fact obligations are best construed as a subclass of duties, namely those duties that are contractual or quasi-contractual with correlative rights *in personam*. This distinction is of no importance for present concerns.

the act in question. This kind of analysis may be termed justificative.

The two different angles of approach are often combined to form modified sanction theories. Thus an imperative approach to the problem of the nature of the requirement to perform a duty has been combined with either a predictive sanction theory or with an imperatival sanction theory. Similarly a normative analysis of the requirement to do the duty has been combined with the third kind of sanction analysis to yield the claim that a duty is an act the performance of which is required by a rule or norm of a certain kind, and the non-performance of which is a reason or ground for sanctions of certain sorts. A justificative analysis may similarly be modified by combination with the third kind of sanction theory. Other less plausible combinations are, of course, possible too.

Since the concept of duty fulfils an important role in discourse concerning a wide variety of kinds of standards of conduct, for example in law, morality, religion, social practices, etc., the various approaches to the problem of analysis must involve sufficient flexibility in their definitions of the general concept of duty to account for the different types of duty. This is typically done by specifying variations in the sources, nature, and character of sanctions analytically involved in the concept of duty, or alternatively by specifying *differentia* in the sources, logical form, or content of the requirement to perform the obligatory act, or both.

Cutting across these different classifications is a further notorious source of contention. The various theories of duty may be distinguished into social-fact or positivist theories on the one hand or non-positivist, more rationalist-inclined theories on the other. Social-fact theories conceive statements about duties to be statements about complex structures of social facts concerning patterns of behaviour, reactive and affective responses to behaviour, critical attitudes, and beliefs. The more rationalist-inclined theories will tend to lay stress not on actual behaviour, critical attitudes, and beliefs, but upon rational justifications for action, or for rules requiring the performance of certain actions, or for sanctions or censure. What people take as a reason must be understood not in terms of social facts *simpliciter*, but in terms of their beliefs, correct or incorrect, as to what is a reason or justification. The notion of reasons or justifications, the antipositivist will argue, cannot be analysed in terms of social facts, but only in terms of a rational system of values and principles.

This typology is by no means the only possible one for classifying philosophical analyses of duty. Nor is it suggested that all important theories of duty can be readily accommodated in it. All that is claimed is that this is one useful way of looking at many attempts to render an explication of the problematic concept of duty.

It should be noted that the notion of a reason for action, and the logically related notions of justifications and grounds for action, and of what ought to be done, occupy a central role in many philosophical analyses of the concept of duty. In the ensuing discussion the notion of a reason for action will be used extensively. No attempt will be made to provide a proper analysis of this philosophically problematic concept, but its use will, I trust, accord with our ordinary linguistic intuitions regarding the correct employment of the term. Nevertheless, a few clarificatory remarks are necessary.

Whenever an action ought prima facie to be done, then there is a reason for doing it. Conversely, whenever there is a reason for doing something, then it ought prima facie to be done. The notion of a reason for action is involved both in the explanation and in the justification of human action. When there is a reason for action then there is a justification of some kind for acting. Various kinds of factors are referred to as reasons, despite important differences in their roles in practical reasoning and justification. Sometimes we simply cite a fact as a reason. Thus the third type of sanction theory stresses that failure to do an obligatory act is a reason for a sanction-applying act. Here a past act of omission is held to be a reason. I shall refer to reasons of this kind, that is backward looking reasons, as 'grounds' for action. Equally we often refer to future facts, for example prospective sanctions, as providing reasons for action. Such citation of grounds or forward-looking reasons do not reveal in virtue of what further considerations such facts are reasons for action. But in many contexts we explain why certain facts are reasons by reference to justifying principles and values which members of a social group accept, or which are conceived of as having a rational foundation (or both). I shall refer to reasons of this kind as 'justifications', although in ordinary discourse the term 'justification' includes both what I call 'grounds' and also forward-looking reasons. I am not suggesting that there is any ambiguity in 'reason for action'; merely that the logical structure of practical reasoning is complex, and that in normal discourse different constituent elements are, depending upon the context, selected as appropriate to cite as reasons. It is instructive to bear in mind that similar considerations apply to identifying a factor as a cause. According to various principles of selection we pick one factor out of an array of jointly sufficient and individually necessary conditions for the occurrence of an event and refer to it as 'the cause'. In a different context and with different interests we could, with equal propriety, select a different factor. So too, analogously, with reasons.

The explanatory role of reasons for action is evident whenever we speak of a person acting for a certain reason. Here a person's conduct is explained by reference to his having a reason, in one sense of the phrase, for acting as he did, and acting on it. It seems plausible to think that the notion of there being a reason links the explanatory and justificatory aspects of reasons for action. For a person subjectively has a reason for acting,[3] one might claim, in so far as he believes, rightly or wrongly, that there is a reason for him to act thus. And a person's actions are explained in terms of reasons for action in so far as we explain that he did what he did because of his belief that there was a reason for him to do it. These crude distinctions between grounds, forward-looking reasons, and justifications, and between acting for a reason, having a reason, and there being a reason, are important in understanding the different theories of duty to be examined. The distinctions are relatively crude, and stand in need of much refinement and explication. But for the purposes at hand they will, I trust, suffice.

In this paper I shall undertake a historical and critical examination of two famous, predominantly sanction theories

[3] We also employ the phrase 'has a reason' or 'had a reason' objectively, i.e. such that it does not imply any cognitive attitude on behalf of the person who is said to have the reason. A person objectively has a reason for acting in so far as there is a reason which applies to him, i.e. a reason for him, to act thus or so.

of duty. I shall first examine Bentham's account, or rather accounts, of duty and obligation. Next I shall survey Mill's writings upon duty and its sanctions, paying particular attention to the relations between his theories and those of Bentham. Finally I shall briefly dwell upon Hart's contemporary modified sanction theory. The upshot of the analysis will be to direct attention to justificative analyses of the requirement to do the duty act, and to stress the different needs which the concept of duty meets in moral and legal discourse which suggests that however appropriate a positivist analysis of legal duty may be, an antipositivist analysis of moral duty is required.

II. BENTHAM ON DUTY

Bentham[4] had many reasons for lavishing special attention upon the philosophical analysis of the concept of duty or obligation. In the first place it is a salient concept in the descriptive language of legal theorists, designating a central feature of any legal system we can conceive. Secondly, being a substantive, it suggests the existence of some corresponding entity to which it refers. This suggestion is deceptive. A duty, Bentham claimed, is a fiction; it is, strictly speaking, a logical construction. That is, sentences in which the word 'duty' appears, while ostensibly about an objectively existing entity—a duty—are really about something else. Such sentences can be replaced by, or reduced to, logically equivalent sentences in which the word 'duty' does not appear. By applying a method of reductive analysis to the concept of duty, a general method of reductive elimination of fictions can be exemplified. Thirdly, the concept of duty was frequently used by Bentham as a striking test case for his idiosyncratic and novel theory of definition. In Bentham's opinion *summa genera* and certain logical and grammatical connectives cannot be defined by *genus* and *differentia*. An alternative method is definition by

[4] In the following discussion Bentham's works are referred to as follows:
L.G.—*Of Laws in General*. *P.M.L.*—*An Introduction to the Principles of Morals and Legislation*. The editions employed are those of the *Collected Works of Jeremy Bentham* (University of London, Athlone Press 1970). *F.G.*—*Fragment on Government* in the Blackwell edition edited by Wilfred Harrison (Blackwell, Oxford, 1960).
Works—*Jeremy Bentham's Works* edited by Bowring (Tait, Edinburgh, 1843). *C.C.*—*A Comment on the Commentaries* edited by C. W. Everett (Clarendon Press, Oxford, 1928).

paraphrasis. Here we take a sentence or a sentential formula containing the word to be defined and substitute a logically equivalent sentence or sentential formula in which it does not appear. Paraphrastic definition, in Bentham's view, is not merely a novel and useful method of definition, but fulfils an important role in ontology, for it is uniquely suited for defining logical fictions, and peculiarly useful in reductive analysis. Fourthly, the concept of duty provided an impressive example of the subsidiary definitional process of archetypation. According to Bentham many terms, especially philosophically problematic ones have images or pictures etymologically built into them. These, if properly interpreted, can provide a clue to the the correct analysis of the terms in question. His favourite example for demonstrating the process of archetypation was the concept of obligation. Finally, Bentham's way of 'fixing' i.e. explicating, the concept of duty deliberately rendered the explicatum a peculiarly useful conceptual tool for a utilitarian censorial jurisprudence by reference to which we may 'rear the fabric of felicity by the hands of reason and of law'.

In the course of his voluminous writings Bentham delineates more than one analysis of duty and obligation. These are often divergent and occasionally incompatible. The most notorious is his predictive, probabilistic, sanction analysis. It is this which is most closely integrated with his theory of definition. One may distinguish the pure form of the predictive theory from its impure form. In the latter version it is combined ingeniously with Bentham's imperatival analysis of duty, a version hardly less notorious than the predictive theory.

The pure predictive theory is succinctly stated in Bentham's 'Logic'.[5]

> An obligation (viz. the obligation of conducting himself in a certain manner) is incumbent upon a man (i.e. is spoken of as incumbent on a man) in so far as, in the event of his failing to conduct himself in that manner, pain, or loss of pleasure, is considered as about to be experienced by him.

The pain or loss of pleasure which results from the non-performance of the obligatory act is called a sanction. Bentham defines a sanction as a source of obligatory powers or motives,

[5] *Works*, Vol. VIII, p. 247; cf. 'Essay on Ontology', *Works*, Vol. VIII, p. 206.

that is pains or pleasures which operate, indeed are the only things which can operate, as motives for action.[6] A pleasure or pain consequent upon an act or omission which suffices to give 'binding force' to a law or any other rule of conduct qualifies as a sanction. Remunerative sanctions, that is rewards, do not suffice to generate obligations.[7] The above definition of obligation is a paraphrastic definition of the generic notion. The various species of duty or obligation so conceived are distinguished according to the agency constituting the source of the probable sanction. In the *Fragment on Government*[8] Bentham distinguishes three kinds of duty. Legal or political duty involves the application of a sanction by an assignable legal official. A religious duty is created by punishment expected from God, moral duty is created by the application of indeterminate sanctions from unassignable members of the public at large. Elsewhere[9] Bentham distinguishes a fourth kind of duty which he calls 'natural'. Here the agency is non-human nature, the sanctions being those pains likely to result from imprudent disregard of the likely causal consequences of naturally dangerous acts, for example walking along precipices, or on thin ice etc. Thus for any sentence in which the word 'duty' appears a logically equivalent sentence in which it does not appear may be substituted. Instead of '*A* has a moral duty to aid his brother' we may substitute 'In the event of *A* not aiding his brother he is likely to suffer indeterminate sanctions of opinion from unassignable members of the public'. The paraphrastic definition provides a method of translation and of reductive elimination of fictitious entities.

The generic concept of obligation has embedded within it two illuminating archetypes. We speak of being 'under an obligation' or of an obligation being 'incumbent upon us' and of duty being 'burdensome'. Here the emblematic image involved is that of a weight pressing upon us, necessitating us to act or refrain from acting in a certain way. Alternatively we speak of being 'duty-bound' or of the 'binding force' of obligations, of being obligated, and so bound to a course of conduct or person. The archetype here, clearly of etymological

[6] *P.M.L.*, p. 34.
[7] *L.G.*, pp. 289 f., although compare *L.G.*, p. 136 and note f.
[8] *F.G.*, p. 107 n. [9] *P.M.L.*, pp. 35 f.

origin, is of a cord or rope tying us to a person or binding us to a course of action. Bentham interprets both archetypes as indicating the motivational necessitation of the probable sanction which, analytically, renders an action obligatory. It should be stressed, however, that the definition of duty which Bentham suggests is not a psychological one. It specifies nothing about the motives for which men *actually* fulfil their obligations. He does, misguidedly I believe, think that the *effectiveness* of obligations is wholly dependent upon men *having* as their reason for fulfilling their obligation the fact that they will probably suffer pain if they fail to do the act in question,[10] i.e. consciousness of the probable sanction is the standard motive for compliance with duty and hence a condition of its efficacy. But it is not a necessary condition for an act being a duty. Bentham's contention is that an act constitutes a duty because there *is* a certain forward-looking reason for performing it, namely the likelihood of sanction, whether anyone *has* this reason or whether anyone acts *for* this reason, is irrelevant.

We shall see later that in fairness to Bentham important qualifications must be introduced into this account of his sanction theory of duty which will serve, if not to deflect some of the standard criticisms, at any rate to soften the blows. Nevertheless this is the standard interpretation of his pure predictive theory and it is certainly not groundless. The theory is a 'naturalistic' one. It detaches the concept of duty from the notion of normativity. It is a social-fact theory, predictive and probabilistic. To assert a point of conduct to be a duty is to predict the conditional likelihood of a future sanction. The pure theory, narrowly interpreted as above, had a deep impact upon subsequent legal and moral philosophy. In an interestingly transmuted form it is one of the more popular currently debated analyses of duty. Before turning to its evaluation and elaborating Bentham's qualifications of it, it is necessary to give a brief outline of his pure imperative theory of duty.

In the *Fragment on Government* Bentham declares:[11] 'An act which is the object of a command, actual or fictitious; such an act, considered before it is performed, is styled a duty or a

[10] See footnote to the above definition of duty in his 'Logic', *Works*, Vol. VIII, p. 247 n.

[11] *F.G.*, p. 29.

point of duty.' Here the requirement to do the duty is explained, quite independently of the concept of sanction, by reference to the fact that the duty act is the object of a command. This analysis is reiterated in *Of Laws in General*:[12] 'Every legal command imposes a duty' and 'A law commanding or forbidding an act thereby creates a duty or obligation.' A similar analysis is to be found in 'View of a Complete Code of Laws':[13] 'To be subject to a certain obligation is to be the individual or other of those whom the law directs to perform a certain act' and 'To direct men to abstain from all acts which may disturb the enjoyment of others is to impose an obligation on them . . .'[14] In the *Principles of Morals and Legislation*[15] Bentham remarks that a law which commands or prohibits acts imposes duties. The matter becomes clearer, however, when, on the following page, Bentham clarifies his conception of legal obligations in particular by combining the pure imperative theory of the *Fragment on Government* with an imperative sanction theory:[16] 'What is it that constitutes a legal obligation in any case? A command, express or virtual, together with punishment appointed for breach of it.'

In 'Pannomial Fragments'[17] on the other hand, the pure imperative analysis and the predictive sanction analysis are combined in a definition which Austin clearly borrowed:

> Obligation has place when the desire on the part of the superior, the obliger, being signified to the obligee, he understands at the same time that in the event of his failing to comply with such desire, evil will befall him, and that to an amount greater than that of any evil which he could sustain in compliance with that desire.

It should be noted that here consciousness of the likely sanction is specified as a necessary condition of an act being a duty.

How should one explain the coexistence of these distinct analyses and the varying combinations of imperative and predictive elements in Bentham's theory? The following conjecture may provide an analytic explanation, whether it is biographically correct or not. If one adopts an imperative theory of law rather than a normative one, as Bentham did, and

[12] *L.G.*, p. 58 and Appendix C, p. 293.
[13] *Works*, Vol. VIII, p. 181. [14] Ibid., p. 159.
[15] *P.M.L.*, p. 206 n. (continuation of note e.2 from p. 205).
[16] Ibid., p. 207 f.2. [17] *Works*, Vol. III, p. 217.

if one desires to propound a general theory of duty in which legal duty is viewed as a species of a wider genus, one is bound to find one's theory under strain. The imperatival features which appear to characterize law are wholly missing from morality (unless conceived as commands of the Deity) and while legal duties appear to be the product of the will of the legislator, moral duties cannot be so accounted for. However, a common feature does appear in respect of the consequences of not performing a duty. The legislator's volition trusts for its accomplishment 'to the expectation of certain events which it is intended such declaration should upon occasion be a means of bringing to pass',[18] and non-performance of moral duty can likewise be expected to result in certain unpleasant 'events' which have motivating force. Hence it is reasonable in one's general account of duty to seize upon this common feature of the probable outcome of non-performance of a duty act. But it is likely to prove irresistible to fill out this thin account of duty in general with a substantial addition of imperative theory when one deals with legal duty in particular. To be sure Bentham's analysis of legal duty is much more sophisticated than his general account would lead one to expect or indeed could warrant. Moreover not only is it often an impure predictive theory, having an imperatival admixture, it is often, as we have seen above, not even a predictive account at all. We shall return to this point below.

Before elaborating the defects of Bentham's sanction theory it is worth dwelling briefly upon its merits. The analysis has five central advantages. Firstly, it demystifies the notion of duty and stands opposed to any intuitionist or emotivist analysis. The existence of duties involves no mysterious transcendent realities, nor does the concept of duty allude to any psychological facts, cognitive or affective. The concept of duty is not logically tied to conscience or to a special moral sense, nor to feelings, attitudes, and emotions. The demystification is certainly desirable, although it is not obvious that this is the only way of achieving it. As we shall see below the severing of any conceptual nexus with conscience was subsequently to become a point of contention. The concept of duty is explained in terms of social (and other) *facts*. Secondly, Bentham provides

[18] *L.G.*, p. 1.

us with a perfectly *general* analysis of duty into which the various social types of duty, for example legal, moral, religious, etc., can, without undue strain, be systematically and uniformally explicated. It is a desideratum of an account of the concept of duty that the varieties of duty be generically related. However, it should also be borne in mind that there is no *a priori* reason for thinking that our concepts are so systematic. Analogical extension plays a central role in the evolution of language, and the price to be paid for a systematic generic explication may be excessive in terms of other criteria of adequacy for explications. Thirdly, Bentham identifies an important connection between duty and sanctions. Whether the sanctions he specifies are the right sort has been questioned. Is there an additional 'sanction of conscience' and is it not at the heart of our concept of duty? Is the nexus predictive and probabilistic at all? Indeed are Bentham and other philosophers who have rendered an analysis of duty and obligation in terms of a sanction right in thinking the nexus to be analytic at all? These questions will be examined below, but be the answers what they may it seems indisputable that there is a connection between duties and sanctions. Fourthly, Bentham's analysis of duty provides a basis for a fruitful analysis of other fundamental legal concepts such as powers, rights, liberties, liabilities, etc. This important feature is especially prominent when Bentham modifies his pure predictive theory by combining it with his imperative theory of law. The general theory of duty Bentham elaborates involves no reference to laws, either legal, moral, or religious, or to rules or norms. But his discussion of legal obligation frequently generates a concept of obligation which brings together elements of his imperative theory of law with a sanction theory of duty. Thus in the *Fragment* he writes:[19]

> That may be said to be my duty to do (understand political duty) which you (or some other person or persons) have a right to have me made to do. I then have a duty towards you, you have a right against me.
>
> What you have a right to have me made to do (understand a political right) is that which I am liable according to law, upon a requisition made on your behalf to be punished for not doing.

[19] *F.G.*, p. 106 n.

I say punished: for without the notion of punishment (that is of pain annexed to an act, and accruing on a certain account, and from a certain source) no notion can we have of either right or duty.

Here we have a sanction theory of duty put to revealing use in rendering an analysis of rights as a 'secondary fictitious entity'. It is interesting to note in passing that though Bentham's beneficiary theory of rights has acquired a certain notoriety, his 'choice' theory,[20] clearly specified here, has gone almost unnoticed. Bentham's sophisticated analyses of legal modalities stem from his grasp of the central position which the concept of duty occupies in this complex network of concepts. Related to this point is the fifth and final one worth emphasizing. This is Bentham's clear realization that legal fictions, as he called them, are merely reflections of the language we employ to describe the law and its operations, to classify aspects of legal situations and relations. He writes thus:[21] 'The affair of its being prescribed a duty and created an offence is only the language we use in speaking of what the law has done. They are different turns of expression of our own concerning what the law has done. . . .'

III. CRITICISMS OF BENTHAM'S THEORY

The most common criticism directed at Bentham's pure predictive sanction theory is to be found in Sidgwick;[22] in recent years it has been revived and extensively elaborated by H. L. A. Hart.[23] The likelihood of suffering a sanction is not a sufficient condition of an act being a duty. Moreover it is not even a necessary condition. Thirdly, as Sidgwick points out in a fashion similar to Moore's subsequent techniques, we can conjoin a statement of the likelihood of sanctions for non-performance with a statement that the act in question is obligatory, without any sense of redundancy or tautologousness.

[20] See H. L. A. Hart, 'Bentham on Legal Rights', below, p. 171.

[21] *C.C.*, pp. 97–8; cf. 'View of a Complete Code of Laws', *Works*, Vol. III, p. 159.

[22] H. Sidgwick, *Methods of Ethics*, Bk. I, ch. III (7th edition, 1907). On page 29 Sidgwick, while producing these forceful criticisms of Bentham's predictive theory of moral duty, mistakenly accepts the predictive theory of legal duty.

[23] H. L. A. Hart, *The Concept of Law* (1961), pp. 10–11, 81–8, and 'Il concetto di obbligo', (1966) 57 *Rivista di filosofia*, 125–40. It should be stressed that Hart's criticisms are directed at Bentham's pure predictive theory only (see 'Il concetto di obbligo', p. 133, note d).

Thus far Bentham's explication diverges profoundly from our ordinary concept. The error is to conceive of the concept as either predictive or probabilistic. To assert a point of conduct to be a duty is neither to assert that anything will certainly occur nor that it will probably occur. The nexus between duty and sanction is not predictive at all. Dereliction of duty, Hart points out, is a *reason* for suffering a sanction. It is true that sanctions for non-performance of a duty act are often predictable. But this is not a consequence of an analytic connection between non-performance and the probability of a sanction. It is a derivative consequence of the fact that failure to perform a duty is considered a ground or reason for applying a sanction. This connection between omission and sanction is analytic.

Was Bentham's theory as simple-minded as this powerful criticism suggests? It may be admitted that in some statements of the general pure predictive sanction theory Bentham's position is indefensible. But a closer examination of Bentham's numerous remarks on the subject reveal greater sensitivity to the issues involved.

The first point to examine is Bentham's elaborate discussion of sanctions. When explaining the legal or political sanction the existence of which creates a legal duty Bentham provides the following definition:

> If at the hands of a particular person or set of persons in the community who under names correspondent to that of judge are *chosen for the particular purpose of dispensing it, according to the will of the sovereign* or supreme ruling power in the state it may be said to issue from the political sanction.[24]

Here it is quite clearly specified that the political sanction does not arbitrarily result from non-performance of a duty, but is applied according to the will of the sovereign. On the following page Bentham adds that the punishment that constitutes the political sanction happens to one by the *sentence* of the political magistrate. This suggests that Bentham is by no means oblivious to an extra-predictive nexus between non-performance of duty and sanction. The suggestion is reinforced by his subsequent remarks on the moral and religious sanction. A punishment of the religious sanction, he writes, is 'manifested *on account* of

[24] *P.M.L.*, p. 34, my italics.

some sin committed'. A punishment of the moral sanction is *occasioned* by the misconduct of the sufferer, it is done *out of* some dislike to his moral character. In all these cases it appears that Bentham views the consequential sanction as having the past misconduct as its ground or reason.

Is this conception of sanction integrated into the analysis of duty? Clearly not always. But when one examines Bentham's analyses of legal duty in particular, especially when the imperatival theory is being conjoined with the sanction (and allegedly predictive) theory, it is clear that the traditional strictures no longer apply. In the *Fragment* Bentham writes 'That is my duty to do which I am *liable* to be punished *according to law* if I do not do.'[25] In the *Principles* he writes 'What is it that constitutes a legal obligation in any case? A command, express or virtual, together with punishment appointed *for breach of it*,'[26] In Appendix A to *Of Laws in General* he writes 'Whatever business the law may be conversant about, may be reduced to one sort of operation, viz. that of creating duties. To make duties, in the first place it must define them: in the next place it must mark out the punishments to be inflicted for breach of them.'[27] To this passage Bentham appends a note as follows: 'When the law gives you a right, what does it do? it makes me liable to punishment in case of my doing any of those acts which would have the effect of disturbing you in the exercise of that right.' Though the analysis of rights here is neither correct nor representative of Bentham's more common view, it is clear that the term 'liable' is not to be interpreted predictively but as meaning 'legally liable'. This is clear too from the preceding quotations.

Of course it should not be surprising to discover that Bentham frequently stresses the liability to suffer a sanction for breach of duty and disregards the secondary and dependent feature of its predictability. For he conceives of law as a social technique for the control of human behaviour by means of a standard motivation. The standard of behaviour is established by the declaration of the volition of the sovereign and the standard motivation created by annexing a subsidiary law, a further command, requiring the application of sanctions for non-

[25] *F.G.*, p. 107, my italics; cf. *F.G.*, p. 106 n.
[26] *P.M.L.*, p. 207 f.2, my italics. [27] *L.G.*, p. 249.

compliance with the primary law. It should be equally obvious that this dual imperative theory of duty cannot readily be carried through for the analysis of non-legal duty.

The standard criticism attacks Bentham's pure predictive account of duty because it allegedly misidentifies the nexus between duty and sanction. A deeper criticism, less easily deflected, attacks the theory not on the grounds of being predictive but on more general grounds. For what is less commonly noted is that Bentham's predictive sanction theory detaches the notion of duty from the notion of a course of action which ought to be followed. Acts which ought to be done are, according to Bentham, those acts which conform to the principle of utility, i.e. acts the tendency of which is to augment the happiness of the community. Only thus can 'ought' be given a meaning.[28] Duties, on the other hand, are acts the non-performance of which is likely to incur a sanction. Thus any coincidence of duties and acts that ought to be done is purely contingent. That something is a duty does not entail that it ought to be done, nor even that it ought prima facie to be done. To be sure, in an ideal, utilitarian, world the two will, up to a point, coincide, not by necessity, but by wise utilitarian legislation and enlightened public opinion. But what one ought to do and what is one's legal or moral duty to do are two quite distinct matters. Thus the legislators ought to legislate for the benefit of the community, but they have no legal duty to do so,[29] and, unless public opinion is utilitarian-minded, no moral duty to do so either.

Yet we do intuitively conceive of some logical link between duty and what one ought to do. If an act is a moral duty, then it seems, there is a moral reason or justification of a certain kind for doing it, and hence one ought, prima facie, to do it. Equally if an act is a legal duty then it is conceived of as an act for the performance of which a specific kind of legal justification can be adduced. As a result of his narrow conception of rationality,[30] his unduly restrictive conception of

[28] *P.M.L.*, p. 13. It should be stressed that there are other, subjectivist, analyses of 'ought' in Bentham's writings.

[29] *F.G.*, p. 107 n.

[30] See H. L. A. Hart, 'Bentham', (1962) 48, *Proceedings of the British Academy*, 316 ff.

what can constitute a reason or ground of action, and his monistic theory of justifying principles, Bentham never contemplated an important alternative to his analysis. This is the suggestion that the concept of duty in general be analysed in terms of an act supported by a justification of a specific kind. Accordingly duty, justification or reason, and what ought to be done are logically linked. Such an account of duty would treat the duty-sanction nexus as secondary and consequential. It is because a duty is an act supported by justifications of a peculiarly pressing kind that we take performance of the duty to be so important, and take violation of the duty as a ground for sanction. The sanction is a subsidiary, not a primary, feature.

Although Bentham denied any analytic connection between 'duty' and 'ought', it is interesting that he himself occasionally slips into this way of talking in spite of its being wholly inconsistent with his theory. In an autobiographical remark in the *Fragment*[31] he says: 'I learnt to see that utility was the test and measure of all virtue; of loyalty as much as any; and that the obligation to minister to general happiness was an obligation paramount to and inclusive of every other.' But the principle of utility tells us what we *ought* to do, not what we are likely to be censured for not doing; nor is it clear that it dictates that we ought always to be censured for not maximizing general utility. A similar backsliding occurs in Bentham's *Principles of the Civil Code*[32] in discussing need as a reason for action: 'The good Samaritan by relieving the wounded traveller saved his life. It was a noble action, a virtuous deed—nay, a moral duty.' But the pure predictive theory of duty clearly does not warrant such a use of 'moral duty'. Bentham's theory stands accused of two defects. It detaches 'duty' from 'ought' and it treats what is secondary as primary. We shall revert to these points subsequently.

So much for quite general criticisms of Bentham's account. Two brief points are worth making about the relation of the analysis to the sophisticated theory of definition. Firstly, though paraphrastic definition is useful and illuminating it is not obviously necessary. Bentham's pure predictive theory can be

[31] *F.G.*, p. 51.

[32] 'Principles of the Civil Code', in *The Theory of Legislation*, ed. C. K. Ogden (1931), p. 190.

phrased in a traditional definition thus: a duty is a kind of act non-performance of instances of which is likely to incur a sanction. Secondly, though the operation of archetypation is both interesting and valuable, it is not obvious that Bentham interprets the archetypes correctly. Clearly the pressing weight and binding cord are emblematic representations of necessitation. Bentham conceives the practical necessitation, the 'binding force', of duty to lie in sanctions. The justificative analysis previously hinted at would argue that this is a misconception of practical necessitation. Duty necessitates because of the pressing reasons for doing the duty act, independently of the sanction. In passing it is worth remarking that Bentham, rather surprisingly, fails to connect the binding-cord archetype of obligation with the archetype of a right. In giving the archetype of a right he stresses the notion of investiture[33] which is, perhaps, appropriate to his beneficiary or beneficiendary theory of rights. But the choice theory, above mentioned, can be attractively illuminated if the archetype of a right is conceived as 'a portion of matter', as he puts it, which is the loose end of the binding rope of obligation. Having a right, transferring a right, relinquishing a right, *releasing* a person from his obligation to one, etc. can readily be conceived as holding the ropes of practical necessitation and so possessing limited sovereignty over the person obligated.[34]

Finally a few comments on the specific accounts of duty. The concept of a natural duty is misguided. Bentham sees that elementary natural necessities provide a foundation for practical necessitations that are the subject of prudential reasoning. Given the desire to avoid falling then the fact that ice is slippery is a reason for walking carefully. If one does not walk carefully one is likely to fall and get hurt. Duty designates a normative necessitation and while the notion of a compelling reason for action is a connecting link between duty and practical necessitation, it is false that a prudential reason for acting which rests on the fact that non-performance of the act in question is likely to have untoward consequences makes the act a duty in any sense. Nor is the predictable unpleasantness rightly called 'a sanction' in the ordinary sense of this term, although Bentham

[33] *Works*, Vol. III, p. 217.

[34] See H. L. A. Hart, *The Concept of Law*, p. 85.

is right in suggesting that it has obliging (but not obligating) force. It is not intentionally applied by an agent on the grounds of non-performance of a required act.

The positivist concept of moral duty which Bentham elaborates may be well suited for anthropological and sociological purposes, but it is ill suited for moralists and moral philosophers. Rendering an analysis in terms of pressures of public opinion does not enable one to distinguish *mores* from morals, nor to assert without contradiction that although no evil consequences will be visited upon you for not doing so and so, nevertheless it is your duty. Bentham's concept of moral duty is analytically tied to social facts, namely affective and reactive behavioural responses to conduct. It is detached from any notion of a moral reason (of a certain kind), and so *a fortiori* from rational morality.

The pure predictive theory of legal duty is open to all the general objections already discussed. Substitution of an imperative sanction theory for a predictive sanction theory may avoid some of the defects of the predictive theory. Addition of an imperative analysis of a duty-imposing law doubtless avoids other difficulties. Though such an imperative theory is, for well-known reasons, unsatisfactory, it is arguably nearer the truth concerning the analysis of duty than any pure sanction theory. For it rightly associates the concept of a legal duty with the idea of a standard of conduct established by the legislator. The stress here is upon the requirement of conformity to a legally established standard rather than upon the legal consequences, whether predictable or commanded, of non-conformity to that standard.

IV. J. S. MILL'S ACCOUNT[35]

One of the main points upon which Mill recurrently criticized Bentham is the deficiency of his psychological theories. In his harsh, anonymously published paper 'Remarks on Bentham's Philosophy' he wrote:

As an analyst of human nature (the faculty in which above all it is necessary that an ethical philosopher should excel) I cannot rank

[35] References to Mill's ethical writings are abbreviated as follows: R.B.P.—'Remarks on Bentham's Philosophy', B.—Bentham, *U.—Utilitarianism.* The edition employed is Volume X of *Collected Works of John Stuart Mill: Essays on Ethics, Religion and Society* (University of Toronto Press, 1969).

Mr. Bentham very high. He has done little in this department, beyond introducing what appears to me a very deceptive phraseology and furnishing a catalogue of the 'springs of action' from which some of the most important are left out.[36]

Purporting to describe the nature of man, Bentham has omitted all that makes us distinctively moral creatures. Although sympathy is included in his list of motives, Mill admits, the most significant ethical motives and emotions are neglected. An analyst of human nature who disregards conscience, the feeling of duty, the love of justice, the moral sense, who obscures the essential human capacity to do an act merely because it is right, has failed in his task.

Mill returns to the same theme five years later in his essay 'Bentham' written in 1838. Bentham's psychology, in particular his endeavour to explain all human conduct by reference to interest is condemned on the same grounds as before:

Man is never recognized by him [Bentham] as a being capable of pursuing spiritual perfection as an end; of desiring, for its own sake, the conformity of his own character to his standard of excellence, without hope of good or fear of evil from other source than his own inward consciousness. Even in the more limited form of conscience, this great fact in human nature escapes him. Nothing is more curious than the absence of recognition in any of his writings of the existence of conscience, as a thing distinct from philanthropy, from affection for God or man, and from self-interest in this world or the next.[37]

Given this persistent preoccupation it is interesting to note how the theme of conscience and its role in moral psychology reappear in *Utilitarianism.* The third chapter, entitled 'Of the Ultimate Sanction of the Principle of Utility', begins by posing a series of related questions. Regarding any moral standard we may ask—What is its sanction? What are the motives to obey it? More specifically, Mill continues, we may query—What is the source of its obligation? Whence does it derive its binding force? In the course of his complex reply to these questions, which he mistakenly takes to be identical, Mill argues that the sanctions of any morality, and so of the utilitarian morality too, are either external or internal. The external sanctions of morality are the Benthamite ones—the hope of favour and fear

[36] R.B.P., p. 12. [37] B., p. 95.

of displeasure from our fellow creatures or from God; these are the external motives for observance of moral standards. But an account which mentions only these misses the most significant sanction, namely conscience—the internal sanction of duty:

> The internal sanction of duty, whatever our standard of duty may be, is one and the same—a feeling in our own mind; a pain, more or less intense, attendant on violation of duty, which in properly cultivated moral natures rises, in the more serious cases, into shrinking from it as an impossibility. This feeling when disinterested, and connecting itself with the pure idea of duty, . . . is the essence of Conscience;[38]

The binding force of the idea of moral obligation, Mill continues,

> consists in the existence of a mass of feeling which must be broken through in order to do what violates our standard of right, and which, if we do nevertheless violate that standard, will probably have to be encountered afterwards in the form of remorse. Whatever theory we have of the nature or origin of conscience, this is what essentially constitutes it.

The ultimate sanction of all morality, Mill concludes, is a subjective feeling in our minds.

On a superficial reading it may appear that Mill is trying to bolster up Bentham's predictive sanction theory of duty by the addition of the internal sanction of conscience. It may seem that Mill's recurrent criticism of Bentham's psychology comes to a head in the claims that Bentham lacked an adequate account of the sense of duty and that his account of the meaning of duty is defective for precisely this reason. Thus Mill has been interpreted as merely adding 'the "internal sanction" of conscience to Bentham's list of the sanctions which are "constitutive" of obligations'.[39] A proper account of conscience in terms of a 'subjective feeling in our minds', Mill is thus thought

[38] *U.*, p. 228.

[39] H. L. A. Hart, 'Bentham', loc. cit., p. 320; Alan Ryan, in *The Philosophy of John Stuart Mill* (1970), p. 209, argues, as Hart does, that Mill's theory of the sanction of conscience attempts to provide an analysis of 'duty'. Unlike Hart, Ryan does not see it as part of a predictive theory: 'He tends to analyse the notion of obligation as equivalent to feelings of discomfort at the thought of not doing an action. Thus "I am obliged to do X" is analysed as "the thought of not doing X causes me pain".'

to argue, will produce a satisfactory predictive sanction theory of duty. Duty is then analysed as an act the non-performance of which is likely to result in an internal sanction. It is, of course, unclear whether the idea of an internal sanction is conceived of as an element in the concept of any social type of duty, or only in that of moral duty.

Three questions arise: Is Mill's criticism of Bentham justified? Is Mill, in the course of his discussion of the ultimate sanction of utility, modifying Bentham's definition of duty or does he have some other target? Is Mill's account of the 'sanction of conscience' acceptable?

It is worth noting that Mill's most common accusations against Bentham on the score of conscience and the moral sense are not so much of conceptual error as of omission of fact. Bentham has left out of his account an important fact about human nature: 'The feeling of moral approbation or disapprobation properly so-called either towards ourselves or our fellow creatures, he seems unaware of the existence of.'[40] Consequently he fails to realize man's capacity for disinterested pursuit of spiritual perfection, 'without hope of good or fear of evil from other source than his own inward consciousness'. To this there are two replies. Firstly, in so far as one retains the utilitarian axiology then the fact that spiritual perfection is conceived of as an end of action can be readily accounted for as long as 'spiritual perfection' is interpreted in hedonic terms. What justifies its pursuit, the reasons for which men ought to aim at it, are the certain, pure, fecund pleasures which it affords. It is interesting to note that Mill believes that it is necessary to supplement the account of the justification for the pursuit of such ends (which he renders in eudaimonic rather than hedonic terms) by an account of motives, namely the hope of good or fear of evil from one's own inward conscience. The fact that Mill, like Bentham, takes for granted such a gap between justification and motivation is extremely important to the understanding of his views. Secondly, though Bentham's account of conscience is unquestionably defective, Mill was wrong to think that he never provided one. In the *Comment on the Commentaries*, which Mill probably never saw, Bentham briefly examines the notion of conscience in the course of a

[40] Mill, B., p. 95.

criticism of Blackstone.[41] Blackstone's notion of an obligation *in foro conscientiae*, Bentham argues, can either be accounted for in terms of the three external sanctions of obligation, or it is nonsense. For there is no other source of motives constitutive of obligations than the legal, moral, and religious sanctions. The will is governed by two motives, the idea of pain and the idea of pleasure. If one wishes to use the term conscience to speak of the faculty of the will in so far as it is determined by the prospect of pain derived from an invisible, divine source, one may do so. It is harmless as long as it is not conceived of as a novel source of obligation.

Would this account satisfy Mill? Clearly not. Bentham's theory of motivation, like his general theory of justification, is consequentialist. Sanctions, whether remunerative or punitive, are the sole source of motives, and they are necessarily prospective. In the 'Remarks on Bentham's Philosophy' Mill objects to this consequentialist account of motives.[42] To be sure pleasure and pain determine all our actions, Mill admits, but it is not only future pleasures and pains that do so, but also present ones which precede the contemplated act. If a man refrains from committing an offence out of fear of a likely social sanction, or even out of a desire to avoid the remorse he is likely to feel, he is not truly virtuous. The virtuous man recoils from the very thought of committing the act; the pain of contemplating himself as performing such an act determines his will and motivates his self-restraint. Such conduct is not determined by a deliberate conscious aim, but, Mill suggests, by an impulse or feeling which has no ulterior end. The virtuous act or forbearance thus becomes an end in itself.

Mill's riposte however seems to be directed at Bentham's theory of motivation rather than at his theory of value. We are not *moved* to action solely by prospective pains and pleasures, and in the case of acts done for their own sake, in particular virtuous acts, we are moved by our conscience, that 'mass of feeling' which is the product of socialization[43] and which can be utilized by the utilitarian pedagogue as much as by an intuitionist. Mill's criticism of Bentham in the matter of

[41] *C.C.*, pp. 55 and 95. [42] R.B.P., p. 13.

[43] Mill's account of the phenomenology of conscience, as well as his theory of duty, is derived from Bain's *The Emotions and the Will* (1859).

conscience is not concerned with his theory of duty, nor indeed with his theory of justification, but with his moral psychology. Bentham, in Mill's opinion, cannot give an adequate account of acts done for their own sake, and hence fails to account for non-hedonic ends in themselves. This suspicion is confirmed in his essay on Bentham. For here again[44] he accuses Bentham of failing to recognize the possibility of pursuing any ideal end for its own sake, whether it be moral desire for perfection, or the quasi-aesthetic ideals of honour and dignity. Morality consists of two parts, Mill declares, an external and an internal part, social control and the training of the will and affections. Bentham's philosophy is concerned only with the former. But to omit the latter is to distort morality and to misconceive moral agency. The role of chapter III of *Utilitarianism* is to show that the classical theory of *motives* is incomplete, and must be supplemented by the addition of the sanction of conscience. It is thus not coincidental that in chapter IV Mill goes to great lengths to show that utilitarianism *properly interpreted* encompasses within the end of happiness (which is held to be the goal of all action) all goals pursued for their own sake. Mill's analytic account of the concept of duty appears only in chapter V of the book.

Before turning to that account some critical remarks on Mill's doctrine are in order. In the first place conscience cannot be conceived as a source of sanctions *stricto sensu*. A sanction is intentionally applied on the grounds of omission of a required act, in some cases with the intention of intimating a reason for future performance of such required acts. Conscience is conceived to operate in two ways, pangs of remorse subsequent to an offence, and powerful feelings of repulsion prior to a projected offence. In neither form is any suffering intentionally inflicted. In the latter case the unpleasant feelings of repulsion precede the act and do not have as their rationale the past commission of the offence. In the former case the remorse is felt on the grounds of having done an evil. Though not intentional, can prospective remorse provide a reason? Only in a secondary and derivative way. For if remorse is to be intelligible it necessarily involves the idea of violation of an accepted standard of conduct. Hence a primary reason for compliance is

[44] B., pp. 95 f.

necessarily the standard of conduct thus accepted and ultimately whatever reasons justify the standard. Prospective remorse could only constitute a sanction in a loose sense in those abnormal cases in which a conditioned remorseful response remains despite conscious and convinced renunciation of the previously accepted standard. Similar considerations apply to conscience when conceived of as involved feelings of repulsion at the thought of sinning. Although these powerful feelings may indeed play a causal role in one's self-restraint, they are essentially intensional, having as their intensional object the prospective offence. They cannot be conceived of as a sanction. They can be thought of as motives only if one employs, as Mill does, a misguided mechanical model of motivation.[45] But both these explanatory routes are redundant, for such feelings of conscience already involve a necessary reference to a reason for self-restraint, namely the thought of the prospective act as wicked.

Mill's difficulties arise because, *inter alia*, he adopts a so-called externalist[46] conception of the relation between obligation and motivation, assuming that there exists a gap between moral justification and motivation which needs to be filled in by a theory of sanctions. Hence he assumes that the question, regarding any moral standard, What is the source of its obligation? is identical both with What are the motives to obey it? and What is its sanction? This question, Mill argues, arises whenever one is called upon to adopt any moral standard. What he fails to realize, because of his externalist doctrine, is that *adopting* a moral standard is itself tantamount to generating such an array of complex feelings and responses. They are not reasons for adopting the standard, but logical consequences of so doing. The questions that arise when one is called upon to adopt a standard are Why this standard rather than another? What is its justification? and not What is its sanction?

In chapter V of *Utilitarianism* Mill briefly outlines his own analytic account of duty. His purpose is to identify the domain of justice within the broader range of morality in general. The

[45] See Mill, *System of Logic*, Bk. VI, chapter II.

[46] See W. D. Falk, '"Ought" and Motivation', *Proceedings of the Aristotelian Society* 48 (1947–8); W. K. Frankena, 'Obligation and Motivation in Recent Moral Philosophy' in A. I. Melden, ed., *Essays in Moral Philosophy* (1958); T. Nagel, *The Possibility of Altruism* (1970), pp. 7–12.

concept of morality he employs is strikingly narrow, for he hives off a large segment of morality, allocating it to aesthetics—conceived unusually widely. The principles of Practical Reason may be distinguished into three groups:[47] prudential, ethical, and aesthetic, concerned respectively with the expedient, the right, and the noble or beautiful. The domain of morality in general is identified with that sphere of action which is right and omission of which is wrong. Such acts are moral acts. These Mill identifies with duty. Morality is essentially the doctrine of duty. He then provides the following analysis:

> We do not call anything wrong, unless we mean to imply that a person ought to be punished in some way or other for doing it; if not by law, by the opinion of his fellow creatures; if not by opinion, by the reproaches of his own conscience. This seems the real turning point between morality and simple expediency. It is part of the notion of duty in every one of its forms, that a person may rightfully be compelled to fulfil it. Duty is a thing which may be *exacted* from a person, as one exacts a debt. Unless we think that it might be exacted from him, we do not call it his duty . . . we call any conduct wrong . . . according as we think that the person ought, or ought not, to be punished for it.[48]

This brief account could readily be expanded. One may conceive of this as a fragmentary analysis of the generic concept of duty. The different social types of duty might then be analysed along Benthamite lines according to the source or sources and determinate or indeterminate nature of the sanction, the reason or ground for which is the non-performance of the duty. It is noteworthy that the notion of conscience is introduced into this analysis, but not as an expedient to avoid a defect in a predictive sanction theory. Rather it is introduced as an element of a theory which conceives of non-performance of a duty act as a ground for a sanction. It would appear, although Mill does not explicitly say so, to be intended as a distinguishing feature of moral duty. We conceive of an act as a moral duty in so far as we think that its omission *ought* to be 'punished' by the opinion of members of society and the reproaches of the agent's conscience.

Mill's fragmentary account (he stresses that he is indicating only part, presumably a necessary condition, of the notion of

[47] *System of Logic,* VI. xii. 6. [48] *U.*, p. 246.

duty), like Bentham's main analysis, is a sanction theory. However it is neither a predictive nor an imperative sanction theory. The duty-sanction nexus is explained in terms of what *ought* to follow the non-performance of a duty, not in terms of what does, or is ordered, to follow. The reason or ground for the sanction is omission of the duty. How does Mill explain the notion of 'ought', or reason? Is non-performance of an act a reason for sanction if, and only if, people actually look upon it in a certain critical light and manifest their critical attitudes in conduct? Or is it rather a reason or ground if, and only if, certain kinds of rational principles justify the critical response? Is Mill's analysis positivist or antipositivist? Mill's position in *Utilitarianism* is not wholly clear. He gives a sociological-cum-genetic analysis of reactive responses which constitute an element of the sense of justice, and then gives a utilitarian account of the moralization of these responses. In *System of Logic*,[49] however, he clarifies his position explicitly. Indicative sentences in which words such as 'ought' appear, differ deeply from those in which only 'is' or 'will be' occur. The difference is not that the former fail, in some sense, to assert something. They affirm, according to Mill, that the act which ought to be done excites the speaker's approbation. But this is peripheral. The speaker's approbation is not a sufficient reason why others should approve, nor indeed is it a conclusive reason for himself. Rather it must be justified by reference to principles which will determine the *proper* objects of approbation. It is the task of the doctrine of Teleology to disclose such principles. The promotion of universal happiness, Mill declares, is the ultimate principle of Teleology.

What of the relation between 'duty' and 'ought', and of the nature of the requirement to do acts which are duties? In the fragmentary account of the concept of duty thus far examined, Mill seems quite oblivious to the important conceptual connection. Nor does he labour to clarify it elsewhere. It is, however, clear from the subsequent discussion of justice that, unlike Bentham, he connects the idea of justice, and so the obligations of justice, very closely to the notion of a rule, and so, in so far as this notion is connected with that of a reason, to the notion

[49] *System of Logic* VI. xii. 6 and 7.

of what one ought to do. 'Justice', Mill writes,[50] 'is a name for certain classes of moral rules, which concern the essentials of human well-being more nearly, and are therefore of more absolute obligation, than any other rules for the guidance of life.' It would not be unreasonable to infer from this and other like remarks that Mill did conceive there to be an analytic tie between 'duty', 'rule', and 'ought'. It would also appear that he did not analyse the notion of a duty-imposing rule by reference to social facts, but rather by reference to the requirements of the principle of utility. The introduction of the notion of a duty-imposing rule, and its analysis in terms of justifications for doing acts of the kind required by the rule, was an important modification of sanction theories. Mill, however, never developed the idea, nor sought to explore its ramifications. Nor is it wholly clear whether his antipositivist account of duties of justice is intended as a contribution to the analytic question 'What does "duty" mean?' or to the moral question 'What are our duties?'.

How does Mill put the notion of duty, thus explicated, to work? Morality has been identified with the domain of duty. The sphere of duty is the range of acts the non-performance of which is wrong and which ought to be punished or censured. Justice is concerned with that segment of morality which consists of duties of perfect obligation. These are duties to which there is a correlative right. Duties of imperfect obligation exhaust the remaining part of morality. These are duties which, 'though the act is obligatory, the particular occasions of performing it are left to our choice; as in the case of charity or beneficence, which we are indeed bound to practise, but not towards any definite person, nor at any prescribed time'.[51] The domain of worthiness, or, as Mill calls it in *System of Logic*, 'Aesthetics', is not part of morality. It is concerned with the desirable or laudable, the noble and beautiful. Performing worthy acts, it seems, is praiseworthy, but their omission is not blameworthy. Morality, as Mill conceives it, is concerned with the social minimum, with what may be *demanded* of men.[52]

[50] *U.*, p. 255. [51] *U.*, p. 247.

[52] Cf. 'Thornton on Labour and Its Claims' in *Collected Works of John Stuart Mill*, Vol. V, pp. 650 f.

V. EVALUATION OF MILL'S THEORY

Mill's analysis of the concept of duty involves substantial advances over his predecessors. It has four desirable features. Firstly, in respect of the nexus between duty and sanction, Mill's suggestion comes very close to the truth. The connection between non-performance of duty and sanction is neither predictive nor imperative. It is rather that dereliction of duty is a ground or reason for sanction or censure. Secondly, Mill's undeveloped suggestion that a normative analysis of the requirement that the obligatory act be performed was a promising move. The concept of duty is thereby correctly associated with the notion of standards of conduct, and rightly allocated to the sphere of normative language. Thirdly, Mill's unclear suggestion that the concept of a duty-imposing rule should itself be analysed in terms of certain kinds of justifications or reasons for doing the duty act points beyond a normative analysis to a justificative one. I shall suggest below that this insight is worth developing. Fourthly, Mill's claim that the concept of moral duty is concerned, in some sense, with a social minimum, is, I think, correct.

These gains, however, on one interpretation of Mill's theory, are thrown away by an over-hasty insistence upon a necessary connection between the concept of duty and the principle of utility. This distorts both the analysis of the connection between duty and sanction, and the analysis, whether normative or justificative, of the requirement to perform the relevant act. While it is plausible to think that failure to perform a legal duty is a ground for a legal sanction and not merely a sign of its probability, it is highly implausible to think that only those acts whose non-performance would, *from a utilitarian point of view*, be justified grounds for sanctions are legal duties. *A fortiori* the claim that only legal rules justified by reference to the principle of utility are duty-imposing would be defective. This confuses expository with censorial jurisprudence and renders the important notion of legal duty useless for expository purposes. It would therefore seem *more* plausible to argue that the generic concept of duty is to be partly explicated as an act the non-performance of which is a ground for censure or sanction. Legal duty is then partly explained as an act the non-performance of which constitutes a legal ground for the application, by an appropriate organ, or a legal sanction (or, minimally, of legal, authoritative, censure). Moral duty would analogously be explained as an act the non-performance of which constitutes a moral reason for moral censure. Although this is insufficient, it is a move in the right direction. It needs supplementation by an analysis of the relation between duty and reasons or justifications for action. Moreover, this account of the generic concept fails to distinguish prudence from duty; for imprudent acts, to be sure, provide reasons for censure. Mill's introduction of the substantial element of the importance of acts that are duties to social well-being may serve to distinguish moral duties, according to utilitarian ethics, from mere prudence. But this is of no avail to remedy the weakness in the generic account. The modification provides a false analysis of legal duty. Furthermore it is not obviously correct for an analysis of moral duty unless, as Mill believed, duties of justice (and other moral duties) can be given a utilitarian rationale. If the notion of justification is to enter into the analysis of duty, it must do so in a more complex and flexible way than that suggested by Mill's rather crude theory.

A further point of criticism is that Mill mistakenly equates what one may exact from a person with what one may punish a person for not doing. Moreover he makes far too much of the idea of compulsion, whether by reference to exaction or to punishment. Such a rigorous account will not fit legal duty satisfactorily, and is inappropriate for moral duty (although, to be fair to Mill, he speaks loosely of being 'punished' by 'the opinion of his fellow creatures' or 'the reproaches of his own conscience'). The more flexible notion of censure needs to be invoked.

More specific criticisms than this are, given the incompleteness of Mill's account, pointless. But a few remarks upon his subsequent employment of the notion thus defined may be appropriate. Firstly, Mill's general conception of the domain of morality is unduly narrow. There is more to morals than avoidance of wrong and fulfilment of duty. There is the domain of self-sacrifice and heroism, of supererogation and favour.[53]

[53] See J. Feinberg, 'Supererogation and Rules' in his book *Doing and Deserving, Essays in the Theory of Responsibility* (1970).

There is also, as Mill points out in criticism of Bentham, the cultivation of moral virtues, not all of which are expressed in the fulfilment of duty, e.g. generosity, kindness, compassion, etc. Secondly, as a corollary of the first point, Mill's conception of the aesthetics of action is too wide. No doubt there is such a sphere. The less utilitarian the culture the larger it bulks. Concepts such as honour, dignity, and the like are quasi-aesthetic. But to identify the aesthetics of action with the domain of worthiness, and exclude the latter from the sphere of morality is misguided. Much that is worthy, laudable, and desirable in action, which is nevertheless not mandatory, belongs to morals. Such acts constitute part of the grounds for the assessment of the moral standing of a person, for the description of his virtues, character, and personality. The possession of such virtues as generosity, kindness, and compassion constitutes part of a moral, not aesthetic, ideal of life. Thirdly, Mill's conception of duties of imperfect obligation is defective. For if duty is identified with the contrary of wrong, and wrong conduct is that which ought to be punished, then it is unclear how charity and beneficence can be considered to be duties at all, for there can be, on Mill's account, no *specific occasion* of dereliction of duty which will be a ground for censure or punishment. To be sure one *ought to be* generous and beneficent. But the performance of acts of generosity is good and praiseworthy without their omission being wrong or (normally) censurable. Such acts belong to the domain of worthiness, which is a segment of morality. A corollary of this is that Mill unwittingly identifies justice with almost the whole sphere of duty. This is clearly mistaken. Finally, it is worth pointing out that Mill's sanction theory must be interpreted as having primary application to kinds of acts rather than individual acts, and that the reason for the sanction in the event of non-performance, is only a prima facie reason. For there are clearly many excuses and indeed justifications for not doing one's duty upon some specific occasions.

VI. HART'S MODIFIED SANCTION THEORY

The most elaborate and sophisticated theory of duty expounded in recent times is Hart's.[54] It is a modified sanction

[54] Hart's most detailed discussion is in *The Concept of Law.* The following sum-

theory, for although duties are essentially and necessarily connected with sanctions, it is also the case that duties are essentially acts the performance of which is required by a social rule. The theory is therefore a normative one. It is also positivist in the sense that it provides a social-fact analysis of duty-imposing rules.

The gist of Hart's theory can be captured by the following schema: A duty is an act the performance of which is required by a social rule of a certain kind, and the non-performance of which is generally held to justify the critical reactions with which it is normally met. The schema must be filled in by specifying the nature of the social rule and the nature of the critical reactions. Hart specified four conditions which must be met by the duty-imposing rule:

1. It must require members of a specified class of persons to do or abstain from a given act upon specified occasions. 2. The rule is thought, by most members of the social group, to be important because it is believed necessary to the maintenance of social life or some valued feature of it. 3. The conduct required by the rule may conflict with the wishes of those subject to it. 4. Compliance with the rule is general. Hart specifies four further conditions which must be met in the event of deviations from the rule: 5. Such deviations are usually met with serious critical reactions, demands for conformity, sanctions etc. The nature of the critical reactions varies from one social type of rule to another. 6. Deviation is generally accepted as a good reason for the ensuing critical reactions. 7. Such critical reactions are themselves regarded as legitimate, i.e. they are not themselves normally met with counter critical reactions. 8. Normative language is extensively used in the expression of such critical responses.[55] Where these eight conditions are satisfied then duties may be said to exist.

I suggested above that Hart's theory is a *modified* sanction theory. The important modification which Hart has introduced relative to the previous two sanction theories is the explicit insistence that duties are imposed by rules, that fulfilment of

---

mary rests exclusively upon the theory propounded in that book. Subsequent references to it are abbreviated to *C.L.*

[55] *C.L.*, p. 56.

duty constitutes compliance with a rule and failure to fulfil one's duty is equivalent to deviation from a rule. Mill hinted at but never developed this important feature. Bentham captured an element of it in his imperative theory of legal duty, but the substitution of a normative account of law instead of an imperative one is clearly a great gain. An equal advantage is gained by the corresponding analysis of moral duty. I shall return to this feature and its important ramifications below. For all that, however, Hart's primary emphasis in his analysis of duty is upon the sanctions for non-performance rather than upon the rule imposing the duty. 'What is important', he writes,[56] 'is that the insistence on importance or seriousness of social pressure behind the rules is the primary factor determining whether they are thought of as giving rise to obligations.' Similarly he emphasizes the employment of normative language in response to deviation from duty rather than in the context of practical reasoning, advice, and exhortation.

Like Mill, Hart conceives the non-performance of duty to be a reason for a sanction. Unlike Mill, however, the account given of this nexus between duty and sanction is in terms of social facts. Deviation normally meets with critical reactions, and these are thought of as justified, i.e. the deviation is considered a sufficient reason for the critical responses, and they are not themselves met with further critical attitudes. This conforms with the general social fact account Hart gives of rules, as well as with his account of duty-imposing rules.

Hart's analysis constitutes a great advance on those of his predecessors. It affords valuable insight into the structure of normative concepts and hence into the nature of the phenomena we describe by this means. The generic account is constructed with the general notion of social standards of conduct in view. With some modifications specific accounts of legal, moral, and other social types of duty are readily generated. Legal duties are imposed by legal rules and their non-performance normally is a condition which provides legal grounds for the application of a legal sanction by a legal organ. Because of the systematic nature of a legal system and the organized application of relatively determinate legal sanctions

[56] *C.L.*, p. 84.

many of the features characteristic of the general concept of obligation must be modified. The rule imposing a duty need not be eminently general[57]—it need not be thought to be important *per se* but only *qua* authoritative law; compliance need not be general, but the law must then be a valid law of a system compliance with most laws of which is general. Some legal duties are not backed up by sanction stipulating laws; nevertheless critical reactions to non-performance of such mandatory legal acts are normally forthcoming from law applying organs, and are normally held to be legitimate.[58] Hart characterizes moral rules of a social group by reference to the eight features[59] specified above in conjunction with the specification of the nature of the social pressure for conformity. Where the social pressure is heavily dependent upon the operation of feelings of shame, remorse, and guilt, Hart remarks 'we may be inclined to classify the rules as part of the morality of the social group and the obligation under the rules as moral obligation.'[60] The ultimate sanction of morality is, it seems, the internal 'sanction' of conscience. For Hart this is an analytic truth. Other social types of duty, e.g. the duties of occupants of certain social roles (e.g. of a host, of a committee chairman), may also be accommodated within this analysis.

Hart's theory is, I think, defective at two points. The first concerns Hart's emphasis upon the stringency of social pressure for conformity to a rule requiring one to do or abstain from some act as determining whether the act in question is rightly thought of as a duty. As I have already indicated, this emphasis seems to me to treat what is of secondary significance as if it were of primary importance. To identify a moral duty by reference to the nature of the critical response assumes that the affective reactions of shame, guilt, and remorse, as opposed to loss of face, embarrassment, and regret, are readily identifiable independently of the prior identification of the offensive act which occasions the reaction as non-performance of a moral

[57] For the notion of 'eminently general' norms, see G. H. von Wright, *Norm and Action*, pp. 79 ff.

[58] See J. Raz, *The Concept of a Legal System* (1970), pp. 149–54.

[59] One should point out that eminent generality is not necessary in the case of content-independent moral duties, e.g. duties created by norm-creating acts such as promising.

[60] *C.L.*, p. 84.

duty.[61] It assumes that the identification of other-regarding criticisms as reflecting upon one's moral standing and character is possible independently of the conception of moral virtues (or vices) as including one's will to satisfy (or not to satisfy) moral standards of conduct which are conceived of as imposing obligations. It is not clear that this is possible, or, if possible, illuminating. Similarly this inversion of the order of significance suggests that the relevant act of omission is a violation of moral duty because it standardly occasions such critical responses. It is arguable that such acts of omission occasion the relevant critical responses because they constitute violations of stringent moral requirements. As in Mill's theory, the reasons or grounds for censure must be considered as only prima facie reasons.[62] It is significant that many acts are duties even though their non-performance is, due to exceptional circumstances, excusable or justifiable, and their performance, in these dangerous and demanding circumstances, is praiseworthy. Nevertheless, such acts are not supererogatory but obligatory. If attention is shifted away from the fact that non-performance is a ground for the sanction to the rule requiring performance, this feature can be readily explained.

In Hart's account the primary emphasis is upon the pressure for conformity to the duty-imposing rule, consequently attention is diverted from the rule and the primary reasons for doing the duty which it imposes, and directed to a secondary feature, namely the sanctions the reason for which is violation of the duty. The rule is thus viewed primarily as a standard for evaluation of conduct, and that largely in the breach rather than in the performance. This is especially marked in Hart's stress upon the employment of characteristic normative language in critical responses rather than in advice, guidance, and deliberation. Hence attention is diverted from the rule as a guide to action which constitutes in itself a reason for action. How is this feature of a rule to be explained? That an action is a duty entails, according to Hart, that its performance is required by a rule. However, if one is to grasp the guiding function of duties the introduction of a further 'fictitious entity', a rule, provides

[61] Or, more accurately, identification of the remorseful agent's belief as the belief that he has failed to do his moral duty.

[62] *C.L.*, p. 167.

insufficient explanation. Eliminating this fictitious entity may shed further light upon the structure of the concepts in question. That one ought to do an action entails that there is a reason for doing it, but tells us nothing about the nature of the reason. That an action is a duty, however, is in itself a reason for doing it. It entails that there are further reasons which justify doing it and reasons which justify its being a duty. I may be ignorant of what these further reasons are, but my ignorance does not entail that I have no reason for doing the action. The fact that it is a duty provides me with one. By contrast if I am ignorant of the reasons for doing an act which ought to be done, then I have no reason for doing it. If I know only that I ought to do it, then I have only the weakest of reasons for doing it, namely that there is a reason (of which I am ignorant) for doing it. But I am in no position to weigh the force of this unknown reason. Even if I know that I ought morally to do the act I cannot weigh this consideration against my inclinations, desires, interests, which speak against it. For there are many morally good actions, i.e. actions for which there are moral reasons of a certain kind, which need not outweigh inclinations, desires, and self-interest on particular occasions. But that an act is a duty is in itself a powerful exclusionary reason.[63] It entails, negatively, that not doing the act on whim or inclination is unjustifiable. It entails that not doing the act because one does not want to is no excuse. It entails that the fact that the act is not in one's interest, or even that it is contrary to one's interests,[64] will not constitute an acceptable reason for not doing it. This much at any rate is necessary, though perhaps insufficient, to capture the exclusionary force of the fact that an act is a moral duty. The exclusionary force of the fact that an

[63] The ingenious notion of an exclusionary reason as a key to the understanding of a mandatory norm has been developed by Joseph Raz in 'Reasons for Action, Decisions and Norms' (forthcoming). An exclusionary reason is explained as a reason which, in every situation in which it applies it is not only a reason for (or against) doing the action in question, but also a reason for not considering at all the force of certain other reasons and desires. It is contrasted with strong reasons which are those which in the situations in which they apply *normally* outweigh the standard reasons and desires likely to be present in those normal circumstances. Much of the ensuing discussion is indebted to Dr. Raz's illuminating paper.

[64] There are clearly limitations upon the extent to which self-interest is required to be sacrificed for certain duties. Morality does not require one to ruin one's life to keep a trivial promise.

act is a legal duty seems to encompass not only this but all extra-legal considerations, limited perhaps *in extremis* by fundamental principles of justice and morality.[65] Whether the subjects of the legal system accept the law as possessing such a status is another matter. Normally the law provides sanctions as motivation additional to respect for the law. The law-applying organs are themselves required to treat legal duties as possessing such status, and to apply sanctions to offenders on the grounds of deviation in those cases in which there are sanction-stipulating laws.

Thus far the implications of the negative, exclusionary force of duty. Positively, however, the notion of moral duty, as Hart indicates, entails that in general performance of acts of the kind in question is necessary to the maintenance of social life or some indispensable, highly valued feature of it.[66] Such reasons justifying the duty-imposing rule are strong or weighty reasons. They are not arbitrary as are many of the reasons justifying rules of etiquette. Nor are they justified by the amusing, interesting, or skilful consequences that acting on them has, as are most rules of games. They are justified by reference to fundamental moral values.[67] Hence the importance we attribute to moral duties. But that an act is a moral duty implies not merely weighty moral reasons for doing acts of that kind, it also implies the exclusion of certain kinds of countervailing reasons. Why? The exclusionary force of moral duty is justified, crudely speaking, by reference to such features as the need for predictability, mutual reliability, the multiplicity of temptations to disregard moral reasons, the importance of training and acquisition of habitual patterns of conduct and the like.

The exclusionary force of the fact that an act is a legal duty has already been mentioned. Positively, however, the notion of legal duty entails a justification of a very different kind from that underlying moral duties. While the justification of

[65] See, e.g. the discussion of the revival of Natural Law doctrines in post-war Germany in H. L. A. Hart, 'Positivism and the Separation of Law and Morals' (1958), 71 Harvard Law Review and *C.L.*, pp. 254 f.

[66] Hart specifies this condition in terms of what is, in a social group, *thought* to be important and valuable. This accords with his social fact analysis.

[67] Or, in the case of content-independent obligations (e.g. those created by promising) by reference to obligation-imposing acts, the status of which is justified by reference to such values.

moral duties is, for the most part, by reference to weighty, content-dependent, reasons, the justification of legal duties is, in the first instance, by reference to authority. As such it is content-independent. Legal duties are created by duty-imposing acts, or some other legally recognized way of establishing standards of conduct. To be sure, the duty-creating status of such facts does itself require justification. But the nature of such justification takes one beyond the confines of analytical legal philosophy. Moreover it is debatable whether this ultimate justification, in contrast with the content-independent justification, is part of the meaning of 'legal duty'.

Though the reasons which justify a certain kind of moral duty are necessarily strong or weighty reasons, it is of course not the case that in every instance of a moral duty there are strong reasons for performing the particular act in question. Some particular acts which instantiate a kind of moral duty are trivial and might, were other things equal, be outweighed by other considerations. However the exclusionary force of the duty is not eliminated by the triviality of the act and its consequences upon specific occasions. Conversely, where a duty is instantiated in circumstances in which its performance is of great consequence but exceptional self-sacrifice is necessary, the exclusionary force of the duty may not apply, for not *all* countervailing reasons are excluded by the fact that an act is a duty. Hence omission, in such extreme circumstances, does not constitute a ground for censure. But the act may nevertheless be conceived of as a duty, even though doing it may, unlike the normal case, be praiseworthy.

The fact that non-performance of a duty is normally a ground for censure or sanction must, I suggest, be seen as a consequential feature of the weight of the reasons for acts of the kind in question, and the nature and extent of the exclusionary reasons for every instance of it.

The second point of strain in Hart's account lies in its excessively positivist nature. This is of no importance for the analysis of duties of positive law. But it is of great importance for the account of moral duty. Hart's analysis may be useful for anthropological or sociological descriptions of the *mores* of a social group. However, much discourse about moral duties is not concerned with *mores* but with morals, not with mere description but with rational justification. A moralist frequently declares an act to be morally obligatory, and will not withdraw his claim upon being told that its omission is not viewed by most members of his social group in the critical reflective way which, on Hart's account, is analytically involved in the notion of obligation. Bentham, as we have seen, drove a wedge between 'duty' and 'ought', reserving the former for discourse about positive law, and the latter for his own critical morality. Hart, in his modified sanction theory, follows Bentham in restricting the concept of moral duty to positive morality. He provides a social-fact analysis of 'duty' in terms of reactive attitudes, critical responses, demands for certain patterns of conduct, and the like. Hence, in the absence of these social facts it must be illegitimate for a moral reformer or critic to declare an act to be a duty in the primary sense of the term 'moral duty'.

To be sure there are various ways in which the Hartian analysis might accommodate this difficulty. Bentham argued that an assertion that there is a moral right is to be understood as a recommendation that there ought to be a legal right. Hart might claim analogously that an assertion that an act is a moral duty, though not recognized as such and not part of positive morality, is to be understood as a recommendation that it ought to be a moral duty even though it is not. But this is inadequate. It is one thing to claim that a certain kind of act ought to be accepted as a duty, that people ought to recognize its obligatoriness. It is another thing to claim that it is morally obligatory. The latter statement does not entail that it is recognized as such by members of a social group. What can be meant by saying that it ought to be a duty?—that there are reasons for making it a duty? Moral duties (barring certain kinds of content-independent duties and duties of co-operative practices) are not made. That there are reasons why it is a duty? To be sure there are, but then it *is*, not *ought to be*, a duty. That there are reasons why it should be recognized as a duty? To be sure there are. Members of the relevant social group may not recognize it as such, through insensitivity, hypocrisy, stupidity, or through distinctive empirical or non-empirical beliefs reflected in their order of values. But lack of recognition does not obviously imply absence of duty.

How important these considerations are for the preferred

analysis or moral duty turns largely upon the general conception a philosopher has of morality. The suggestions made above imply that the notion of moral justification cannot be wholly accounted for in terms of social facts, of what people take to be justified. The notion of moral duty cannot be prized off the concept of what ought to be done. Hence the notion of moral duty cannot be completely detached from that of rational justification of action. These contentions verge upon the fundamental problems of moral philosophy, upon the problems of whether there is, and to what extent there is, a rational foundation for ethics. This is not the place to go any further.

VII. CONCLUSION

If the foregoing critical remarks about the various theories of duty are plausible then the possibility of a general theory of duty in which the various social types of duty are displayed as species of a uniform genus recedes into the distance. Such an attractive explication of the concept cannot do justice to usage, nor can it meet the different needs which our untidy and ramshackle concept of duty meets in the domains of law, morality, religion, etc. The phenomena of law, morality, social practices, and religious ethics differ profoundly despite the numerous similarities, interconnections, and analogies. The needs for certain kinds of conceptual distinctions vary from one domain to another. It should not therefore be surprising that the concept of duty, prominent in each of these domains, should reflect the structural similarities as well as the differences. This much is evident from the Hartian analysis, and further supported by the above critical remarks and modifications.

I have suggested that a pure sanction theory of duty is unsatisfactory. But it has not been disputed that the sanction theorists focused correctly upon one important constituent of the general concept of duty. Though predictive and imperative analyses of the nexus between non-performance of a duty act and the consequent sanction are inadequate, the suggestion that the omission must be seen as a ground for sanction or censure is illuminating. The main general defect of sanction theories is, I have suggested, to place excessive emphasis upon the sanction and too little upon the duty-imposing standard of conduct. For duty is a guide to action while the threat of a sanction is a 'goad', and the former function should be seen as prior to the latter. The concept of a duty-imposing norm can be further analysed in terms of justifying reasons, thus laying greater emphasis upon the guiding function of duty. The combination of weighty justifying reasons and exclusionary reasons goes some way to elucidating the concept of a mandatory norm, and serves to bring out further distinctive features of duty-imposing norms. However, even given this explanatory apparatus, the differences between legal duty and moral duty are far-reaching. For even though it has been suggested that a straightforward social-fact analysis of a duty-imposing norm obscures the roles of justifying and exclusionary reasons, the extension of the analysis of a legal duty to the content-independent justification characteristic of law and to the exclusionary force of legal duty does not imply that a positivist analysis is inappropriate. Nor does it imply that a modified sanction theory is incorrect, even though it may be necessary to relax the classical requirement of a legal sanction for every legal duty. By contrast the notion of a sanction in the strict sense plays an insignificant part in our notion of a moral duty, and although the more flexible notion of censure is involved, it is, not surprisingly, less significant than the distinctive justificative characteristics of moral duty. Equally, a positivist analysis of moral duty fails to capture some of the salient features of the concept. In particular it fails to illuminate what has, to many moralists and philosophers, appeared an essential element in morality in general and moral duty in particular, namely their reasonableness.

I / Practical Reason and the Logic of Requirement[1]

Roderick Chisholm

1. To deal with the problems of practical reason we must understand certain general principles about what I will call 'the logic of requirement'. Some of these principles, I believe, have not yet been clearly articulated. I will attempt to formulate a number of them here and to discuss their philosophical significance.

The following passage from Leonard Nelson's *Kritik der praktischen Vernunft* should be sufficient to convey what I mean by 'the problems of practical reason':

What rules guide us when we pass a judgment on what is duty? The first answer that presents itself is: In general we are guided in such decisions by certain rules of morality. In general, when we are confronted with an ethical decision, we have a rule at hand that indicates to us what is to be looked upon as duty. Such rules are, for example, the rule of courtesy in social intercourse, of honesty in the communication of our thoughts, of readiness to help those in need, of loyalty toward our friends, of tolerance for the weaknesses of others. But on closer scrutiny we find that such moral rules are not, strictly speaking, universally valid. It happens to us often enough that these rules fail us. We find ourselves in situations not provided for in this set of rules, or in situations in which a given rule is applicable

[1] With the permission of the editor of the *American Philosophical Quarterly*, I have incorporated certain passages from my article 'The Ethics of Requirement', which appeared in that journal, Vol. I (1964), pp. 147–53.

but in which we feel ourselves justified in violating the rule. This second situation occurs whenever there is a conflict between one rule and another. For example, we are sometimes confronted with an inner conflict when we wish to observe the rule of courtesy as well as that of honesty. The decision as to which of these rules is to be given preference cannot lie in either of the two rules in question. In the case of such conflict one moral rule must be waived in favor of another; here we require a principle of selection enabling us to know which rule we are to waive and which we are to uphold. In other words, we require a strictly universal criterion to determine the validity of each of the two rules in question; and this criterion alone can properly be called the moral law.[2]

But let us make the subject of the final sentence plural: 'such criteria alone can properly be called laws of morality.'

2. We will consider the logic of the following types of argument:

(A) (1) *p* occurs
(2) *p* requires that *S* perform *A*
∴ (3) *S* has a duty to perform *A*

(B) (1) *q* occurs
(2) *q* requires that *S* perform an act incompatible with his performing *A*
∴ (3) *S* has a duty not to perform *A*

(C) (1) *r*, as well as *q*, occurs
(2) *r* and *p* does not require that *S* perform *A*
∴ (3) The requirement, imposed by *p*, that *S* perform *A* has been overridden

The second premiss in an argument of the form of (A) would formulate what Nelson calls a 'rule of morality'; the second premiss in an argument of the form of (B) could be said, in a certain sense, to formulate an extension of such a rule; and the

[2] The first edition of Nelson's book appeared in 1917; a second, unchanged edition is published by Felix Meiner Verlag (Hamburg, 1972). An English edition, entitled *Critique of Practical Reason*, translated by Norbert Guterman, is published by the Leonard Nelson Foundation (Scarsdale, N.Y., 1970). The above passage is from p. 116 of the English edition; it appears on pages 126–7 of the German edition.

second premiss in an argument of the form of (C) might be said to formulate a 'rule of moral permission'. The conclusions of arguments of the form of (A) and of (B) could be said to formulate '*prima facie* duties'. And the conclusion of an argument of the form of (C) could be said to describe a situation in which such a duty could be said, in Nelson's term, to be waived.

I would assert the following: (1) A significant part of our practical reasoning—our exhorting, justifying, and excusing, to ourselves and to others—can be cast in these three forms. (2) Each of the arguments is a valid logical argument. Moreover (3) the three arguments may be said to be consistent with each other in the sense that one may consistently affirm the premisses and conclusions of all three arguments, where *A*, *p*, *q*, *r*, and *S* are replaced, completely and consistently, by actual terms. And, finally, (4) once we have made the explications that are necessary in order to see the second and third of these points, we will have grasped certain concepts which will help us in dealing with a number of fundamental puzzles about what we ought to do.

3. We must understand, then, the concept I have tried to single out with the term 'requirement'.

Examples of requirement, as here understood, are: making a promise requires keeping the promise; wronging a person requires compensating the person; virtue (if Kant is right) requires being rewarded; performing a sinful act requires punishment and repentance. Other examples of requirement have been studied by the Gestalt psychologists: 'It is a basic fact of perceptual experience that some things belong or fit together, and that others do not. A curve may demand a certain completion and seem to reject all others; this completion appears as appropriate to the nature of the curve.'[3] As the quotation suggests, the terms 'fitting' and 'unfitting' might also

[3] Maurice Mandelbaum, *The Phenomenology of Moral Experience* (Glencoe, 1955), pp. 95–6. Compare Wolfgang Köhler, *The Place of Value in a World of Facts* (New York, 1938), especially ch. 3 ('An Analysis of Requiredness'). Köhler refers to M. Wertheimer, 'Some Problems in the Theory of Ethics', *Social Research*, vol. 2 (1935), pp. 353 ff.

be used to express the phenomena of requirement. Thus '*p* is fitting to *q*', in one of the senses in which philosophers have used this expression, could be taken to mean the same as '*p* requires *q*'; in another one of the senses in which philosophers have used it, it might be taken to mean the same as '*p* does not require not-*q*'.

We will take as our primitive locution the schema '*pRq*'–'*p* when it obtains requires *q*'—where the letters *p* and *q* may be replaced by terms designating states of affairs. The schema '*pRq*' may be read in English either as '*p* would require *q*', or as '*p* when it obtains requires *q*', or as '*p* is such that if it were to obtain it would require *q*'. ('States of affairs' will be understood in what I take to be the usual way. For example: states of affairs stand in logical relations to other states of affairs; some of these logical relations constitute the subject-matter of the logic of propositions; for every state of affairs *p*, there is another state of affairs which is the negation of *p* and which obtains, takes place, or occurs when and only when *p* does not obtain, take place, or occur. I will use 'obtains', 'takes place' and 'occurs' interchangeably.)

To facilitate exposition let us begin with a definition:

DI *p* requires *q* = Df *p* obtains and *pRq*

In other words, *p* does require *q*, or *p* in fact requires *q*, when *p* is such that (i) it obtains and (ii) if it were to obtain it would require *q*. Thus the defined '*p* requires *q*', unlike the undefined '*pRq*', implies that *p* obtains. (This contrast between the defined '*p* requires *q*' and the undefined '*pRq*' points to a certain ambiguity in the ordinary use of 'requires'. Sometimes philosophers who talk about the ethics of requirement use the locution '*p* requires *q*' in the sense here defined, and sometimes they use it in the sense of our undefined '*pRq*', i.e. '*p* when it obtains requires *q*'. The expression '*p* confirms *q*', which resembles '*pRq*' in a number of significant respects, has an analogous ambiguity. Sometimes '*p* confirms *q*' is used to refer to a relation that holds necessarily between propositions, or states of affairs, without implying anything as to the epistemic status of p; but sometimes 'p confirms q' is used to imply, not only that a certain relation holds between p and q, but also that p is known to be true, or that it is evident that p is true.)

I will now attempt to set forth certain general principles that hold of requirement as here understood. I will presuppose a principle of substitutivity according to which logically equivalent expressions may replace each other in any R-formula. The list of principles is by no means exhaustive. Additional principles will suggest themselves when we consider some of the concepts that may be defined in terms of requirement. It will be simplest, I believe, to formulate the principles as axiom schemata:

The first principle reflects our commitment to states of affairs:

A1 $pRq \supset (\exists x)(\exists y)(xRy)$

Consider, for example, 'Jones promising to meet his friend, when it occurs, requires Jones meeting his friend'. This implies that there *is* something—namely, Jones promising to meet his friend, which is such that when it occurs it requires Jones meeting his friend; and it implies that there *is* something—namely, Jones meeting his friend, which is such that Jones promising to meet his friend, when it occurs, requires it. But when we say of the first of these two things that when it occurs it requires the second, our statement does not imply that either one occurs. More generally, 'pRq' does not imply either that p obtains or that q obtains. And 's obtains and pRq' does not imply either '$(p\&s)Rq$' or '$pR(q\&s)$'.

Our second general principle tells us that the relation of requirement is like the relations of logic: if it holds between any two states of affairs, then it holds necessarily between those states of affairs.

A2 $pRq \supset N(pRq)$

Our third principle is reflected in the principle that 'ought' implies 'can'. If one state of affairs is such that when it occurs it requires a certain other, then the two states of affairs are logically compatible with each other

A3 $pRq \supset \sim N[(p\&q)$ does not obtain$]$

Our fourth principle tell us, on the other hand, that two states of affairs that are logically compatible with each other may yet have requirements that are *not* logically compatible with each other:

A4 $(\exists x)(\exists y)(\exists z)\{\sim N[(x \& y)$ does not obtain$] \& xRz \& yR\sim z\}$

There is, therefore, the possibility of a *conflict* of actual requirements. That is to say, there may occur one state of affairs which requires a certain thing *q* and another state of affairs which requires not-*q*. If I promise one man to go and promise another man not to go, then there is something requiring me to go and something requiring me not to go. A man may be subject to conflicting requirements through no fault of his own. For example, he may find himself in the position of being the only one who is able to rescue either, but not both, of two equally worthy men in distress.

We may compare 'confirms' once again: one true proposition may confirm *q*, and another true proposition may confirm not-*q*. Indeed, one proposition that is known to be true may confirm *q*, and another proposition that is known to be true may confirm not-*q*.

We add two obvious principles pertaining to disjunctive and conjunctive states of affairs:

A5 $(pRs \& qRs) \supset (p \vee q)Rs$
A6 $(pRq \& pRs) \supset pR(q \& s)$

If two states of affairs are each such that they would require a given state of affairs, then their disjunction would also require that state of affairs (A5). Every state of affairs is such that it would require the conjunction of all those states of affairs it would require (A6).[4] It should be noted that we cannot affirm the converse of (A5), viz.,

[4] These two principles were suggested to me by Ernest Sosa.

$$(p \vee q)Rs \supset (pRs \,\&\, qRs)$$

For suppose, what (A4) allows, that (i) p would require s but (ii) the conjunction of p and r would not require s. Then the principle of substitutivity for logically equivalent expressions would allow us to infer, from (i), that $[(p \,\&\, r) \vee (p \,\&\, {\sim}r)]$ would require s. And then the converse, above, of (A5) would allow us to infer that $(p \,\&\, r)$ would require s, which contradicts (ii).

But the following, closely related formula would seem to be axiomatic:

A7 $\quad (p \vee q)Rs \supset (pRs \vee qRs)$

One might put this principle, somewhat loosely, by saying that if a given state of affairs requires a certain other state of affairs, then, of the possible ways of extending or making 'more determinate' the first state of affairs, one at least will also require the second state of affairs.

4. Among the consequences that can readily be drawn from our axioms are the following:

T1 $\quad pRq \supset {\sim}N(p \text{ does not obtain})$

T2 $\quad pRq \supset {\sim}N(q \text{ does not obtain})$

T3 $\quad pRq \supset {\sim}(pR{\sim}q)$

T4 $\quad (pRq \,\&\, sR{\sim}q) \supset \{{\sim}[(p\&s)Rq] \vee {\sim}[(p\&s)R{\sim}q]\}$

T5 $\quad pRq \supset [(p\&s)Rq \vee (p \,\&\, {\sim}s)Rq]$

A self-contradictory state of affairs would not require anything (T1) and would not be required by anything (T2). No state of affairs would impose incompatible requirements (T3). Thus if, in accordance with the possibility countenanced by (A3), two states of affairs that are compatible with each other happen to impose requirements that are incompatible with each other, then at least one of those requirements is not imposed by the conjunction of those two states of affairs (T4). Much of the sting of (A5), then, is removed by (T3) and (T4). Principle (T4), then, allows for the possibility that, although p is such that if it were to obtain it would require q, there occurs a wider state of affairs that entails p and that does not require q. But principle T5, which is a consequence of (A5), tells us that this is *only* a possibility. For, according to (T5), it is also possible that, if p requires q, then, for every wider state of affairs that obtains and entails p, that wider state of affairs also requires q.

We can say, then, that there may be requirements that conflict with each other (A4). But if there occurs something p which requires q, then this same thing p does not also require not-q (T3). Similarly, if there is a true proposition p which confirms another proposition q, then p does not also confirm not-q. If p and s have incompatible requirements, the larger situation, consisting of both p and s, will not have these incompatible requirements (T4). The analogy with confirmation is obvious, once again.

5. Our theorem T4, above, may be given this alternative formulation: if two states of affairs are such that they would impose incompatible requirements, then one or the other of those incompatible requirements would be *overridden* by the conjunction of the two states of affairs. The concept of a requirement being overridden is central to the logic of requirement and we will now consider it briefly.

Let us first define the case where one state of affairs is such that it *would* override the requirement that would be imposed by another:

D2 The requirement for q, that would be imposed by p, would be overridden by s = Df (i) pRq, (ii) $\sim[(p\&s)Rq]$, and (iii) $p\&s$ is logically compatible with q.

If s is such that it would override the requirement for q that would be imposed by p, then: p is such that it would require q, but the conjunction of p and s is *not* such that it would require q, and the conjunction of p and s does not entail the negation of q.[5]

[5] The third condition in the definiens of D2 is needed because of the consequences that would otherwise follow, given our general principles, from the assumption that a requirement for q had not been fulfilled. Without the third condition we would have to say that if p required q, and not-q obtained, then the conjunction of p and not-q would override the requirement q imposed by p.

We may now say that a state of affairs *does* in fact override a certain requirement if the state of affairs obtains and is such that it would override that requirement:

D3 The requirement for *q* that is imposed by *p* is overridden by *s* = Df (i) the requirement for *q* that would be imposed by *p* would be overridden by *s* and (ii) *p*&*s* obtains.

W. D. Ross has given us a clear example: 'If I have promised to meet a friend at a particular time for some trivial purpose, I should certainly think myself justified in breaking my engagement if by doing so I could prevent a serious accident or bring relief to the victims of one.'[6] His promise (*p*) to meet the friend requires his meeting the friend (*q*), but the accident or the dangerous situation (*s*) creates a new situation (*p* and *s*) which does not require that he meet the friend.

In Ross's example, of course, the new situation not only overrides a requirement but creates a new one—the requirement to prevent the accident or to relieve distress—and the new requirement is incompatible with the requirement that is overridden; the requirement for *q* is replaced by a requirement for not-*q*. But a requirement for something *q* may be overridden without being replaced by a requirement for not-*q*. If I am required to go to Boston in order to meet a friend, and then learn that he is dead, the requirement may be overridden without my being required not to go to Boston.

6. An overriding may itself be overridden. If, as I go to assist the man in distress, I learn that an even greater disaster will result should I fail to keep my appointment with the friend, then this new and more inclusive situation may require me once again to keep the appointment with the friend. Thus there may occur a set of events (there may be a set of true propositions) *p*, *q*, *r*, *s*, and *t*, such that:

p requires *q*
p and *r* requires not-*q*

[6] W. D. Ross, *The Right and the Good* (Oxford, 1930), p. 18.

BPR

p and *r* and *s* requires *q*
p and *r* and *s* and *t* requires not-*q*

Once again, therefore, we find that requirement is like the logical concept of confirmation. For there may be true propositions, *p*, *r*, *s*, and *t*, such that:

p confirms *q*
p and *r* confirms not-*q*
p and *r* and *s* confirms *q*
p and *r* and *s* and *t* confirms not-*q*

The following propositions provide an example: 'Most of the people in this room are Democrats, and John is in this room' (*p*); 'John is a Democrat' (*q*); 'Most of the people on the left side of the room are not Democrats, and John is on the left side of the room' (*r*); '45 of the 50 people who arrived on time are Democrats, and John arrived on time' (*s*); '99 of the 100 people who voted for the measure are not Democrats, and John voted for the measure' (*t*). We do not say, in such cases, that one confirmation has been 'overridden' or 'defeated' in virtue of another, but we could.

Let us consider still another feature of this example of confirmation. Should we say that, in the situation described, the proposition *q* is probable, or should we say that it is improbable? One of the clearest answers to this question is suggested by Bernard Bolzano. We may say that a relational, or relative, probability of a proposition for a given person is the probability which the proposition has in relation to any part of what the person knows to be true. Thus, for a man who knows the propositions, *p*, *r*, *s*, and *t*, to be true, the proposition *q* has various relational probabilities—depending upon which of these propositions it is that *q* is being related to. But the absolute probability of a proposition, for any given person, is the probability which the proposition has in relation to the totality of those propositions which the person knows to be true.[7] Abso-

[7] Bernard Bolzano, *Wissenschaftslehre*, vol. 3 (Leipzig, 1930), pp. 267–8. Bolzano also made a distinction between a real or objective probability and a supposed or subjective probability which we might

lute probability is thus 'toti-resultant'. Normally, when we speak of 'the probability' of a proposition, we are referring to its absolute probability. And it is absolute probability that should constitute the guide of life.

7. From the fact that a state of affairs q is required by a certain state of affairs p such that p obtains, we may not infer that q is a state of affairs that *ought* to obtain. For the requirement imposed by p may be overridden by some other state of affairs s. But from the fact that a requirement for q has thus been overridden, we may not infer that q is a state of affairs that 'need not' obtain—i.e. a state of affairs such that it is not true that that state of affairs ought to obtain. For there may be some *other* state of affairs that requires q—indeed, some wider state of affairs that includes (entails) both p and s. We will say that a state of affairs ought to obtain provided there is a requirement for it that has not been overridden:

D4 It ought to be that q obtains = Df. There is an x such that x requires q and it is false that the requirement for q imposed by x is overridden.

The relation between what is merely required and what ought to be is thus analogous to the relation between what was called relative and absolute probability above. Thus one might also consider defining the 'ought to be' by reference to what is required by the totality of relevant considerations. But D4 is simpler and, I believe, accomplishes the same purpose.

8. Another pair of concepts that are useful in formulating certain ethical issues are singled out by the following definitions:

D5 p would indefeasibly require q = Df (i) pRq and (ii) there is

put as follows: a real or objective probability of a proposition, for a given person, is the probability which that proposition bears to something that the person knows; the supposed or subjective probability is the probability the proposition bears to something the person thinks (possibly mistakenly) that he knows. (Unfortunately, Bolzano's own definitions are marred by the fact that he attempts to get along with an epistemic term which is weaker than 'knows'.) The more important parts of Bolzano's book have been translated by Rolf George as *Theory of Science*, The University of California Press: Berkeley and Los Angeles, 1972). Compare pp. 359–65 of the English edition.

no x such that the requirement for q that would be imposed by p would be overridden by x.

D6 p indefeasibly requires q =Df (i) p requires q and (ii) p would indefeasibly require q.

If we know that p indefeasibly requires q, then we can know that, no matter what wider states of affairs may happen to obtain, q is such that it ought to obtain.

There is a temptation to say that most ethical disputes are concerned, not merely with what requires what, but with what *indefeasibly* requires what. But any dispute about what indefeasibly requires what will turn upon some question about what requires what. (If you think, and I do not, that promise-making indefeasibly requires promise-keeping, then presumably there will be some state of affairs p which is such that I think, but you do not, that p would override the requirement imposed by promise-making. Our dispute would then turn on the question whether the conjunction of p and promise-making requires promise-keeping.)

The concept singled out in D6 is also relevant, of course, to the problems of theodicy.[8]

9. We are now in a position to introduce three definitions enabling us to see the validity of the three types of practical inference with which we began. The three types of inference were exhibited by:

(A) (1) p occurs
(2) p requires that S perform A
∴ (3) S has a duty to perform A

(B) (1) q occurs
(2) q requires that S perform an act logically incompatible with his performing A
∴ (3) S has a duty not to perform A

(C) (1) r, as well as p, occurs

[8] I have discussed this point in 'The Defeat of Good and Evil', in *Proceedings and Addresses of the American Philosophical Association*, vol. XLII (1968–9), pp. 21–38. This paper is reprinted in J. E. Smith, ed., *Contemporary American Philosphy: Second Series* (George Allen & Unwin: London, 1970), pp. 152–69.

(2) *r* and *p* does not require that *S* perform *A*

∴ (3) The requirement, imposed by *p*, that *S* perform *A* has been overridden.

To remove a certain ambiguity, to be noted below, let us re-express the conclusion of argument (A) by saying '*S* has a *prima facie* duty to perform *A*' and that of argument (B) by saying '*S* has a *prima facie* duty not to perform *A*'. We now add definitions of these two concepts:

D7 *S* has a *prima facie* duty to perform *A* =Df. There is an *x* such that *x* requires *S*'s performing *A*.

D8 *S* has a *prima facie* duty not to perform *A* =Df. There is an *x* and a *y* such that (a) *x* requires *S*'s performing *y* and (b) *S*'s performing *y* is logically incompatible with *S*'s performing *A*.

Definitions D7 and D8 enable us to see that arguments (A) and (B) are valid. Our earlier definition D3—the definition of the concept of *overriding*—enables us to see that argument (C) is valid. The three definitions together, taken with what we have said about the logic of requirement, are sufficient to justify the following remark that was made at the outset; namely, that the three arguments (A), (B), and (C), may be said to be consistent with each other in the sense that one may consistently affirm the premisses and conclusions of all three arguments, where *A*, *p*, *q*, *r*, and *S* are replaced, completely and consistently, by actual terms.

We may now define 'the ought to do' by reference to 'the ought to be':

D9 *S* ought to perform *A* =Df. It ought to be that *S*'s performing *A* obtains.

Having defined 'the ought to be' in terms of requirement, and having characterized requirement in terms of relations holding necessarily among propositions or states of affairs, we may say, with Samuel Clarke, that our duties are a function of the eternal relations of fitness that hold among things.[9]

10. Thus, if I am not mistaken, we have a clear-cut distinction between what it is that a person ought to do and what it is

[9] Samuel Clarke, *Discourse upon Natural Religion* (London, 1706).

that something may require him to do. We have defined the nonrelative term 'ought' by reference to the relative term 'requires'. I suggest that the way in which we have drawn this distinction may throw light upon a number of questions of moral philosophy. I shall mention six such questions.

(i) We can now better understand the distinction W. D. Ross wished to make, in saying that certain acts are '*prima facie* duties' and others are 'duties proper'—that certain acts are '*prima facie* obligatory' and others 'absolutely obligatory.' We may say that a man has a *prima facie* duty to perform a certain act *a*, if there is a requirement that he perform *a*, and that he has a duty proper to perform *a* if he ought to perform *a*.

There are circumstances under which it makes good sense to say: 'You ought to do it even though you are under obligation not to do it.' In this use, the expression 'You ought to do it' is more authoritative, more stringent than 'You are under obligation to do it.' We could say to the man of Ross's example, 'You ought to miss the appointment, in order to prevent the accident, even though you are under obligation to your friend not to miss the appointment.' The man's *prima facie* duty is the duty to keep the appointment, and had it not been overridden by the danger of the accident, it would have been his duty proper. The distinction between *prima facie* and absolute duty is thus the analogue of Bolzano's distinction between relational and absolute probability. Ross's 'duty proper', like Bolzano's 'absolute probability', is 'toti-resultant'.[10]

[10] Professor Strawson has argued that Ross's distinction is untenable on the ground that it comes to little more than the following: *x* is *prima facie* obligatory provided *x* has a property such that everything having that property tends to be obligatory; and *x* is absolutely obligatory provided *x* has no property such that, having that property entails being absolutely wrong. The first definition obviously leaves something to be desired, and the second leaves us with the concept of wrong, which involves all of the difficulties of obligatory; 'besides having this theoretical defect, the suggested model is, of course, practically absurd'. P. F. Strawson, 'Ethical Intuitionism', *Philosophy*, vol. 24 (1949). It must be conceded that without a concept such as that of overriding which I have attempted to define, Ross's distinction would involve serious theoretical difficulties.

(ii) This type of distinction enables us to solve at least one of the theoretical problems which the fact of moral conflict involves. A man may be able to formulate two practical arguments having premisses that are true, but conclusions that contradict each other: '*a*'s occurring obligates me to do *b*; *a* has occurred; therefore I ought to do *b*. But *c*'s occurring obligates me not to do *b*; *c* has occurred; therefore I ought not to do *b*'. Shall we say—what seems implausible—that there really are no such conflicts? Or shall we say—what seems intolerable—that a person may have conflicting absolute obligations?[11] We may avoid both extremes by saying that the two arguments are formally invalid: The premisses refer to *prima facie* obligations, or requirements; and the conclusions refer to absolute obligations, or what it is that one ought to do.

A valid practical argument, with premisses referring to requirement, and with a conclusion referring to what one ought to do, would have this form: '*a*'s occurring requires me to do *b*; *a* has occurred; and nothing has occurred to override this requirement; therefore I ought to do *b*'.

Thus we may say that there are moral conflicts and also, if we choose, that whenever there is such a conflict, there is a reasonable and proper way out. As our theorem T3 makes explicit, we may assume that if there occurs something *p* which requires *q*, then this same thing *p* does not also require not-*q*. And we may also assume that, wherever there are conflicting requirements, then at least one of the requirements is overridden. The difficult problem is that of deciding which.

(iii) Let us now consider one of the problems involved in supposing that people are capable of acquiring knowledge in ethics. Our ethical judgements, if some of them constitute knowledge, resemble those judgements which are traditionally called '*a priori*' in the following way: An 'intuitive induction'

[11] A clear formulation of the theoretical problem may be found in John Ladd's 'Remarks on the Conflict of Obligation', *Journal of Philosophy*, vol. 55 (1958), pp. 811–19. Ladd attempts to get between the horns, but I believe he is committed to the first of the two courses noted.

or an 'experiment in the imagination' seems to be all that is needed to establish a universal generalization. To know, for example, that malice is reprehensible wherever and under whatever conditions it occurs (if one can know such a thing), it would seem to be necessary only to know what malice is, or to contemplate a single instance of it. Thus we have said, in A2, that the relation of requirement holds *necessarily*. Yet our ethical judgements, unlike those which are traditionally called *a priori*, are notoriously corrigible. Not only do we fail to agree with each other; we come to realize that many of our own ethical judgements, even those made under conditions which seem ideal for such deliberation, have been mistaken. The problem, then, is this: How can an *a priori* judgement be so obviously corrigible?

I suggest that we are now in a position to solve the problem in the following way. A judgement to the effect that something *p* requires something *q* may be *a priori* and incorrigible; so, too, for the judgement that *p* and *r* taken together do not require *q*—i.e., the judgement that the addition of *r* to *p* overrides *p*'s requirement for *q*. The judgement that there is in fact a requirement for *q* and that this requirement has not been overridden—hence the judgement that *p* ought to obtain (or that *p* ought to be true)—is not *a priori*, but requires a survey of all of the relevant *a posteriori* evidence that is available.

(iv) These distinctions may also throw light upon the nature of moral disagreement and of *akrasia*. If, as often happens, two people agree upon all the facts and accept the same principles of morality and yet find themselves in disagreement about a particular moral issue, then at least one of the people has failed to consider the moral relevance of some particular fact. In consequence he has failed to see that some requirement has been overridden, or that some overriding has been overridden. And the incontinent man may be said, in the following sense, to 'do what he knows he ought not to do'. His act is one such that his information and moral principles imply that it ought not to be performed; but he restricts his view to only a part of the relevant situation, making use only of enough of his information to be able to draw the conclusion that the act is not one which ought not to be performed.[12]

(v) What is the status of 'Small Moralls'—the requirements of etiquette and esthetics? We may say that these requirements are 'small', for not much is needed to override them. But they are requirements, and therefore when they are not overridden—when the only question is whether or not to follow the requirements of 'good taste'—then they are absolute obligations. Our principle (A5) and its consequence (T5), tell us that, if *p* requires *q*, then it is possible that, for every wider state of affairs that obtains and entails *p*, that wider state of affairs requires *q*. Every requirement, however small it may be, is such that, under certain possible circumstances, it would be an absolute obligation.

(vi) Finally, let us consider what is sometimes called 'subjective' obligation. What shall we say of the man who has an obligation to perform a certain act *a*, but who believes that he has an obligation to do something which is incompatible with his performing *a*? We can hardly say that it is obligatory for him to do what is not obligatory. But it would be equally wrong to say that his beliefs about what is obligatory have no moral relevance. What we must conclude, I think, is this: The fact that a man believes that a certain act is obligatory is morally relevant precisely because it is a fact which requires him to perform that act; but the requirement is one that may easily be overridden. An erring conscience may not bind, but it does require.

Comment: 'Reasons, Requirements and Practical Conflicts'

BY J. RAZ

Professor Chisholm is obviously right in stating at the beginning of his illuminating paper that many of the more important problems of practical reason concern the ways in which the demands of practical reason may intersect and conflict. I find myself in complete sympathy with what I take to be his main thesis, namely that practical reason can give rise to diametrically conflicting demands and that talk of diametrically conflicting demands does not always lead to contradictions, for a conflict of demands results from a difference in the grounds for the demands. I further agree that such conflicts are often resolved when we consider the demands of the conjunction of the states of affairs giving rise to the conflicting demands, for we may find that one demand overrides the other or that they cancel each other.

Having expressed my sympathy with Professor Chisholm's main thesis let me also confess that I was not convinced by his implicit claim that the principles of the logic of requirement he expounded today go a long way towards solving the main problems of practical reason. I shall comment very briefly on three subjects:

A: Types of conflict of practical reason.
B: Reasons for action and the Logic of Requirement.
C: Types of overriding.

A: TYPES OF CONFLICT OF PRACTICAL REASON

The key terms in Professor Chisholm's theory are 'requirement', 'ought' and 'duty'. The meaning he assigns to these terms is only remotely related to their meaning in ordinary English discourse. Though the point is never made by Professor Chisholm, I take it that he is completely unperturbed by this fact. His aim must have been merely to define a set of technical concepts with the help of which one would be able to talk intelligibly about conflicts of practical reason. In this I believe that he was successful.

But the scant attention he paid to the logic of ordinary discourse means that his success is very partial and incomplete. A comprehensive theory may very well include a set of technical concepts providing a framework for precise and clear discourse. But to show that they fulfil their function one must, firstly, analyse the logic of ordinary discourse on matters involving conflict of reasons and, secondly, show that the proposed conceptual framework can be used for the same purposes. We must be convinced that it either reflects the basic features of ordinary discourse or that it can usefully replace it. To the extent that Professor Chisholm refrains from dealing with these matters he leaves important problems unsolved, including some which are essential for any attempt to pass judgement on his theory. All that I can hope to do here is to make a few unsystematic remarks in an attempt somewhat to clarify the nature of the problems involved.

1. *Some problems about ordinary discourse:* There are conflicts of rules and of principles. Conflicts of rights, of duties and of reasons, etc. To deal with the problems of conflicts in practical reason one must explain the nature of each of these cases of conflict and the relations between them. I believe that all these kinds of conflict can ultimately be explained by reference to conflicting 'ought'-statements, of the type 'x ought to A in C' and 'x ought to B in C' where it is impossible for x to do both A and B in C. Conflicting 'ought'-statements can both be correct. An 'ought'-statement is correct if there are reasons for the agent to perform the act in those circumstances. Since there can be conflicting reasons there can be correct though conflicting 'ought'-statements. It must be admitted that there is an air of paradox in the statement that it may be true both that I ought to keep my promise and that I ought to break it. The

apparent paradox can be explained away as the product of pragmatic implicatures. Because of the pragmatical requirement that the speaker should not hold back relevant information my saying to John, you ought to keep your promise, has the pragmatic implicature that I do not believe in any reasons overriding those for keeping the promise. The same, of course, is true of John, and therefore, if he tells me that on the contrary he ought to break his promise, there is a genuine conflict of opinions for we are both stating our views on the balance of reasons. But this is so because of the pragmatic implicatures, not because of the meaning of 'ought'.

2. *The importance of partial conflicts:* It is not my purpose here to solve any of the problems I mentioned. I merely intend to indicate some of the more important problems that a theory which, like Professor Chisholm's theory, is designed to solve the problems of conflict in practical reason must tackle. Let me mention yet another type of conflict disregarded by Professor Chisholm.

If there are reasons for x to do A in circumstances C and if at the same time there are reasons for x to do B in C and if x cannot do both A and B in C then x is faced with a case of a diametrical conflict. Professor Chisholm's is a theory of diametrical conflicts. My characterization of a diametrical conflict is incomplete for it leaves unexplained the nature of the factors because of which x cannot do both A and B in C. Professor Chisholm's explanations are incomplete for the same reason: nowhere does he explain what he means by the incompatibility of actions. I do not wish to enlarge on this theme but let me note in passing that Professor Chisholm comes near to mentioning the problem in his comment on his third axiom saying that $pRq \supset \sim N[(p\&q)$ does not obtain$]$. This principle, he says, 'is reflected in the principle that "ought" implies "can" '. He is of course right, all the more so because he was careful not to say that his axiom *reflects* the principle that 'ought' implies 'can'. Clearly that my doing A is not logically incompatible with my doing B does not entail that I can do both. We do need, however, a fuller explication of the principle that 'ought' implies 'can' in order to be able to characterize the nature of diametrical conflicts which are the only type of conflict with which Professor Chisholm is concerned. So long as Professor Chisholm's logic can explain only those conflicts which are due to logical incompatibility it remains impotent for it is unable to deal with the majority and the most troublesome cases of diametrical conflicts.

However important is the problem of diametrical conflicts, it must be admitted that non-diametrical partial conflicts are much more common, and one may well wonder whether Professor Chisholm's logic as it is does in any way illuminate their nature.

If an agent has reasons to do *A* and reasons to do *B* and if his doing one of those acts will affect any aspect of his ability to perform the other act then he is confronted with a practical problem of (at least) a partial conflict. To make my meaning more precise let me introduce examples of three types of partial conflicts of practical reasons and contrast them with the clear case of diametrical conflict in which I have reason both to keep an appointment and to help a man injured in an accident but cannot do both.

(*a*) Assume an agent has both a reason to perform a generic act *A* in circumstances of type *C* and a reason to perform a generic act *B* in C^1. There is no assumed incompatibility between the two generic acts and a person can usually do both. Usually, but not always. In certain circumstances it is impossible to perform both and sometimes conditions *C* and C^1 obtain in conjunction with further factors making it impossible for the agent to do both *A* and *B*. One can usually both tell the truth and keep one's word, but sometimes they prove to be incompatible and a choice has to be made. In such cases one's reasons to do *A* in *C* partially conflict with one's reasons to do *B* in C^1 because in certain circumstances there is a diametrical conflict between the reasons for *A* and those for *B*.

(*b*) In order to introduce the second type of partial conflict we have to distinguish between various generic acts by the degree of their specificity. Kicking a ball is a more specific act than lecturing which is more specific than teaching. Acting fairly or to everyone's benefit are highly unspecific acts. Saying 'Hello' or drinking a cup of tea are highly specific acts. In general the specificity of an act is in reverse to the number of heterogeneous acts the doing of which on different occasions counts as doing the action in question. Unspecific acts are acts which can be done by doing any of a large variety of other acts.

A reason for performing *A* partially conflicts with a reason for performing *B* if some ways of doing *B*, though not incompatible with doing *A*, are incompatible with some ways of doing *A*. In other words if there is an act B^1 by which *B* can be done and which is incompatible with the doing of A^1 which is a way of doing *A*. To the extent that a reason for an act is also a reason for any act by which it can be done, the second type of partial conflict can also be characterized in terms of diametrical conflict: A reason for *A* conflicts with a reason for *B* if *A* can be done by A^1 and *B* by B^1 and the reasons for A^1 and for B^1 conflict diametrically.

(*c*) The third type of partial conflict concerns cases where there are reasons to achieve two goals and where the full realization of one goal though compatible with the realization of the second goal to a certain extent is incompatible with its realization in the highest degree. A government having reasons both to secure growth and to maximize equality is confronted with a typical case of partial conflict of both the second and the third types. It is not difficult to see that this type of partial conflict can also be characterized by reference to cases of diametrical conflict which it engenders.

B: REASONS FOR ACTION AND THE LOGIC OF REQUIREMENT

I mentioned some of the problems of conflict of practical reason not dealt with by Professor Chisholm merely to correct the impression of the great simplicity of this philosophical field which might be created by his paper. As I have already said I find much to agree with in his treatment of diametrical conflicts of practical reasons, which is the problem with which he is most directly concerned. His reluctance to interpret his key term *R*, nevertheless must make one postpone judgement until some further clarification is provided.

1. *Reasons for action and 'requirements'.* We mention both facts and rules and principles as reasons: 'You should give him the book because you said you will.' 'You should not lie to him because one should not deceive people.' It may be tempting to say that the first item in an *R*-relation is a fact which is a reason, and that some true *R*-statements are statements of rules and principles. If this interpretation is correct it raises a few questions which I am sure Professor Chisholm could easily answer in his reply. Can we apply this interpretation to *R*-statements in which the state of affairs required is not one of an agent performing an act or refraining from one? Can it be applied to the following of his examples: 'A curve may demand a certain completion and seem to reject all others?'

The fact that an act would realize or promote some value or that it is good or bad in itself is a reason for action: 'This tax law should be adopted because it will increase equality.' Are values appropriate items for the *R*-relation? 'Deceiving is wrong because it is incompatible with human dignity or with regarding people as ends in themselves.' Should we say that human dignity requires that one will not deceive? If malice is wrong in itself what is it that requires that we shall not act with malice?

2. *Professor Chisholm's principle of non-contradiction.* This seems to be an appropriate name for T3: $pRq \supset \sim (pR{\sim}q)$. I have no objection to this principle, but it should be clear that its application is far from straightforward. Imagine that I witness one man shoot another from a passing car. This, let us assume, requires both that I attend to the injuries of the victim and that I shall pursue his attacker, but doing one of these acts entails the non-performance of the other. Is not this a case of one state of affairs requiring both *p* and not-*p*? Of course, Professor

Chisholm will be able to deal with this and similar examples with relative ease. My point is that to defend his theory he must employ an elaborate theory of identity of states of affairs which might well be counter-intuitive and counter-productive. What would normally be regarded as the same state of affairs differently described will turn out to be two different states of affairs. Furthermore, he will have to employ some elaborate theory of the completeness of reasons. If p appears to require both q and not–q it must be that it is really p and r, and not p by itself, which requires either q or not–q. I would be grateful if Professor Chisholm would elaborate on this point.

3. *The special case of interpersonal conflicts.* Some conflicts of practical reason are interpersonal. This is the case whenever one person has a duty the performance of which will make it impossible for another person to discharge his obligations. Should this affect the considerations of the first person, and if so in what way? Such conflicts call for a special consideration which is not provided by Professor Chisholm. His logic applies to interpersonal conflicts for according to it it is possible that p requires s (i.e. that x will do A) and that q requires t (i.e. that y will do B) whereas it is necessarily true that not (s and t). This means that if (p and q) requires s and does not require t then the requirement for t is overridden by that for s. If we accept that if pRs and s entails not t then $pR\sim t$ it would follow from T4 that if pRs and qRt and N(s and t does not obtain) then 'either not [$(p\&q)R\ s$] or not [$(p\&q)\ R\ t$]' is a theorem. This means that in every interpersonal conflict at least one requirement overrides the other. This result shows that because Professor Chisholm has not confined his logic to personal conflicts A3 $pRq\supset\ \sim N$ ($p\&q$ does not obtain) is wider in certain respects than the principle that 'ought' implies 'can' and cannot be justified by it. The result that in every interpersonal conflict at least one requirement overrides the other can be justified, if at all, which I doubt, only by assuming that every interpersonal conflict generates a personal conflict. If the performance of a duty of mine will prevent somebody from discharging a duty then I

have a conflicting duty not to perform the act. I wonder whether Professor Chisholm does maintain this. The fact that he defined (in D8) a *prima facie* duty to refrain from acting in a way which precludes taking the duty of another as a ground for my duty to refrain makes one wonder whether he really intended his logic to apply to interpersonal conflicts at all.

4. *The plausibility of T5.* Professor Chisholm's fifth theorem (which is derived from A7 by substitution) reads: $pRq \supset [(p\&s)Rq \vee (p\&{\sim}s)Rq]$. This means that if both ${\sim}[(p\&s)Rq]$ and ${\sim}[(p\&{\sim}s)Rq]$ then it is not the case that pRq. Since it is necessary that either s obtains or that ${\sim}s$ obtains the theorem means that there is no requirement which is necessarily overridden. This would have been plausible enough but for the fact that 'an overriding may itself be overridden.' Let us assume that the following is the case:

(1) pRq
(2) sRu
(3) ${\sim}sRv$
(4) N[($q\&v$) does not obtain] & N [($p\&u$) does not obtain]

I do not think that the conjunction of these statements is necessarily false. It does, however, amount to a conflict of requirements. Let us, therefore, further assume that the conflicts are resolved in the following way: the requirement for q that would be imposed by p would be overridden both by s and by ${\sim}s$. But the requirement for q that would be imposed by the conjunction of $p\&t$ would be overridden only by ${\sim}s$. It would not be overridden by s. If this is the case then the following is true:

(5) ${\sim}[(p\&s)Rq]$
(6) ${\sim}[(p\&{\sim}s)Rq]$
(7) $[(p\&s)\&t]Rq$

The conjunction of (1), (5) and (6), however, contradicts T5. Do we have any reason for concluding that the conjunction is necessarily false? If the fact that the requirement for q that would be imposed by p would always be overridden (as shown by (5) and (6)) would have meant that it is necessary that it is not the case that *q* ought to obtain (cf. D4), then we should have accepted the conclusion. But since (7) shows that this is not the case, because the overriding of the requirement for *q* may itself be overridden, we have no reason to accept the conclusion. It may well be a necessary truth that:

(8) $[N{\sim}(\text{it ought to be that } q \text{ obtains})] \supset {\sim}(pRq)$

But, it seems to me false that *q* is not required by *p* if that requirement is necessarily overridden. I would, therefore, suggest that T5 and with it A7 must be either rejected or modified at least if we wish to preserve Professor Chisholm's other assumptions.

It might be useful to illustrate the sort of situation I have in mind by an example. I am not confident that I have a good example but let me lay the following one:

Promising John that I shall kill him (*p*) requires killing him (*q*). John is either sane (*s*) or insane (${\sim}s$). Both impose requirements (different in each case) which are incompatible with killing him and override that requirement, in so far as it is imposed by my promise. But if John has an incurable and very painful illness (*t*) the overriding is overridden. So that in these circumstances I am required to do what I promised. (This may not be the case if John is insane. His sanity may be essential for the requirement to stick.) It is worth noting that his illness in itself (*t*) certainly does not require killing him. It is only my promise that does so. The illness is only relevant for the overriding to be overridden. Therefore, it is not open for Professor Chisholm to say that in the cases I have in mind it is always *t* that requires *q* and never *p*. He could, of course, maintain that *p* does not require *q* at all and it is only the conjunction of *p* and *t* that requires *q*. The example I have chosen was meant to show that by doing so he would contradict sound moral beliefs. If this example fails to do so, others will no doubt succeed.

C: TYPES OF 'OVERRIDING'

Professor Chisholm's explanation of the notion of overriding makes clear how one can talk of practical conflicts being resolved. It does nothing to explain how they are resolved. To the extent that it suggests that all cases of overriding are essentially alike it is grossly misleading. I shall briefly survey several cases of conflict and of overriding in order to show the different considerations involved. Some of my examples will demonstrate how widely Professor Chisholm's concept differs from the ordinary one. Before I start I wish to mention one important case of such discrepancy. If pRs and qRt and s entails not t, then if $(p\&q)R(s \vee t)$ but $\sim[(p\&q)Rs]$ and $\sim[(p\&s)Rt]$ then according to Professor Chisholm both requirements are overridden, whereas ordinarily we would say that none of them is overridden.

1. I promised John to make him a gift of my dog on the first of July. Therefore, I have a reason to do so. On the first of June John released me from my promise and I no longer have a reason to give him my dog. This is not a case of conflict nor does Professor Chisholm claim that it is. Yet it is a case of overriding in his logic. There is, of course, nothing wrong in stretching the concept of overriding to cover cases where no conflict exists. It may, however, be thought somewhat unfortunate that such cases should be drastically separated from others which seem to resemble them. Imagine, e.g., that John did not release me from my promise but that my dog died on the first of June. $p\&r$ does not require q, but this is no longer a case of overriding since $p\&r$ is incompatible with q. Professor Chisholm's requirement of compatibility in the definition of 'would be overridden' does not seem adequate to its task.

2. John, who had invited me to a dinner party greets me with a wanton and humiliating insult when I arrive. His invitation and my acceptance of it are reasons for me to behave politely and not to give offence. His subsequent insult is reason for making clear what I think of his behaviour. This is incompatible with polite behaviour, but the nature of his insult is such that I have no longer any reason for behaving politely. The requirement to be polite is not merely outweighed it is completely cancelled out. If I behave politely I will not be doing something

which I have at any rate some reason to do, for now I have none at all.

3. My daughter is getting married and setting up an independent household. I have reason to give her a dish-washer and a washing machine. Both will save her time and work. I can give her either of them but not both. I should give her the washing machine because it will save more of her time and energy. The reasons for giving her a washing machine override those for giving her a dish-washer, but they do not cancel them out. I still have reason to give her a dish-washer, even though it is overridden. In this respect this example differs from the previous one.

4. I have reason to to provide my daughter with a washing machine but I have also reason to pay her university fees. I cannot do both. The latter reason overrides but does not cancel the former one. In this respect this case resembles the previous one. But the calculation is different. Both the washing machine and the dish-washer serve the same goal—making life more comfortable. A university education will serve my daughter in a different way than having a washing machine. It will broaden her horizon and enable her to acquire a profession and with it economic independence. My present choice involves judgement concerning the relative importance of different values, whereas my previous choice involved merely an estimate of the relative utility of two courses of action with respect to one value.

5. Gordon, an employee of a large financial concern, is offered a deal by which he can make a considerable sum of money by forging one document. He needs the money very badly and therefore has a reason to accept the offer. He is uncertain as to the moral merit of the case. Forgery and breach of faith are usually wrong but he is aware of a powerful argument purporting to establish that in the circumstances the forgery will not be morally reprehensible at all. He turns down the offer, not because he believes that the act would be morally wrong and the moral considerations outweigh the self-interested ones, but because he thinks that he cannot trust his judgement. He is

afraid that the temptation is such that it will affect his judgement and therefore he refuses to consider the pros and cons and acts in his normal way. I should make it clear that Gordon did not assess the risk that the temptation will affect his judgement and did not add this likelihood of making a mistake to his calculations. He considered the possibility of doing so and dismissed it because he found that he could not trust himself to evaluate the likelihood of a mistake due to temptation. This is a case of a conflict of reasons and yet it differs fundamentally from the previous cases mentioned. Gordon has decided to act as he did not because he believed that the reasons for his action outweigh the reasons against it, but because he believed that he has reason to refrain from fully considering the merit of the case. Later on he may conclude that on the merits he should have accepted the offer and yet continue to believe that he was right in refusing to assess the various factors involved. He acted on a reason for action of a special kind which I shall call an exclusionary reason for it is a reason for disregarding other reasons which do apply to the case. I do believe that Gordon's reasoning may very well have been valid. But more important is the fact that people do act, rightly or wrongly, on exclusionary reasons and that the theory of practical reason is at fault for not recognizing their presence, let alone their importance.

6. While serving in the army Jeremy is ordered by his commanding officer to appropriate and use a van belonging to a certain tradesman. He, therefore, has reason to obey the order. His friend urges him to consider his action carefully. Maybe that the loss to the tradesman outweighs the utility to the war effort of following the order and that it also outweighs the danger to Jeremy of disregarding it. If this is so, he contends, the general effects of disobeying on the army's morale and discipline will be on the whole beneficial. Jeremy, however, refuses to engage in this reasoning. An authoritative order, he argues, is an exclusionary reason. It is a reason to perform the act required *and* to disregard countervailing reasons. He admits that it does not exclude all countervailing reasons. If he were to be

commanded to perform a moral atrocity he would refuse. Exclusionary reasons do not usually exclude all contrary considerations. But his, he thinks, is an ordinary case and the exclusionary reason should prevail. Without commenting on the merit of this particular case let me say that Jeremy is right in thinking that the concept of an authority in practical reason entails that its authoritative directions are exclusionary reasons for action. Many explanations of the concept failed by disregarding this.

7. I agree with Professor Chisholm that whenever one has a duty to do *A* it is required that one shall do *A*, or as I prefer to put it, one has a reason for doing *A*. But Professor Chisholm maintains that the contrary is equally true: whenever one has a reason to do *A* (it is required that he should do *A*) he has a duty to do *A*. This makes it impossible for him to deal with the problem of supererogation. Michael has reason to use his earnings for the benefit of his family. He also has reason to donate two-thirds of it to Oxfam. Assume that he does not donate the money. Some will say that he acts wrongly for the money would produce much better results if donated to Oxfam. Others will maintain that he did nothing wrong in not donating the money. The latter may be mistaken but it would be odd to maintain that they are committed either to factual mistakes or to contradiction. Is their position coherent? Assume that they accept that donating the money to Oxfam will do more good than spending it on one's family. They maintain that the donation would have been an act of supererogation and yet that Michael did nothing wrong. They are precluded from saying that the needs of one's family are more weighty reasons than the more pressing needs of other people for this would mean that had Michael donated the money he would have acted on the lesser reason. And yet they are equally precluded from saying that the reasons for the donation are more weighty for they maintain that Michael did nothing wrong in not acting on these reasons.

The way out of this dilemma is through the notion of an exclusionary permission. As Professor Chisholm has mentioned in passing, sometimes saying that an act is permitted is simply saying that there are no reasons for avoiding it. But the notion has several other uses and one of them is that of the exclusionary permission. Saying that I have an exclusionary permission to do an act does not entail that there are no reasons for not doing it but it does entail that there are reasons which entitle me to disregard, to exclude from my considerations some reasons for not doing it. Exclusionary permissions differ from exclusionary reasons in that they do not require that I shall disregard the excluded reasons. They merely entitle me to do so. I do wrong when I do not disregard reasons excluded by exclusionary reasons, whereas I am not doing any wrong when I consider reasons I am permitted to disregard, indeed I may even be acting virtuously.

Those who treat supererogation in the way described above believe that people have an exclusionary permission to disregard certain very weighty reasons but that they act virtuously if they do not do so. Michael did nothing wrong in resolving the conflict of reasons the way he did but not because he acted on the more weighty reason but because he had an exclusionary permission to disregard it. The reasons for asserting such exclusionary permission probably involve belief in a certain autonomy of the individual *vis-à-vis* the needs of other individuals, but this is a different story.

I have mentioned some points which call for clarification. I have also challenged Professor Chisholm on four issues: A3 and interpersonal conflicts, the plausibility of T5, his last condition in the definition of overriding and the promised dog and the problem of supererogation. My main purpose, however, has been to indicate some of the complexity of the problems of conflict of practical reasons and in particular to commend to you the notions of exclusionary reasons and exclusionary permissions.

Acknowledgments

Wesley Newcomb Hohfeld, "Some Fundamental Legal Conceptions as Applied in Judicial Reasoning," *Yale Law Journal* 23 (1913), pp. 16–59. Reprinted by permission of The Yale Law Journal Company and William S. Hein Company from the *Yale Law Journal*, Vol. 23, pages 16–59.

H. J. McCloskey, "Rights," *Philosophical Quarterly* 15 (1965), pp. 115–127. Reprinted with the permission of Basil Blackwell Ltd.

David Lyons, "Rights, Claimants, and Beneficiaries," *American Philosophical Quarterly* 6 (1969), pp. 173–185. Reprinted with the permission of the *American Philosophical Quarterly.*

Joel Feinberg, "The Nature and Value of Rights," *Journal of Value Inquiry* 4 (1970), pp. 243–257. Reprinted with the permission of Kluwer Academic Publishers.

H. L. A. Hart, "Bentham on Legal Rights," in *Oxford Essays in Jurisprudence* (Second Series), A. W. B. Simpson (ed.), Oxford: Clarendon Press, 1973, pp. 171–201. Copyright © Tony Honore 1987. Reprinted from *Making Law Bind: Essays Legal and Philosophical* by Tony Honore (1987) by permission of Oxford University Press.

Ronald Dworkin, "Taking Rights Seriously," in *Oxford Essays in Jurisprudence* (Second Series), A. W. B. Simpson (ed.), Oxford: Clarendon Press, 1973, pp. 202–227. Copyright © Tony Honore 1987. Reprinted from *Making Law Bind: Essays Legal and Philosophical* by Tony Honore (1987) by permission of Oxford University Press.

D. N. MacCormick, "Rights in Legislation," in Law, Morality and Society, P. M. S. Hacker and J. Raz (eds.), Oxford: Clarendon Press, 1977, pp. 189–209. Reprinted with the permission of Oxford University Press.

Carl Wellman, "Legal Rights," in *Uppsalaskolan—och efferat*, Stockholm: Almqvist and Wiksell, 1978, pp. 213–221. Reprinted with the permission of Almqvist & Wiksell International.

J. Raz, "On the Nature of Rights," *Mind* 93 (1984), pp. 194–214. Reprinted with the permission of the Oxford University Press.

Judith Jarvis Thomson, "*Self-Defense and Rights*," in *Rights, Restitution and Risk*, Judith Jarvis Thomson, Cambridge MA: Harvard

University Press, 1986, pp. 33–48. Reprinted with the permission of Harvard University Press.

W. D. Ross, "What Makes Right Acts Right?" *The Right and the Good*, Oxford: Clarendon Press, 1930, pp. 16–47. Reprinted with the permission of Oxford University Press.

H. L. A. Hart, "Legal and Moral Obligation," in *Essays in Moral Philosophy*, A. I. Melden (ed.), Seattle WA: University of Washington Press, 1958, pp. 82–107. Reprinted with the permission of University of Washington Press.

R. B. Brandt, "The Concepts of Obligation and Duty," *Mind* 73 (1964), pp. 374–393. Reprinted with the permission of the Oxford University Press.

James K. Mish'Alani, "'Duty', 'Obligation' and 'Ought'," *Analysis* 30 (1969), pp. 33–40. Reprinted with the permission of the author. Appeared in *Analysis*.

John Ladd, "Legal and Moral Obligation," in *Political and Legal Obligation: Nomos XII*, J. Roland Pennock and John Chapman (eds.), New York: Atherton Press, 1970, pp. 3–35. Reprinted with the permission of Atherton Press.

P. M. S. Hacker, "Sanction Theories of Duty," in *Oxford Essays in Jurisprudence* (Second Series), A. W. B. Simpson (ed.), Oxford: Clarendon Press, 1973, pp. 131–170. Copyright © Tony Honore 1987. Reprinted from *Making Law Bind: Essays Legal and Philosophical* by Tony Honore (1987) by permission of Oxford University Press.

Roderick Chisholm, "Practical Reason and the Logic of Requirement," in *Practical Reason*, Stephen Körner (ed.), New Haven: Yale University Press, 1974, pp. 1–17. Reprinted with the permission of Yale University Press.

J. Raz, "Comment: Reasons, Requirements and Practical Conflicts," in *Practical Reason*, Stephen Körner (ed.), New Haven: Yale University Press, 1974, pp. 22–35. Reprinted with the permission of Yale University Press.